D0985869

Northwestern University

STUDIES IN *Phenomenology &*

Existential Philosophy

GENERAL EDITOR
John Wild

ASSOCIATE EDITOR
James M. Edie

CONSULTING EDITORS

Hubert L. Dreyfus
William Earle
Dagfinn Føllesdal
Marjorie Grene
Aron Gurwitsch
Emmanuel Levinas
Alphonso Lingis
Maurice Natanson
Paul Ricoeur
George Schrader
Calvin O. Schrag
Herbert Spiegelberg
Charles Taylor

The Function of the Sciences
and the Meaning of Man

Enzo Paci

Translated,

with an Introduction, by

The Function of the Sciences and the Meaning of Man

PAUL PICCONE
and JAMES E. HANSEN

NORTHWESTERN UNIVERSITY PRESS
EVANSTON   1972

Copyright © 1972 by Northwestern University Press
All rights reserved
Library of Congress Catalog Card Number: 71–186545
ISBN 0–8101–0378–8
Printed in the United States of America
Second printing, 1980

Originally published in Italian under the title
Funzione delle Scienze e Significato dell'Uomo,
copyright © 1963 by Il Saggiatore, Milan.

Material from Karl Marx, *Early
Writings,* translated and edited by
T. B. Bottomore, © T. B. Bottomore, 1963,
is used with permission of McGraw-
Hill Book Company, New York, and
Pitman Publishing, London.

Paul Piccone is instructor of philosophy at the
State University of New York at Buffalo.
James E. Hansen is assistant professor of
philosophy at Brock University in Ontario.

1st paperback printing 1980

Contents

Acknowledgments

WE WOULD LIKE TO ACKNOWLEDGE the following people and institutions for their aid in our translation. First, we want to thank Professor Marvin Farber for having introduced us to phenomenology and for encouraging us to translate this work, and Professor Rollo Handy for his valuable help in the early stages. We also thank Maria Coles and Sylvia Federici Kosok for aid in translating, Karen Wharton and Margaret Littlejohn for their swiftness and accuracy in typing the many versions of the manuscript, and Alex Delfini, Joseph Wolberg, David Cornberg, Carl Ratner, and especially Sylvia Federici Kosok for their comments and criticisms. We also thank the State University of New York and Brock University for grants which helped make this translation possible.

P. P.
J. E. H.

Translators' Introduction

THROUGHOUT THIS CENTURY both phenomenology and Marxism have been major cultural and historical forces, each developing its own tradition. However, they have usually been regarded as radically different and fundamentally irreconcilable. Phenomenology allegedly dealt with pure consciousness and the structure of knowledge, while Marxism was presented as a socioeconomic doctrine primarily concerned with material forces and historical changes. Safely entrenched behind the boundaries of their respective domains and isolated by their jargon, phenomenology and Marxism ignored and dismissed each other as irrelevant and misguided. Furthermore, to the extent that the phenomenologists were devoted to analyzing phenomena insofar as they are presented to consciousness, while the Marxists busied themselves in attempting to alter those socioeconomic forces they considered to be the moving powers of history, the two positions never seriously confronted each other as more than cultural oddities.

Nevertheless, as Paci points out here, in the course of their respective developments, something peculiar happened to both phenomenology and Marxism: phenomenology discovered its foundations within the Marxist problematic, while Marxism, torn by an internal crisis, rediscovered a phenomenological basis that had been presupposed but not often clearly elaborated. After half a century of uninterrupted intense phenomenological investigations, Husserl was finally confronted in the *Crisis* with the problem of history, which, along with the problem of materiality (the

Dingvorlesung) and determined activity or praxis (what Husserl calls constitutive operations), forms the foundations of Marxism. Husserl did not seem to have any reservations about his philosophical radicalism and, in the Vienna lecture, did not hesitate to claim that "I, the supposed reactionary, am far more radical and far more revolutionary than those who in their words proclaim themselves so radical today." [1] What is the basis of this Husserlian radicalism? From his early investigations of the *Philosophie der Arithmetik,* to his unwavering criticism of the naturalistic attitude, and eventually the "crisis"—which turns out to be a result of the naturalistic attitude—the *leitmotif* of Husserl's work is the return to the subject as the *real foundation.* Meanings are constantly referred to the human operations that consitute them. Even modern science is seen as failing and eventually leading to the broader social crisis still existing today, because Galileo and those who followed him systematically occluded the subjective operations which constitute scientific meanings. Scientists thus fail to thematize the abstractive process which is presupposed by all mathematical sciences. Concrete entities (the plena) are purified into ideal forms which can then be quantified to infinity and scientifically articulated. This objectivistic bias that substitutes ideal forms for concrete reality, and subsequently takes the *constituted* articulation of abstractions (science) derived from these forms as the criterion of all reality, ends by altogether excluding the subject from scientific discourse or—even more dangerous—by dealing with the subject as if it were just another object among objects. Science thus becomes its own criterion.

"The modern epoch translates ἐπιστήμη as 'ratio.' Thus, mathematical natural science comes to be considered as the highest knowledge of the beings of all of nature [*seienden Allnatur*]. As mathematics, this transcends prescientific sensuous nature, yet beyond it there is no longer a metaphysical in-itself that appears

1. Edmund Husserl, *The Crisis of European Sciences and Transcendental Phenomenology: An Introduction to Phenomenological Philosophy,* trans. David Carr (Evanston: Northwestern University Press, 1970), p. 290. This of course does not mean that Husserl was politically radical. Except for the omission of several appendixes, the Carr translation includes the entire text edited by Walter Biemel and originally published in German in 1954. An earlier English translation of what is known as the "Vienna lecture" can be found in Quentin Lauer's translation of Edmund Husserl, *Phenomenology and the Crisis of Philosophy* (New York: Harper and Row, 1965), pp. 149–92.

through this knowledge as if the latter were a mere appearance of it." [2] Trapped within a self-contained system where means and ends become indistinguishable, this pseudo-rationalism camouflaged as "scientific neutrality" is divorced from the creating subject who originally constitutes it, and it becomes another tool of the manipulation and oppression of man. This is to be expected: the science meant to dominate and control nature ends by controlling and dominating man himself when he is considered at the level of mere objects. The crisis, therefore, far from being a sharp departure from the rationalism of the Enlightenment, is its historical fulfillment. As Adorno and Horkheimer have indicated, the philosophy of the Marquis de Sade is not an antiscientific aberration, but a consistent extension of the very *scientific* neutrality of the Enlightenment.[3] This, however, is not the end of scientific rationalism, since Husserl's analyses show that what failed was only a dogmatic naturalistic rationalism which, in its professed self-sufficiency, turns out to be based upon a broader irrationalism. In this, "rational" science and "irrational" ethics are rigidly separated, with serious consequences. To the extent that science preempts rationality, its justification cannot be scientific—unless the justification is circular—and the justification thus falls outside of any "neutral" science. Hence, science's justification is necessarily irrational, and science is thereby not at all superior to the lowest of all human activities—hence, de Sade. It is in this context that Husserl discusses the *telos* of the sciences which has been lost, in addition to discussing the lifeworld out of which science originally arose.

The theme of the life-world, however, has met much resistance, not only from professional phenomenologists who would

2. Edmund Husserl, *Die Krisis der europäischen Wissenschaften und die transzendentale Phänomenologie: Eine Einleitung in die phänomenologische Philosophie*, ed. Walter Biemel (1954; 2d printing, The Hague: Nijhoff, 1962), Beilage X, p. 420.

3. See Max Horkheimer and Theodor W. Adorno, *Dialektik der Aufklärung* (Amsterdam: Querido Verlag, 1947). A similar thesis is defended by Max Horkheimer in his *Eclipse of Reason* (New York: Oxford University Press, 1947). Unlike Adorno's later work on Husserl, *Zur Metakritik der Erkenntnistheorie* (Frankfurt a. M.: Kohlhammer, 1956), where a distortion of phenomenology is systematically confronted with the Hegelian dialectic and, consequently, rejected as a form of positivism, in this early work both Horkheimer and Adorno not only articulate a thesis very similar to Husserl's, but they also favorably quote that part of the *Crisis* which had been published in *Philosophia* in 1936 and which was the only part publicly available at the time they wrote their text.

prefer their Husserl to be merely another idealist,[4] but from other quarters as well, where the theme of the crisis is seriously studied.[5] However, the life-world is fundamental to any philosophy that seeks to avoid naïve realism or idealism and give an adequate analysis of knowledge.[6] The difficulty is that neither idealism (the consideration of reality as entirely constituted by projected categories) nor realism (the belief that reality has the same structure that we conceptually apprehend, or that the conceptual structure *is* the real structure) adequately thematizes the relation between concept and object. The failure to thematize concept-object relations is connected to a much more fundamental difficulty, to wit, that neither view is able to furnish criteria of truth or knowledge. Idealism fails because any criterion it offers must be strictly system-generated and thus incapable of applying to the system as a whole. Realism fails because any concept derived from such a system is limited by the conditions of derivation, i.e., any criterion of knowledge or truth can apply only circularly. In both cases, we confront limited categorial systems of concepts. The concept-object relations cannot be thematized without begging the question. The only way to escape such a static system of constructs is to develop a philosophy which has a basis and a goal that cannot be grasped in necessarily limited systems of categories. For Husserl, the basis is the life-world.

The concept is not and cannot be mechanically *derived* from

4. See David Carr, Introduction to Husserl's *Crisis*, p. xli. He writes: "If we take seriously the 'pregivenness' of the life-world, upon which the author repeatedly insists, Husserl's early idealism seems to be in difficulty." What is not at all clear, however, is whether Husserl was ever an idealist.

5. See William Leiss, "Husserl's *Crisis*," *Telos*, no. 8 (Fall, 1971).

6. The types of idealism are perhaps too varied to specify. We have three in mind here: subjective idealism, transcendental idealism, and objective idealism. The first is characterized by a single scientist (e.g., Bohr), who constructs a system of categories in terms of which the world can only be meaningfully construed. The second is characterized by a specifiable set of categories—perhaps the "categories of the understanding"—which are trans-subjective, but which nevertheless posit categorial conditions which their domain must meet in order to be known or even exist (where "existence" might be a category of the understanding). The third type of idealism—objective idealism—is restricted by the supposition that the structure or nature of the cosmos or world is delineated by categories imposed on it from without, i.e., in order for existence to be structured, it must be categorially constructed by a being or consciousness which is separate from or external to that which is constructed.

the object, but must be constituted in terms of a *telos* that furnishes a precategorial criterion of relevance.[7] It is here that Husserl's analysis turns to the precategorial world as the world of human operations, and the problem of materiality becomes central. Without extensively reconstructing Husserl's profound analyses concerning these matters—which Paci does in the second part of this volume—we should note that "need" is the precategorial foundation upon which everything else depends. Need is thus determining. The life-world is the world of needs and of their satisfaction by means of labor. Among other elements, the life-world provides the basis for the creation of conceptual mediations which alone can guarantee the proper relationship between means and ends, thus differentiating labor from meaningless activity.

Formulated in a different way, the crisis is the result of the substitution of the categories devised to deal with the domain of needs in the life-world for that very same life-world. Hence the *telos* implicit in the life-world becomes transposed to the same level as the means to attain it, thus destroying the meaning of both. Husserl confronts the problem of history precisely when he tries to temporally locate the sources of the crisis, for, unlike some existentialists, he never hypostatizes the crisis to the level of a metaphysical crisis grounded in the very nature of existence —which would make the crisis irresolvable in principle. As Banfi has pointed out, "The theme of the crisis is a typical moment of German cultural consciousness and thought during the period following the first world war." [8] However, unlike analyses such as Simmel's or Heidegger's, Husserl's interpretation is historical, and, rather than reifying or glorifying the crisis as something insuperable or even positive, he seeks its essential *causes.* If the crisis consists in the occlusion of the *telos* of humanity with the development of modern science at the beginning of the modern age, there must be a reason for the occlusion that can be discovered by means of a rigorous analysis of the origins of modern science. For Husserl, this entails an analysis of the elimination of psychology as a *science of decisions* by reducing it to behaviorism.

Nevertheless, the *Crisis* ends abruptly at this crucial point—

7. The *telos* and the criterion of relevance must themselves be precategorial for, if they were categorial, they would have to be constituted according to some other criterion of relevance and *telos.*

8. Antonio Banfi, "Husserl e la Crisi della Civiltà Europea," *Aut-Aut,* nos. 43–44 (1958), p. 2.

xxiv / TRANSLATORS' INTRODUCTION

precisely when Husserl attempts to articulate his analysis of the roots of the crisis. We are left, at best, with a speculative solution which creates more problems than it solves. The crisis turns out to be an essentially philosophical crisis, and only subsequently does it involve all of humanity. Husserl believes that it is the failure of philosophy to retain the original *telos* which guided the whole of Western history up to the Renaissance. The philosophers' forgetting of this *telos* is the source of the naturalistic "scientific" attitude and all the ensuing problems. When the problem is posed thus, there can be only one answer. What is needed is the development of a new *subjective* philosophy which, unlike the *objectivistic* systems developed since the Renaissance, would lay major stress on the subject, the life-world, and the all-important *telos*. Needless to say, such a philosophy is his phenomenology—which, however, has not received the attention that it deserves. Thus, as Husserl says, *"the dream is over."* [9] The old and misunderstood Husserl at the end of his life gives up in the face of the coming holocaust which death alone prevented him from experiencing.

Husserl does not explain, however, why the philosophers lose the *telos*, and why this happens precisely when it does. Here Husserl would have had to give an intersubjective, i.e., social, explanation of the historical event of forgetting, or of the birth of the Enlightenment. At this point a developed phenomenology coheres with Marxism as a dialectical account of how men make themselves and their institutions in the laboring process. This is the same process that the knowledge examined by phenomenology was supposed to mediate. Hence, phenomenology as a whole can already be found *within* Marxism as a necessary and essential moment of the whole structure, and the crisis of the sciences can be seen as a *special* case of the capitalist crisis. In fact, if with Marx we characterize the capitalist crisis as consisting in the reversal of subject and object through the laboring process whereby the subject objectifies himself in the object which, separated from the creating subject, comes to confront him as an alien and determining entity redefining him as a mere object, then the crisis of the sciences is part of the same process. Instead of dealing with production and distribution in general, Husserl deals with science as the product of *specialized* workers, i.e., scientists. The results, however, are the same. Whereas, with Marx, commodities and capital as the *created* objects come to control

9. Husserl, *Crisis*, p. 389.

the worker (the creating subject), in Husserl, science (the creation of the scientists) comes to control the scientists. All these parallels, and more, are fully elaborated in Part III of this volume, where Paci shows how the very source of Husserlian radicalism, the constant stress of the subject as the root of all, also turns out to be Marx's source: "To be radical is to grasp things by the root. But for man the root is man himself." [10]

II

OF COURSE, Paci's work also took place within a determinate historical period which determines it and gives it a *function*. Written in the late 1950s and early 1960s, at the height of the Khrushchev thaw when it seemed as if the Cold War were about to end and rigid and dogmatic Marxism was ready to give way to a new critical Marxism, Paci's book is one of the leading contributions to a broad cultural attempt that saw the development of a massive amount of literature, ranging from the Marxist-Christian dialogue [11] to less impressionistic works such as Havamann's *Dialektik ohne Dogma?* [12] Meant to contribute to a "reconstitution" of Marxism and phenomenolgy, Paci's book is a rigorous attempt to show how the problems dealt with by Marxism arise within phenomenology and how, at the same time, the entire phenomenological problematic is implicit in Marxism. His book thus presupposes the crisis of Marxism itself—which has yet to receive either a Marxist or a phenomenological analysis.

Generally speaking, the crisis of Marxism is structurally isomorphic to both the crisis of capitalism and Husserl's notion of the crisis of the sciences. In capitalism, as we have said, the subjects (workers) produce the objects (capital) which are "estranged" from the producing subjects. In the sphere of pro-

10. Karl Marx, *Early Writings*, trans. and ed. T. B. Bottomore (New York: McGraw-Hill, 1964), p. 52.
11. See Roger Garaudy, *Marxism in the Twentieth Century*, trans. René Hague (New York: Charles Scribner's Sons, 1970).
12. Robert Havamann, *Dialektik ohne Dogma? Naturwissenschaft und Weltanschauung* (Hamburg: Rowohlt Taschenbuch Verlag, 1964). This text is a collection of lectures delivered in East Berlin dealing with a critical reexamination of Marxist philosophy.

duction, we have "the inversion [Verkehrung] of the subject into the object." Here, the "laborer appears as bare objective [gegenständliche] labor-power." [13] As a bare object, the laborer (who is considered only insofar as he is an objective repository of labor-power) comes to be circulated in the exchange market just like any other object.[14] As a result, we have a queer situation wherein the original subject, without whom there would be no objects to exchange on the commodity market, becomes an object to be exchanged like any other object. According to Husserl, the scientist (e.g., Galileo) constitutes his science and for some mysterious reason the creating scientist subsequently becomes estranged from the science, which loses sight of both the life-world and the telos which necessitated it. Subsequently, in behavioristic psychology, the scientist himself becomes redefined as a mere object, while the objectified science, to the extent that it determines what is rational and what is not, becomes the subject. In Marxism, the theory itself is originally created in a certain historical stage to mediate a specific political practice (proletarian revolution). However, as the object (Marxism as the mediation of proletarian class consciousness and its historical conditions) became separated from the subject (the proletariat) toward the end of the nineteenth century, it became (in the official versions of the Second and Third Internationals) a deterministic fixed doctrine used to justify the union leaders' manipulations of the working class before 1914 and bureaucratic privilege under Stalin and his successors.

The Marxist explanation of the crisis of capitalism has already become part of the cultural heritage. In the process of historical self-becoming, the creation of capitalist economic relations allows man to free himself of feudal restrictions, thus permitting the creation of certain bourgeois institutions, such as science. Thought by their originators to embody universal ideals, these institutions contradict themselves and, rather than becoming means of human emancipation, develop into tools of manipulation and domination of one class (the bourgeoisie) over another (the proletariat). In the process, however, capitalism creates the proletariat as a class which is in an objective position to qualitatively change capitalism and, through socialism, realize precisely

13. Karl Marx, Capital (Moscow: Progress Publishers, 1962), III, 45. We have amended this translation in the interest of clarity.
14. See Marx, Capital (Moscow: Progress Publishers, n.d.), I, pt. 2, chap. 7, sec. 1, "The Labor-Process or the Production of Use-Values," 177–86.

those universal goals that capitalism vitiates. The phenomenological explanation of the crisis of the sciences can be seen as a *special* case of the crisis of capitalism—at least to the extent that science is the product of scientists' labor, and in a capitalist society this product is subject to the dynamics of commodities in general.

The crisis of Marxism, however, remains to be theoretically articulated. Paci himself here merely lays some foundations. Yet the Marxist phenomenology or phenomenological Marxism that results from his investigations, if understood not as a deviation from either phenomenology or Marxism but as the de-mystification of both, is fully adequate to deal with this critical problem. If Marxism is seen as articulating the objective *consciousness* of a specific class developed in the course of a certain type of creative activity, then it is not in principle qualitatively different from the *commodities* produced by such an activity or the (scientific) *techniques* required by it. Thus, capital, science, and Marxism are three different products of the *same* sociohistorical process of capitalist development. The crisis of Marxism, analogous to the crisis of the sciences and capitalism, is essentially the separation of subject (workers) and object (their objective consciousness: Marxism), with the subsequent reification of the object to the level of an objective science (in Husserl's sense) totally independent of the concrete subjects that were to be its executors.

This is not the place to analyze the reasons for these three manifestations of the crisis, which, over thirty-five years after Husserl wrote about it, is still very much with us. Paci's book presupposes that only an approach that is both phenomenological *and* Marxist can allow even a proper formulation of the problem. Although such a philosophical marriage may seem strange to English-speaking readers, for whom the two aspects have always been kept separate, this theme has been well elaborated in Western Europe since World War II. Paci's work is only the latest and most systematic account in a long list that extends from Marcuse and Tran Duc Thao to Goldmann and Kosik.[15] Let us here attempt to sketch the intellectual background of Paci's book. One of the earliest efforts to make a synthesis between phenomenology and Marxism can be traced back to Herbert Marcuse, who,

15. For an elaborate account of the works of the Marxist critics of phenomenology, see Guido G. Neri, *Prassi e Conoscienza* (Milan: Feltrinelli, 1966), pt. 3, pp. 128–208.

in 1928, immediately following the publication of Martin Heidegger's *Sein und Zeit*, wrote a long essay dealing with phenomenology and Marxism.[16] Lucien Goldmann has argued that the crucial confrontation between phenomenology and Marxism had already taken place much earlier, and even Lukács' early works, such as *The Soul and the Forms*, can be seen as situated "in the crossing-point of the three great currents of German academic thought of the period: the neo-Kantianism of Heidelberg, the elucidation of the concepts of meaning and understanding by Dilthey, and Husserlian phenomenology." [17] Thus, the very vitality of Georg Lukács' Marxism as outlined in *History and Class Consciousness* [18] consists, according to Goldmann, in "the decisive progress that the work entails by substituting the phenomenological idea of *atemporal* meaningful structure . . . with the Marxist and dialectical concept of meaningful structure which is both dynamic and temporal, based on the idea of the Totality." [19] Furthermore, he sees the birth of German existentialism as an attempt to answer Lukács:

> We hold that it is impossible to understand such a philosophical Renaissance [existentialism] anxious and decadent, unless it is seen in relation to the fact that it is always elaborated in relation

16. Herbert Marcuse, "Beiträge zu einer Phänomenologie der Historischen Materialismus," in *Philosophische Hefte*, no. 1 (July, 1928), pp. 45–68. This essay has been translated into English in *Telos*, no. 4 (Fall, 1969), pp. 3–34. The same issue of *Philosophische Hefte* also includes a note by the editor, Maximilian Beck, indicating the close connection between the Marxian notion of *class* and Heidegger's *das Man* and *Mitsein*. According to Beck, both *class* and *Mitsein* mediate the individual and society in general.

17. Lucien Goldmann, "Introduzione" to the Italian translation of Georg Lukács, *Teoria del romanzo* (Milan: Sugar, 1962), p. 13. It would have been more correct if Goldmann had substituted Kierkegaard and Sorel for Husserlian phenomenology. As Lukács put it in the 1967 Preface to the new edition of *History and Class Consciousness:* "On the one hand, Kierkegaard has played a significant role in my early development and in the immediate pre-war years in Heidelberg I even planned an essay on his criticism of Hegel. On the other hand, the contradictions of my social and political views brought me intellectually into contact with Syndicalism and above all with the philosophy of Georges Sorel." See Georg Lukács, *History and Class Consciousness*, trans. Rodney Livingstone (Cambridge, Mass.: M.I.T. Press, 1971), pp. ix–x. For a broader analysis of this issue, see Andre Arato, "Lukács' Path to Marxism (1910–1923)," *Telos*, no. 7 (Spring, 1971), pp. 128–36.

18. This work was originally published in German in 1923.

19. Goldmann, "Introduzione," p. 43.

to a provisionally absent thinker [Lukács], forgotten and isolated in silence, who nonetheless has preceded such a Renaissance, by outlining the area and the level of the discussion, the problems to be dealt with, but who has always asserted man's dignity, the value of clear consciousness, courage and hope. . . . It is not by chance that the two most important thinkers of such a philosophical rebirth, Heidegger and Jaspers, belong to the same generation as Lukács and come from the very same restricted university circle: that of the southwest German "school." [20]

Hence, according to Goldmann, what Merleau-Ponty called "Western Marxism" [21] (as opposed to the "orthodox Marxism" of official Communist parties) has been, from its very origin at the end of World War I, inextricably connected with phenomenology —even if in an unacknowledged way. And this is not all: even Heidegger's *Sein und Zeit* had already been interpreted by Goldmann in his doctoral dissertation as "mainly a confrontation with Lukács' work: the answer in polemic with it from a viewpoint of anxiety and death." Heidegger allegedly did so by transposing all of Lukács' discourse "on a metaphysical level by mainly modifying the terminology, without ever mentioning Lukács." [22]

Although a close reading of Lukács' later works, such as *Die Zerstörung der Vernunft*, shows that he has some limited knowledge of Husserlian phenomenology—despite the fact that when he attacks phenomenology he confuses Scheler's and Heidegger's variety of phenomenology with Husserl's [23]—it is undeniable that the cultural climate of middle Europe between the two world wars was saturated with these issues. Whether or not Heidegger consciously intended his work to be an answer to Lukács, it was in fact taken to be one, not so much because of the profundity of Heideggerian existentialism, but because of the inner contradictions of Lukács' position and the crisis of the European working-class movements—the repository of hope for all Marxist thinking of the period. In reaction to the mechanistic Marxism of the Second International that had degenerated into reformism

20. *Ibid.*, pp. 48–49.
21. See Maurice Merleau-Ponty, *Les Aventures de la dialectique* (Paris: Gallimard, 1955), chap. 2, "Le Marxisme 'Occidental,'" pp. 43–80. An English translation of this crucial chapter has appeared in *Telos*, no. 6 (Fall, 1970), pp. 140–61.
22. Lucien Goldmann, *Mensch, Gemeinschaft und Welt in der Philosophie Immanuel Kants* (Zurich: Europa Verlag, 1945), p. 244.
23. For an excellent analysis of Lukács' critique of phenomenology, see Neri, *Prassi e Conoscienza*, pp. 128–35.

and political impotence in the first part of the century, Lukács sought dialectically to articulate a dynamic Marxism free from the metaphysical shackles of scientism and positivism. He tried to achieve this articulation by vindicating the Hegelian heritage of Marxism and uncompromisingly approaching every problem in terms of the Totality. The whole effort, however, was fundamentally vitiated by Hegel's objective idealism. This prevented Lukács from dealing with *real* historical forces and disrupted his analysis, which rotated around uncritically accepted categories that had long since ceased to be adequate to sociohistorical reality. It is thus not surprising that *History and Class Consciousness*, a book glowing with revolutionary fire on every page, was one of the most untimely Marxist books of the century, appearing precisely when it had already become evident that the real possibilities of Marxist revolutions in Western Europe had disappeared. The problem with Lukács' book was that, despite the rhetorical lip-service it paid to materialism, it operated with an idealistic dialectic which brilliantly articulated Marxist categories transposed *tout court* out of Marx without, however, retaining their grounding in sociohistorical reality, i.e., without retaining their materiality. Notwithstanding its penetrating philosophical analyses of reification, social democracy, and bourgeois thought, *History and Class Consciousness* was, in practice, a beautiful dream altogether lacking any mediation whereby it could meaningfully relate to the desperate realities of middle Europe in the 1920s. Lukács himself must have been painfully aware of this, for in the very last essay of the book, "Towards a Methodology of the Problem of Organization," and in another little booklet written immediately thereafter on Lenin, he practically repudiates his entire theoretical apparatus in favor of the early Leninist notion of the party and its mechanistic consequences. Thus, ironically enough, he gained the much needed mediation at the price of precisely the theoretical framework that had to be mediated.[24]

24. As Merleau-Ponty points out, Lukács tried to retain his dialectical edifice within the limited field of aesthetics to which he dedicated the better part of his life: "Although he [Lukács] has generally accepted the lessons of philosophical Leninism and like everyone else he speaks the language of reflective consciousness, thus leaving the door open for less comprehensible detours and giving a free hand to the history makers, in principle he still upholds the autonomy of truth, the possibility of reflection, and the life of subjectivity in the cultural realm where these cannot be subordinated to a tactic or it will mean their death. Everything happens as if, having accepted the unavoidable in action and in historical engagement, he now attempts to

Lukács became a Stalinist, which considerably dulled his theoretical edge. The same was not true of a whole host of young radicals whom Lukács himself mentions as being greatly impressed by his Hegelian Marxism.[25] Unwilling to accept what was presented as the "Leninist mediation" (which on Hegelian grounds turns out to be a romantic *external* mediation and, consequently, an undialectical pseudo-mediation), these young radicals remained faced with the problem of having to mediate their theory and the reality to which it was to apply. It is not surprising, therefore, that when, a few years later, Heidegger published *Sein und Zeit,* people such as Marcuse took it to be the kind of mediation needed to make Hegelian Marxism viable once again. With its stress on the things-themselves, phenomenology seemed to remedy the egregious deficiency of Hegelian Marxism, i.e., its inability to relate to the existing state of affairs:

> A fundamental distinction must be drawn between the immanent meaning of an ideology and its historical sense (location). One of the most fundamental theses of historical materialism is that the *definition* of an ideology (its immanent meaning) is not consistent with its *historical meaning.* Historical materialism is interested only in the latter, since only the latter can be dealt with by its dialectical method. The explication of immanent meaning requires precisely an approach completely opposed to the dialectic.[26]

This approach, of course, is Heideggerian phenomenology. Lukács himself had already separated "immanent meaning" from "historical meaning," [27] but he had assumed throughout that Marxism could easily deal with both, despite the fact that he had also severely curtailed Marxism's domain of application by altogether

---

preserve for the future the conditions necessary for a healthy culture." See Merleau-Ponty, "Pravda," in *Les Aventures de la dialectique,* pp. 91–92. An English translation of this chapter has appeared in *Telos,* no. 7 (Spring, 1971), pp. 112–21. The quoted passage appears on pp. 117–18.

25. Lukács, *History and Class Consciousness,* p. xxii.

26. Marcuse, "Contribution to a Phenomenology of Historical Materialism," *Telos,* no. 4 (Fall, 1969), pp. 27–28.

27. Thus, he writes: "On the one hand, all the categories in which human existence is constructed must appear as the determinants of that existence itself (and not merely of the description of that existence). On the other hand, their succession, their coherence and their connections must appear as aspects of the historical process itself, as the structural components of the present." See Lukács, *History and Class Consciousness,* p. 159.

excluding nature from the realm of investigation of dialectical methodology.[28] Confronted with the contradiction and openly attacked in the political arena, Lukács chose to discard the entire problematic, even though the political attacks of Zinoviev and Kautsky had nothing to do with the *real* shortcomings of his work.

Marcuse's proposed synthesis, however, did seek to remedy the real problems of Hegelian Marxism. Yet Jürgen Habermas' claim that this early effort was to become the basis of later attempts is not altogether correct,[29] because of the altogether different subjects of Marcuse's later investigations (e.g., Freud). The *forced* synthesis of the two mechanically juxtaposed frameworks (dialectic and phenomenology) is bound to fail from the very beginning, for either phenomenology ends up absorbed in the dialectic and ceases to be phenomenology, or the dialectic is frozen in the phenomenological foundation and ceases to be a dialectic.

Merleau-Ponty seems to have understood this very well, and his philosophy of ambiguity sought to handle both without ever really mixing them. Thus his political writings—at least up to 1955—are dialectical through and through, while his other philosophical efforts remain strictly phenomenological. To the extent that, as Paci shows, both Marxism and phenomenology are not separate but are parts of the same broad perspective, what Merleau-Ponty achieved was not a phenomenological or a Marxist perspective, either of which would have excluded the other, but a phenomenology that paved the way for structuralism and a

28. In fact, Lukács had reproached Engels for attempting a dialectics of nature: "It is of the first importance to realize that the [dialectical] method is limited here to the realm of history and society. The misunderstandings that arise from Engels' account of dialectics can in the main be put down to the fact that Engels—following Hegel's mistaken lead—extended the method to apply also to nature. However, the crucial determinants of dialectics—the interaction of subject and object, the unity of theory and practice, the historical changes in the reality underlying the categories as the root cause of changes in thought etc.—are absent from our knowledge of change" (*ibid*, p. 24, n. 6).

29. Thus Habermas writes: "After the war, the left existentialists of Paris and the philosophers of praxis of Zagreb and Prague substituted the analysis of the life-world of the late Husserl for Heidegger's analysis of being, yet both 'schools' are based on a phenomenological foundation of a Marxism that Marcuse had himself anticipated." See Jürgen Habermas, ed., *Antworten auf Herbert Marcuse* (Frankfurt a. M.: Suhrkamp, 1968).

tamed Marxism that gave way to social democracy. Although efforts to reconcile phenomenology and Marxism often take the form of a *synthesis,* such efforts are from the beginning condemned to failure, since they result in two ideologies unable to accommodate each other. Only by seeing Marxism as the outcome of phenomenology, and phenomenology as an inextricable moment of Marxism, can one attain any sort of reconciliation which simultaneously produces a more relevant phenomenology and a nondogmatic Marxism.

Before Paci, the most important man attempting to develop a phenomenological Marxism and a Marxist phenomenology was Tran Duc Thao, who moved within the same cultural milieu as Sartre and Merleau-Ponty. As early as 1946, Tran Duc Thao published a long article on "Marxisme et phénoménologie," where, among other things, he gave a phenomenological interpretation of the Marxist notions of "structure" and "superstructure." [30] Unlike Marcuse's, Tran Duc Thao's approach is not a forced synthesis but a genuine articulation of the two positions within their own frameworks. This article, however, met much opposition in orthodox Marxist circles [31] and, as Tran Duc Thao became increasingly involved in communist politics,[32] he eventually came to reject the whole attempt in his *Phénoménologie et matérialisme dialectique* (1951). This work, however, creates more problems than it solves. Put forth as an attempt to show that it is impossible for phenomenology to resolve its own inner contradictions

30. Tran Duc Thao, "Marxisme et phénoménologie," in *Revue Internationale,* 1946. In the same issue there is an article by Jean Domarchi on "Les Théories de la valeur et la phénoménologie" which operates very much within the same frame of reference. In fact, Domarchi writes: "In the first chapter of *Capital,* Marx carries on in the same way as the phenomenologists. Through a discursive process very close to Husserl's reduction, he has determined the essence (or the eidos) expressing the economic meaning of a thing, and he has subsequently described how, on the level of the *world* (especially the capitalist world) the thing *appears* as a commodity, i.e., it takes on a form that *masks its authentic economic existence*" (*ibid.,* p. 159).

31. See Pierre Naville's reply in the next issue of the same journal, entitled "Marx ou Husserl," where not only Tran Duc Thao but also Sartre and Merleau-Ponty are directly or indirectly rebuffed.

32. For an account of Tran Duc Thao's intellectual development in the late 1940s, see Roberta Tomassini, "Fenomenologia e Materialismo Dialettico in Tran Duc Thao," in *Critica Letteraria,* no. 9 (July, 1971); and Pier Aldo Rovatti, "Introduzione" to the Italian translation of Tran Duc Thao, *Fenomenologia e Materialismo Dialettico* (Milan: Lampugnani-Nigri, 1970).

other than by becoming dialectical materialism, the presentation turns out to be inconclusive. The volume really comprises two separate books: the first one is a brilliant commentary on Husserlian phenomenology, and the second one is a mediocre reiteration of the theses of Soviet "dialectical materialism." (Lukács had already expressed roughly the same theses in his *Existentialisme ou Marxisme* [1949].) [33] Notwithstanding this turnabout, it is not altogether obvious that Tran Duc Thao *actually* rejected *in toto* the phenomenological approach, and his latest work on language indicates a strong reliance on tacitly accepted phenomenological techniques.[34]

33. We should remember that the late 1940s and early 1950s are the most dogmatic and Stalinist years of Lukács' entire career. The other main work of this period, in addition to *Existentialisme ou Marxisme?*, is *Die Zerstörung der Vernunft*, where Western philosophy from 1948 to the present is presented as an increasingly irrationalistic apologetic. In fact, as Neri has shown (*Prassi e Conoscienza*, pp. 128–35), and as we have already mentioned, during this whole period Husserlian phenomenology is summarily dismissed by being confused with the Heideggerian and the Schelerian variety. In this dogmatic rejection, Lukács was a typical representative of the orthodox Marxist treatment of the subject. For a later work on the same level, see Jean T. Desanti, *Phénoménologie et praxis* (Paris: Editions Sociales, 1963), devoted exclusively to Husserl's *Cartesian Meditations*, which are found to be caught in a vicious circle. A major exception to the "official" treatment of Husserlian phenomenology can be found in the work of Antonio Banfi, who, as a leader and senator of the Italian Communist party, always paid very close attention to Husserlian phenomenology and other "decadent" philosophical trends. Although highly critical, he never summarily dismissed either Husserl or existentialism. For a good example of his account, see his posthumously published work, *La Ricerca della Realtà* (Florence: Sansoni, 1959). Also relevant is the fact that Paci, Neri, and the whole school of phenomenological Marxism in Milan originates from Banfi.

34. Tran Duc Thao's latest works comprise a series of four articles published in *La Pensée* under the following titles: "Le Mouvement de l'indication comme forme originaire de la conscience," no. 128 (August, 1966); "Du geste de l'index à l'image typique (I)," no. 147 (October, 1969); "Du geste de l'index à l'image typique (II)," no. 148 (December, 1969); and "L'Avéole de la dialectique de la connaissance," no. 149 (February, 1970). For an analysis of these works, see Silvia Federici, "Viet Cong Philosophy: Tran Duc Thao," *Telos*, no. 6 (Fall, 1970). The same issue of *Telos* also includes the English translation of one of Tran Duc Thao's articles, "The Rational Kernel in the Hegelian Dialectic" (originally published in *La Pensée*, no. 113 [February, 1965]), while no. 8 of *Telos* includes the English translation of his "The Hegelian Dialectic and Its Real Content" (originally published in *Les Temps Modernes*, no. 36 [1948]).

Finally, one of the most important figures who has attempted to articulate rather than merely analyze the phenomenological basis of Marxism is Karel Kosik, whose *Die Dialektik des Konkreten* is one of the high points of Marxist philosophy reached in Eastern Europe in the postwar period.[35] Through a devastating criticism of Heideggerian philosophy, Kosik reexamines key Marxist notions such as praxis, labor, consciousness, and economy. His analysis is free of the mechanical sloganeering typical of "official" Diamat lines. The result is a phenomenological Marxism of a quality unmatched since Lukács' work. Such a Marxism, however, by indirectly debunking established myths—e.g., the theory of knowledge as reflection, the consideration of class structure as reducible to ready-made categories whose real function is actually to occlude social reality, and the consideration of the economy as a limited sphere of human activity—turned out to be too explosive for the official ideology. Inextricably connected with the Czech "New Course," of which it was one of the best theoretical articulations, Kosik's work was suppressed by the Soviet intervention of 1968. Forgotten in Eastern Europe and partly ignored in the West, Kosik's work seems bound to the same fate as Lukács' *History and Class Consciousness*.

What is the status of a Marxism with phenomenological tendencies today? Systematically rebuffed in the East, where it constitutes a serious threat to the established ideology, and ignored by official Western Marxists, phenomenological Marxism can be articulated only by those seeking a fresh start in a chaotic context. It is precisely to this chaotic context that Paci's analyses are addressed, both as rigorous reconstructions of Husserl's phenomenology and as genuine expressions of the original spirit of Marxism, long since hidden under ideological covers motivated by dubious political goals. Paci's analyses supply a new point of departure for a reconsideration of both philosophy and politics—which, in terms of Paci's own account, are different aspects of the same predicament.

JAMES E. HANSEN
PAUL PICCONE

35. Karel Kosik, *Die Dialektik des Konkreten* (Frankfurt a. M.: Suhrkamp, 1967). The original Czech edition, however, dates back to 1961. An English translation of the first part of this work has appeared in *Telos*, no. 2 (Fall, 1968), and no. 4 (Fall, 1969).

PART I

The Crisis of the Sciences
and the Problem of Time
in Phenomenology

1 / The Crisis of Science as the Crisis of the Meaning of Science for Man

[1]   *The Crisis of Science and the Crisis of Existence*

AT THE BEGINNING OF *The Crisis of European Sciences* or, more precisely, in the lectures delivered in Prague that constitute the beginning of the volume, Husserl asks himself: "A crisis of our sciences as such: can we seriously speak of it? . . . This may be true of philosophy, which in our time threatens to succumb to skepticism, irrationalism, and mysticism." [1] Husserl recognizes that scientists, sure of their method, have some reason for protesting against those who speak of the crisis of science (p. 4). The crisis of which Husserl speaks, however, does not concern the sciences as such. Rather, it concerns what they have meant and what they could mean for human existence (p. 5). Thus, from a Husserlian viewpoint, despite the sciences' continued successes, a crisis of the sciences does exist. The crisis of psychology does not concern psychology alone. It has a "central" meaning because in psychology the enigma of subjectivity reveals itself in an undeniable way. This enigma decides both the content and the method of psychology, and subsequently influences the content and method of the other sciences. Psychology does not allow itself to be reduced to a "factual science." Its central position with respect to the other sciences consists precisely in

1. Edmund Husserl, *The Crisis of European Sciences and Transcendental Phenomenology: An Introduction to Phenomenological Philosophy,* trans. David Carr (Evanston: Northwestern University Press, 1970), p. 3. All subsequent parenthetical page references in the text are to this edition of the *Crisis.*—TRANS.

this: it resists this reduction, while the latter, since the second half of the nineteenth century, seem to have allowed themselves to be reduced to "factual" sciences. Modern man accepts being determined by the "prosperity" and success of the sciences. He accepts being, or, rather, wishes to be, a "mere man of fact," which entails the reduction of the "subjective" to the factual, and thus the transformation of psychology to a factual science. Psychology reveals the impossibility of this transformation and how, in attempting it, man allows its tendency to destroy his "subjectivity," his freedom in the world, and his freedom to rationally shape himself, his life, and his history. Men are the subjects of this freedom. Science is in crisis when, in wanting to reduce itself to a factual science, it "abstracts from everything subjective" (p. 6). To abstract from man's possibility of shaping the world is to abstract the "meaning" of human life. It amounts to believing that the "meaning of life" is not a problem, or that it is a problem which could not possibly be approached rationally or, broadly speaking, scientifically. Science can offer a solution to the problem of the meaning of life: in fact, this is precisely the function of "scientificity." * The crisis of the sciences is due to the sciences' renunciation of their own scientificity—a scientificity meant as a horizon of life, as meaning and as purpose of life. The factual, that which is objectively ascertainable, is not the only truth. The idea of rationality that gives life to any science and gives a meaning to life is also true. Truth does not rest in objectification but beyond it, on the rational movement that transcends any of its expressions and that gives meaning to any partial expression precisely when it lifts these expressions to an infinite rational movement, to a "meaning." The crisis is due to the pretense of realizing truth in the factual, to the pretense of reducing meaning to the objectivity of the expression. The expression is reduced to a factuality lacking any "intentional"

---

* Although the term "scientificity" is somewhat clumsy, it is necessary to preserve it throughout the text, insofar as it is intended as the antonym of "scientism." "Scientificity" is our rendering of Paci's *scientificità*, which is in turn his rendering of Husserl's *Wissenschaftlichkeit*. Scientificity is the essential character of science. It refers to the open-ended and nondogmatic character of science as an ideal, the character which leads to the possibility of constructing a universal store of knowledge. Scientism, on the other hand, is what becomes of science when it is dogmatized and reduced to dealing exclusively with particular bits and pieces of data. For Husserl, classical scientificity has been occluded by contemporary scientism.—
TRANS.

sense, any ideal unity of meaning. This is the resumption of the theme of the first of the *Logical Investigations*. It is not, however, a mere resumption; rather, it reveals a continuity in Husserl's thought from 1898 to the *Crisis*.

Since phenomenology is based upon intentionality, it opposes any pretense of reducing truth to factuality, either in the natural sciences or in the "social sciences" (*Geisteswissenschaften*). Life, psyche, and spirit are not understandable as factual phenomena from which "the specifically human questions" (p. 7) have been banished. Science itself has not always "understood its demand for rigorously grounded truth in the sense of that *sort* of objectivity which dominates our positive sciences . . . [and] is the basis for the support and widespread acceptance of a philosophical and ideological positivism" (p. 7).

According to Husserl, true knowledge is such not because it is factual or "objective," but because it is rigorously founded. It was the need for a foundation that made it possible during the Renaissance for science to have meaning as a molder of a new humanity, of a new life—new because founded on truth. The limiting positivistic conception of science misunderstands the decisive function of science itself.

What was essential in antiquity, and what the Renaissance wanted to restore, was a *philosophical kind of existence*. Existence is philosophical insofar as it can freely conform to philosophically founded principles: philosophy liberates not only the philosopher but every man as well. Renaissance Platonism seeks not only the ethical reconstitution of each of us, but also the remolding of the world, of political and social life, according to the principles of a universal philosophy (p. 8). Philosophy is a totalizing science of which the other sciences are particular branches. With Descartes, philosophy appears as the unity of a theoretical system founded on evident, infinitely perfectible principles. Positivism has rejected the problems that were included in the concept of metaphysics. Now, it is true that traditional metaphysics has declined. But its problems present themselves in a new guise and have their own indissoluble unity in the fact that, whether implicitly or explicitly, they contain the problems of reason in all its individual forms. If man posits a "metaphysical" problem, it is because he raises himself to the level of reason, which transcends factuality. "Metaphysical," in this sense, is what is valid—it is that which remains as authentic in time and history. Moreover, it is that which continually guides us to the foundation of what is valid. The problem of the relationship of permanence and becoming-in-time, of the moving and the *nunc stans,* is the problem of what is authentic because it is grounded. But it must always be grounded anew, and it should never be lost in factuality, which is estranged from the foundation, i.e., from intentional life, which is both the life-world (or the precategorial *Lebenswelt*) and the infinite ideal of rationality.

What emerges triumphant in the Renaissance is faith in philosophy and its method. Subsequently, however, this faith weakens, and the project of a philosophical reconstitution of humanity fails, along with the notion of philosophy as the basis of a rational humanity. Why has the project failed? The era of Hume and Kant, which is also our era, is one which passionately struggles to understand the reasons for the failure of "rigorous" philosophy as the basis of all the sciences and of a new rational humanity. According to Husserl, the ideal of a *philosophia perennis* and of a universal philosophy reappears in its most authentic meaning in phenomenology. It is in this sense that philosophy is rigorous: to the extent that, in the last analysis, it is the active constituting process of a new humanity. We are tempted to say that this rigorous science (*strenge Wissenschaft*) is a new science (*neue Wissenschaft*) in Vico's sense. Up to now mankind has done some philosophy while itself remaining outside of philosophy. It has done some science, but it has also reduced science to factuality, and it wants to reduce man to factuality. Phenomenology wants to return his "subjectivity" to man. It wants to return man to himself, freeing him from every fetishism, from the mask behind which humanity has been hidden or "veiled." Phenomenology is the disoccluding of what is "veiled." It is the revelation of humanity to itself, of the *phenomenon* of humanity to itself. It is a phenomenon constituted and self-constituted according to a truth that man originally carries within himself and that he loses in the "mundane." The constitution, then, is the renewal of humanity through the return to the original and teleological sense of reason. To the extent that man, in the name of reason, rejects his mask, he discovers his own truth. He sees his proper, authentic nature, where what appears is what really is, and where, at any rate, *what is* never appears in a definite way. As such, our most secret nature, what we actually are in the most profound sense, first and foremost, is also the rational ideal, the teleological end, and the final goal.

The ideal of a universal philosophy asserts itself at the beginning of the modern era. Insofar as it is a matter of an ideal which has to ground human existence, the crisis of philosophy and science is the crisis of existence (p. 12). If reason alone can give a meaning to being and existence, to being and truth, to things, to values, and to ends, the collapse of faith in reason cannot express itself other than as an existential crisis. The history of philosophy is a struggle for existence in accordance with an end, a struggle for the meaning of existence. The crisis of our era is the expression of the struggle of humanity for its own self-understanding, for its own transformation and its own meaning. The crisis requires a transformation that is as engaging as it is radical: the transformation that man must demand of himself (p. 13). Philosophy fights for the authentic sense of humanity. If a philosophy is possible today, its duty is not to surrender to man as he is, but rather to rebuild man, to open the way for an authentic man. Metaphysics, understood in a new sense, is "possible" to the extent that a new humanity is possible, or, as we would say in Vico's sense, philosophy has to constitute a new humanity. The realization of metaphysics is both progressive and infinite. Its meaning cannot be exhausted within a philosophical "system." Metaphysics, as philosophy or as a new science, has to bring to light and realize what is hidden and latent. It has to transform what is latent into purpose, into a *telos*. Within man there is a latent humanity—and here we interpret Husserl in a radical sense—a humanity which has not yet been born but which can be born if man so desires, if man assumes the responsibility for becoming what he can become.

History can appear as the progressive self-revelation and self-realization of what is hidden. And what is hidden is the authentic original man: both his meaning and his *telos*. Husserl sees the movement as one from *latent* to *manifest reason*. It aims at realizing that end which, in his opinion, first presented itself in Greece—humanity founded on philosophy. For Husserl, philosophy as a new science is "the historical movement of revelation." The revelation is to become a "phenomenon": it is phenomenology. What becomes a phenomenon is that which is within ourselves, implicit but hidden. It is our true life. We do not yet live according to our true life and therefore do not live according to reason. We do not really exist, but are in a sort of pre-existence. Our duty is to realize our existence in history, to come really into being in history. History has not ended, and we can say that Marx was correct in claiming that we are still in prehistory. This is how we interpret Husserl's claim that "Philosophy and science would accordingly be the historical movement through which universal reason, 'inborn' in humanity as such, is revealed" (pp. 15–16).

The rationalism of the Enlightenment was, and most certainly is, a naïveté. But to renounce the rationalism of the Enlightenment does not entail renouncing authentic rationalism. Naïve rationalism believes that philosophy has nothing to do with existence. But we now know that this very same belief is our misery. Philosophy in crisis is the crisis of existence, the "existential contradiction" (p. 17). Philosophy is not at all "academic," or "cultural," or "superstructural" with respect to existence. It is a function of existence, and, because of this, philosophers are functionaries of mankind (p. 17). As such, they are in history and they must historically understand the crisis of philosophy and its task. Even without knowing it, man has always been he who can and must become authentic. Mankind has always been moving toward the "phenomenological reduction," and must constantly do so. The reduction, the authentic intentional life, explains the past, the present, and the future.

Let us try to understand the meaning of what has been said. Phenomenology wants to lead man to self-consciousness, to self-foundation, to self-constitution, to transcendental foundation. This is possible if the "mundane" is bracketed. Here the mundane means the barely factual, the "positive" of positivism, i.e., meaning reduced to the factuality of discourse, the subject reduced to an object. Objectivism and factuality are masks behind which man is hidden and fetishized. Therefore, the transcendental foundation requires the transcendental reduction to pure subjectivity, i.e., to transcendental subjectivity. Even if not identical with man, the transcendental ego does not differ from the original man in his rational reality, who is, in every sense, authentic man. He is not an abstraction. To the extent that he is man, even if a minimal man, he is present to himself: he is *in the first person*, in presence, in time as presence. Presence here is the primary origin, and it constitutes the truth of the evidence. Evidence, always limited and finite, is the pledge and the proof that man can bring to light what is latent within himself, what he has hidden, what is not yet human, what is not rationally or philosophically grounded. For the philosopher who wants to constitute humanity and ground it upon philosophy, evidence is therefore the starting point, the beginning. But because evidence is always partial and finite, this evidence and the foundation of humanity are always posed as a task for the future, as a *telos*.

After all, if man is now an integral part of the evidence, he has also been so in the past, and if the evidence is now the result of the transcendental reduction, then man has always been moving toward the transcendental reduction. His life has always implicitly contained truth and, to the extent that it was even minimally authentic life, it was within truth—even if hidden, fetishized, and objectified. There has always been a precategorial, prescientific life within the very fetishized factuality of the sciences, within the negation of the life-world (the *Lebenswelt*). It is because of this that history has a meaning: from the past, in the present, for the future.

The reduction to transcendental life is the foundation of scientificity and not of factuality; it is a reduction to transcendental subjectivity and to the *Lebenswelt:* a reduction to life present to itself, to presence. This presence, which is never absolute, has a genesis (a past) and a future (a *telos*). If we bracket the "mundane" and include in it "factuality" and the categories that are fetishized, objective, and scientific, and go on to trace the history of the sciences as they have pretended to substitute their absolutized categories for the precategorial life (the *Lebenswelt*), then we see that precisely for this reason the sciences have failed in their "philosophical" function. Furthermore, we realize that the philosophic function was precisely the function of science and the sciences, and that, "historically," the sciences have failed in their function. The historical analysis allows us to recapture the *Lebenswelt* behind its fetishization. It becomes the explanation of the crisis. The reduction to the *Lebenswelt* appears to Husserl precisely when he historically analyzes the failure of the philosophical task. In a certain sense it is the factuality into which the sciences have fallen, their very success (as fallen), which reveals the *Lebenswelt*. Something has been betrayed in spite of their success; rather, the failure has occurred *precisely because of their success*. This is the enigma: why has the very success of the sciences provoked the crisis? This cannot concern the sector where the sciences are successful, but it does concern the sector of the function of science for life and history.

I can consider the reduction to the *Lebenswelt* only on the "historical" level. In a certain sense, I can locate myself in the past and consider the present free of "factualism" and myself free of any fetishization as if I were already inserted into the *Lebenswelt*. But in this case I lose my authenticity at the very moment that I believe I have reached it. Rather, I should return to myself, to my presence, and perform on myself the operation which I have seen lacking in history. The reduction will then appear to me as a transcendental reduction to the present *qua* present, i.e., to pure subjectivity. Husserl sometimes speaks of the reduction to the *Lebenswelt* as if it were a first reduction, and of the transcendental reduction as if it were a second reduction. As a matter of fact, the reduction is complex and therefore can appear in numerous aspects, in different temporal acts, according to various modalities. This is because the reduction itself is never definitive and absolute. In a sense, the transcendental reduction includes all others and leads us to a subjectivity which is not mythological; it is my life oriented toward truth, the life which I somehow always live behind my masks. The masks themselves can and do reappear in daily life, and then they are lived as if they were real. The life-world itself can always be obscured anew. It can be deceived, and in order to be rescued it must return to that pure subjectivity which brackets everything—even life— and which, above all, appears as a result of the transcendental reduction. Pure subjectivity discovers within itself not the myth of a closed consciousness but, once again, life: a life beset by the danger of being lost, and containing the possibilities of being rescued. The two possible ways in which the reduction is presented reveal the world (*Lebenswelt*) and the ego. But to the extent that the world is alive, it is also the "subjective" world. Similarly, "subjectivity," to the extent that it is transcendental, is also the inherence of subjectivity in the world.

Life and transcendental consciousness, the ego and the world, are not absolute. They are moments of the loss and of the recovery of life, of its occlusion and awakening, of its presence and absence, of its relative possibility of wakening and re-presenting the occluded, of the rediscovery of presence in absence. Even if, as has been said, there is a dualism of the *Lebenswelt* and absolute subjectivity, it is a contradiction between the various ways in which the same concept of reduction appears. The contradiction disappears if it is considered in relation to the primary and more profound sense of phenomenology, which is to be seen in the structure of time. Within time, being awake (i.e., life as presence) is not possible without the pauses of sleep and death. After all, it is due to these pauses, to the very limit of any re-presentation (irreversibility), and, finally, to the very crisis of the sciences recognized as a crisis, that it is possible for existence repeatedly to understand its own meaning and to move again toward its own *telos*.

[2]   *The Phenomenological-Historical Genesis
        of the Crisis*

THE HERITAGE OF Euclidean geometry, mathematics,
and Greek natural sciences directly influences, even if in a different way, the beginning of the modern era. Science appears according to a new principle that was alien to the ancients. Ancient
science was encompassed in a finite and closed sphere: it had not
arrived at a recognition of the possibility of an infinite task, a possibility inherent in "geometrical" space. Geometrical space is
ideally defined a priori in all of its possible determinations. Notice: only ideally. It is closed insofar as it allows the construction
of all the spatial forms that it potentially contains. Proceeding
gradually to infinity according to a univocal method, we discover
in a preliminary way what we assume as true from the beginning. Ideal space allows science to dominate an infinite sphere.
A closed ideal form makes possible a systematic and infinite
integration of what, within that form, appears as already ideally
determined. The same happens in formal mathematics that opens
to infinite horizons. Algebra, mathematics of the continuum, and
analytic geometry originate in this fashion.

An infinite universal science begins to appear. The infinite
appears as rational and, therefore, as controllable through a
preliminary idealization. As such, this idealization is a priori.
The development of the research into what is ideally a priori
determined can be infinitely explicated within the sphere of the
idealization that has made the research possible. Thus, the mathematical idealization of nature limits the sphere of an infinite
system to the "manifold" of nature. For Galileo, all that can be
constructed in pure form, and, in general, the mathematics of the
pure spatiotemporal form, is obviously included in nature (pp.
21–24). The Galilean mathematization of nature and pure geometry is obvious. Husserl denies this obviousness. He wants to
seize the origin of idealization in order to discover its most authentic meaning.

Therefore, we can notice:

1) The historical investigation of the origin of the contraposition of objectivism to subjectivism becomes the investigation
of the origin of the idealization which allows the construction of
the mathematical science of nature. An investigation of a "histori-

cal" type "also" presents itself as a "phenomenological" investigation. If the idealizations are on the level of science, their modality (that from which they derive—the world from which they arise, which is, after all, the "life-world") is not. This indicates the pre-scientific dimension from which science historically originated, and from which it still originates today when we phenomenologically inquire into how it comes about. Notice this relationship between "historical" and "actual" phenomenology. They both seek an origin. But that which explains the origin and starts from the origin is both what has done so in the past and what can do so today. At play here is the problem of time, the problem of the present which remembers and "re-presents" the past;

2) A relation between the finite and the infinite comes about in the idealization that is inclusive, determined, and determining. Before the idealization there is the infinite as indetermination. Subsequently, the infinite becomes ordered research in a determined field;

3) Finally, we must distinguish between what we reconstruct of the path taken by Galileo, insofar as we do so within ourselves (and in doing so, in reflection and in the re-presentation, we are aware of it), and what remained unconscious and hidden (even though obvious) in Galileo. Here we apply the general principle of phenomenology whereby we cannot only re-present the past in the present but, in re-presenting it, we can now make explicit what in that past (in the present which is now past) remained unconscious and hidden. What remained hidden was active, functional, and functioning. Therefore, there was a functioning intentionality operating in Galileo that becomes conscious in the actual reflection when we re-tread and reexamine the historical origin. Then it is not simply the case that the actual investigation of the origin "coincides" with the origin at that time; rather, the actual investigation, unlike the earlier one, is self-conscious, and can be so precisely in the "coincidence."

From the tradition, Galileo inherits a formal geometry applied to the empirical forms. For him, the spatial figures of experience seem to coincide in an obvious way with the geometrical idealities. The empirical-intuitive geometrical figures are the "bodies" of experience. Their "typical character" is fluctuating and approximative, and the same can be said of their "completeness," which is gradual (they are, for example, more or less flat or circular). The perfection of the technique tends toward an ever greater completeness. The process of perfecting takes place within the horizon of limiting forms, and it tends toward the ideal of a domain of pure forms. The forms on the one hand determine an inclusive realm, and on the other hand open to an infinite horizon. Thus, they constitute a field of work governed by ideal objectifications that can always be rediscovered (insofar as they are determined) and can always be perfected anew. There is not only a generic limit whereby we could speak of a movement to infinity, but, in an indetermined way, *the limit is also that of a determined ideal object, of a horizon of ideal objects, e.g., the geometrical ones.*

Once determined, the ideal objects also remain available because they are expressed and *sedimented* in the language. Now, the ideal objects are derived from the idealization of the empirical forms, from the forms of the *Lebenswelt* or *Erfahrungswelt* (world of experience). This is their origin and this is their original meaning-structure [*formazione di senso*]. But this origin can be occluded, it can be forgotten, as happens with Galileo where the meaning-structure, the meaning, is no longer consciously known. At any rate, the language can fix the ideal objects. The meaning-structure has been forgotten, but it has been sedimented in the language which allows us to deal operationally with the objects, even if the origin of the objects (and, therefore, their meaning) has been occluded.

Among the idealized forms derived from lived experience, there are some privileged ones, e.g., the point, the straight line, and the plane. Departing from these, we can construct univocally determined forms by means of a systematic method, i.e., we can construct all the forms that are thinkable in terms of the same structure. The method leads back to the practice of measuring. From measuring we arrive at the idealization (as happens, e.g., in land surveying). Therefore, measuring obtains between the world of experience and the world of ideal objects, and it allows us to understand the origin of the experience of these objects (pp. 24–28). It represents a functional relationship between experience and the limiting mathematical ideas. Galileo assumes this relationship as obvious, and even disentangles it from the technique of applied geometry without worrying about the origin of the ideal forms in the *Lebenswelt:*

Galileo . . . did not feel the need to go into the manner in which the accomplishment of idealization originally arose (i.e., how it grew on the underlying basis of the pregeometrical, sensible world and its practical arts) or to occupy himself with questions about the origins of apodictic, mathematical self-evidence. [P. 29]

Now, phenomenology is interested precisely in the origin.

Without worrying about the origin, Galileo attempts to ideal-ize the bodies by transposing them into forms, thereby extracting all their specific qualities from their sensitive plenum, in accord-ance with the model of the relationship between experience and geometrical ideas. In their concreteness, the "full" bodies are interconnected in a reciprocal inherence and in a spatiotemporal connection which has its own typical modes, its "habits." The complex of full bodies is in a spatiotemporal relation of "pres-ences" that has its own causal style and presents itself as an infinite total unity (this is a characterization of the unitary and infinite totality of the corporeal presences within the space-time of the *Lebenswelt*). The causal style of the presences makes hypotheses about the past and the future possible. Mathematics has idealized the indetermined, generic, and corporeal world, thus arriving at ideal objects. Infinity is preliminarily defined, thus permitting a method. Through measuring, from which mathematics has arisen as a science of bodies transformed into ideal forms, mathematics itself is applicable to the empirical-intuitive world. Thus, through the formalization of the presence of the full bodies, and through the formalization of hypotheses about the past and the future, it makes possible inductive predic-tions of a new kind. That is, starting from individual, given, and measured forms, it allows us to calculate with certainty other forms, unknown and inaccessible to direct measurements. Math-ematics suggests a universal science of nature applicable to all corporeal and concrete plena and their specific qualities. This application cannot be direct, since it is possible only for abstract forms and not for plena; thus it must be indirect. Both bodies and forms belong to the same world. In every intention we assert something of a unique world, one and the same world. Husserl points out that this is the way of thinking which motivates the idea of a new physics (p. 33). This idea is inherent in the prob-lem of the mathematization of the plena.

A sensitive plenum has its own specific sensible qualities: smell, sound, color, feeling. These qualities are properties of actual experienced bodies (they are not the "sense-data" which are already abstractions). They are properties experienced in a lived experience—the prescientific experience of the *Lebenswelt*. The specific qualities of meaning cannot be measured precisely. The exactness is due to an increasingly more perfect empirical measurement from which the ideal forms are derived. These are part of a universal form of the world that is the geometry of the forms. It is the universal form that presents itself as a formal, constructible world. The structure of the world implies that all plena have their own geometrical forms and that bodies have specific sensible qualities. But these are not analogous (Kant would have said "homogeneous") to the mathematical, geometrical, and spatiotemporal forms, and they are not articulated in a form of the world that is specifically theirs. They cannot be idealized, and, therefore, they cannot be directly mathematized. Indirect mathematization is possible because the specific qualities are similar to the forms and inhere in them in an essential way. Even if they are not analogous to the real plena, the ideal forms are related to them. The relation indicates that there is a concrete, universal causality. In his astonished admiration of the grand and decisive work of Galileo, Husserl here applies the principle according to which the prescientific, concrete world is supported by a *causal relation* (as he himself has clarified in *Ideen II*).

Causality and indirect mathematization reveal a horizon which anticipates but does not yield the infinite manifold of the particular essences. The causal connection and the changing of the plena do not have their own *direct* counterparts within the sphere of the forms. According to Galileo, however, all that appears as real in the specific sensitive qualities must have its mathematical index in the sphere of the forms, a sphere already completely idealized. (This is today obvious from a "physicalist" point of view, whereby color and sound are resolved into sound and heat waves.) From this the possibility follows of an indirect mathematization. As such, mathematics is applied to nature and can construct all events of a concrete causality, the causality of the plena (pp. 34–37).

There are numerous "throwbacks" which unite the plena to the forms: e.g., the functional dependence, already observed by the Pythagoreans, obtaining between the pitch of a sound and the length of the vibrating chord. In the Renaissance the entire concrete world must be shown to be translatable into a precise mathematization, *if* adequate measuring methods are possible. The idealization had built an infinity. Now this is projected onto the plena, which appear infinite and therefore able to be infinitely disassembled and separated. The concrete world appears pervaded with infinity. (This is true of the problem of abstraction of mathematical infinity as projected to the *Lebenswelt*, and it is a problem which also concerns the Kantian dialectic, i.e., the antinomies of pure reason. But it is a problem that still awaits a complete phenomenological analysis—which, in turn, would be the analysis of the finite-infinite relation within the framework of perception. This analysis also seems to be lacking in Husserl.)

On the basis of what has been described, Galileo arrives at a general hypothesis (which he does not see as a hypothesis): the hypothesis of universal induction that dominates the entire intuitive world. He will systematically want to seize universal causality.

Idealized universal causality embraces all the particular forms—even what happens on the fringe of the plena has to be studied methodically. In the investigating process, Galileo attempts to elaborate the most appropriate methods of measurement. His hypothetical anticipation implies the ubiquitous existence of causal connections expressible in mathematical formulae. If we think of how what we call a hypothesis arose, experience necessarily agreed with him, since the hypothesis originated precisely in experiences (an origin which had remained occluded). Husserl says that Galileo's discovery (which lacked the awareness we have when we reenact his operations) was a *mixture of instinct and method* (p. 40), because his operations remained mysteriously occluded.

The indirect mathematization of the intuitive world, the world of plena, gives rise to general numerical formulae that can thereafter be applied to particular cases subsumed under them. These formulae express general causal connections or "natural laws." The laws of real dependence must be expressed in terms of "functional" numerical dependences.

The Galilean hypothesis becomes a project: it is not verified once and for all. It always remains a hypothesis, and its only possible verification is, in fact, an infinite succession of verifications. What reappears here is the relationship between the determined (and the determinable) and the infinite. The "true nature" of the natural sciences is an idea which extends to infinity, an idea which is composed of infinite theories whose verification is bound to an "infinite historical process of approximation" (p. 42).[2]

The empirico-intuitive world is an approximation of exact, typical forms. Because of the indicated connections, these forms can construct a picture of the probable, empirical regularities of

2. The theory of the infinite theories of a science of essential types of possible theories poses the problem of the "theory of the manifold" (Grassman, Hamilton, Cantor, *et al.*). See E. Husserl, *Logical Investigations*, trans. J. N. Findlay (New York: Humanities Press, 1970), I, 239 ff.; and Husserl, *Formal and Transcendental Logic*, trans. Dorion Cairns (The Hague: Nijhoff, 1969), pp. 90–98.

the life-world. The formulae allow predictions of what can be expected in the *Lebenswelt*. Notice that within the domain of the *Lebenswelt* mathematics is but a particular praxis. It is understandable that the search for the formulae was, and is, captivating. So is the temptation of "taking these formulae and their formula-meaning for the true being of nature itself."

The formulae are determined in ever more general numerical propositions, and the progress of algebra allows the arithmetization of geometry. The empirical intuitions are transformed into purely numerical forms. With the algebraic calculus, the geometrical meaning becomes secondary.

> One calculates, remembering only at the end that the numbers signify magnitudes. . . . Later this becomes a fully conscious methodical displacement, a methodical transition from geometry, for example, to pure analysis, treated as a science in its own right. [Pp. 44–45]

With Galileo, we arrive at an arithmetization, or *universal* formalization, that prepares the way for the "theory of the manifold" and logicism. With his *mathesis universalis* Leibniz poses himself at the center of this process. In the constitution of the logico-formal idea of a world in general, the "theory of the manifold" is the essence of the universal science of definite manifolds. This is how Husserl has traced the origins of logic and of contemporary logicism (pp. 44–45). Logic becomes a technique, an art, a complex of the "rules of the game." By now, the original meaning of the game in the *Lebenswelt* has been lost.

The passage from the experience of the *Lebenswelt* to the technique is not only legitimate but also indispensable. What matters for Husserl is that it be conscious.

> It can be this [i.e., conscious], however, only if care is taken to avoid dangerous shifts of meaning by keeping always immediately in mind the original bestowal of meaning [*Sinngebung*] upon the method, through which it has the sense of achieving knowledge about the *world*. Even more, it must be freed of the character of an *unquestioned tradition*. [P. 47]

What is not investigated is what remains as obvious, or what is mechanically applied in the occlusion of the origin, in the occlusion of the *Lebenswelt*. The indispensable technization falls into alienation if it loses its meaning and the meaning of science for man.

2 / The Occlusion of the Life-World and the Meaning of the Transcendental

[3]   *The Occlusion of the* Lebenswelt
      in Galileo: The Circle
      and Dialectic of Time

ACCORDING TO HUSSERL, Galileo substitutes the categorial dimension of mathematics for the truly experienced and experienceable world, i.e., for our real daily world, the *Lebenswelt*. Idealized nature becomes superimposed on prescientific, intuitive nature (p. 50). Every category arises from the environment, from the surrounding world in which each of us lives, from the precategorial *Umwelt*. Every category has a goal which is part of the life-world and refers to it. However, only the world where the scientist lives as a man, our living world, is questionable within the infinite and open horizon of what has yet to be investigated. We live our corporeal mode of being within the *Lebenswelt*, which may be constituted by the dynamic synthesis of our senses and movements. For Husserl, this is the constitution of the *transcendental aesthetic*. He has investigated this area in *Ideen II* and further analyzed it in the unpublished manuscripts of Group D. Husserl says that in the life-world we find neither geometrical space nor mathematical time. Generally speaking, we find no "idealizations" in the *Lebenswelt*. In fact, idealizations are the result of a series of operations which *initiate and remain* within the life-world. If this origin is "occluded," the idealizations are taken for reality, and abstraction is substituted for concreteness.

The life-world, in its aesthetic aspect, in its style, in its spatiotemporality, does not disappear if we invent an art or a

technique of the Galilean mathematical-geometrical variety that
we call physics. We employ this technique to make predictions,
but the basis of its functioning is always the spatiotemporal
structure of the *Lebenswelt* as it reveals itself to perception and
as we experience it "in the first person." To perceive is also to
"plan," and "to direct oneself toward in advance" (*Vorhaben,
Vormeinen*). If, as we try to understand Husserl, we keep in
mind his studies of time, we must observe that the temporal
presence includes not only retention and remembrance, but also
protention and recollective anticipation; this is why prediction
is possible.¹ It seems, then, that the origin of the technified
scientific prediction and its meaning must be studied within the
temporal structure.

The life-world is misunderstood and occluded when it is
dressed up in and obscured by the clothing of abstract mathematical ideas (*Ideenkleid*) and separated from their origin, i.e.,
from lived experience (pp. 51–52).

When the *Ideenkleid* of mathematics is separated from the
real life-world and assumed to be true and objective nature, it becomes true reality. It causes us to take as true being that which is
only a symbol or a method which perfects the rough, temporal
predictions as they are perceived and lived. Absolutized and
separated from reality by means of the "misplaced concreteness"
of its methods (Whitehead's expression concurs perfectly with
Husserl's usage), science becomes a sort of mechanism whose
real operations remain hidden.² This is how Galileo discovers his
art, his technique, his method. But by believing that true being is
the being of the method, he again covers his own discovery at the
same time that he unveils it (p. 52). The mechanism is handed

---

1. For an elaboration of the problem of temporal modalities, see
my text, *Tempo e Verità Nella Fenomenologia di Husserl* (Bari:
Laterza, 1961), where an attempt is made to clarify the Husserlian
analysis of time, beginning with his *Vorlesungen zur Phänomenologie des inneren Zeitbewusstseins* (Halle: Niemeyer, 1928). [This
latter text shall hereafter be cited in the English edition: *The Phenomenology of Internal Time-Consciousness*, ed. Martin Heidegger,
trans. James C. Churchill (Bloomington: Indiana University Press,
1964).—TRANS. (All subsequent translators' notes will be in brackets.)]

2. Concerning the relationship between Husserl's and Whitehead's viewpoints, see H. Spiegelberg, *The Phenomenological Movement* (The Hague: Nijhoff, 1960), I, 78–79. Also see my "Über einige
Verwandtschaften zwischen der Philosophie Whiteheads und der
Phänomenologie Husserls," *Revue Internationale de Philosophie*, no.
56–57 (1961), pp. 237–50.

down, but it is no longer bound to the meaning-structure given to it by its origin in the *Lebenswelt*. The historical meaning of the original formulation is lost: therefore, the actual foundation is lost. It is from this foundation that, even now, technology originates. The loss of this foundation is the loss of intentionality, the loss which motivates the crisis. Therefore, for Husserl, who searches for the historical origin of the crisis, Galileo (for whom abstract nature, dressed up and obscured, is for the first time clearly substituted for the *Lebenswelt*) is a name representing an entire series of situations, both preceding him and deriving from him. We ourselves are in the situation represented by Galileo. Phenomenology must free itself from the abstract dressing, from the occlusion caused by the fetishized, ontologized, and objectified science that prevents us from experiencing life as it is, from experiencing *things-themselves* as they are, from experiencing the *Lebenswelt* whence all meaning originates, and from experiencing life in its function as the "giver of meaning."

We must always rediscover the original basis beneath the covering and the occlusion, and this is possible only through the reduction which phenomenology invites us to perform, starting from the living present. The living present is lost in the world: it is in the loss of the world (*Weltverlorenheit*). The transcendental reduction allows us to find what Husserl indicates as absolute subjectivity. (We must be careful here not to give a metaphysical or dogmatic meaning to the adjective "absolute.")

We must make the following comments here: absolute subjectivity, or transcendental life, is not only pure consciousness. It is also corporeality, sensitivity, and intermonadic life—life that experiences the world (*welterfahrendes Leben*). In the occluded present, the reduction allows us to discover the life that experiences the world, and the world that is experienced within ourselves—the world that becomes subjectified within the concrete relation of monads, in their internal relatedness (*Ineinandersein*). This intermonadic being is the intersubjective "we," but it is also life itself in the first person. It is the life of perception, of aesthetic intersensibility (transcendental aesthetic), of instincts themselves, of needs and impulses (including the need for food, and the sexual instinct). The concrete living presence is the result of the transcendental reduction. This is not the abstract transcendental ego separated from the ego which we are, and it is not separated from that concrete world in which we have always been living, which is always presupposed and never deniable insofar as it is lived in perception. But the living presence (the present time) also contains the past, and retains and recollects the past that constitutes it, even if that past is occluded. The living presence contains its historical genesis, and the historical genesis contains the living presence: the point of arrival of the genesis, the present, coincides with the present that I rediscover by means of the reduction. The coincidence is never absolute. From the present I attempt new re-presentations and new historical geneses: the historical geneses themselves can generate the need for new reductions. In our opinion, if we fail to consider these perspectives—decisive in all of Husserl's work—we run the risk of understanding nothing of what Husserl says in the *Crisis*.

With Galileo, the consciousness of the origin of the sciences in the *Lebenswelt* has been occluded. But something has remained with me, and today I can rediscover the *Lebenswelt* and subsequently investigate it within the history which has led me to its occlusion: I can disocclude history. Or, rather, the historical investigation that I make into the actual occlusion can reveal what is occluded of the past, and thereby what is occluded in the present. Can full understanding of the *original*, as the beginning that explains the actual, be attained solely by departing from the occulded present that should disocclude it? We must insist on this circle, which Husserl saw only vaguely. It is a fact that historical research does not proceed mechanically according to an entirely clear, preestablished continuity from the present to the past and from the past to the present. The circle is temporal, and time includes interruptions, pauses, and recollections. Pauses and detachments delimit temporal periods: the individual durations of the monads from birth to death. It would be illusory to represent a past that arrives at the present by a continuous and direct line, and to represent a present that goes back to the past in the same way: there are temporal and historical leaps. Retention and protention are continuous, but this is not the case with remembrance and anticipation. I do not hear a symphony without a beginning and an ending; I hear one that has both. If I forget it, and afterward try to remember it, I can do so with a certain freedom. I could not do this with a symphony played *ad infinitum*. The pauses themselves, and the *distinctions between periods*, enable me to leap, to remember this or that period of the past without having to go through and relive all of it. I can forget what I did four years ago, and remember what I did ten years ago. I may want to re-present my infancy without fully presentifying my youth. I jump back into the past: a simple and linear "flowing back" into the past is impossible.[3]

It must be borne in mind that in fact I do not return to the past, but re-present it in remembrance, i.e., I recall (in an activity which is in the present). If in fact I do not flow back, but instead leap with "seven-league boots," [4] it is because I am dealing with the actual time of memory and not with the past time of what is being remembered. Historiography is free to skip from century to century precisely because it starts from the present, or because it follows a new interest in which the present becomes detached from itself owing to a new horizon.

I believe that here it is helpful to apply my principle of *temporal irreversibility*.[5] The irreversibility of the flow of experience (*Erlebnisstrom*) allows me to start out from the present, and only from the present, in order to relive the genesis which has led to the present. It is the present which comprehends and disoccludes the past, because the present is life that can remember death without *actually* bringing back to life what is dead. Death is an inevitable pause of life, and it is life that dies in order to live again, that comprehends the past for a new future, that renews the thought of dead philosophers. In one unpublished manuscript, Husserl writes, "It is the living who wake up those who are not living," and, in another, "Without life there is no death." [6]

Because of temporal irreversibility, the relationship with the past, with past life, is an intermonadic relationship. Since the past does not repeat itself and I am unable to relive my birth, my

3. See the unpublished manuscript C 13 II, p. 2, in Gerd Brand, *Mondo Io e Tempo* (Milan: V. Bompiani, 1960). [The numbers of these manuscripts refer to the Husserl-Archiv numbering given to the collection of manuscripts in Louvain. Some of these manuscripts have in fact been published in various places (as in this case) but are still called "unpublished" because they have not been brought out in the official Husserliana series of texts. When possible, Professor Paci refers the reader to published sources for these manuscripts.]

4. Brand, *Mondo Io*, p. 193.

5. See my text, *Tempo e Relazione* (Turin: Taylor, 1954).

6. See the unpublished manuscript K III II, pp. 14–15, and B I 14/X, p. 22.

factual origin, I am reborn in the present in a new sense, in the teleological sense of becoming. Husserl's "circle" contains the *origin as past* and the *origin as present,* in addition to containing the transformation of the "past" origin in a *telos* for the future. As always in Husserl, the meanings of the fundamental terms are threefold (because they are inserted into the three dimensions of time). In our interpretation, which is both a restatement and a correction, the impossibility of present life's returning to the past (irreversibility) allows me to be free in the present to re-present what has been detached from me by occlusion and death. Death is the guarantee of freedom. It is now possible to discover the occluded in the past in order to transform the present and proceed into the future. The unreachable past origin projects itself into the future, becomes *telos.* The primary principle that I seek, for which I long, becomes a new task for the future. It is while questioning the past (but not by becoming the past) that I understand the present and the interest of the present for its own transformation. Since everything originates in present life, in this dialectic the *origin as past,* in passing from the *origin of the present,* becomes the *origin as future,* and therefore *telos.* Sometimes this complex temporal dialectic has remained hidden to Husserl, even though he has laid down its premises. Here it is merely indicated. It involves a complex network of connections and implies an elaboration replete with very difficult consequences for phenomenology in a temporal-relationistic sense. We shall describe the fundamental operation of the outlined dialectic as that operation whereby, in the present, the past reverts into the future. The flowing, living life, as presence, is precisely the transformation of the past into *telos.* This involves irreversibility, discontinuity, the leap, and death. But it is also the only way of allowing what has been dead to live again. It amounts to the discovery of the unrealized, occluded *telos* and its continual elaboration in the present.

Husserl himself warns us that there is a cyclical relationship between the past and the present, insofar as the present must comprehend the past and the past must explain the present. Furthermore, he says that we must proceed in a broken fashion, i.e., by zigzagging. We have attempted elsewhere to clarify for our purposes the more profound sense of this zigzagging (p. 58).

[4]   *Objectivism and Transcendentalism:*
       Dualism, Objectified Psychology:
       Becoming-Conscious
       and Decision-Making

THUS HUSSERL'S GENETIC RECONSTRUCTION inserts itself into the temporal dialectic. Time conditions and passively
constitutes me (*passive genesis*). However, it is in time that I am
free. This means that I always reconsider time in its transcendental foundation, in its living presence. In other words, I have
no choice but to depart from the subject and, therefore, from the
present. While disoccluding itself, this living presence can disocclude the past and again ground itself in the past for the teleological sense of the future. In its finitude, in its division into periods,
in the temporalization of the monads (in its irreversibility), temporal becoming is my limit. But it is a limit that allows for the
freedom of the transcendental foundation of time within time.
Becoming is not merely "factual" or a simple succession of causal
events. According to Husserl's expression, it is relived "from the
inside" (p. 71), from within the internal consciousness of time.
The expression "from the inside" does not refer to the "idealistic"
consciousness, but rather to the living person in his intermonadic,
physical, instinctive, corporeal, psychological, and spiritual concreteness. Husserl analyzes even impulses, hunger, and the
sexual appetite "from the inside." [7] In the present reflection, the
analysis from the inside summarizes time and reverses it into the
telos. It is the life of intentionality that is functioning in the self-
consciousness of "interest" and purpose of life. As such, it is
intentional life in time. It is constitutive, intermonadic, and intentional life. It is *constitutive* because it is in time that the sensible,
the perceptual, the corporeal, animated life and spirit, constitute
themselves and are active.

Intentional life is the overturning of the past origin *in the*

7. See the unpublished manuscript E III 5, in the appendix to
Tempo e Verità. [For an English translation, see Husserl, "Universal
Teleology," in *Telos*, no. 4 (Fall, 1969), pp. 176–80.]

present taken as the actual origin. In this sense, intentionality lives in the world and gives history a teleological-intentional meaning. Human existence is teleological and has meaning insofar as it is the continual intentional overcoming of estrangement. It is man's life, the life of the concrete monad in its psychophysical concreteness. If Husserl says "from the inside," it is because a certain school of psychology, following the example of Galileo's physics, fetishizes man and captures only the external aspect, i.e., the psychophysical objectification (pp. 62–65). Psychophysical objectification, through which the human *Lebenswelt* is occluded in the same way that the living world of nature and aesthetic life (transcendental aesthetic) are occluded in Galileo, arises from the dualism that separates the body from the psyche, the *res extensa* from the *res cogitans*. Here the body is reduced to the level of a "thing" or an "object" similar to the objects of mathematical physics. In Husserl there is no *cogito* which is not incarnate in the living body (*Leib*) and in the aesthetic concreteness of time. And there is no "spirit" except in the intentional life of the dialectic of time. The life of the spirit is the previously discussed dialectical reversal. Factual birth, the factual, temporal origin, which in the present is always the renewed rebirth and re-presentation of the historical past, is the .spirit as teleological life. There is an intermonadic relationship even with those who "have been," the dead. It is clear that "spirit" should not be fixed as a metaphysical entity or as a substance analogous to the *res cogitans*.

The occluded character of the *Lebenswelt* is thus connected to the dualism of the *res cogitans* and the *res extensa*. This, in turn, is at the origin of the contrast between "objectivism" and "transcendental subjectivism." Both the misunderstanding of the *Lebenswelt,* and dualism, are inherent in the loss of intentionality and teleological direction. Subsequently, dualism determines the crisis of psychology that is located, so to speak, midway between objectivism and transcendentalism. The history of psychology, the aporetic center of modern thought, is an excellent example of the alienation of the *Lebenswelt* and the impossibility of reducing the "psychic phenomenon" to a fetishized object, and therefore the impossibility of destroying intentionality, or, as we would say, the absurdity of the dualism of the physical sciences and the social sciences.

According to Husserl, this dualism originates with the hypostatization of Galileo's physicomathematical science as the *unique* and *exclusive* model of all science. This abstraction has projected itself upon life: life itself has become dualistic. In occluding the *Lebenswelt,* Galileo conceives, and must conceive, of nature as a world of bodies (object-bodies, not living bodies) closed in themselves. His viewpoint is related to Descartes's dualism. The psychic sphere differentiates itself and stands in opposition to the closed world of bodies. The very idea of a rational philosophy is conceived in terms of the model of mathematical physics. Thus, psychology will have to reduce itself to the natural science of psychical objects, even if separated from the physics of the *res extensa.* The mathematization of the psychical sphere was already undertaken by Hobbes and Locke. Classical rationalism is shot through and through with the pitfalls of this dualism, which does not allow any understanding of the problem of reason and which therefore will lead to the critique of reason. Philosophy done *ordine geometrico* (Spinoza) corresponds to the birth of naturalistic psychology. Berkeley's and Hume's importance lies in the fact that with them naturalistic psychology reveals itself as insufficient. For Hume, skepticism is radical. The ideal of a rationalistic philosophy that originated out of the model of Galilean mathematical physics is shaken to its roots (p. 67). This lays the premises which will lead to the revolution of Kantian transcendentalism, post-Kantian philosophy, and, today, phenomenology. "This greatest of all revolutions must be characterized as the transformation of scientific objectivism—not only modern objectivism but also that of all the earlier philosophies of the millennia—into a transcendental subjectivism" (p. 68). This revolutionary intentionality aims at constructing a new humanity. The revolution can be carried out in the dialectic of time, i.e., in the dialectical reversal.

According to Husserl, the struggle between objectivism and transcendentalism gives us the "meaning" of the history of the modern spirit (p. 69). For objectivism, being is "already given" objectively: it is being according to the physicomathematical "categorial" model. For transcendentalism, being is the prescientific *Lebenswelt:* the daily world in which we live and have always lived. This world is "subjective," i.e., it is direct intermonadic life, the interrelation of presences in the first person. It is the mode of experiencing in which the world experiences and is experienced, where the world has the validity of truly lived being, given with the evidence of the things-themselves. "Psychological" life is in the *Lebenswelt* as life that experiences the world (*welterfahrendes Leben*). It is not an object. Phenomenology uncovers and always rediscovers this life. It is "a final form of transcendental philosophy . . . which also

contains, as a suspended moment [*aufgehobenes Moment*], the
final form of psychology" (p. 70).

The preceding historical considerations re-present and give
new life to what has been sedimented. Consequently, they are
teleological and are the expression of a responsible critique
(p. 72). As we have seen, to rediscover what is original in history means to orient oneself toward the *telos* within the responsibility of the actual present: "But to every primal establishment
[*Urstiftung*] essentially belongs a final establishment [*Entstif-
tung*] assigned as a task to the historical process." The historian's
work becomes inserted into the temporal dialectic. It always
grasps anew what is sedimented, objectified, alienated, dead,
in order to make it alive again. True historiography is a process
of continually bringing back to life (*immer wieder lebendig zu
machen*). It is the rediscovery of the hidden historical meaning (pp. 72–73). Once again the historical-genetic origin becomes the goal: beginning and goal meet one another in a
circle.

The circle, however, is but the expression of the dialectic.
It is the continuous renewal in the present, of the past, for the
future, of the *Lebenswelt* for its *telos*. In us who activate this
renewal, the renewal itself is will, decision, interest, and praxis.
The becoming-conscious, the responsible criticism, is the criticism for the decision (p. 73).

[5]   *The Historical Background
        of Modern Thought*

GENERALLY SPEAKING, Descartes is for Husserl the true
and real founder of modern thought, while, on the other hand,
like all of us, he is part of a tradition. "Descartes has behind
him the history of philosophy, a community of philosophers that
goes back to Thales. But *Descartes begins anew.* 'We philosophers
of the present,' this philosophical present, also begin anew."
We have predecessors and ancestors. Our beginning anew is,
then, connected to a "memorative historical presentification, to
the degree that we can perform it." We presentify in ourselves,
in our presence as philosophers of today, the presence that was
the "present state" of dead philosophers. They are "awakened in
memory" in the "historical-recollective awakening of present
philosophers and their philosophies." We accept certain parts of

the heritage, and critically reject others.[8] We refute the occlusion and attempt to disclose what remained hidden to the philosophers of the past. As such, they live again in us, in the *philosophia perennis* that is constituted in the dialectic of tradition and renewal, of the "always present" and the "new." In the "always" there is the new beginning, and in the "anew" there is the renewed sense, the ulterior unveiling and the meaning that the tradition acquires in us. The dialogue between us and the tradition is a discussion that is always renewed: the discussion between Husserl and Descartes constitutes a pairing (*Paarung*) of a particular type with a dead philosopher who nonetheless lives anew in Husserl. Ultimately, there is the intermonadic relation and the renewal of the intermonadic presence.

Philosophy is presence in time, and in time philosophy founds itself over and over again in each philosopher. Past presence relives in present presence to the extent that each philosopher discovers the same basic exigency: the new start. Consciously or unconsciously, to start anew is to carry out the transcendental reduction and to aim toward its target. But the reduction is never absolute, and for this reason it continually reappears in time, and reproposes itself to each philosopher. What remains is the same intuition and *telos* that give unity to the history of philosophy.

> The intentional unity and identity of all philosophies imply the unity and identity of a constant world that always changes its historical content, and within which all the philosophers live and constantly know themselves as in the historical world.[9]

This historical world is the life-world which must always find itself and start at the beginning in order to do so. The life-world tends to "cover itself up" because each philosopher, in being born, is "lost in the world," in the mundane. The same can be said of a group, of a "trend," or of a "period." I do not remain "within procreation." "I am born" and I am in the mundane, and those who are born will always find themselves in it. The task remains for everyone to rediscover the life-world by means

8. E. Husserl, *Die Krisis der europäischen Wissenschaften und die transzendentale Phänomenologie: Eine Einleitung in die phänomenologische Philosophie*, ed. Walter Biemel (1954; 2d printing, The Hague: Nijhoff, 1962), p. 392. [These quotations are from Beilage V, which has not been included in the English translation. We shall cite from the original German text (our translation), as the English edition is incomplete.]

9. *Ibid.*, p. 393.

of the epochē of the mundane. The intention of being born again from within, i.e., the intention to start anew, always remains.[10]

Notice, in what we have said, the connection between the reduction to the *Lebenswelt* and the transcendental reduction, in addition to the connection between intermonadicity and teleology. The critique of the tradition is the critique of the "mundane" tradition. More precisely, it is a critique of the fact that I have been born of parents: in being born in this way I have my "occluded" being, my being lost in the mundane. To find myself anew is to reduce myself transcendentally. It is to find the original *Lebenswelt* within me, as if, in the present, I should be born again by means of the transcendental reduction. But I cannot in fact be reborn. Now I can only re-present the hidden and fight the mundane and the occluded that inheres in my actual presence.

Because there is an intermonadic relation in each monad, we could say that everything which is hidden in me is also what is, and has been, hidden in other monads. Similarly, what has been revealed in me can be so again, and more clearly, according to the *telos* of the revelation of the reason hidden in the historical process. Husserl has probably not sufficiently analyzed the situation of "rebirth," concerning which we shall venture some observations. The description of birth is bound with the loss of oneself in the world, a factual loss which is never completely redeemable since time is irreversible. The unredeemable, the mundane, is always present precisely because each one of us exists in the finite: we are born in one time and we die in another time. To the extent that it is hidden, the mundane is a constitutive element of the dialectic, and I always find it in front of me. Therefore the reduction must always be resumed. On the other hand, even if the mundane which has been partially won reappears in me, and does so precisely because I am born in it, yet I also contain the original *Lebenswelt* in the diachronic, historical sense. This *Lebenswelt* has already been revealed (e.g., in the historical origin of geometry and science in the *Lebenswelt*), and is intentional and functioning life, even if hidden and unrecognized. Ontogenetically and phylogenetically, there is in history, and in my presence where history renews itself, an originating, functioning intentional life: I will always have to

10. *Ibid.*, p. 394. For the expression "within procreation," see the unpublished manuscript E III 5.

investigate it, and every subject and every intersubjective community will also investigate it by departing from its actual presence.

Remaining firm on the principle of presence, we can notice that every monad is finite, even though it encloses the infinite. My functioning life, my life as a monad, is a functioning life that I have inherited and that is also lived in the monads of the past. While rediscovering it in me, I find not only what is mine, but also what is at the root of other monads. They are also finite and individuated, as I am. The history of my individuation is my history. It has, however, a common background with other histories, and if it discovers that background, to the degree that it rediscovers it, it resumes the history of the other monads. Thus, the continuity, the unity of history, also appears as the continuity of intermonadic revelations, as the revelation of humanity hidden to itself, as the revelation and the general actualization of humanity that constitutes itself historically in an infinite path and according to its own authenticity.

In the suggested perspective, which is only indirectly Husserlian, humanity must always fight against what is inauthentic, against prejudice, against the mundane, against the fact that the monad has already been born in the world. It must not only already be born, but it must make itself present within the living presence of the *Lebenswelt*. This new birth, that fights the already-given birth, would be the absolute reduction. Since this is impossible in the present, it poses itself as a *telos*: the *telos* of humanity amounts to being born within its own authenticity. The true man is yet to be born: authentic man becomes the idea that guides the history of humanity, since man always poses himself as a problem to himself—because man "is not yet" himself in the same way that humanity is not yet itself.

Within historical continuity, within the continuity of the aim for the foundation of man and civilizations, each historical period is the expression of a type of humanity, of a culture, of a civilization. It is a definite historical period with its own character and individuation. Similarly, all monads are also "definite." Within the individuation of a period, and in any civilization, the entire problem of humanity presents and reproposes itself, even if the "answers" given to the problems are different. In a certain sense, there is always a crisis, and it is also true that *every epoch has its own crisis*. This reflects the general crisis. The answers of every epoch (and of different peoples and cultures) are valid for the entire intermonadic humanity as answers inserted into the answer of the humanity that is posed as a problem. To believe in definite answers is to fall back into the mundane and fetishization. Humanity must continually shape itself anew. Thus, that which constitutes it is its intentionality "within": the continuity of its "intention," of its teleologically oriented history, does not lie in its finite expressions, but in the intentionality that has given rise to them.

The preceding considerations are not clearly stated in the *Crisis*, even though they are suggested by some of Husserl's unpublished manuscripts. They are derived from our interpretation, from a relationistic development of phenomenology, and from an as yet vague indication of future analyses. These are connected with the background upon which is based the reconstruction of the history of modern thought that Husserl makes in the *Crisis*. And they are ultimately connected to the dialogue that Husserl always re-undertakes with Descartes, with the Cartesian radicalism of "beginning anew."

[6] *The Occlusion of the Transcendental*
     and Its Progressive Unveiling
     as the Meaning of History

VACILLATIONS ARE NOT LACKING in Husserl's constantly renewed dialogue with Descartes. These vacillations are a consequence of the way the reduction appears as the transcendental reduction and as the reduction to the *Lebenswelt*. According to Husserl, Descartes suspends the mundane. The transcendental reduction suspends the obvious life in order to rediscover it as a problem in the historical reconstruction, i.e., in the relation between tradition and renewal. In addition to the background of the historical reconstruction, we find intersecting in Husserl, sometimes with very little clarity, considerations about the mundane and the *Lebenswelt*. If the "hidden" meaning of Descartes is the transcendental reduction, what remains hidden to Descartes is transcendentalism itself. In fact, he misunderstands his discovery in a "psychologistic" sense. He again reduces the ego to an "objectified" soul, and he "again covers" subjectivism which, for Husserl, is the "Archimedes' point of philosophy."

Husserl notes that Descartes does not understand that "all such distinctions as 'I' and 'you,' 'inside' and 'outside,' first 'constitute' themselves in the absolute ego." It should be noticed here that the "absolute" is not meant to take the place of the metaphysical: the ego about which Husserl speaks is "absolute" because we cannot *actually* start anywhere but from ourselves. The influence that scientific objectivism has on Descartes prevents him from systematically questioning the "I think," and what inheres in the acts of the ego in which it operates intentionally. In losing the meaning of transcendental subjectivism, Descartes ends with an analysis of mind (*mens*). And this leads directly to an objectivistic psychology (p. 82). What Descartes has discovered and at the same time covered again is intentionality itself, the fact that the world is not merely objectivity but is also the *cogitatum* of the *cogito* (pp. 82–83). Descartes thinks that the world can be known *more geometrico*. This line develops in Spinoza and Leibniz, up to Kant, who remains entangled in objectivistic rationalism, mainly in connection with the "thing-in-itself." The function of English empiricism is precisely that of reacting against the already given and objectified transcendence of rationalism. By criticizing objectivistic rationalism, empiricism contributes to the foundation of an authentic transcendentalism (pp. 83–84). But Locke too allows himself to be taken in by psychologistic objectivism, which reveals itself in the theory of psychic sense-data. These sense-data, understood as rationally, artificially, and objectively constructed "things," impress themselves on an "object-soul" understood as *tabula rasa*. On the other hand, Hume sees all rationalistic constructions as "fictions." All categorial constructions are fictitious: there is no rationalistic objectivity. With Hume, rationalistic objectivism reaches its own self-destruction.

Hume, however, does not ask which activity operates in his philosophy. Therefore, transcendental consciousness remains hidden along with the transcendental reduction (pp. 84–88). Locke does not see that consciousness is always present in *Erlebnisse,* because it falls back into objectivism. On the other hand, the authentic philosophical motive hidden in Hume's skepticism is the refutation of that objectivism by means of which he unknowingly leads us to the awareness that the objective sciences are constituted by subjective operations. The transcendental motive remained hidden to Berkeley and Hume, even if their critique was a critique of dogmatic objectivism. By influencing Kant, Hume paved the way for transcendentalism and classical German idealism, especially since he forced Kant to face the problem of the transcendental foundation of science.

In Kant, the sciences are founded on assumed sense-data, and on a priori forms. They are founded by the intellect and not by philosophy, which seems to operate in the background as the functioning intentionality in the shaping of the categorial ("as the secret art of nature"). According to Husserl, the Kantian transcendental is neither totally subjective nor totally transcendental. Because of the incompleteness of Kant's transcendentalism, phenomenology has to return to "the knower's reflecting upon himself and his knowing life," a return whereby we can establish what is of value "for him." Broadly speaking, transcendentalism is a philosophy that discovers its own source in the ego. "This source bears the title *I-myself,* with all my actual and possible knowing life, and, ultimately, my concrete life in general" (pp. 97–98). The philosopher can understand this ego if he himself lives this "subjectivity functioning as primary source" (p. 99). Kant's philosophy leads us to this path of subjectivity conceived as the "primal locus of all objective formations of sense and ontic validities" (p. 99). Objective sciences are based upon "a never questioned, deeply concealed subjective ground" (p. 100). Husserl concludes, then, that one must acquire *direct experience* of the long-felt but constantly concealed dimension of the 'transcendental' " (p. 100).

The transcendental as subjectivity, the ego that Descartes covers up after having discovered it, reproposes itself as a problem in and after Kant. Husserl says that what must not be lost is what Descartes loses and Kant does not fully recover: the absolute subject. The absolute subject is discovered in an epochē that must not only be seriously actualized, but must be "always functioning" (p. 109). This epochē brackets everything, even the *Lebenswelt:* that which remains is only subjectivity as constituting intentionality. In section 49 of *Ideas,* this subjectivity is treated as emptied of the world. The reduction to "absolute" subjectivity which is without the world, but which constitutes it, is the extreme reduction. Thus, the transcendental reduction would be the true and proper reduction in whose name Husserl, as we have seen, reproaches Descartes for not having understood that all distinctions between "I" and "thou" are constituted in the absolute subject.

Yet subjectivity without the world contains it. It is not the bracketed world, but the new world, which is not already fulfilled but is to be found in subjectivity itself and is intentionally constituted by it. With the same vigor with which Husserl insists upon the absolute subjectivity that negates the mundane, he insists upon the fact that this subjectivity, cleansed of the mundane, is not empty but contains "concrete life in general." Subjectivity is the very ego "with all my constitutive, real, and possible life." Then, the transcendental ego is not a categorial abstraction, and its absoluteness is not to be understood in a dogmatic and metaphysical sense. The so-called absolute ego is also *my own concreteness of man* in which the *cogito* is bound to the body (as it turns out, in the fifth of the *Cartesian Meditations*). Constitutive intentionality is constitutive to the extent that the ego itself is concrete sensibility, concrete body, concrete perception, concrete feeling, concrete instinct, and concrete impulse. Therefore, it is intentional activity. The *ego cogito* is not an axiom; it is original life. It is the source in which the ego discovers itself through reflection as functioning, living presence.

Subjectivity is the *entire world* to the extent that it is subjective, intentional activity. The fact that philosophy has its source in the ego does not mean that the ego is consciousness without the world, and therefore that the ego shapes, creates, or posits the world in an idealistic sense. It means that the world lives as functioning activity in the ego and not in a realized meaning, already presupposed, as "mundane." Instead, nonmundane transcendence is made explicit by intentional immanence which is "sensation," "perception of," and "impulse toward something." It is transcendence toward which immanence "explodes." The transcendental object, the whole of the transcendental objects toward which the ego itself explodes as intentionality are the *cogitata* of the "felt," the "perceived," the terms toward which intentionality directs itself. These intentional objects are the "unity of meaning." In them, the world acquires meaning and purpose, since from this viewpoint the teleological direction of the meaning of the world and the world itself become a horizon. This is the horizon of all the horizons that inhere in each act of feeling, perceiving, desiring, and willing. The possibility of directing oneself toward this horizon of meaning, whose meaning is *constituted* by the ego itself in all of its acts of subjective life, is a function of the negation of the mundane, of the world as already constituted. From this it follows: (1) When it is said that the ego itself is "without the world," what the ego is without is the mundane; (2) Since the total reduction is impossible, the ego itself is never completely free of mundane prejudices and must always bracket them; (3) The liberation from the mundane is, therefore, an infinite task; (4) The mundane is what covers and occludes the concrete intentional life of the ego itself with

all its concrete acts in its concrete life, i.e., the *Lebenswelt;*
(5) The *Lebenswelt* is concrete life in its original evidence and,
therefore, in its living presence; and (6) The living presence is
never absolute but is relative, and must always again become
living presence by fighting the mundane. Thus it poses itself
before the mundane as free, unbounded, *absolute* subjectivity.
In this sense it can be said that the true and proper reduction is
the transcendental reduction.

In its exigency of absoluteness, the reduction opposes the
mundane. *Confronting the mundane,* its absoluteness is an
exigency. It is operating only partially, and never completely, so
that the concrete ego or monad is self-presence, living self-
evidence, and a finite monad. Were it not so, there would be
neither different degrees of evidence nor a multiplicity of
monads.

Husserl avails himself of the preceding distinctions even if
he sometimes seems to forget them, as he in fact does. This has
given rise to misunderstandings about the term "absolute," which
has many meanings in Husserl. What happened to Galileo and
Descartes seems to happen to him too, i.e., in some expositions
of his thought he covers up what he discovers. What must be
rediscovered is that the transcendental reduction is relative insofar as it is concrete and actual, insofar as it lives in the presence
of the monads in different degrees—even if it is always present.
But since presence is in time, the fact that it is always present
does not mean that it is absolute in the exhaustive and total
sense. If time is always presence, it does not mean that presence
is always absolute, since in that case time would not have a present and a future: it would not be time. If the transcendental reduction is absolute, it is so as infinite task and as an exigency, as
telos, always implicit in every finite monad. But it is never completely explicit. Its becoming explicit happens in historical time,
in the presence which remembers the past, re-presents it, and with
the past extends forward toward the future, the aspect, and the
"meaning" of the future in the pre-recollection (*Vorerinnerung*).
In the present which presentifies the past and becomes future,
the intentional meaning is constituted so that the renewal of the
teleological meaning is always the re-presentation of the forgotten, the freeing of historical investigation from occlusion, the rediscovery of the occluded *Lebenswelt,* the renewal, as rediscovery,
of the actual *Lebenswelt.* It is the teleological task that appears as
the horizon and as the intentional meaning projected to the future. The transformation of the world is carried out in relation to

the intentional objects that appear as ideal unities, as that toward which immanent life explodes and toward which it transcends itself. The ego itself is absolute subjectivity. But this absolute subjectivity is both the relative autonomy of the *Lebenswelt* from the mundane, and the presence as functioning and evident life that constitutes its own meaning as an ideal teleological horizon. Presence in time, in order to locate itself as the constituent, must disocclude itself and re-present the past, rediscover itself within the hidden or forgotten presence, and meaningfully constitute the future. Now, in the present, in the past, and in the future, the occluded is the mundane. It is that which covers intentional life. Freedom from the mundane, then, *does not happen all of a sudden, and it is never completely realized.* It takes place in history, in that history which the presence re-presents in order to be rediscovered along with its own meaning. It is because of this that presence must always be reconquered anew in time, and it is because of this that, insofar as it is meaningful, history turns out to be the continuous rediscovery of the presence and its meaning.

The "absolutism" of subjectivity that Husserl discusses has, however, various meanings, even if Husserl himself suggests the proposed interpretation. Certainly, some of Husserl's readers could say that it is an interpretation or, maybe, a correction. I do not believe this to be the case, but if it is, the correction would be required by the coherent development of Husserlian phenomenology.

PART II

The Foundation
and the Function
of the Sciences

3 / Phenomenology as New Science

[7]   *Functioning, Kinesthetic Corporeality.*
        Transcendental Aesthetic.
        Toward a Phenomenology of Labor.
        The Prerogative. The Meaning of Praxis
        in the Horizon of the World.
        The Transcendental Foundation and the
        Process of Infinite Rationalization

AS WE HAVE MENTIONED, Husserl discusses Kant again
at the beginning of the third part of the *Crisis,* the first section
of which deals with the problem of the *Lebenswelt.* He writes
that Kant was not aware of the fact that his philosophical constructions were based upon uninvestigated presuppositions. The
Kantian intellect acts unknowingly when it constitutes that form
of meaning (*Sinngestalt*) which continually develops in the
intuitive life surrounding us (*anschauliche Umwelt*) (p. 109).
Kant does not elaborate the close connection between intellect
and sensibility. (It can be argued, however, that he has really
confronted this problem in the transcendental schematic.) According to Husserl, Kant does not arrive at the direct foundation
of the scientific operations that should have been based on
original sources. Kant unconsciously presupposes the surrounding life-world (*Lebensumwelt*) where we always live in our *lived*
experience. This life-world is not investigated, nor is it used as
the original source of scientific operations.

The experience of the world is continually valid for us

according to those modes of validity of certainty, possibility, and appearance (in this connection, see the third of the *Cartesian Meditations*). The world so experienced is unitary and continuously corrects its own contents (pp. 104–6). For Husserl, the correction is possible because there is always an evolution of the modes of appearance, which are, for instance, the various perspectives of vicinity and distance. Perception itself is a modality. This, in fact, is the theme Merleau-Ponty has attempted to develop. More specifically, perception is the central modality. Perception gives us the original world of intuition where things, as the evidence of variable contents, appear in the first person. Furthermore, there is an evolution of presence in the first person, i.e., of being present. The evolutions and their modifications are the presentifications (*Vergegenwärtigungen*) and modifications of the presence.

A modification of the being that is present in person is the being which has been present in person or, in the future, the being which will be present in person. The intuitions brought to the present "recapitulate," according to their own modifications, the manifold of the appearances in which something is represented in perception (pp. 105–6). This is possible because phenomenology is the return to experiencing, sensible life. Perceptions are corporeal. Even though not everything can be reduced to corporeality, perceptions are inconceivable if they are not recognized as moments of the life of sense-organs.

Phenomenology must take into account the various aspects of touch, sight, hearing, etc. The living body (*Leib*) lives in the operations of its perceptive organs. So understood, the functioning of perceptions must be brought back to the ego as concrete body, and, therefore, to the movements of the ego. This is the problem of kinesthesis with which Husserl deals specifically in the manuscripts D, which are devoted to the transcendental aesthetic. The ego is not merely the *ego cogito*, but also the "I move" and the "I do." Even inactivity and passivity are modalities of kinesthesis. The various aspects in which corporeal perception appears are not contiguous. They are complementary and together they contribute to the formation of the general kinesthetic sense. We have, then, a kinesthetic-sensual total situation (*kinästhetisch-sinnliche Gesamtsituation*) (p. 106). Husserl has his own conception of sensibility, the "ego's active functioning of the living body or the bodily organs." This functioning essentially belongs to each corporeal experience (p. 106).

Husserl insists on the distinction between the real body

(*Leib*) and the body as a thing. In *Ideen II* we discover a thing-corporeality in us. Sartre ignores these premises, even though they pave the way for the thesis of the *practico-inert*.

Notice that this is not a matter of the corporeal appearances of the "things-themselves." The corporeality of things is connected with kinesthetically functioning corporeality (*fungierende Leiblichkeit*). Things are woven, in the habits and in the passivity of the ego, into its original corporeal history. So understood in a new sense, the body is an organ. Activity and passivity are particular kinesthetic forms. Action appears as the functioning of every corporeal perception.

According to Husserl, there is a potential kinesthetic system which is actualized in every individual kinesthetic action; i.e., there is a kinesthetic background of connectedness, which subsequently lives in the particular specifications of the sense-organs. Thus, each organ has two aspects: a general one connecting it to the background, and a specific one. If the sense-organs aim at a unified perception, it is because they explicate an original background that becomes the unitary *telos* toward which perception aims.

Phenomenologically, the "appearances," or the phenomena of the world, are my own bodily appearances. In this sense they are subjective. The appearances belong to active kinesthesis. However, it is always possible that the subject may face obstacles which are perceived as extraneous objects. At the beginning of phenomenological experience, the body is inorganic and inert (*Körper*) and, as such, is different from the real living body (*Leib*). Thus, it appears extraneous. In subsequent developments of phenomenological experience, the organic bodies are not the only extraneous elements. Other living bodies, or other subjects, also appear extraneous. This is how the *cogito*, by starting out with its own body, confronts the problem of extraneous subjects, and in the end constitutes intersubjectivity (p. 108).

The importance of the preceding passages lies in the fact that the dialectic between what is one's own and what is extraneous is posed there on the kinesthetic level. (The whole topic is, of course, related to the subject matter of the fifth of the *Cartesian Meditations*.) It seems that by going beyond Husserl, the elaboration of this viewpoint can lead to a genuine phenomenology of labor foreseen by Husserl when, among the various egological and kinesthetic modes, he discusses "lifting," "carrying," and "pushing."

Generally speaking, labor is the meeting of *Leib* and *Körper*.

Since the *Leib* is always threatened by degradation to the level of the *Körper*, it can become an objectified body by being exploited and fetishized by an exploiter. Therefore, the meeting of *Leib* and *Körper* is closely related to that of life and death, and that of capital and labor. It is easy to make connections here with the dialectic of certain famous passages of Hegel's *Phenomenology of Mind* and Marxism. Husserl comes very close to these positions in some of his unpublished manuscripts.[1]

A switch from *Leib* to *Körper* is possible when a *Leib* considers another *Leib* as a *Körper* and steals from it, as it were, its *Leiblichkeit*. What is called capitalism, with its fetishizations, can reveal its origin in a phenomenological reconsideration of the dialectic of master and slave. At the beginning, such a dialectic is the struggle for life, and it tends to take away life. From our viewpoint, it coincides with the disposing of someone else's subjectivity. The fact that Husserl has posed these problems in connection with the critique of Kantian transcendentalism, interpreted as a transcendentalism that does not take into account sensitivity, corporeality, and aesthetic experience (transcendental aesthetic, in the Husserlian sense), makes it possible for his critique of Kant to appear as a critique of aesthetic experience, i.e., as a *critique of corporeal experience*.

According to Husserl, someone else's body can never be perceived as one's own. If I feel and live my own body, that means that I can act and move from retention and protention to remembrance and anticipation. For this and other reasons, the action of subjects in intersubjective relations is always connected with time and its modifications. The body is "one's own" to the extent that it is detached by retention and can be historically considered in remembrance. The real body is not a prisoner of a closed present. It is kinesthetically active, since it can consider itself from a spatiotemporal distance. *The ego can do something. It can act, insofar as it is in historical temporality and establishes a relation with the past in connection with a project for the future*. Subjectivity is the historically founded possibility of movement and action. To have this possibility means to have a *prerogative*.

For Husserl, then, *it is the possibility of having a prerogative that allows praxis*. Here, the return to subjectivity appears as a return to action in time bound to the past and directed toward a teleological future. Subjectivity, as praxis, is actual commitment directed toward a finality.

1. For example, see the unpublished manuscript E III 6, pp. 5–6.

It is clear that in Husserl there is a close relationship between subjectivity and praxis. This is the relationship that Sartre will discover independently, in the *Critique de la raison dialectique,* by skipping the Husserlian foundation. This relationship is connected with the dialectic of interest and disinterest. When Husserl defends the knower as a "disinterested spectator," by disinterest he means disinterest in instrumentalism and the mundane fetishization. The phenomenological reduction must be freed of fetishized interests in order to be directed to teleological and historical interests. Thus, "scientific" disinterestedness appears as the prerogative of giving an intersubjective, and hence social, meaning to history. Phenomenology teaches us that subjectivity is the possibility of freeing oneself from fetishization. Knowledge itself is a prerogative that transforms obscure and fetishized things into things that become representable—into things that become *phenomena.*

The scientific disinterest that Husserl defends is the condition that allows for the possibility of a non-fetishized interest. If the theoretical ego becomes a spectator, this activity as a spectator, this freedom from fetishism, transforms the fetishized mundane interest into a historical-teleological and intersubjective interest. Therefore, we must distinguish between mundane praxis and praxis free of the mundane. The latter is in a dialectical struggle with the former, and takes place in the historical, intermonadic level.

The praxis free from the mundane provides the *opening* to the world as a universal horizon. It is historical insofar as it reconstitutes an open world which is the world of the intermonadic "life with others" (*Miteinander-Leben*). This life with others (p. 108) must also be understood as the explication of a hidden life. Only the teleological horizon of a social life that appears as the end of history can aim at infinitely explicating the reason occluded in history, in the course of history. Living reason is explicating what is hidden. It is the awakening of the slumbering. It is the passing from the unconscious to the "awakened consciousness of the world." This awakened consciousness of the world is a prerogative that becomes praxis. It becomes an activity on the background of a passive "having of the world."

Husserl's ideal leads him to value the active subjects in their awakened acting, aware of their purpose, alive in their rational praxis obtained through the disinterest of the theory (which negates the mundane or fetishized interest). The subjects act on the background of a purely passive "having of the world." They transform passivity into activity. In the final analysis—and this is a fundamental achievement—it is precisely theoretical disinterest which allows philosophy to become the active transformation of the world that overturns passivity into activity in terms of the passive "having of the world" (*auf dem Grunde der passiven Welthabe*). We give a general meaning to our particular actions and, therefore, we "thematize" in a dialectical contrast with this background of passive having [*dell'avere passivo*] in the teleological horizon. Here we can see how the specification (or supposed separation) of the functions of the sense-organs becomes synthetic and active in a general kinesthesis, and how it aims at a universal subjectivity within the horizon of the world. The objectified corporeal must become thematic in what we could call a system of thematizations. It is strange that Husserl does not speak of such a system. He does make it very clear that to "thematize" means to live in time according to a *telos*. The theme is perceptive awareness. To thematize means to draw conclusions, to outline, to plan, and to mediate actively between projects and purposes (p. 109).

The purpose of thematization is the transformation of passive into active objects. An object must become a means for a purpose, an organ, a theme. For one to become concerned with an object before the phenomenological reduction can mean that one forgets oneself in the object and forgets its end. In the second part of the *Crisis,* Husserl criticizes technology precisely insofar as it comes to be taken (if employed) as the occlusion of the goal, i.e., the teleological meaning of life and history.

Technology has occluded the meaning-structure and therefore does not answer to the innate *telos* of life that it nonetheless carries. It is from this fact that the contradiction of technology, history, and society arises. Marx would say that the sorcerer's apprentice is no longer capable of positively reestablishing the relationship between technology and society. For Husserl, what the sorcerer's apprentice does not know is phenomenological reflection. It is the awakening of the historical meaning that, for Husserl, is also a linguistic awakening, as we shall see in connection with Appendix VI (pp. 353–78).

In conjunction with the foregoing, one must remember that phenomenological reflection is *in* time and *for* time. It is the reversal of praxis through the epochē. It is the *return to the living structure through the liberation from mundane superstructures,* and it is, therefore, the foundation of authentic life. This foundation is one of the aspects of what Husserl calls the transcendental foundation.

The transcendental foundation gives us the teleological meaning obtaining in the intermonadic relationship between egos. This relationship reveals to us the meaning of being (*Seinsinn*). This is why Husserl speaks of *us* as subjectivity (*Wir-Subjektivität*) (p. 109) and of the intermonadic thematization that is dialectically outlined upon a residue and a background. In the ultimate analysis, we may reach the conclusion that the intermonadic, thematic project is the barrier of civilization against the threat of death. It is the continuous struggle against the dark, the anonymous, and the hidden [*l'oscuro, l'anonimo, il nascosto*]. Intermonadic, historical teleology is the foundation of society and the foundation of individuation. This foundation is "general" and synthetic. It is not the loss of oneself in the separation of the organs, in the technical fragmentation and fetishization.

The transcendental foundation that gives us the teleological meaning is possible because the life-world and the corporeal world are prescientifically valid (p. 110). We live in a community. In this community it is "obvious" that we have a body of our own, and that we have always been in corporeality and time. Husserl thinks that this obviousness has never been investigated, not even by Kant. Rather, it is the constant presupposition of scientific thought and, ultimately, also of philosophical thought (p. 110).

In the always presupposed life-world, there is an implicit infinity which must be made explicit. The implicit infinite, the whole always present in the part, must become a task, a *telos*. The infinite is hidden in functioning life. By making it explicit, science transforms it into a task. The idea as an infinite, teleological idea must give rise to a method of continuous verification. While prescientific life implicitly contains the infinite as chaos, theortical praxis elaborates theories and techniques that transform the hidden infinite in a progressive revelation, and into a progressive functioning. In other words, prescientific life contains the possibility of being transformed into a life organized according to a *telos*. "True science" consists in this teleological transformation. In this sense, it is needed by the *Lebenswelt* insofar as the *Lebenswelt* needs techniques, theoretical praxis, and elaborations of teleological theories. What is extraneous to prescientific life, what requires its foundation according to a *telos*, is precisely the theoretical elaboration and explication of the rational potentiality that it encloses (p. 111). Husserl returns to prescientific life to elaborate a theory and a praxis in order to transform the mundane into an explicit research which can give the meaning of reason to life. This research is infinite, not in the sense whereby the infinite is occluded in the life-world but in the sense that the disocclusion becomes an inexhaustible task. The task, infinite because inexhaustible, allows the concrete elaboration of scientific research. This is what Husserl sought, both in the *Logical Investigations* and in the *Formal and Transcendental Logic,* when facing the problem of the theory of the manifold. For Husserl, to defend obviousness against Kant means to clarify the historical and teleological meaning of the transcendental foundation.

[8]   *The Meaning of the Spiritual Operation*
        as the Rationalization of Functioning Life,
        and the Teleological Unity of Life.
        Superficial and Profound Life.
        The Science of the Lebenswelt
        as the Science of Operations

ACCORDING TO HUSSERL, the world that Kant presupposes as obvious is the domain of subjectivity, understood as functioning kinesthetic corporeality. Kant has not seen that subjectivity so understood is ubiquitous. Subjectivity must not be neglected. If philosophy is to be a rigorous, well-founded science, it cannot leave the domain of the subjective immersed in anonymity (p. 112).

A unitary, teleological meaning must be discovered in functioning and anonymous life, and in the subjectivity that lives in all the sciences. The sciences arise out of an anonymous subjectivity that hides a unity of meaning within its obviousness. This subjectivity must be investigated. Husserl says that the universal operation by means of which we give meaning to anonymous subjectivity is spiritual. This operation is subjective and tends to bring to light the functioning life. The world is thus constituted as a teleological world insofar as it overcomes every "given externality" and constitutes it as a scientifically revealable operation. In the final analysis, the transformation of the anonymous into a phenomenon is revealed in the teleological unity that reveals the hidden roots. The meaning of the Husserlian critique of externality and, therefore, the meaning of Husserlian subjectivism is here presented as an illumination of anonymous subjectivity and its internal, organic life. Husserl says:

> It is like the unity of a living organism, which one can certainly consider and dissect from the outside but which one can understand only if one goes back to its hidden roots and systematically pursues the life which, in all its accomplishments, is in them and strives upward from them, shaping from within. But is this not simply a metaphor? Is it not in the end our human being, as the life of consciousness belonging to it, with its most profound world-problematics, which is the place where all problems of living inner being and external exhibition are to be decided? [Pp. 113–14]

If Husserl had studied the *Critique of Judgment* with greater care, he might have been able to find many anticipations of his position in Kant. However, it must not be forgotten that Husserl accuses Kant of remaining bound to naturalism and, specifically, to naturalistic psychology. Despite this, Husserl observes that Kant had noticed the difference between "naturalistic" and pre-scientific life that conditions all science. Naturalism remains on the surface. Phenomenology reveals a new dimension. Thus, it counterposes a profound life (*Tiefenleben*) to the superficial life (*Flächenleben*). Even if it is unnoticed, profound life functions in all experience. Helmholtz once tried to imagine some surfaces with only two dimensions. We can imagine these surfaces so that there would be no suspicion of the existence of a third dimension, i.e., depth. If we assume that the surfaces could think and reflect, they could not know the third dimension of which they are actually a part. Now, in relation to this hypothetical example, the surface corresponds to mundane life, to the mundane *modus operandi* of the scientists. The scientists would exist as if they were locked in two dimensions and, to this extent, would not be able to notice that the two dimensions are actually aspects of a three-dimensional world and are, consequently, superficial aspects of a deeper truth. This deeper and more active truth, which remains hidden if we do not investigate subjectivity, is what Husserl calls functioning spiritual life (*fungierendes geistiges Leben*).

Yet, as Husserl points out, notwithstanding that the sciences have remained in superficial life, they have achieved many successes. This can be explained by the fact that this success is limited to given technical results. It does not always affect the meaning of the methodological procedure of science and, there-fore, the teleological meaning. The problem of the success of the sciences appears repeatedly in Husserl. His clarifications are not always entirely convincing. Certainly, the technology that loses the teleological meaning falls into slumber and occlusion. Maybe it would have been better to deepen the utility and the function of the technical operation, and also its functioning in the pauses where the teleological meaning is lost. This last problem is in-vestigated by Husserl in the unpublished manuscripts Groups C, E, and K. It is present as the problem of the pauses of the vital activity, the function of sleep, and, finally, the function of death.

This must be placed in relation to the dialectic of what is awake and living, and what is asleep and sedimented. That which is sedimented loses its meaning but retains a possibility for repeti-tion, as happens with constituted and fixed language which, how-ever, carries out its function.

In connection with Freud, we can say that, if technology tends to dull the senses, this tendency to forget the *telos* can also be viewed as a suppression. A phenomenological analysis should probably clarify the difference between the function of the pauses of technology and the technology that becomes suppression. For-getting oneself in technology can be considered the suppression of the end which will eventually be reached by technology. That is, it can be the suppression of the consequences of a technolog-ical operation. Technology can be connected both with life and its goal, and with the negation of life itself, the "death instinct." De-parting from this premise, logic as a technology can be revealed as ambivalent. Certainly, logic must ultimately be based on a teleological meaning. But it is also true that logic can lead to for-getting its objective and, therefore, to the forgetting of the *telos*.

In section 33 of the *Crisis*, Husserl observes that the problem of the *Lebenswelt* can initially appear within the more general problem of so-called objective science. Science is a realization of the human spirit. Historically, it presupposes an intuitive point of departure. Prescientific knowledge has a constant function in the praxis of the physicist. If we speak of objective science, it is because we think of a universal science whereby all the *Lebens-welt*, and not only the domain of physics as a science, should be-come a universal teleology. In fact, what has to be made mean-ingful is the entire *Lebenswelt*. Therefore, if the *Lebenswelt* is initially a partial problem, in the end it is posed as a total problem of universal science (p. 123). We must study the activities of life and the operations of the scientists in their teleology, not the domain of a science separated from all others. What science also seeks in its search for objectivity is the revelation of the profound life that grounds science. It is the phenomenological revelation of the third dimension that we mentioned in relation to Helmholtz' example. "It is not the case that, in the end, through what first appears as a special subject in the theory of science, that 'third dimension' is opening up, immediately destined in advance to engulf the whole subject matter of objective science (as well as all other subject matters on the 'plane')?" (p. 123). This is how Husserl poses the problem of phenomenology as the universal science of the life-world, a science that must underlie all scientific operations.

[9]   *Scientific Universality as the Negation*
        of Fetishized Objectivity
        and as the Revelation
        of the Hidden Meaning of Objectivity.
        Existence as Life of the World
        and as the Source of Verification

THE CONCEPT OF A SCIENCE of the life-world is further clarified by Husserl in the six parts of the fundamental section 34.

He says that the life-world must not remain as it appears in normal, anonymous life, in the daily praxis. It must become scientific. According to the tradition, this means that it must become "objective," i.e., universally true. As we have seen, however, for Husserl being scientific is not the same as being objective in the sense of "objectified." "And yet, paradoxically, we uphold our assertion and require that one not let the handed-down concept of objective science be substituted, because of the century-old tradition in which we have all been raised, for the concept of science in general" (p. 124). For Husserl, science must be rigorous. In order to be rigorous it must not be objectified. It must be subjective. And even when it is subjective it must not be particular, but general. This poses, among other things, the problem of intersubjectivity.

The *Lebenswelt* demands tasks different from the traditional ones. Authentic and full scientificity must consider relational problems. It must not, e.g., treat the logical problem separately. The " 'life-world' makes possible and demands perhaps various different, though essentially interrelated, scientific undertakings." The problem that must be solved is that of how the *Lebenswelt* functions. How is it possible to realize this peculiar scientificity, which has hitherto always been supplanted by objectified scientificity? First of all, we must think of experience "in all its modes of perception, memory, etc." This is the experience that Husserl has indicated as kinesthetic corporeality, by contraposing to Kant the whole of phenomenology and, therefore, the entire complexity of the life of experience. The modality of perception, and therefore all of the transcendental aesthetic, must not be falsified by categorial objective science. The atomic sense-data are not the starting point, since they are already abstract constructions. Rather, the starting point is "the 'merely subjective-relative' intuition of prescientific world-life." So understood, relative and prescientific life is the subjective world of the *doxa* (pp. 124–25).

For Husserl, therefore, universal science is the science of the prescientific life-world. The particular sciences avail themselves of the life-world for their purposes but, as Husserl says, to avail oneself of the life-world does not mean to know it scientifically. The use that Einstein makes of Michelson's experience is not based on a Michelson reduced to a scientific object, on a Michelson as an object of psychophysics: in the eyes of Einstein, Michelson is a man in his concrete reality (p. 125). Einstein does not construct the man, or the world, or the environment in which Michelson works. Rather, he places himself in a relationship with the prescientific man of whom he has an immediate experience. In other words, Einstein refers to Michelson's real existence and his concrete work. Even while performing his scientific operations, Einstein is, like everyone else, in the world of existence. And existence is subjective-relative existence, the *doxa*. For the scientist, the logical-mathematical ideal truths which we must constantly approach emerge from existence. Yet the life-world continues to function in the scientist at the same time that he does mathematical physics.

It is clear from the above that functioning life is existential life. What must be stressed is the fact that, for Husserl, existential life is the source of evidence (*Evidenzquelle*) and the source of verification (*Bewährungsquelle*). The distinction between Husserl's and the existentialists' concepts of existence is that, for

Husserl, existence implies evidence, the foundation, verification, or, in other words, *subjectivity in the first person.* Objective science avails itself of existence. Phenomenology, as universal science, experiments and knows existence as the original source of verification and as the basis of truth.

[10]   *Experienceability of Life in Time.*
         The Temporal Foundation of Essences,
         Categories, and Ideas. The Lebenswelt
         as the Ground of Scientific Truth.
         Phänomenologie als neue Wissenschaft

THE WORLD OF THE *Lebenswelt* is not a construction. Husserl insists on the fact that the *Lebenswelt* is intuitible in principle, since he wants to distinguish it from the objectified world which is a "logical substructure." The scientific world, understood as the objective world, is derived from Galileo's natural science. The substructure is something we cannot experience. Instead, the *Lebenswelt* allows an evident, convincing, and original experience in the first person.

The *Lebenswelt* is "experienced . . . in immediate presence, or, in memory . . . , and every other manner of intuition is a presentification of the thing itself" (pp. 127–28). This passage is important because it implies that the *Lebenswelt* is temporality and temporal experienceability. In turn, this temporal experienceability is in the modes of the evidence such as the present and its modifications. What is not a substructure *can be experienced in time.* Husserl emphasizes the fact that the science of the lifeworld has the fundamental task of revealing the original primacy of temporal experienceability that underlies every logical construction. Temporality is both presence and modification of the presence. As such, it is the basic functioning life. This entails that the science of the *Lebenswelt* is the science of the operations of basic life, understood as presence in time and as modifications of the presence. In temporality so intuited, we find the "primal self-evidence in which the life-world is ever pregiven" (p. 128). The modifications of the presence allow, among other things, the various degrees of evidence (*Evidenzstufen*). Ultimately, intuition itself is to be brought back to the evidence, i.e., to the temporal operating of the presence in its modifications. It must always be remembered that life can be experienced only in temporality, and that reflection itself is in temporality.

If life can be experienced, it can be experienced directly through intuition. Intuition catches certain forms in life that have something of a typical and permanent character. A typical form represents a constant way in which life appears. Typical patterns and models can be seen as typical forms of the immediate, i.e., as mediations (p. 129). Because of this, it becomes clear that the operations of temporal subjectivity make the sciences possible. They are a kind of doing in time, a type of praxis. Therefore, Husserl poses the problem of the typical as the problem of the types of temporal operations. This can bring to mind the fact that "essence" itself can also appear as an operation—as a mode of operating of transcendental, subjective life. The categories themselves can be interpreted as typical operations of the temporal operating of the *Lebenswelt* (this is the theme of *Erfahrung und Urteil*). So explained, the categories can be brought back within original intuition, i.e., to the way that the temporal *Lebenswelt* is intuitively revealed. This feature of the *Lebenswelt's* appearing as intuitive revelation allows the transcendental aesthetic.

Aesthetic appears here as the basis of categorial logic. The patterns, the various types of operations, the intuitive schematizations, and what Husserl calls infinite ideas, "e.g., the infinity of the number series" (p. 128), must arise from the heart of transcendental aesthetics. At the source of all this there is the conception of the foundation of the categories as based on intuitions having their origin in time. This is tantamount to basing all the categorial sciences upon the *Lebenswelt* and its science, which is rendered possible by the self-intuition and self-evidence of the temporal presence.

If we consider science as the "totality of predictive theory," we discover that science is "rooted, grounded in the life-world, in the original self-evidences belonging to it" (p. 130). This is why science is always connected with the world in which we concretely live: as is often said, the world "corresponds" to the categories. Predictive, logical theories can be considered (as by Bolzano) as truth itself, or as ideal units of meaning. But the foundation of meaning lies in temporal life. The ideal units of meaning derive from temporal operations because the *Lebenswelt* is "the grounding soil of the 'scientifically true' world" (p. 131).

As operating subjects, the scientists operate on the terrain of the *Lebenswelt*. The scientists themselves are concrete monads insofar as they are operating subjects. Consequently, the temporal operations of the *Lebenswelt* are inserted into teleological intermonadicity. This, in turn, is closely connected with the foundation of the transcendental aesthetic.

Husserl points out that the *Lebenswelt* and objectivity have a cross-reference. We have the conflict of the two worlds which, although separate, are also inseparably united. Husserl sees this cross-reference as causing considerable difficulties, and characterizes it as "enigmatic." Here phenomenological clarification is faced with a paradox. Yet philosophy must be possible despite this paradox. As the science of the *Lebenswelt*, philosophy must be inserted into the paradoxical relationship between the *Lebenswelt* and scientific objectivity. If it is possible to clarify this paradox, it is because Husserl's scientificity is a "new scientificity": "Of course, it is a new sort of scientific discipline that is required for the solution of the enigmas which now disquiet us; it is not mathematical, nor logical at all in the historical sense" (p. 132).

The above not only allows a phenomenology as a rigorous science (*Phänomenologie als strenge Wissenschaft*), but, as has been said, it allows a phenomenology as a new science (*Phänomenologie als neue Wissenschaft*).

This can occur as a result of becoming aware of the conflict and cross-reference between the *Lebenswelt* and scientific objectivity. The conflict obtains its meaning in teleological reflection. The need for a new kind of consciousness, i.e., a consciousness of the *Lebenswelt*, is revealed precisely by the indicated new awareness. Husserl says that the science of life is not the result of an "intellectualistic enterprise" (p. 132). It is demanded by the necessity of basing the sciences on the operations that we perform in time. We can know these operations in temporal reflection which is both history and the foundation of its meaning of truth.

We perform the operations in time and, therefore, we can give a meaning to being, i.e., we can base the meaning of the truth of being in time. In passing, we could apply Vico's principle whereby *mathematicam demonstramus quia verum facimus*. With this principle, mathematics would be removed from its objectification and brought back to the *Lebenswelt*, or, more precisely, to the operations that found mathematics in the *Lebenswelt*. Generally speaking, if we apply Vico's principle, whereby *verum et ipsum factum convertuntur*, to Husserl, the *verum* phenomenologically becomes the sense of *fieri* that frees itself from the *factum* by means of intentionality. The existence of a science of the *Lebenswelt* is due to something other than an intellectualistic enterprise. The objectification typical of Galileo's science is brought back to the subjective-relative sphere, to the *doxa*. However, it should not be forgotten that the *doxa* is the concrete life of teleologic-monadic temporality.

Those who speak of intellectualism, and of Husserl's desperate intellectualism, believe that a science of life amounts to a reduction of life to a scientific intellectuality and, therefore, that it ends by misunderstanding the *Lebenswelt*. Clearly, if the scientificity of the science of the *Lebenswelt* poses itself as a new scientificity with respect to the traditional kind, this is because it is based on the capacity of consciousness to illuminate what is hidden in precategorial life. This does not entail a reduction of precategorial life to an intellectualistic rationality or a dogmatic dimension.

Phenomenology is never a construction, but it is a revelation, which means precisely that it is not the construction of a metaphysical system. It means that phenomenology is not metaphysics in the traditional sense, even if it can be considered metaphysics in the only possible and genuine sense. Husserl points out that "all problems of truth and of being, all methods, hypotheses, and results conceivable for these problems . . . can attain their ultimate clarity" only by returning to the *Lebenswelt*, i.e., by means of the presumed intellectualism. "This will then include, certainly, all ultimate questions of legitimate sense and of nonsense in the busy routine of the 'resurrected metaphysics' that has become so vocal and so bewitching of late" (p. 133).

As we have seen, the problem functioning in the *Lebenswelt* is universal, while the problems of the objective sciences are particular. The operations that ground the science of the *Lebenswelt* are not the operations of a disembodied transcendental ego. They *are the operations of individualized ego that operates in its functioning unity with other egos and monads in intermonadic life*. The new science is based on the world of "community life," in the "world of straightforward intersubjective experiences" (p. 133).

Compared with the new universal science, a science without any relations to the *Lebenswelt* "loses its self-sufficiency" and becomes "a mere partial problem." Husserl has thus reversed the initial positions. The science of the *Lebenswelt* that appeared as a partial problem ultimately turns out to be the "totally self-sufficient subject of investigation," the problem of the foundation of all other sciences by means of phenomenology, and, therefore, the "genuine and most universal problem" of the new science.

[11]   *Vocational Time and Teleological Life.*
       The Religious Character of the Epochē
       Understood as Liberation
       from Fetishization. The A Priori
       of the Lebenswelt. *Horizon of Things*
       and Horizon of the World

IN SECTION 35, Husserl outlines an analysis of the *transcendental epochē*. The new science is to be reached gradually by means of successive steps that appear as successive suspensions of judgment. Now, the first epochē must be an epochē of objective science. What should be bracketed is the basic idea of science considered as objectivity. Only by rejecting objectivity will a new science be possible. We must remember that to bracket science does not mean to negate the specific work of the scientists. Scientists do not disappear. They remain with their "vocational time" (*Berufszeit*). Vocational time is certainly connected with the danger of fetishization and separation of the vocational from the life-world. But what counts is that the teleology of the life-world gives a meaning to vocational time, that the vocation be at the service of the universal teleology of humanity and not the contrary. The theme and interest of the life-world insert themselves into the vocational times. The new science must not be identified with the bourgeois vocations. Otherwise, as Husserl points out, irrationalism would prevail, insofar as rationality would be fetishized in the vocation and thus separated from the teleological historical meaning of humanity in history. The science of the *Lebenswelt* thus must not be interpreted as a technique that places itself on the same level with the others. The science of the *Lebenswelt* gives meaning to the techniques but is not reducible to a neutral technique (p. 136).

The problem of time is inserted into the problem of the successive times of the epochē. To perform an epochē means also to perform an epochē of the partial interests and their fetishization, and of the society that can compel some of its members or groups to fetishization. The epochē must free the individual in *society*. The progressive establishment of an intermonadic society represents the negation of the fetishization which reduces each individual and group to a pure means without a *telos*. It is because of this that Husserl sees the epochē as "a religious conversion" that must ground "mankind as such" (p. 137).

Hence the epochē of the objectified sciences is connected with the epochē of fetishized interests, and it is the struggle against the reduction of man to technical functions. It is the freeing of the individual and society in the intermonadic teleology that gives a meaning of truth to being.

Husserl again discusses the problem of the science of the *Lebenswelt* in section 36. The *Lebenswelt* is both relativity and *doxa*. Even though the *Lebenswelt* is relative, the science of the *Lebenswelt* discovers a general structure, without becoming an objectified science. The *Lebenswelt,* in the prescientific framework, has the same structures of objective science. All that becomes categorial in science already has its own *concrete structure* in the *Lebenswelt*. For example, the *Lebenswelt* is spatiotemporal. But this spatiotemporality is not a category, since it is lived spatiotemporal experience and kinesthetic life. In the *Lebenswelt* there are also bodies, but they are not the same bodies of the science of physics. Therefore, generally speaking, if there is an objective a priori of science, in reality the true a priori is that of the life-world (p. 140). Now it is the a priori of the *Lebenswelt* that must become a scientific theme in a new sense, i.e., the universal theme of a new science. If we speak of an objective a priori of science, we must distinguish it from the a priori of the *Lebenswelt* and subsequently derive it from the latter. If we speak of mathematical evidence, this evidence must find its own meaning-structure and legitimacy in the evidence of the *Lebenswelt*. It is thus clear that mathematics must be based on evidence understood as lived presence in the first person and, therefore, on time and its modifications.

According to Husserl, it often happens that, even when we think otherwise, we remain captives of the objectivistic metaphysics that hides within the sciences. The epochē of the sciences also frees us from such a metaphysics.

Husserl considers it a fundamental result of phenomenology that the universal a priori of the *Lebenswelt* must precede and found the a priori of the sciences. The precategorial a priori must in turn be explained by a special "new science." Only this science, phenomenology, can really ground the objective sciences on an authentic scientific basis. The same can be said of logic. The science of the *Lebenswelt* is the foundation of logic on the universal, prelogical a priori.

According to Husserl, the new science must aim at a "pure theory of essence of the life-world" (p. 141). This statement must not be misunderstood. The essences must not be separated from the temporal constitution of life itself. As we have seen, the essence can appear as a modality of temporality. It can appear as the complex of typical modalities of temporal life upon which both essences and categories are ultimately founded. Of course, to search for the typical forms of the life of the *Lebenswelt* also means to search for the invariable forms of that which varies in life. It is because of this that Husserl speaks of an investigation of the forms of the *Lebenswelt*. What is being investigated here is that which is invariable in the general formal structures of the evolution of the *Lebenswelt*.

For Husserl, the meaning of any discourse concerning the world is determined by spatiotemporal form. The world is the totality of things in the spatiotemporal form (p. 142). Thus, things become spatiotemporal *onta*. This poses the task of an ontology of the life-world (ontology of temporal life) that would reveal the essence of the spatiotemporal *onta*.

If we speak of an ontic reality, we speak of a reality in which we live, even if it has not been revealed in a phenomenology, in a science of the *onta*, i.e., in a science of particular things. Since we live in space and time, we always experience things, or *onta*, as partial multiplicities. Ontologically, we only live in some "details," in some perspectives, in some aspects of the world.

To transform the ontic into the ontological means to recognize the relationship among the *onta*. As has been discussed, it also means to realize that in every partial thing, in every part, a universal horizon is potentially present. This universal horizon is never given in its totality. It is what Husserl indicates as the world, or, more precisely, as the horizon of the world. Therefore, to transform the ontic into the ontological amounts to transforming unrelated things into relations, to grasping the presence of the universal horizon of the world in each of its spatiotemporal individuations. We have already indicated how this is where the meaning of the praxis in the horizon of the world resides. If phenomenology is an ontology, it is not so in a dogmatic or metaphysical sense. It is an ontology to the extent that it is the science of a progressive revelation, insofar as it is an active connection, the transformation of every spatio-temporal individuation in the horizon of the world. This horizon of the world is *always* present *in us,* even if it is never fully conquered.

This horizon is present in every partial spatiotemporal in-dividuation, even if it is hidden. The ontology that reveals the essence of the spatiotemporal *onta* is the progressive explication of the horizon of truth of the world that is implicit in every reality and finite individuation. In the ultimate analysis, this is *phenomenological relationism.* So understood, ontology is, *tout court,* phenomenology. Therefore, in order to be sustained, it does not need a fictitious ontology in either the traditional or the Heideggerian sense, because *it has arisen precisely in order to overcome the fetishization of being.*

4 / Universal Correlation and Philosophy as the Transformation of Being in the Meaning of Truth

[12]   *Direct Experience and Reflection.*
        Scientific and Subjective Constitution
        of the Life-World

IN SECTION 38 OF THE *Crisis*, Husserl observes that there are two different ways of considering waking life (*Wachleben*) within the general picture of the *Lebenswelt*. The first regards it as life internal to the horizon of the world. The second approaches it as the consciousness we all have of *how* everything we experience within the horizon of the world *appears to us*. The first is natural, direct, and normal. In it, the world is the totality of those things that appear in the constant flow where we know and live. There, we gradually become interested in the objects that appear to our thoughts and activities as if, being particular, they were immediately part of a general plan or intentional horizon animating them all. In the second case, we are aware of how objects appear, and we turn our attention to the subjective forms through which they are given to us. In the first instance objects are entities, and in the second they are modalities of representations: they are as we represent them to ourselves. The first way is ontic, the second ontological. Phenomenology is ontology if it studies the forms of *how*, the modalities of appearance and self-revelation. Normally, these things are directly lived without our bothering with how they are lived *by us* and are valid for us.

The first (the ontic mode) is broader than the second (the phenomenological). In the first we unconsciously experience more than in the second, since in the second what we experience is consciously apprehended as a subjective operation. In the second, reflective mode, we know that the world had already been directly given to us before reflection, and what we had not yet discovered in the already given world. The "before" indicates that reflection acts in time. I can reflect on what has passed and, in the present, I can awaken what has been forgotten. Of course, this does not mean that, in the present, the present subject *poses or creates* the past in a metaphysical-idealistic sense.

There is no dualism between the first and second modes. The second is a development of the first, even if everything we have directly and unconsciously experienced in the first does not pass into the second. The ontological is not a different level or a level parallel to the ontic. Instead, it is a self-evolving of the ontic into the ontological, a development of the *Lebenswelt* into consciousness of the *Lebenswelt*. The *Lebenswelt* (the *directly* flowing and constant life, with its objects, its interests, its activities, and its ends within the world) does not disappear in order to reappear in consciousness. The first level is not *res extensa* and the second is not *res cogitans*. The first is not irrational existence and the second is not rational thought. Furthermore, the first is not without specificity or structure, and the second is not an abstract, categorial construct. The *Lebenswelt* has its own structures. Unseparated from this *Lebenswelt*, the categories are but the evolution of the structures of mundane life to the level of consciousness, i.e., of the "natural" way in which we are "within the world." The categories, then, are modalities which we discover by reflection and through which we live the *Lebenswelt* and experience the world. The study of these modalities is the science of the life-world. The evolution of the *Lebenswelt* to consciousness is a temporal process. Consciousness is also reflected life which maintains and retains the *Lebenswelt*, and which continuously discovers it as that which is prior to reflection. While I reflect, the direct life (which is always broader than what I can know about it phenomenologically) keeps on working and functioning. It is a constantly flowing and functioning life. Thus, at a later time, I am able to study what was previously functioning, without being aware that I am studying it as one of my modes of experiencing or, better yet, as a subjective form of experiencing.

Husserl points out that it is through reflection that I grasp the world prior to reflection, i.e., the world where I live and experience here even before reflecting. Hence, it is only *in reflection* that I can say that the life-world is "pregiven." The direct world evolves and remains alive when, through reflection, I distinguish between the subjective acts whereby I think of the world, and the intentional contents of thought. What I think is not a categorial abstraction: it is always the *Lebenswelt* which, remaining such, evolves in its meanings. Hence we do not think about abstract objects or about "thoughts." We do not deal solely with abstract ontological objects of thought. Phenomenology is consciousness of the ontic, i.e., of the living world. When studied in the *modes* through which it appears, this world produces phenomenological analysis and reflection and, therefore, a science of typicity and meaning.

Reflection takes place in time, where the ontic becomes ontological. More specifically, reflection is the temporal life of the ontic that is immediately given and becomes consciousness and presence in life. As a philosopher, I always begin from the presence and the evidence, i.e., from ontological awareness. But since, while it continues to live, the presence retains the life that has "just" been lived, to begin from the presence means to recognize that precategorial, prereflective, direct, and functioning life is also pregiven to reflection. In other words, *it is precisely in reflection, in consciousness, and in self-consciousness, that I discover that the world is pregiven to consciousness.* If we think about what Husserl says, we readily understand that consciousness discovers that it does not posit the world. Contrary to traditional idealism, consciousness discovers precisely that the world is pregiven. This is the basic tenet of the phenomenology of the life-world. Therefore, the epochē of all the objective sciences is insufficient: what must be analyzed is how we experience what is pregiven (p. 145).

I grasp the past that has been present and retain what has been seen in it by reflection. But I also retain that which has not been seen and becomes reflection now, in the actual present. I can retain in a concealed way, without having reflected upon it, that which I have lived. By reflecting, I can reveal what has remained hidden and, in the future, I can even reveal what remains hidden in present reflection. Thus, the future can be considered as the ideal of the revelation of the hidden, as the clarification (in reflection) of the hidden life, as the *telos* of life. In remaining alive, this life evolves in rationality and, by so doing, becomes the true life which progressively acquires the meaning of truth.

[13]   *Dialectics and Meaning.*
         Phenomenology as the Universal Science
         of the "How"

ACCORDING TO HUSSERL, the evolution, from the direct
way of living in the world to the study of the ways through
which the world is given to "us," presupposes a complete change
of our interests. In the second case, unlike the first, we do not
live only within the world without thinking about overcoming
what we live. This is so even if we "preliminarily" have the vague
feeling of an intentional horizon lying "behind." In the second
case, we live in order to overcome the already constituted world,
to direct ourselves toward a new world that we can conceive
and whose realization we can seek to effect. *Here the interest
has changed,* since the interest is no longer concerned with the
given world but with a world evolving from it by means of
reflection. This evolving-in-reflection goes behind the direct
world. Reflection aims toward a teleological and intentional
meaning. The world no longer interests us for what it is, but
for the meaning it can have and for the meaning which we can
give to it and realize. When realized, this meaning becomes immediate. At this point, however, a new meaning appears and
must be grasped by the new reflection which protends toward
the future in protention and anticipation. Hence, even if I have
reflected in that present that has now become the past, I must
reflect again, and I can say, with Husserl, that reflection has
always been. This does not contradict the fact that what has
"already been reflected upon" can appear in the first mode, the
direct one. What has "already been reflected upon" may have
been forgotten, and past reflection may no longer be reflection
in the present. Thus, it may appear as an already accomplished
reflection, or as a reflection that has been occluded.

As a "new science," phenomenology's domain is the world of
the *Lebenswelt* in its evolution, moving through reflection, from
the direct to the indirect mode, and reflecting upon how the
world obtains and can obtain for us. Phenomenology is the
universal science of the *how*, of the way in which we have lived
and now live, and of the way we can and must live the *Lebenswelt* in functioning and operative subjectivity (*fungierende
leistende Subjektivität*). The *Lebenswelt* must become the uni-

versal domain of a life that has a meaning and goal. As the universal science of the how, phenomenology is the science of the "ultimate foundations," the science of the original "meaning-structure" (*Sinngebung*).

[14] *The Primacy of Reflection.*
       The Intentional Revolution

THE HISTORICAL INVESTIGATION of the *Crisis* has led to the discovery of what has occluded the *Lebenswelt,* and, as such, has reduced the categorial and scientific to the prescientific level. It has led us to the domain of the world that is always given prior to the sciences that depend upon it. However, this discovery does not yet mean that the *Lebenswelt* can be studied by a science only if it is raised, in reflection, to the analysis of how the world which is prior to both consciousness and reflection appears to us in consciousness. We discover the *Lebenswelt* in history, and we find it in the very same constructions that have hidden it. How can we know this *Lebenswelt*? We know that we can know and transform it into a scientific theme only if we do not see it as objective. In phenomenological reflection, we study the subjective modes through which it appears to us. This is why Husserl says that, having freed the *Lebenswelt* from the sciences, we must reduce it to the "universe of the purely subjective" whereby the world exists *for us* (p. 147).

Husserl insists that the transcendental epochē must not only give us the separate objects (or the various things that gradually appear within the horizon of the world), but also yield a universal horizon with an autonomous, intentional meaning and goal. Only reflection can yield these results. Reflection is an extension of the direct mode of living. It participates in life without reflecting upon the indirect and teleological mode of life that gains self-consciousness in the actual presence. As we have seen, it is in the presence, and because of reflection in the presence, that I can say that the world was "pregiven" to me. I cannot say this as long as I directly participate in the world's functioning. This is why Husserl says that "simply living on in this manner, one does not need the word 'pregiven'" (p. 145). When I say that the *Lebenswelt* is already given before reflection, I say so in the reflective presence. But reflection concerns the modes of subjectivity and presence. Therefore, it is in reflection, in the original subjectivity, that I discover the *Lebenswelt* as such. I see the *Lebenswelt* as it is and, therefore, I see that, in terms of the science of the *Lebenswelt*, natural life becomes the functioning life that produces validity, i.e., it experiences the world as it is really lived before any scientific or categorial construction. If I remain in a natural mundane attitude, I do not know what its function is: I do not approach it scientifically or investigate, discover, and reveal it. However, if I change my attitude and place myself on the level of reflection, I am able to understand the *Lebenswelt*, its function, and its sense. In reflection, I do not construct categories by which the *Lebenswelt* is negated or occluded (as happens, e.g., in Galileo), but I clearly see how the *Lebenswelt* acts, operates, and lives. The change does not concern the negation of the precategorial by means of the categorial, or the negation of life by means of rationality. The change concerns my attitude, my decision to discover the rational meaning of the *Lebenswelt*. It involves a change from passive acceptance, where one does not raise questions concerning the functioning and meaning of the *Lebenswelt*, to an active decision which, on the contrary, investigates both. The reader might think that the transcendental epochē is the negation of the *Lebenswelt*, but this is not so. The natural attitude that must be negated is that which passively lives in the *Lebenswelt* without questioning its meaning. The transcendental attitude does not negate the *Lebenswelt* and the pregiven world. Rather, it denies that it should be accepted as already done and accomplished.

That the world has always been given, and that we always live in it, does not mean that we know its intentional meaning. This is the task of the transcendental attitude, which recognizes that the world is always given but that it must continually renew its proper meaning. It aims at discovering such a "meaning and ontic validity, and continually attains these in new forms, in our conscious life" (p. 148). If the passage from the first to the second way of living is an evolution—since it is always the *Lebenswelt* that is first lived directly and only later in reflection —then the same passage also implies taking a dialectical, revolutionary position on the intentional level. This is so if, in the investigation of the *Lebenswelt*, I discover, by reflecting, that it has meaning insofar as it tends toward a teleological, ideal unity. In terms of time, from the viewpoint of the actual present, the evolution of the *Lebenswelt* toward reflection is the presence of the past in the present (retention). As this presence gradually fades away and becomes what it has already been, i.e., the present as past (what has historically happened), I am conditionally free. Even if I am always conditioned, I become an "I can" or an "I do," striving toward a universal historical goal. In this process, particular themes are subordinated in the autonomous and universal theme that I can grasp in a genuine realization of the epochē. Life does not obtain in the "direct" mode in which I live or in its immediate interest. This interest is the historical *telos* which obtains in my individual life and in that of all others. From this viewpoint, the transcendental epochē is a *total* transformation (*Umstellung*) (p. 148).

[15]   *The Being of the World*
       as the Intentional Meaning of Truth.
       Time and Meaning

FOR HUSSERL, the validity of natural life is never "separated." It is connected to the general validity. More or less consciously, it is also connected to that which is not experienced in the actual moment, that which is not clearly perceived and remains in the background (*Hintergrund*). It lives, then, in a vast horizon which can be neither directly nor consciously perceived. In this sense, the direct *Lebenswelt* is always inherence in a horizon (*Horizonthaftigkeit*). Therefore, the horizon is always indicated in its totality, even though it is only lived and perceived in its parts. If I want to suspend the direct *Lebenswelt*, I can do so only if the parts inhere in the total horizon. It *seems* that the epochē must be carried out all at once, "with one blow" (p. 150). This is the dialectical "leap" of the attitude which is posed at the intersection where anything in direct life is bound to everything else. It is given in a whole which is immediately "here" as *Dasein*. This *Dasein* is not a problem (*fraglos*) because it is a universe of things immediately at hand: "*Universum der Vorhandenheiten*" (p. 150). The "being-at-hand" (*Vorhandenheit*) is thrown off by the transcendental epochē in terms of which the world is no longer valid in its being-at-hand. We must decide "once and for all" (p. 150) about this attitude that rejects mere utility as such. We must do this so that we will stand by the decision. The world remains "at hand," *but its meaning does not reduce to the fact that it is so:* this produces a radical change of the meaning of life.

In fact, the epochē is precisely *the liberation from the pre-given world, considered as if its meaning were already concluded and definitive.* Reflection frees us because it allows us to recognize the intentional meaning of the world and gives the latter a new teleological meaning. It is liberation from the occluded which holds us prisoners. Therefore, it is a phenomenological revelation of that which imprisons us by remaining occluded. The world obtains already, even if we do not know why. As such, it does not obtain freely for us. By means of the epochē we make sure that the world really comes to obtain for us.

Even before the epochē, the world used to live in subjectivity, but I did not know this. With the epochē and reflection I always discover anew what obtains and obtained for subjectivity. Husserl says that because of this, the philosopher continuously places himself in the attitude whereby the meaning of the truth of being is never pregiven but is continuously produced by intentional subjectivity. That which previously had an occluded meaning now reveals its true meaning. We must add that it is modified on the basis of this new meaning insofar as it comes to be revealed in relation to the infinite and teleological task of discovering meaning and truth. The epochē negates pregiven being in order to continually constitute it, where being is understood as intentional truth which is never exhausted in the given, in what is already objectified, in what is at hand and already has a meaning. The world is "being" because consciousness constitutes it as the meaning of truth always to be discovered anew. The being of the world is not already there in its *Dasein,* but in its meaning of truth. The true being of the world is its progressive self-revelation as truth, as phenomenon. Phenomenology discovers that *the world has being insofar as it has a meaning,* to the extent that the truth inhering in it is discovered and becomes the aim and intentional meaning of human life. The transcendental relationship of the world and consciousness means that the truth of the world is always in the subjectivity that lives in it. Subjectivity is first occluded in the world and then revealed in the actual presence. Finally, it becomes the teleological and intentional meaning that guides us through a future of progressive revelation, discoveries, and realization of truth in time.

Since truth is meaning, it is constituted in the transcendental relationship. Since being is meaning, the being of the world is constituted in subjectivity. Transcendental consciousness (subjectivity), as the being of the world that is constituted in consciousness, is not the acceptance of a pregiven being (which is not true being). Rather, it is the active constitution of meaning: forming subjectivity (*gestaltende Subjektivität*) (p. 151). The reader should not think of consciousness as a *res cogitans* separated from body and matter. Forming subjectivity is also corporeal subjectivity that feels alive and is discovered alive. For Husserl, to reflect upon the body is not to negate it, but is rather to give it an intentional life. The same is true for both "things" and matter. Thus, to reflect upon the world is not the same as to negate it (since it is always pregiven). Rather, such reflection gives it a meaning. Philosophy is not a negation of reality. It discovers that true meaning of reality that remains hidden and forgotten in the nonphilosophical attitude, with the consequence that man and civilization, instead of giving life and meaning to the world, become lost in the mundane.

The transcendental reduction "reduces" humanity to the "phenomenon" humanity, i.e., to its teleological meaning which is correlative to meaning-producing subjectivity. Husserl observes that subjectivity so understood is absolute (and we discover anew how the adjective "absolute" must be grasped in its true meaning) (p. 153). Husserl insists on the fundamental fact that absolute subjectivity, as he means it, is not a metaphysical invention or construction. It lives: it is life that lives in us even though it is hidden and unrecognized. Philosophy does not invent it; philosophy discovers it and continually changes it from the occluded to the revealed, from the potential to the actual, from the passive to the active. *Philosophy does not create the world but gives it a meaning of truth.* And the life of truth is already potentially, implicitly, hidden and present in the world. What we must do is render it explicitly active in order to transform the world. Mundane or hidden being is not true being. Yet it contains true being in its meaning. As such, to constitute being, and to see it as the goal, is tantamount to continually rediscovering (i.e., disoccluding) what is hidden and lost in normal, direct, and immediate mundane living.

Every step forward is the constitution of the world according to truth. The familiar ground of the world in which being is what it appears to be is abandoned for a meaning which is both the principle and the goal, the origin and final meaning of consciousness. The initially occluded true being that we live in transcendental subjectivity can be discovered in the present and realized in the future. In different ways, true being has "already obtained" its "validity" prior to any science and scientific or philosophic construction. As a matter of fact, it obtains as subjectivity in the presence: what has been, had been presence, in the same way that what will be, will be presence. Furthermore, according to its modalities (as remembrance and representation), the present "that has been" is in the actual presence in the same way as what will be (as anticipation and prefiguration).

From this viewpoint, presence is *nunc stans:* everything happens in presence, within the subjectivity of a presence where the world has its validity. Presence is origin, actuality, and goal at the same time. However, in the presence the world changes, is lost and found again, and ends and begins anew. The modes of presence are thus the self-distinctions of present subjectivity in the stasis of the past, present, and future.

The humanity that lives in time, with its individuals, its various social units, and its civilizations, is frozen presence understood as *nunc stans.* It is the self-alienation (meant in the positive sense) of transcendental subjectivity which, "since always," has alienated itself and, therefore, even though it is present life, has always had a past, has a present, and will have a future. Consequently, it lives in finite times. Transcendental humanity becomes objectified in determinate civilizations. It has had an original past which is now occluded, has a present conditioned by the past, and will have a future. From this viewpoint, the real past is also original—the past as the infinite origin which must continuously be investigated and brought to light as a "phenomenon." It must be noticed that absolute subjectivity is "functioning." The transcendental reduction allows the continuous revelation of the present that has always been active, is active now, and will be active in the future. The functioning *nunc stans* can be revealed only by transcendental subjectivity, which reflects on the functioning and, in the present, always reveals it by "seeing it" in the past and protending itself toward the future, in the ideal of a complete revelation which is really infinite. Therefore, although it is realized and lives in time, reflection is always in the present. It is temporality that remains self-identical, although it is temporalized in temporal stases. Transcendental subjectivity is embodied life that lives in its limited and finite expressions, and which continues to live precisely because of this. It is life which lives in time. It begins and ends in time. Simultaneously, it is regenerated and maintained precisely by being frozen in time. It is temporality that persists, and temporalized permanence. Philosophy does not construct this perennial and changing life, but only philosophy can talk about it. And only phenomenology, for which *truth* is more important than what is pregiven, can give a meaning to being. What counts for all of us is not simply to exist, but to exist for a goal, for a positive meaning, for truth. Philosophy is the expression and meaning of life.[1]

Philosophy does not deduce life. Rather, it is life which, in reflection, persists and is renovated by continuously giving itself an intentional meaning. It always avoids the occluded by continuously reconstituting itself in truth and by transforming being into the meaning of truth. In philosophy, life is recognized as the self-determining life which is expressed and actualized in temporal finitude. But it can also be recognized as life which, precisely by means of philosophy, becomes reengaged, since it does not become exhausted in any determination but always begins anew in every monad, in every monadic pairing (*Paarung*), in every group and civilization. Philosophy is the human activity in which life resumes the journey toward truth by continuously returning to its own origin and by becoming transformed in the horizon of truth, i.e., by always reconstituting being into intentional meaning.

[16] *Genesis and Transcendental Reduction. Time and the Ethos of Rational Life*

THE PATH TO THE TRANSCENDENTAL EPOCHĒ indicated in the *Crisis* begins with the critique of the constituted sciences. In such a historical and genetic critique, Husserl discovers the *Lebenswelt* and its transcendental correlation with consciousness. As we know, the transcendental epochē appears in the *Crisis* as a second reduction with respect to the first reduction to the *Lebenswelt*. However, precisely because of the transcendental correlation, the first and second reductions are very closely connected so that, generally speaking, one can begin with either of the two. Even though this is not clear after a first reading, one implies the other. In the historical analysis of the second part of the *Crisis*, Husserl himself discovers the *Lebens-*

---

1. This viewpoint is present as early as the Husserl of the *Logical Investigations*. See E. Husserl, *Ideas: General Introduction to Pure Phenomenology*, trans. W. R. Boyce Gibson (New York: Humanities Press, 1931), p. 347: "Logical meaning is an expression."

welt, since he has somehow already performed the transcendental reduction that makes such a discovery possible. For methodological reasons, he carries out the investigation as if this had not happened and, therefore, the transcendental reduction appears as the second reduction.

Ideas lacked this progressive, genetic, and historical explanation. The reduction has been carried out with one leap, and we know that this is not possible because there is no gap between the *Lebenswelt* and consciousness of the *Lebenswelt,* between the ontic and the ontological. This is true even if the reduction is a dialectical leap, a radical change or "radical transformation" leading to the intentional meaning and *telos* that goes beyond the partial and particular interests within the world. Hence, the *Crisis* deals once again with the reduction of *Ideas* (the "Cartesian" reduction). But it deals with it through the genesis whereby (as for the ego of the *Cartesian Meditations*) the reduction is carried out for the ego "in its own history." *Ideas* has made the genetic analysis of the *Crisis* possible. Similarly, the *Crisis* resumes, corrects, and at the end radically alters the reduction of *Ideas* by associating it with the genesis of the *Lebenswelt* and its correlation with consciousness.

The genesis of the *Lebenswelt* is possible for the transcendental reduction (and this is itself prepared by the genesis). That which in the *Crisis* is called the first reduction presupposes the second, which is itself entailed by the first. In an absolute sense, it is always a matter of the same reduction, because transcendental subjectivity is always presence, and it is always present even if hidden. It is temporality that sees itself as *nunc stans.* But the absolute (which—to reiterate—must not be understood as a metaphysical substance) is determined and temporalized in the temporal stases. Therefore, it discovers its own genesis in the presence, just as it prepares the meaning of the future and poses itself as the *telos.* Absolute subjectivity is always present subjectivity and expression. By expressing itself it reveals the meaning of truth in the functioning, rediscovers the past origin, reveals the present, and appears as the teleological ideal.

Phenomenology lives in a dialectic which unravels and persists. This permanence is eternal, but its expression is temporal: philosophy as expression and reflection grasps permanence in time. Therefore, it is correct to say both that the transcendental reduction presupposes its own genetic history and that this genetic history presupposes the transcendental reduction. As a matter of fact, subjectivity always appears as *nunc stans* in any moment of the genesis, in the actual genesis, and in the future. On the other hand, in temporalization it appears as preparation for the present in the same way that, in the present, it prepares for the future. It is always active as functioning life, while it always remains to be carried out as teleological and conscious life. So understood, life is the fluent and constant life of the totality of the monads which, in a gradual process *ad infinitum,* moves toward the universal *telos* by transforming its own being in truth. A science of the life-world is possible if the radical change of attitude allows us to free ourselves from fetishized things and to observe how they are lived by us. This is the theoretical interest that goes beyond particular interests and rises to a teleological meaning.

The life-world which has the general function of being the terrain of humanity (*Boden*) is the subjective-relative world of the *doxa.* Phenomenology wants to be a science of the *doxa* that leaves its real and concrete structures to relativity. This science requires an ethical decision, an initial act where transcendental subjectivity begins to operate. "In the beginning there is the deed" (p. 156). This means that transcendental subjectivity is theoretical-active (*leistende Subjektivität*) and is operative after the epochē. The attempt to explain the positive sciences, the clarification of their hidden functioning, leads to the science of the modalities of the "Heraclitean flux." Science is the will of science which is living rationality. For this reason, the norm is not an abstract law, but active theoretical life which is real as living *ethos.*

[17]   *Phenomenology of the Thing. Relationistic Reconsideration of Phenomenology*

THE "HERACLITEAN FLUX," or the subjective-relative world which obtains as such, has the various aspects of touch, smell, etc., in the perception in which it appears. Moreover, new aspects or various phases of each of these aspects appear. The same thing is given to me and I represent it to myself according to various modalities: when I see only one of its sides, I know that it is only a side and not the complete thing. I know more than what I see, more than what I actually perceive. In successively seeing a thing from various sides, I retain what I have already seen in the various perspectives. By holding (*Behaltung*) (which is also a retention in time), I put together both what precedes and what follows. This putting-together (*Zusammen-genommenheit*) of all the sides reveals to me the thing in its organic unity. Although I had already previewed this unity, I never stop discovering the thing by viewing it from different angles (consider the history of art, and how various painters see the same thing). The modes of appearing are a function of the vicinity and distance of something with respect to the position of my body, and of its internal and external movements [*cinestesi*].

In its various perspectives the thing is present in each of the perceptions I have of it, even if I only perceive one of its aspects. I know only one side, but I presume that there are others. I presume it according to an intentional presumption (*Meinung*) which is yet to be verified, just as when I conceive that the thing, when seen from another side, will appear in some determinate way. Yet I have not seen it, though I mean to do so. The intention is present and empty: it will be filled when I actually look and have the actual perception of the presumed vision.

Every perception of a thing implicitly contains the other aspects of the thing. If I touch something with my eyes closed, the vision that I have of it when I open my eyes is contained in the tactile perception. Every mode of perception, my ways of perceiving, and every particular perception, contain the other perceptions which, if perceived, would give me the thing in its organic totality. Each perspective whereby the thing is perceived is the perspective of the thing-horizon, of the "total" thing. Yet, such a "totality" is never explicitly given to me. It appears as that at which all perceptions and representations aim, and which are therefore "respresentations of" the total horizon of the thing. Therefore, they are intentional representations in respect to that horizon.

I can have various representations of the "same" color and of the "ideal" color. No matter how different they may be, they are still representations of that color which is never wholly given to me. They are, therefore, representations of an ideal color, of the meaning of that color, or of the ideal unity of sense which is but its meaning. The sense and meaning of things and colors become explicit in time in syntheses that sometimes break down, and at other times are united for the purpose of aiming at a general synthetic unity or synthetic horizon. Each temporal representation of the same color, from different positions and distances, has an identity of meaning. This is progressively enriched when I remember what I have seen, what I see, and what I anticipate I will really be able to see ("fulfilling" the intention) or not (leaving the anticipation empty and recognizing that I was wrong). This is an incomplete phenomenological description of how something is temporally lived in all its aspects, and according to the progressive constitution of its intentional meaning. It is the description that Husserl outlined for the first time in the unpublished *Dingvorlesung* of 1907.

To the extent that it is possible, the phenomenological description of the thing occurs because there has been a shift from the natural to the reflective attitude, or from the direct to the indirect way. The indirect way is no longer interested in what is mundanely given, but in the *how*, in the way in which the world, as it has been seen, is subjectively experienced. The shift requires that total change of interest that follows the transcendental epochē, and it is this shift which allows the constitution of the meaning of truth in the correlation of the world and consciousness of the world. The latter is not invented or metaphysically constructed; it is constituted in subjectivity and is experienced in the first person. The reduction to subjectivity may appear as a second reduction with respect to the first reduction (or the reduction to the *Lebenswelt*) obtained by the epochē of objective science. However, we have seen that the two reductions are correlative insofar as life is always on the path of self-consciousness, or on the path of the *telos* where truth appears as the goal.

The epochē of objective science must allow for a subjective science of the *Lebenswelt*. The *Lebenswelt* must not be fetishized but must be caught in its subjectivity, its relativity, and its appearing as *doxa*. We can catch it this way if we do not remain tied to mundane objects and if, in our theoretical commitment, we turn ourselves to *how* they are given to us. An analysis of the "thing" is an analysis of the *how* and offers us an example of the science of the *Lebenswelt* in action: it is the beginning of explicating what is given to us by sensations and perceptions. Such a beginning has been possible because we have renounced directing ourselves toward objects with a mundane attitude; we have renounced dealing with them as if they were already constituted. Instead, we have dealt with the way they reveal themselves to us, how we represent them in our subjectivity, how we live them by treating them as concrete experiences in spatio-temporal life, in vicinity and distance, and in the constitution of the various syntheses that offer a progressive meaning of truth in continuous self-correction.

Hence, the *Lebenswelt* is given in intentional representations that aim toward an ideal unity, i.e., a teleological and intentional meaning. This is the true meaning, the transfiguration of being into truth in the intentional representation of the world lived in transcendental subjectivity.

Reflection reveals to us that we live the world in every perception that we have of it in space and time. Perception thus implies the connecting and the continuation of intentional representations constituting a progressive development aiming toward truth and intentional meaning. The tactile perception of something implies aural and visual perceptions. The view of one side implies the view that I could have of the other sides. In the intentional presumption (*Meinung*), I expect new perceptions to be a certain way rather than others, and they may or may not turn out to be what I expected. In the negative case, new perceptions can compel me to correct even what I believed I had perceived previously, and what I thought I had correctly represented to myself. Therefore, the true meaning of a thing demands some corrections in its progressive formation, as may be required by the coherence of the perspectives, by the intentional and synthetic agreement which I seek and which must continuously explain and correct any disagreement (this is how Husserl explains errors).

The analysis of the *how* is an analysis of intentional representation. Every perception implies other possible perceptions. Every partial representation of something implies the final horizon of that thing and, finally, the meaning of truth. I do not perceive only the color or the geometrical form. I do not smell only one odor or hear only one sound. What I now perceive implies a whole series of perceptions that tend to cohere toward the final representation of the thing and its true meaning. Every representation is part of the total horizon of the thing that, as such, implies a teleological and coherent horizon, even if I may not be aware of it. Consciousness clarifies one aspect of the perception. But the other aspects are also present and functioning, even if they are not clarified. As Husserl puts it, they are cofunctioning. What also functions in all that I perceive is everything that I do not focus upon: even what I barely perceive and do not yet perceive. What is functioning at this moment without my being aware of it may become, in a following moment, a representation connected to the preceding ones. As such, the synthesis of intentional representations (their coherent horizon) is a progressive explication of what is functional in each particular perception. Thus the science of the *Lebenswelt* appears as the progressive explication of what remains implicit in each perception. Every perception has a clear focus where it is a representation. This focus is surrounded by cofunctioning perceptions implied by the central perception. These cofunctioning perceptions must be made explicit. Every evident, present, and conscious perception is inextricably related to cofunctioning and obscure perceptions, and, as a limiting case, to what is not perceived (pp. 159–60).[2] Every part implicitly contains the whole. The phenomenological description must gradually explicate in time what remains implicit. Every perception implies a multiplicity of other perceptions that are not yet actual: otherwise we could never experience the world or gradually represent it in space and time according to an ideal and teleological horizon. The horizon is already obscurely present in every aspect and part. The implicit presence of the whole in the parts—which operates even if I have not rendered it explicit and conscious—is an a priori correlation of the part with the whole, of a perception with other possible perceptions, or of an aspect of the thing with other aspects that cohere with it. It is the a priori presence of the whole in the part. It is an implication, in the part, of the relation to the whole: it is the presence of universal correlation. This is what Husserl calls the *a priori of the correlation*. It is for this reason that relationism, i.e., the philosophy that I outlined from 1951 to 1954, was bound to evolve into Husserl's phenomenology: only by starting with phenomenology, by starting all over again, was it possible to begin a new path.

The perception from which I depart is the present, actual, and focal perception. But this clear and evident perception is a priori correlated with all that is not now present in this moment and situation. Evidence is surrounded by not-evidence, still-hidden evidence, and potential evidence. The presence contains a priori the entire universe: its finitude a priori contains the infinite, and in an obscure and hidden way. As present, it contains the infinity of the past and the future. As space, it contains, in my location, the whole infinity surrounding such a location: it contains what is closest to me as well as what is most distant from me. The universal a priori correlation implies the copresence of what is now here in a conscious, explicit, and

2. See my text, *Il Nulla e il Problema dell'Uomo,* 2d ed. (Turin: Taylor, 1959), pp. 179–91.

evident way, and implies what is not yet, what was, and what is elsewhere in a non-evident way.

Phenomenology is the revelation of that which is not explicitly present and evident. Phenomenology's task is to bring to light and to the life of evidence what is hidden, occluded, confused, and engulfed in error. This task can only be accomplished by starting from that evidence which is in *us:* the subject, the subjects in intersubjectivity. Since what surrounds evidence is implicit in it, and since the implicit is infinite, the task of phenomenology is both temporally and historically infinite. The purpose of history is to render the hidden horizon present, true, and rational. This infinite transformation is always the simultaneous *transformation of myself, others, and the world.* My horizon, which is also intersubjective and historical, is ultimately intentional.

The a priori of the correlation unfolds in time. To the extent that it functions, the operative ego is both hidden and implicit and explicit and evident. Therefore, subjectivity contains something hidden and something revealed. I can gradually unveil what is hidden by departing from what is revealed in the evident presence (myself). Perception contains evidence and also potentially contains what is not yet evident. If I reflect upon perception, I can reveal what is functional in it, not at the time in which it functions, but after it has passed (as retention) and is, therefore, observable. Since present perception passes, although I retain and observe it, it happens that I first perceive and then notice the perception. I first immediately live what is functional and then reflect upon it. Similarly, life perceives and notices itself in the flowing of time: it lives and comes to know itself. It is both the *Lebenswelt* and the science of the *Lebenswelt.* It is the presence of the functional ego and the revelation of that which is functioning in reflection. That is why Husserl says that, in reflection, subjectivity perceives and notices itself in perceiving: it functions and at the same time becomes aware of its functioning. The functioning is anonymous, but reflection takes the anonymity away from it. The functioning level passes to the reflective level, where it is noticed and revealed in a life which is perception and awareness of perception: a life which perceives and becomes self-aware in perception (*wahrnehmendgewahrend*).

Functioning life is the *Lebenswelt* containing the a priori of the universal correlation. Husserl sometimes says that, so understood, it is unity: it is the absolute, unique, and functional ego.

But this unique ego implicitly contains the whole. If it did not reflect upon itself it would not be aware of containing the world. What I reflect upon contains others and is in time: prior to, contemporaneous with, and after the others. It is important to notice that the universal correlation can only live and be revealed in time and its modalities.

The first modality is the presence in which life is given as such: it is evidently present in the "first person," or, as Husserl sometimes calls it, in flesh and bones (*leibhaft*). For the past, as indicated, there is the modality of retention that Husserl terms "primary recall." In addition to primary recall, when that which is directly held begins to be forgotten, we have remembrance, or secondary recall (*Wiedererinnerung*). The operation that characterizes direct presence is presenting activity (*Präsentation* or *Gegenwärtigung*). The operation of remembrance does not aim at what has just passed (as retention does) but at the past present. It brings the past present back to the actual present: it is, therefore, a presentification of the past, or a re-presentation (*Vergegenwärtigung*). The counterpart of retention in the direction of the future is protention, or the expectation of what is about to happen. It is the approaching of the future which for me is really a leaning toward, a protention toward the future in the present. To the remembrance corresponds rememorative anticipation (*Vorerinnerung*), the prefiguration of the future which is not yet in the horizon of what is about to happen and which I imagine as the future that I will remember once it will have happened. As a matter of record, the modalities of time, which are the modalities of functioning presence and its unfolding and self-recognizing in reflection, were described for the first time by Husserl in his famous lectures on the *Phenomenology of Internal Time-Consciousness* of 1904–5.[3]

These lectures, however, do not make it clear that temporal modalities characterize the *Lebenswelt* and allow reflection upon the *Lebenswelt* in the *Lebenswelt*. Moreover, temporal modalities discover the *Lebenswelt* in reflection insofar as they constitute its very structure of *doxa* and of the subjective-relative occluded in forgetfulness. If revealed, the latter becomes a phenomenon in actual and evident presence. Functional life is revealed in time, and it is for this reason that reflection is essentially temporal. Functioning life, which implicitly contains the whole, comes to

3. See E. Husserl, *The Phenomenology of Internal Time-Consciousness*, ed. Martin Heidegger, trans. James C. Churchill (Bloomington: Indiana University Press, 1964), pp. 44–45, 50 ff., 75, 79–80.

be revealed and explicates the whole through temporalization. It does so by dividing itself in the present which becomes past and in what persists in the present to be reflected upon. Under examination, the functioning ego, which remains unique and temporalizing, appears temporalized to itself. The functioning and hidden uniqueness, the *nunc stans*, is known only when it does this. When I want to understand all of this, I must reflectively see the functioning ego in self-consciousness, allowing the becoming of the world to flow and generate through me. The infinite and progressive vision of the functioning ego is at the same time its clarification, its science, its transformation, which depart from the evidence that I am to myself. Methodologically, this evidence is absolutely primary. The functioning ego persists before, in the actual moment, and afterward. Intentionality obtains before the evidence as well as after its genesis, from the *I* as the origin of the evidence to the historical genesis of the evidence that is discovered to be antecedent. The recognition of this leads to the disocclusion of history and poses the task of disocclusion as the *telos*, i.e., as the meaning of the truth of the intentional horizon.

Let us return to the phenomenological description that Husserl undertakes in section 45. In description, we start from evidence. This evidence, however, is also evidence of our own body, of the body we "feel" alive as our own (*leibhaft* or, as Sartre and Merleau-Ponty translate it, *corps propre*). But our body does not live by itself, remaining motionless: it moves, it is active, it operates, it is moved by other things and other bodies. The concrete I is an "I can," "I move," and "I do." Everything that it perceives as external is in relation to its internal mode of feeling and its "own" mode of feeling other things and living bodies of other egos. Kinesthetic movements are interrelated, and our way of representing the world is a function of this kinesthesis. If I move in a certain direction, I presume that things will appear to me according to certain perspectives and according to an "if-then" (*Wenn-so*) relationship: if I move this way, then I will see that if I do x, y will result. The various movements tend toward an intentional unity: they conform in terms of this intentionality. When I move in a certain way, I do not always see or hear what I expected to see or hear. In some instances, I become aware of the fact that my presumption was illusory. Thus, the unification of kinesthetic movements continuously corrects illusory expectations so that the corresponding representation is subject to a continuous verification. A perception implies other perceptions that I can have if I move my perceiving body. The perceptions are arranged in a perceiving body and within a horizon of perceptions. Other possible perceptions inhere in the individual perception. The horizon of the perceptions of something inheres to the horizon of the perceptions of something else, and in a horizon that contains both the first and the second. Hence, things have both an internal and an external horizon. The world is represented to us in pieces and connections of pieces. Every horizon implies other horizons: the horizon given to me is the horizon of other horizons, of other ways whereby the world can be given and obtain for me.

Every horizon tends to agree with other horizons; there is an intention of horizons.[4] Every particular horizon, each piece, inheres in a total and open world that must continuously be explicated. The world does not obtain on the level of constituted horizons but is a unity of horizons that I must constantly experience and relate in an open perspective. The representation of the world is a synthesis that is always in process, a unification that is always making and correcting itself in the explication of the movements of my body and other bodies, in the constant attempt to reach a unity of the world.

In every representation and piece I have the foreboding of a unity of the world, of the unity of the horizon of all horizons. This unity indicates the possibility of a representation which organically contains all my actual representations. Similarly, the latter contain the final unity which is factually unreachable: the *telos* of the world.[5] The world is in an eternal movement where it is made and unmade. It is constantly corrected and changes its illusory or false mode of presentation in each of its parts and in me. The world is thus present in each part and can be understood in each part because it is contained in it. In the parts, however, the world appears only in a certain aspect. Only parts of it appear evident, even though these parts imply those other parts which are not yet evident or explicit. As Leibniz puts it, the world appears in a certain way to every monad. Therefore, the transformation and perfection of the world presuppose intermonadic life and reciprocal agreement between the monads that are connected in relation to one another: "The world exists not only for isolated men but for the community of men" (p. 163). The world lives in the life of the monads that participate in each other (p. 163).

The *Lebenswelt* is intermonadic and intersubjective life. It is

4. See *Horizontmeinung*, in C 7 11, p. 6.
5. See K III 6, pp. 9–11.

in this life, with all its movements and actions, that the world is lived and can be transformed according to a horizon of truth that is the horizon of all horizons already implicit in every horizon and part. Thus, phenomenology as the science of the *Lebenswelt* appears as the science that must transform the world according to a meaning of truth. It must give a meaning of truth to intersubjective operations, to the actions of men. In this sense, the world can aim at the ideal of an infinite agreement.

[18]   *Universal Relationism*
         and Transformation of the World
         According to Its Intentional Meaning

As MENTIONED, the science of the *Lebenswelt* is the science of relative subjectivity, of the *doxa*. The horizon of the world is implicit in every subjectivity, and every relative representation inheres in the horizon of the world. Therefore, the world is correlative to the way it is given and represented in the "Heraclitean flux," where the same thing appears in different perspectives aiming toward agreement. These perspectives are the intentional representations and presumptions that can be confirmed or corrected. The world is made and transformed in the spatial and temporal process with its active and passive kinesthetic modalities. It is the temporal elaboration of functioning life *in the time of every monad*. The monads can deceive themselves, but they can also correct their illusions and mistakes.

The functioning life which is elaborated in the time and space of the world can give the world a meaning of truth. Therefore, the world occurs in its representations, in its appearing, and in its becoming a phenomenon. The functioning world is the same world that is revealed in the monads and that aims at a unity of meaning in them. Consequently, the world and consciousness are not separate. It is always the same world which first functions "unconsciously" and then in reflection. Correlation obtains between the world and the consciousness of the world in subjectivity, which is first direct and then indirect. The world is initially obscure and subsequently clear. It becomes gradually clarified in a progressive enrichment of meaning. Now, every part that is represented, every piece of the world, is such that, as a part, it contains the relations with its horizon, and this horizon contains other horizons. To reiterate, then, every aspect and every perspective implies the universal correlation. Each thing is represented relative to each subject and monad. This seems obvious, but it really means that every perception implicitly contains an intentional horizon that has to be explicated. Every perception implies a series of relationships that can be clarified by reflection. This series is implicit a priori. Being appears in the parts, in the kinesthesis and the temporal modalities, because it lives in the monads. Its "reality" is what is lived in intentional evolution, and it is constituted in the egological subjects and their community. Phenomenology's task is to transform hidden being into true being. This process reappears in Marx's dialectic of appearance. Being becomes real when it is revealed and coincides with the phenomenon. Being is the revelation of what hides behind false, mundane, and fetishized appearances. It forms its own sense (*Seinsinn*) in successive intentional representations, in their agreement. From this viewpoint, being is that which appears as the phenomenon. There is as much being as there is appearance (*soviel Schein, soviel Sein*).[6] Here, "appearance" means the revelation of what is hidden.

Being becomes true in its intentional representations. It is true within the limits of its evidence, within its modes of evidence and representation. There are numerous ways of revelation: this multiplicity (or relativity) of correlation is not accidental but is an essential necessity that gives rise to a rich and powerful system of a priori truths. Every being (which is so insofar as it lives in a subjectivity and according to how it appears in subjectivity) necessarily lives as it does and cannot appear otherwise. The modes are numerous and relative, but they inhere in each other and, as such, constitute a system. Every revealed being implies all others. It functions as the index of the systematic multiplicity of its modes of representation and revelation (p. 166). Something that now appears concretely as color indicates its possible mode of representation as surface. A representation of a sound indicates a visual representation, and one side of an object indicates the way the others will appear. The same can be said of the

---

6. E. Husserl, *Cartesian Meditations: An Introduction to Phenomenology*, trans. Dorion Cairns (The Hague: Nijhoff, 1960), p. 103.

presence, concerning how it will persist in retention, how what has just passed and the remembered past will appear, how the future is expected and previewed, how something will be seen from different distances, how it will be perceived "if" I change position in relation to other representations and monads.

All of these and other modalities form a system that inheres in every representation. There would be no experience, no being, if there were not an entire a priori system of modalities of self-revelation, of the modalities of the meaning of truth. Therefore, every event occurs and is represented in a certain way because it is related a priori to the structured multiplicity of the system. No event can be realized, represented, and true unless it appertains to an a priori systematic correlation of modalities. The systematic multiplicity inheres in every mode of representation through which the subject represents the total horizon of the system in a given representation. Every representation is intentional insofar as it tends to realize such an a priori system. The subject can live it in all its aspects, according to a progressively cohering synthesis, only if it corrects the discordances and transforms them in the temporal explication. As such, the a priori system of the possible ways becomes progressively real, and the modalities come to be concretely fulfilled. Every object of experience is correlated to the system of its modalities: this is what Husserl considers his greatest philosophical discovery. According to what he says, it goes back to 1898 (pp. 166–67, footnote). This discovery coincides with the discovery of intentionality. The intentionality of the subject is that which strives for the system in every representation and subject. The system is such that every *cogito* can discover the implicit *cogitata* in the *cogitatum*. In fact, intentionality can be defined by the formula: *ego cogito cogitata qua cogitata*. The *cogitatum* is that which the subject represents and which lives in him, as perception, feeling, and action. However, every perception in its mode of self-givenness implies the whole system of modalities of self-givenness whereby every intentional act necessarily strives toward the entire system of modalities and directs its representations and *cogitata* according to the intentional meaning of truth of the system.

The horizon that must be revealed in phenomenological analysis is always present in every subject. But it is as if this horizon were hidden in the subject and could not appear. The analysis thus must face obscurity in order to bring the horizon to light. The subjects, or monads, as centers of evidence in the first person, can transform the given world and constitute a true world by departing from their own subjectivity. Therefore, the constitution is intersubjective. Every monad contains such a hidden functioning capacity that implicitly contains what can be revealed. A unique operating ego operates in every monad. However, the operating ego always functions within an active intersubjectivity without which there would be no world valid for all—a world always on the *path of self-constitution.* In intersubjectivity, the world aims at clarifying its meaning in the direction of a rational ideal that guides its progressive constitution. This constitution is the task of all subjects and the monadic community of subjects. To explain the world, to institute a science of the *Lebenswelt,* means to go back to the intentional origins, to how the world comes to be constituted in every subject and in the possible agreement of various subjects. Husserl stresses the fact that every perception is a perception by subjects in time and space. This is not the time and space of the sciences or of mathematical logic, but is *lived* time and space. The evidence of present perception is always the starting point, but the presence contains more than just the actual perception of the now (*Jetzt*); it contains the "continuum" of perceptions, intentions, remembrances, and anticipations. Being as truth that is constituted in temporal modalities becomes so in continuous syntheses, rendering possible the "discrete" syntheses. These occur when there is an interruption of consciousness. When this happens, my past ego is no longer recognized by my present ego and appears extraneous. This is the meaning of the presence of a plurality of egos within my own ego, which makes it possible to understand the relation between me and others as united by a reciprocal empathy (*Einfühlung*).

Therefore, the only functioning ego is in a horizon which is obscure, clear, implicit, and present at the same time. What counts, however, is that, even if unique, it is intersubjective. It includes the different modes whereby I live in time my different egos which, besides being part of me, are also part of others. The implicit whole is thereby explicated in the ego's functioning and through its clarification; i.e., the functioning world is constituted according to its rational meaning in the evidence. That hidden and yet clear whole which is the ego in flesh and blood, the concrete individual who lives and reflects, aims at a unity of meaning where the meaning of the truth of life and the world gradually comes to light in order to transform the fetishized mundane world.

The task of reason is the ideal of a total clarification and a total truth. Phenomenology is the infinite clarification and changing of the world: it is the constituting of the world *in praxis* where it is conquered and reconquered according to its most profound, rational, and logical meaning.

5 / Phenomenology and the Ideal of a Rational Society

[19]   *Ego-Pole and Object-Pole.*
        The Intentional Sense
        of the Society of Monads

ACCORDING TO HUSSERL, operative life is expressed and revealed in time: the world is represented and experienced in time. The "subjective" life is the life which experiences the world (*welterfahrendes Leben*). "In my egological sphere . . . I always find myself as an ego experiencing the world." [1] The ego-world relationship is intentional between two poles: the ego-pole on the one hand, and the object-pole on the other. The object-pole is that of the objects appearing to and experienced by the ego. The world obtains for the ego. The ego and its unity, its uniqueness, and its temporal changing, contains all the forms through which the world can be represented. The ego represents the world through various modalities in which the world is given as the being of the phenomenon in revelation and representation.

If I turn my attention to egological representations, to the *cogito,* I see the world in the ego-pole. If I turn my attention to what is represented by the ego—the *cogitata*—I see the world in the object-pole. The ego-pole is intention, and the world of its objects is intended. It must be remembered that functioning life, which is always broader than the egological functions that I assume as the theme of my analysis, is realized in the ego-pole and its various forms. These are the forms through which the ego experiences and *knows* the world as its *cogitatum.* Thus, the ego-

1. Unpublished manuscript C 7 II, p. 19.

[87]

pole implies an activity which functions even if the ego does not reflect upon it and *can be captured only by reflection*. In the object-pole, the idea of a perfectly clear, revealed, and rational world corresponds to the internal activity of the ego-pole. This idea, which is but the meaning toward which the world aims, its teleological sense, its truth, its true being, and *the meaning of truth toward which history aims*, is never completely realized. Therefore, it requires investigation, clarification, and infinite reconsideration which asymptotically tend to the limit of truth. Such reconsideration constitutes being as the truth and meaning of being.

In phenomenological self-awareness, the world aims at the idea of a rational and true world. It is an intentional truth, an intended final object, a totalization of all the partial intentional representations, a horizon which inheres in all partial horizons and gives them their meaning. The totalization of a final truth, therefore, where the meaning of all partial beings agree, corresponds to the internal activity of the ego-pole. Implicit functioning intentionality corresponds to its infinite explication in time. Rational revelation, guided toward the rational agreement by phenomenology and the path of philosophy and humanity, corresponds to obscurity. To the extent that it is guided by phenomenology, the historical process reveals what is hidden and temporally constitutes being as truth. Being is infinitely constituted because the facts to be revealed, and the events which humanity must organize in its practical and theoretical activity according to a rational idea, are themselves infinite. The aim of all representations is not just the ideal agreement; it is also the *teleological idea of a society* where all the monads are fully themselves and realize their full individuality to the degree that they are able to come to an agreement in a rational and free relationship.

Therefore, the ego-pole contains the operative ego which, in revealing itself, constitutes the object-pole not only as *cogitatum* but also as a totality of *cogitata* representing the teleological idea of truth as a final terminus and as a rational agreement of all beings. The ego-pole also includes unclear actions. The object-pole is constituted by the clarification of this obscurity, by its revelations (phenomena), aiming at a total revelation. If, in order to study the ego-pole, we abstract it from the object-pole—although they can never actually be separated—we can ask the following questions. What are its characteristics? What is its form? Can the ego-pole be clarified, and thus appear in its functioning and its structure? If the clarification of the ego-pole is not done, it will remain hidden and we will be able to see its revelation only in its *cogitata,* in the object-pole. Phenomenology would then illuminate the intended, but it would never illuminate the subjects; it could study the intended objects, as perceived or thought, but it could never study constitutive operations, which would remain hidden and obscure.

Therefore, the operative ego, insofar as it is anonymous and hidden, does not constitute a world of truth. It constitutes such a world, however, when it becomes self-conscious, when it acts according to certain functions and structures which are but the modes through which the world is represented and through which the world thinks in its meaning of truth, i.e., the world as a set of phenomena which order themselves in the final idea of truth. The ego-pole can constitute an uncovered objective world by uncovering what it contains as unrevealed within itself. By continuing to discover the hidden aspects of its own functioning, by grasping its own obscurity, the ego-pole constitutes a mode of being of the world as truth, i.e., the meaning of something aiming infinitely at the truth. According to Husserl, the subjective-constitutive act can be investigated, and, therefore, its internal life can be investigated. If this is the *Lebenswelt,* to investigate it means to constitute a science of the *Lebenswelt* and to start constituting such a science by clarifying the structure of the ego-pole.

It is important to understand what Husserl means by the study of the ego-pole and its structures. If the ego-pole were to remain hidden it would not constitute the intentional, true world of the *cogitata.* Certainly, the hidden ego lives in the ego-pole, but the ego can intend a true and rational world only to the extent that hidden subjectivity becomes self-aware. This happens in the self-reflection of the ego. All of this can happen *only in time.* On one hand, it must *always be the same ego* which functions and reflects upon its own functioning, while it functions anew in order to reflect anew. On the other hand, this same ego occurs in *different moments* even if functioning life is always unique, present, and *nunc stans.* Now, in self-revelation, the unique functioning ego (which contains temporality in its permanent flowing) becomes temporalized and displayed in different temporal worlds, in *different modalities of the presence.* The functioning ego is temporality as static presence, as implicit temporality. The evidence is the expression of what is hidden in the functioning ego. *Departing from its own, evident presence,* the subject can, in time, in the different temporal modalities, reflect upon the activity which operates within it. It can reveal the hidden primarily through retention. Because of the primacy of reflection, the reflective ego discovers the functioning in the presence. The presence "holds" the functioning, it can reflect on it, and, by means of reflecting, it can clarify what has "just passed." Therefore, the structures and modalities of time are the structures of the ego-pole. The functional ego, the temporality which is internal and contained in the ego-pole, in becoming progressive evidence, in discovering in the actual evidence that which has been, comes to know itself in the structure of the temporal modalities. It changes from temporality (*Zeitlichkeit*) to temporalization (*Zeitigung*). Temporalization is the explication of that which is implicit in the functioning ego, and the unaware ego, by becoming aware, by revealing to itself its own hidden depth, becomes self-temporalizing. We must remember that I know all of this by departing from awareness. In its own obscurity, the ego contained the still unexplicated time embedded in the *nunc* understood as stasis. In the awareness of reflection I discover and can continuously rediscover the stasis of unawareness. The ego discovers its own hidden temporality only through reflection and by becoming temporalized in different times. Being is truth only in the concrete, temporal modalities and horizon. This self-temporalization is, *so to speak,* a function of hidden being. Let us say "being" in the more common, nonphilosophical sense. The being of which we speak in order to make ourselves understood is an unconscious and unexpressed being which must be self-temporalized in order to express itself and be real.

It is in self-temporalization, in concrete history, and in reflecting reflections upon it that we become aware that we are being temporal and that we were unknowingly functioning. Furthermore, reflection is not an abstraction but concrete history and temporality. Strictly speaking, functioning life becomes aware of having been obscure, or mundane, *only in reflection.* Although functioning life is only within finite evidence directed toward a final evidence and truth as the teleological idea, it is *only in reflection* that it is discovered as presence, evidence, and self-transparence.

As presence "in the first person," evidence is possible because in concrete temporality we discover ourselves as temporal life in its various modalities. Ultimately, our unity discovers itself as multiplicity and finitude by discovering itself as evidence. Even if an infinite horizon of truth inheres in all evidence aiming toward a final horizon, every evidence is finite. It is in the aiming that the meaning becomes constituted as the progressive and infinite realization of truth. Here is one of the differences between Husserl and Heidegger. For Husserl, the I in the first person becomes revealed, clear, and self-aware through self-temporalization in multiplicity and history. For Husserl, temporal finitude is reflection. Without reflection and its temporal modalities, the subject remains obscure and closed in its unexpressed unity. On the other hand, for Heidegger, real being is what Husserl considered unexpressed, obscure. According to Heidegger, when being falls into the finite world, it becomes lost and hidden precisely because it becomes finite and part of a multiplicity. For Husserl, this becoming finite makes possible the progressive self-constitution in history *according to truth,* and this constitution renders human civilization possible. For Heidegger, being originally becomes false and can no longer aim toward the goal of truth because it falls into history. The only thing left for it to do is to return to the hidden, original being. Temporal being is concretized in finite existences by multiplying itself, coming into being, and dying. This is true for both Heidegger and Husserl. But, for Husserl, finite beings are the monads in an intermonadic relationship where subjects are united in pairings (*Paarungen*) and groups whose meaning is given by the intentional *direction* inherent in every individual and group. This direction becomes outlined according to a universal teleology.[2]

Universal teleological life is continuous and discrete at the same time. The teleological and subjective life of the monads falls asleep in death and awakens in birth. Similarly, the individual pauses in his conscious life and presence. These are the pauses of sleep or fainting, or, more generally, drowsiness. Awakened life can appear as if constituted by pauses of sleep in the same way that the individual falls asleep and wakes up.[3] The individual ego is formed by a multiplicity of awakened egos. *Universal, teleological life is concretely constituted by a multiplicity of individuals who are born and die.* Husserl very closely connects the problem of sleep and being awake, and of birth and

2. See unpublished manuscripts E III 1, E III 2, E III 3, E III 4, E III 5. These are manuscripts in which intersubjectivity is connected to the teleology which gives sense to each individual and finite life.

3. C 17 V, p. 38.

death, with intersubjectivity, the relationship between the ego and other egos.[4]

For Husserl, then, birth and death are a function of universal teleology that inheres in the horizon of every individuality, every *Paarung*, every group, and every period of civilization. Teleological life becomes civil, historical, and dialectical, aiming at the progressive constitution of social reality according to the limiting idea of an ideal society. This is so because teleological life is individuated and embodied in the birth and in the death of individuals, groups, and historical periods. This inherence is similar to the way that the ego operates in every subject in the first person, becomes clear to itself, and can, by self-revelation, progressively constitute itself according to the meaning of truth. Husserl does not mention the problem of dialectics, but lays the basis for a rational nondogmatic and nonillusory comprehension of the *real dialectic* which lives in historical time and in the concrete relations between individuals and groups. Historical intentionality is compromised, and the crisis comes into being, when one group makes itself absolute and aims at making the other into a pure instrument or fetishized objectivity. But even in such a case, the contradictions that arise from the crisis end by reaffirming the historical meaning and its intentional direction toward a rational society because it destroys itself as a negativity and *negates itself as a negation*.

This indicates the fundamental reasons why Husserl developed the problem of the ego-pole (p. 171). The science of the *Lebenswelt* is possible only if we investigate the functioning ego and its structures. To the extent that it is functional, the ego remains the same. It is constituted in the permanence of an individualized, concrete monad to the extent that it is historical continuity. Therefore, it is constituted in time, where we find the synthesis and continuity of the various egos which continually aim at a new synthesis.

> The same ego, now actually present, is in a sense, in every past that belongs to it, another—i.e., as that which was and thus is not now—and yet, in the continuity of its time it is one and the same, which is and was and has its future before it. [P. 172]

In time, the ego can undertake a dialogue with itself as if it were a different subject. The ego contains the alter ego. The relationship between the ego and the other, elaborated in the fifth of the *Cartesian Meditations*, already obtains in the history of one

4. C 17 V, pp. 30–40; A VI 14, p. 6; K III 6, pp. 350–55.

monad. Even though it is a matter of the same ego, there are certain pauses between me and my alter ego. Between lived youth and maturity there is a time during which I forget, fall asleep, and end by finding myself to be someone else who must subsequently take the past ego from oblivion and re-present it. Husserl widens the horizon of the internal intersubjectivity of each individual to the collective life of various individuals. In the universal, teleological life, everyone is rooted in the same *functioning life which, seen as a mundane object, is the pregiven world*. Everyone is individualized and embodied in different times and lived histories, separated not only by their moments of sleep and wakefulness but by birth and death. Individuals live in one another in a reciprocal empathy (*Einfühlung*), because they live in the same intentional life, which is also instinctive life, impulse, sensuality, and the implicit teleological background which is not yet self-aware.[5] The same common background can be brought to light not by a sole individual but, and maybe ultimately, only by a meeting of individuals and monads through a conscious *Paarung*. This is how the "I-Thou" relationship (*Ich-Du-Synthesis*) arises, which in turn generates the relationship of reciprocally aware monads in a common life aiming toward a rational goal and constituting history in its rational sense. This is what is meant by the "we" (*Wir-Synthesis*). Thus the ego-pole is related to others in temporal life which is the simultaneity of common life. In turn, this is the relationship which in the present connects past and future life. It is clear, therefore, that Husserl ends by discovering that the only functional ego is also, and at the same time, intermonadic life and the "social" synthesis. The social synthesis is "our" intentional becoming. Husserl says that "it is universal sociality (in this sense, 'mankind'), the 'space' of all ego-subjects" (p. 172).

[20] *Clarification of the Unique Functioning Ego
and Transcendental Intersubjectivity*

THE UNIQUE OR TRANSCENDENTAL EGO *is, as a matter of fact, transcendental intersubjectivity*. This point, which seemed so "miraculous" to Merleau-Ponty, is at the foundation of all phenomenology. In fact, the transcendental ego is each one of us in

5. E III 9, p. 11.

his concreteness as a human being in flesh and blood. We are the transcendental egos.

Husserl tries to clarify this point when he remarks that "it is my—the philosopher's—psychic faculty. Can the ego which posits itself, of which Fichte speaks, be anything other than Fichte's own?" (p. 202). To understand what Husserl means here, we can put it as follows: the transcendental ego or subject *does not exist.* Only concrete men, concrete monads, exist. For me, in the first person, only that which I directly live and experience exists: my own body, the world that surrounds me, the planet Earth upon which I live. This position must be understood in a *strictly empirical* sense. If I begin from my present ego, it is not because I *choose* to start from that ego: it is because I cannot do otherwise. The ego and the world I experience are a *Faktum.*

I depart from myself in the first person, because the opposite, i.e., not departing from myself, is impossible. That is, my presence to myself in the first person cannot be the opposite of what it is. We can then say that this presence is *apodictic,* certain, and undemonstrable, since any demonstration would once again be based on the apodictic evidence of the *cogito.*

Still, Husserl's discourse can be misunderstood. It is important to insist continually upon the fact that the ego in Husserl is not a theory of the ego or a discourse concerning the ego. It is myself in flesh and blood: I who write or my reader who reads. The experience of phenomenological teaching shows that this very simple fact is difficult to understand because he who hears of this ego does not think of himself in flesh and bones, or of others like him. Instead, he thinks of the word, category, or scientific or philosophical theory of the ego.

It is at this point that the suspension of judgment (the epoché) occurs. The aim of the epoché is to make everyone recognize himself for what he really is. It is the epoché that compels every ego to free himself from the theory of the ego or subject, so that he can discover himself in the first person. If every subject performed this operation he would discover himself in his reality, and—through the intersubjective constitution discussed in the fifth of the *Cartesian Meditations*—he would discover that all the subjects are *unique and functioning egos like himself.* In order to do this, the ego that does not find its own reality because of theorizing must bracket all philosophies, sciences, and theories. Only then will he discover himself in his own singular evidence. But this singularity belongs to him just as it belongs to all egos which discover themselves as concrete egos. This unique, singular ego is only himself, but he is so in the same way in which all other egos are themselves. His own *structure* in the first person is the *same structure* of every ego in the first person: his uniqueness is multiplicity, his singularity is universality. To be so, in flesh and blood, is to be transcendental, like all other egos. What allows me to make this discovery is the extreme phenomenological reduction to the unique ego. It is thus clear that when I speak of the transcendental ego in the Husserlian sense I am speaking of my singularity in the first person. This is similar to Kierkegaard's singularity in the first person. But by speaking of my singularity, I speak of all egological structures *like mine*. Therefore, precisely by speaking about singularity, I speak about universality, and by speaking about my uniqueness I speak about multiplicity. By speaking about my concrete, real ego, I speak about the transcendental ego.

Yet misunderstandings and ambiguities might remain even after these observations. The traditional philosopher who uses concepts and categories and *forgets that they are concepts and categories* will always say that if the ego is *one* it cannot be *many*, and that if the subject is *unique* there cannot be *intersubjectivity*. In fact, even a thinker with the phenomenological experience of Merleau-Ponty did not understand that *it is not a matter* of categories or philosophical theories, as he thought when he considered phenomenology the *mediation* between those philosophical theories called *idealism* and *realism*. In our experience in the first person, we always simultaneously perceive the one and the many, and on the *precategorial level* we *always* perform operations which, among other things, are diversified and unique. It is absurd to isolate uniqueness and multiplicity and subsequently pretend to reunite these abstract categories in a categorial synthesis. In reality, they were originally united before I reduced them to categories and performed operations in order to convert them into categories. Otherwise, the synthesis would always be abstract precisely because it is a categorial synthesis.

The same must apply to the ego. The ego is the ego of all subjects. Yet it is the unique ego. It is the real ego because it is transcendental, and it is transcendental because it is intersubjectivity and transcendental society.

[21]   *Reconsideration of the Science*
of the Lebenswelt *and the Meaning*
of an Ontology of the Lebenswelt

ALL THAT HAS ALREADY BEEN SAID makes a science of
the *Lebenswelt* possible. Such a science is possible only if the
structures of the ego-pole can be investigated. In turn, these lead
to the structures of intersubjective, intermonadic, subjective life.
The structure of the *Lebenswelt*, then, is resolved into the structures of intersubjectivity that inhere in every individual subject,
in every monad. The ontology of the *Lebenswelt* is presented as
the typical structure of intermonadic, temporal life which intentionally aims at a universal goal, "an absolute intersubjective
ideal," "an absolute, transcendental intersubjectivity" which can
appear as universal sociality. Intersubjectivity thus constitutes
the final meaning of reality. The transcendental reduction, which
must always be performed anew, always reproposes the intersubjective, rational constitution. It is therefore self-perfecting, the
teleological goal of an infinite progress. The structures of historical and temporal life are the structures of the *Lebenswelt*,
which clarifies itself, discovers its own meaning of truth, and becomes science. These structures characterize what the *Lebenswelt* essentially is and constitute a typology of its modalities.

The science of the *Lebenswelt* has nothing in common with
logical and mathematical sciences. It is not a constituted science
because it is in the *Lebenswelt* that it is temporally possible to
constitute any science. Nor is it a metaphysics in the traditional
sense, since the science of the *Lebenswelt* is temporal and historical life which discovers the rational meaning of reality by
being posed as science. Ontology is the revelation of the hidden
which is constituted as truth according to structures that are
typical of revelation and constitution. True being is that which is
revealed in intentional phenomena oriented toward a goal, toward an infinite ideal truth which is inherent in every phenomenon. Being is never completed, objectified, and fixed in
closed forms, although the structures in which being lives and

becomes alive are permanent. Truth is neither static nor objectified. Whatever is objectified, as the natural sciences are when they are not brought back to their constitutive operations, has lost intentional meaning. Objectified being has lost its own meaning of truth. Therefore, the true ontology of the *Lebenswelt* is the science of the *Lebenswelt*, i.e., phenomenology. Phenomenology does not need to be transformed into an ontology in the traditional sense, into a theory that definitely tells us *what being is*. Being is intentional; it lives and forms itself. It is the meaning of life to the extent that life is true, and, for Husserl, life is true in the meaning of truth which "being" has to the extent that it is intentional. The meaning of being is the meaning of the truth which is alive in being. If this meaning is lost, it can be found again only by one's uncovering it, or by correcting oneself and changing the world. It can be found anew only to the extent that one lives for truth.

Phenomenology teaches us that the realm of the always-present *Lebenswelt* is constituted according to a necessary and essential structure. The science of the *Lebenswelt* investigates and illuminates such a structure: this is the only possible ontology, which is nothing other than phenomenology. The problem of ontology becomes a one-sided problem if what is meant is the metaphysics of a being unformed by the essential structures of phenomenology and not intentionally constituted in intersubjectivity and universal teleology.[6] Ontology is problematic if it is not intentional, but is always objectified, so that it has lost its meaning from the very beginning. It ends by accepting things as they are, without grounding being in transcendental subjectivity, i.e., without intentionally constituting the meaning of the truth of being and the structures according to which such intentionality lives.[7] In this case, phenomenology is no longer a science of living men who are intentionally constituted. Instead of a phenomenological or intentional anthropology, we have an objectified and naturalized anthropology.

6. E III 4, p. 48.
7. See E. Husserl, *Cartesian Meditations: An Introduction to Phenomenology*, trans. Dorion Cairns (The Hague: Nijhoff, 1960), p. 137.

[22] *The Assumption of the Paradox*
in the Investigation.
Sociology and Anthropology.
Phenomenology and Encyclopedia

As WE HAVE SEEN, the first reduction which appears as the reduction to the *Lebenswelt* gradually ends by requiring the transcendental reduction. On the other hand, the transcendental reduction needs the reduction to the *Lebenswelt*, and it becomes increasingly more necessary as the problem of a science of the *Lebenswelt* is investigated. For many of Husserl's interpreters, the two reductions are complementary and ultimately reduce to one. This is true not only for the reduction to the *Lebenswelt*, but, with reference primarily to Husserl's teachings during the Göttingen period, it also holds for the eidetic reduction. In fact, the eidetic reduction aimed at a first philosophy capable of capturing the original or essential forms of life. We find the project of a first philosophy of this kind in both *Ideen II* and *Ideen III*, and it is even continued in the two posthumously published volumes of the *Erste Philosophie*. The project of a universal first philosophy once again appears in the science of the *Lebenswelt*.

The new science must capture the structures of the subjective-relative world of the *Lebenswelt* in its essential forms. In fact, if the *Lebenswelt* is relative, then its structures are not relative, since all the sciences must be based on them so that their constitutions have a "meaning-structure." The structures of the *Lebenswelt* must be captured from within. They must be resolved into subjective structures in which transcendental, subjective life is a life which experiences the world. From the very beginning, the reduction to the *Lebenswelt* contains the transcendental reduction. One is a function of the other owing to the correlation between life and consciousness of life, between life which experiences the world and reflection.

The above analysis presupposes that life permeates evidence and reflection. This permeation, which in its simplest form is made possible by retention, in turn presupposes the entire problem of time in the same way that it also presupposes universal correlation, i.e., the possibility of assuming every being as the index of an a priori system of relations. As such, the principle of phenomenology whereby being is true insofar as it is phenomenon (*soviel Schein, soviel Sein*) is fully applicable. This can also be expressed by the formula *ego cogito cogitata qua cogitata*. In turn, universal correlation requires both intermonadic life and universal teleology. It also requires a phenomenology of the inherence of the various perspectives of things in their horizon, and of the inherence of the horizon of things in the meaning of truth. Such inherence enables the world to reveal itself as the teleological horizon which is already implicit in every horizon. This last problem-area is connected to those investigations which, in Husserl, are presented under the heading of the transcendental aesthetic, and which are carried out mainly in the manuscripts D. The problem of the reductions involves the whole of phenomenology and the possibility of phenomenology as science. The path leading to phenomenology by way of the problem of the *Lebenswelt* must culminate in the foundation of a science of the *Lebenswelt*. It should be clear by now that such a path implies both the transcendental path and the transcendental reduction.

Phenomenology becomes impossible for those who perceive the two reductions as separate and contradictory. It is not fruitful to follow such a lead, and it is advisable to stress the internal coherence of Husserl's thought as much as possible, even if this is paradoxical. From this viewpoint it is possible to discover the working of the second reduction in the very heart of the first one. This is exactly what we have done in our reconstructive commentary.

Despite this, it must be made clear that phenomenology, because of the nature of its method, is always bound to reconsider the problems with which it deals. Husserl's intuition is to ground a new science as "subjective" and "not objectified." It seems that phenomenology as science should have an uninterrupted continuity. Transcendental philosophy is neither a "natural" science nor mathematics. However, what is true for mathematics is also true for transcendental philosophy, within certain limits and on a certain level. As Husserl puts it, transcendental philosophy must place itself in the "spirit of finality." Now, it seems that the spirit of finality does not always lead mathematics to begin anew. In philosophy, on the other hand, every philosopher must begin anew (as indicated in the *Cartesian Meditations*). In fact, the foundation of philosophy as a science depends upon the transcendental reduction. If the transcendental reduction guarantees phenomenology its scientificity in the "subjective" sense, it is also true that the transcendental reduction breaks the continuity. The reduction cannot be carried out once and for all, but must constantly be resumed. The continuity between philosophers and philosophies is broken by the transcendental reduction and by the different ways in which it is carried out. On the other hand, the continuity of philosophy is required precisely because every result is not completely accepted as such but must be reduced through the epochē and again brought back to its transcendental foundation. This is so even if such a continuity is not analogous to the other sciences and cannot be maintained even on the "subjective" level. Husserl does not want to give up the transcendental reduction or the continuity of philosophy as a science. This is revealed in the way in which Husserl exposes the progressive deepening of his thought. For example, in section 45, Husserl gives a phenomenological description which is already the active science of the *Lebenswelt*. However, as soon as this science begins to consolidate, he must go back to the transcendental reduction. Sometimes in the exposition the movement in which the active science reveals itself is suddenly interrupted by the movement of the renewed reduction. This happens in all of Husserl's works, and particularly in the *Crisis*.

Actually, the transcendental reduction should be carried out at the same time that the science of the *Lebenswelt* is actualized, and the science of the *Lebenswelt* should constantly be constituted in the transcendental reduction. When this does not happen, one gets the impression that there is discord between the two reductions. The specific reasons for this impression of discord should be fully investigated phenomenologically. They are certainly connected to the problem of time and the continuity and discontinuity of transcendental consciousness. Consciousness is not always awake. Its being awake entails sleep, and its continuity entails pauses (sleep, death). Now, the problem of pauses is connected to the problem of the individuality of the monads, their finitude, their temporal birth and life, and their universal teleology. Transcendental life is the life of every monad, and, to reiterate, the transcendental ego is the concrete individual from which every Cartesian reflection on the *cogito* departs. The transcendental or "absolute" ego is simultaneously the concrete ego in flesh and blood. It is the "animated" and individuated ego living in the precategorial world of the *Lebenswelt*. It so happens that the transcendental reduction allows me to find myself as I am, and that the "myself" that I am is at the same time the absolute transcendental ego. Prior to everything else, it is inevitable that this problem-area will engulf the problem of intersubjectivity and the problem of myself as ego-proper. I am an ego-proper, which is a problem but which already contains the possibility of its solution. In turn, the ego-proper is related to other egos, and every one of these is also an ego-proper. Phenomenology must return to the beginning, but this return must at the same time be a continuity. These problems introduce others. They are not indications of a failure; rather, they are the index of a task. Even the phenomenologist, when he acts as a revealer, can become an occluder without knowing it. This is what happened to Galileo, but he did not know it. The phenomenologist knows that this can happen to himself as well as to Galileo, and because of this possibility he needs at the end to be "disoccluded" by another phenomenologist. Husserl himself often unknowingly occludes his own investigations and discoveries. To understand him in the phenomenological sense means to clarify, deepen, and continue his work, while at the same time seeking hidden lines as well.

We should remember that every new reference to the continuity of the reduction and its acknowledgment does not negate the previous investigations. In Husserl it always indicates the emergence of new "fields." In the *Crisis* the return to the transcendental reduction, with which the first section of the third part of the work ends, paves the way for the deepening of the problem of the science of the *Lebenswelt* into the problem of psychology as a phenomenological and subjective science. The latter is the theme of the second section. Reference can be made to both the first and second sections, where there is a problematic which could lead to still a new path. This problematic could lead to a revision of the transcendental reduction, to a new field already implicit both in the science of the *Lebenswelt* and in psychology as a phenomenological, subjective, or "intentional" science. This new field is the theme of sociology as a new science, a theme suggested in many unpublished manuscripts.[8] It is still the fertile (and for various reasons the decisive and fundamental) theme of anthropology as a new science. We should note that such an anthropology will not be a fetishized or analytical anthropology of *Dasein*. It will be an intentional anthropology. Husserl does not explicitly say it, but this theme is connected to at least two others: (1) transcendental aesthetics, which in

8. See the pertinent unpublished manuscripts in R. Toulemont, *L'Essence de la société selon Husserl* (Paris: Presses Universitaires de France, 1962).

manuscript D culminates in a new kind of natural philosophy (especially in D 17 and D 18); and (2) a phenomenological science of history connected to the general problem of the social sciences. The latter is implied not only by *Ideen II*, but also by manuscript K.

Having continuously to face the paradox is inevitable for the working method of phenomenology. Only in this fashion can phenomenology continue on its course. However, we should note that this is not always understandable in its truest sense. It is not so obvious as it would seem that phenomenological clarification (*Klärung*) should necessarily find itself confronting what has not yet been investigated. Even the dialectic of the hidden and revealed poses certain very particular problems and must be studied closely. Among other problems faced by the phenomenologist is that of risking constructing a philosophy outside of the meaning-structure (*Sinngebung*). ("To construct" is used here in reference to the fact that Husserl warns that phenomenology cannot be a construction.)

The most serious problems of *Sinngebung* are to be found in the relationship of sleep and consciousness. This relationship must be patiently investigated. It is connected to the problems of psychology, sociology, transcendental aesthetics, intuitional and subjective anthropology, and history. Moreover, it is connected to the problem of the foundation of the "formation of meaning" of logic and the sciences, and to the problem of a phenomenological science as a "totalizing" science of man and world. Husserl's phenomenology leads to the encyclopedia. It aims at becoming first science, the "branches" and "terms" of which constitute an organic synthesis. It is always *in fieri*, guided by a *telos* which is inherent in every theme. The encyclopedia is contained in phenomenology. Its continuity is entrusted to its own continuous foundation, to the active and continuous answer of reason to oblivion, weariness, and death. It is also connected to the struggle against alienation, fetishization, barbarism, and evil. Phenomenology cannot avoid the difficulties that clutter its path. It cannot declare itself positive in advance. Its positive quality lies precisely in not denying and rejecting difficulties and paradoxes, but in accepting them as situations and indexes of the need for investigation and transformation. Husserl says that the destiny of phenomenology is

to become involved again and again in paradoxes, which, arising out of uninvestigated and even unnoticed horizons, remain functional and announce themselves as incomprehensibilities. [P. 181]

[23]   *Paradoxes and Obscurity. The Dialectic*

SECTION 52 OF THE *Crisis* presents three paradoxes which are essentially meant to indicate the new character of phenomenology.

The epochē and the discovery of universal correlation within subjectivity have transformed both our way of looking at the world and our disposition toward it. The new disposition is rooted in subjectivity, in humanity as subjectivity. The epochē prevents us from taking what is objectified into consideration. Yet truth is "objective," at least in the sense in which the sciences also search for it. We can wonder if there are two truths. Is it not paradoxical that there is a subjective truth and an objective truth? We know how to answer this question. Those operations which constitute objective truth in the sciences are subjective operations in the sense that they are founded and can always be founded anew. To the extent that it is true, the objective is what is constituted. As such, it comes under the heading of constitution. The surprising result of all that has been said so far is that everything comes under transcendental subjectivity, under the transcendental life which constantly constitutes the world in time. The change of disposition is, once more, the rejection of the prejudice of the already given. This is the rejection of "naturalism." The world is pregiven. We are already in the precategorial world, but only to the extent that we discover and illuminate certain hidden operations. Here, the already given is not a prejudice. It is what we experience in the first person. In the actual situation, we find the past which has constituted us. We find in a new way the world in which we always live. However, we find it by starting from the presence, from the subjectivity present to ourselves. The world which is before and outside of us is resolved in our way of living in time and space, in temporal modalities. To the extent that we bring these categories back to originary operations, we ground the categories and the sciences in the presence in which we live and experience the world before the categories. The objective truth of the sciences obtains only insofar as its foundations are not *forgotten,* insofar as I can find the originary functions in the present. There is only one truth, that which is founded by subjective operations. It is that which I can reconstitute in the presence and will be able to reconstitute in the future.

On the other hand, as we know, truth lies not only in the operations but also in the *meaning of truth*. The sciences lose their meaning when we forget the *telos* and the intentional operations. In such a case, their objective truth is *objectified,* naturalized, and alienated. The paradox that Husserl discusses is resolved if we remember the difference between objective and objectified subjectivity. We should also remember what has been said about the precategorial foundation, the temporal structure of the *Lebenswelt,* and subjectivity as actual presence. The paradox brings us back to the temporal dialectic, to subjectivity and intersubjectivity which operate in time according to the meaning of truth. The subjects operate in the world for the constitution of a rational intersubjective society where the scientific meaning of the objective will always remain; yet objectification as alienation will have to go. To the extent that the paradox is explained by means of all that has been said so far, it leads us back to the temporal and historical dialectic and its goal, the dialectic: the rational society as humanity's *telos*.

The second paradox forces us to wonder whether, having abandoned natural and mundane interests, we can still be interested in something. Husserl answers that it is not a matter of *actually* leaving the world, but of giving the world a new meaning and living according to a meaning of truth. That which is abandoned is the mundane, the already made world which refuses to renovate and reshape itself according to the *telos* of truth, not for immediate ends. Mundane life lives according to certain goals. But in the particular goals it neglects the *telos:* it does not live in the particular goals according to the *telos*. The epochē must give us a meaning. And it does so if we turn to the things-themselves, to what we really remember about the past, and if we project toward the future by beginning from the actual presence. In fact, we are always in the world. With the epochē we start from the beginning and rediscover ourselves and the *telos* in the temporal dialectic. What we must remember is that it is impossible to perform a total epochē. Something obscure and mundane always remains in us that must be made explicit. Because of this, both the obscure past and the obscure present always pose the task of unveiling for the actual presence. Everything becomes a task: the world as the true world, intersubjective society, and truth. The world must be constituted by struggling against the mundane, its prejudices, and its mistakes. Therefore, there is always a dialectic of the mundane and the intentional life that is directed toward a true world. The mundane is obscure. There is always a struggle, then, between the clear life directed toward a truth, and obscurity. There will always be such a struggle. But will there always be a struggle against objectification, against the reduction of man to an object, and against the objectification of the sciences which have lost the meaning of their own task and function? Can the crisis of objectification, understood as alienation, be overcome? We know that this is possible. Husserl thinks that even if there is a perennial dialectic, it is our historically determined crisis that forces us to struggle against the loss of the function of the sciences, against the alienation of man and the objectification which reduces him to a natural thing, to a physical body similar to those of the natural sciences.

Once again, Husserl's second paradox leads to the dialectic, its modalities, and its *telos*. Many points in Husserl are obscure because of his failure to distinguish between the positive and negative senses of objectification. Sometimes Husserl says that subjectivity objectifies itself in the world—experiences and transforms it, and thus gives it a new meaning. When subjectivity is objectified, it becomes an object, and the possibility of acting by beginning anew is lost. Subjectivity is objectified in the negative sense in the same way that it is negative for the sciences to become fixed in fetishization. At other times, Husserl says that the ego estranges and alienates itself in the world, and he means that the ego experiences and lives in the world. Here, estrangement and alienation have a positive sense. What Husserl fights is estrangement and alienation in the negative sense, where alienation is understood in a sense very close to Marx's, even though Husserl is unaware of it.

Even the second paradox thus leads back to the problems of the dialectic and the constitution of a rational society. And both the first and the second paradoxes lead back to the situation of crisis in which intentionality is lost, and in which the ego becomes lost by becoming an object.

The third paradox reminds us that the *Lebenswelt* is as relative as the *doxa*. We live in time, in the "Heraclitean flux," which is made up of *individuals*. Phenomenology is a science; as such, it aims at what persists as typical in the flux as its meaning. The paradox is resolved if we remember all that has been said about phenomenology as a new science. Phenomenology is the science of the *doxa*. So presented, it fulfills Husserl's scientific ideal as formulated in the *Logical Investigations* and the *Formal and Transcendental Logic*. This ideal entails the problem of individuality. As the subject, the individual poses himself in the problems of the constitution of a society of individuals understood as a rational society. As the becoming of individuals, even the Heraclitean flux leads back to the dialectic and the constitution of a society of subjects.

The paradoxes of phenomenology become clear through our investigation of their meaning and the numerous themes entangled and mixed in them. The clarification forces us to analyses that Husserl never faced, and to amplifications of the phenomenological horizon in new directions.

The phenomenological dialectic is a dialectic of the hidden and the revealed. It is possible, however, that the hidden may not appear as such, but as something hiding, as an already revealed truth; that is, it is possible that the hidden may appear as error. In this case, the negative imposes itself and must therefore be "unmasked." What must be brought to the level of revelation is not only the hidden, but also the hidden that appears as "revealed," the false that appears as true, the nonbeing that appears as being. This is the same problem Plato faced in the *Sophist*. True being is the being of the Idea, of the vision, what is seen, what allows itself to be seen, and what reveals itself. But nonbeing cannot be nothingness: it must be something if it has the power to appear as being and if it can always appear as such. Plato says that nonbeing is otherness and that, as such, it is something. Husserl faced this problem in the third of the *Cartesian Meditations*, where nonbeing appears as a "modality of simple being." [9]

Transcendental consciousness is constituted according to various modalities—recall the modalities of time which are modifications of the presence (retention, protention, remembrance, and memorative anticipation). Present evidence is finite; it captures only a nucleus (*Kern*) which flows into the "adumbrations" (*Abschattungen*). The nucleus is the clear present. The adumbrations are retention and expectation, remembrance and anticipation of the future. Within the spatial dimension the nucleus is the position of my body, both when it is at rest and when it is in motion. What I see, touch, or hear is immediately close, less close, or distant; and what is close can become distant. Just as presence is in time (the hour, a fixed point), so there is a normal point of departure in space. It is a point of origin of orientation in relation to which it makes sense to speak of prox-

9. *Cartesian Meditations*, p. 58.

imity and distance. The kinesthetic movements also presuppose a fixed point, e.g., the ground of the Earth for its inhabitants.[10] On the other hand, things are not given to me only as things-themselves, but also in their appearances or phantasms. That part of the thing which appears as a phantasm (e.g., what I see from a distance) becomes the thing in relation to the complex verification of my body's kinesthetic movements. Furthermore, my body is in relation to other fixed or moving bodies on the terrestrial ground. Thus, what I hold in my memory may not be what was in the present which has been, and what I remember can be different from what has happened. The past must be awakened (in the *Weckung,* or reawakening), rediscovered (in the *Aufdeckung,* or uncovering), and reproduced (in the *Wieder-holung,* or reproduction). Husserl studied the problem of space in relation to time, and the problem of kinesthesis (and the phantasms) in the transcendental aesthetic, i.e., in the unpublished manuscripts D. On the other hand, the modalities of the awakening, the uncovering, and the reproduction are analyzed in some of the unpublished manuscripts C.[11]

I can see things both in the spatial kinesthetic and their center, and in the temporal modalities. Hence, my representation of the thing is not reality, and my expectations and presumptions are not satisfied. The evidence, as the mode whereby reality is given, is not fulfilled. There are various types of evidence. All evidences are modalities of a partly fulfilled central modality of a finite fulfillment which nonetheless remains a fulfillment (*Erfüllung*). The center is real; yet it is surrounded by possibilities, presuppositions, and expectations that might not obtain. Finite perception is surrounded by infinite possibilities. Possible and impossible horizons, visions and appearances, are inherent in the central perception. There can be empty evidence with respect to reality (but not the image). These are expectations which may or may not be fulfilled. Therefore, in the center there are the modalities of the probable and the improbable, the possible and the impossible,[12] which are next to the presence of the evidence in the first person.

The basic phenomenological principle is that it is always possible to depart from a presence, from actual evidence (an *Erfüllung*). This evidence will be only a gift of a finite and de-

10. D 18.

11. For manuscripts D, see D 10, D 12, and D 13. Concerning manuscripts C, see primarily C 2 III, C 7 I, C 13 III, and C 16 I.

12. *Cartesian Meditations,* pp. 58–59.

termined center, a light which flows into the penumbra. This relation presupposes that there must be a center of light at the basis. The evidence must have a nucleus of certainty: it must be a basic revelation. Even though it is finite, it must be apodictic. However, this evidence will be inadequate, since the penumbrae and obscurity are temporally and spatially arranged around the present nucleus. Dimness and obscurity can appear as being when they are not being, or as truth when they are not true. The dialectic permits the mistake because it is a dialectic of center and periphery, finite and infinite. According to Husserl, in the transcendental revelation the infinite is not in the object, and it is not certain and present to itself outside of the subject. It must be in the subject. In fact, all spatial and temporal modalities are modalities of subjective presence. The possibility of error must therefore reside within subjectivity. Subjectivity does not contain only what remains the same, what Plato calls the self-same. Within subjectivity there must also be an other that can appear as nonbeing or apparent evidence. In its apodictic certainty, the *cogito* constitutes itself only in doubt and is dialectically related to it.

Transcendental subjectivity contains doubts that it must continually overcome. It is certainty precisely because it contains doubts that it must continually be transformed into certainty. The *ego cogito* is self-certain only when it recognizes an uncertain alter ego. For this reason, at the beginning there is no ego, but rather a kind of *Paarung* of doubt and certainty. The doubting ego that has not yet reflected and recognized that it thinks while doubting, and that, as such, is certain as thought and *cogito*, always precedes the ego which is certain of its doubting. This is so even if I recognize this "precedence" only in the present. Yet, even while doubting, the preceding ego contains certainty (because it thus doubts and is certainly thought or *cogito*). However, this certainty is hidden and is revealed in reflection. Reflection is that evidence which was already there, but which only now knows that it was there. Therefore, the self-certain ego holds or retains the ego which was certain without knowing it and which functioned as certain before the reflection. The ego retains, and for this reason can be a revelation of, that hidden part. The ego can speak of the hidden because it is in the evidence now, but it can be evident precisely because it was not so already. Of course, while I reflect, something still remains hidden which always arises in me. Functioning life reflects upon itself as past, but not at the moment in which it is reflecting. It will do this later and, once again, it will have to reflect in time. In fact, reflection is in time and is temporalization. The dialectic is within the very heart of the evidence. The evidence is what it is precisely because it is finite and in a continuous relation of center and periphery. The evidence continuously requires self-correction in relation to the present and the future, in its dialectic with otherness.

[24]   *The Rise of the Problem of Materialism.*
        Master and Slave.
        The Situation of Crisis

THE EGO AS THE UNIT containing the totality of the world is hidden, and that which is hidden is something different from the evident ego. Yet it is in me, since in the evidence I only explicate what is hidden within me. In a dialogue with myself I discover within me an unknown ego which I must always bring to light. I discover an "I within me" of which I am the revelation: my reality is this revelation, and my evidence is my continuous self-discovery. It is important to notice that what is hidden within me projects its penumbra, its shadows, and, ultimately, its obscurities in the periphery surrounding my nucleus. I do not see everything in space and time. This discovery may allow an independent interpretation and development of the problem beyond Husserl's positions.

That "other" which is not-myself or which surrounds me (my surrounding world) is obscure to the extent that I do not reveal myself to myself. The obscurity surrounding me is the obscurity which has not been revealed within me. In relation to the *ego cogito,* my dialectical alter ego is obscure and I do not understand it: I must reveal it. My *Paarung* with myself as obscurity is a *Paarung* in which one of the elements, the element whence my clarity seems to arise, remains hidden. (It "seems" because in reality what is original is clarity and evidence.) If we speak of the original ego (*Ur-Ich*), we mean both the evident ego and the alter ego. Around me, in the projection of the surrounding world hidden within me, others remain hidden and incomprehensible to the extent that I contain an incomprehensible alter ego. It is important and perhaps decisive to notice that, if the surrounding world can be considered as hidden, as a projection of my obscure (and latent) ego, it can also be said that my ego can be interpreted as a projection or *interiorization of the world*. My noninvestigated interiority is then the projection of the world. To the extent that the "external world" is incomprehensible, it may be that it is revealed as what negates or destroys my clarity. Then my obscure alter ego becomes an enemy and I become opposed to it. Analogously, the others who live in my *Umwelt* appear as my enemies. They become responsible for my lack of absolute clarity: yet it is the alter ego within me which is also responsible and, in some sense, is the first to be responsible. I negate subjectivity with reference to my alter ego and others. By so doing, I reduce the subjective to "objectifications": there is no longer something hidden within me and others that reveals itself, and which both I and others must reveal. Maybe the same world that we have assumed to be projected in my obscurity disappears. Maybe the world projected into me is the *material* "external" world. Among other things, what is coming to the fore in this dialectic is the *great philosophical problem of materialism*. The problem of obscurity, then, is no longer an intimate or "interior" problem. It is no longer even a problem of my own body. The problem concerns the matter of which I am made, which is the same as that of which inert things are made. To know myself on this level means to know both the opacity and the resistance of the matter of which I am made, along with all other things, including the planet Earth and the universe. But to know matter means to enter into praxis, into *work* with matter itself. What is being said here is connected to what has been said about the phenomenology of labor that is also related to the problem of matter.

The world appears extraneous to me to the extent that it is material. It is as if I were to become an object extraneous to myself. The others become, or must become, objects, tools, and things. As the subject I am the master, and the "objectified" others are the slaves. What reappears here in a new form is the Hegelian dialectic of master and slave of the *Phenomenology of Mind*.[13] We must point out that my mastery is illusory: the objectification of others is my own objectification. Therefore, the dialectic of subjectivity and objectivity, the already discussed *paradox of a true subjective science*, leads to the problem of the evidence and constitution of truth in space, time, and history.

13. G. W. F. Hegel, *Phenomenology of Mind*, trans. with an Introduction and Notes by J. B. Baillie (London: George Allen and Unwin, 1949), pp. 234 ff.

The constitution implies the ego-other relationship, hidden life and reflection, and error and truth. It centers around the relationship of finite and infinite, spatial and temporal, center and periphery. In turn, this can be seen as a relationship of what is hidden and what is revealed. This dialectic makes error possible and becomes destructive when the hidden is objectified and closed. It occurs when the relationship of the hidden and the phenomenon is assumed in such a way that revelation, as the foundation of meaning, is no longer possible. The ego then alienates itself by simultaneously objectifying the world and others. As already indicated, this is the situation of crisis. The ego is the center of revelation. *It is not a tool of that revelation.* As life which reveals itself on the human level in universal teleology, the ego is the monad man. This entails the possibility of phenomenology as a new science of history and as a new subjective, phenomenological, and intentional anthropology. Here for the first time we find the broad theme of anthropology inserted into the very heart of phenomenology. Husserl has broached this fundamental point, even if not too clearly.

Man's meaning is both transcendental and subjective, insofar as it is the infinite self-revelation of being, the self-constitution of being as truth, the self-transformation of the being of the world into truth, and the self-transfiguration of being into intentional meaning. If this self-constitution fails, so does intentionality. If the ego is objectified, if it is reduced to the level of an object, it rejects the meaning of the revelation. It rejects itself. The dialectic of obscurity and revelation is infinite, and infinity cannot be enclosed within the finite. To attempt to enclose the infinite in the finite would amount to the objectification of the infinite, the closure and the renunciation of intentionality. But if the dialectic of the hidden and the revealed is infinite, the identification of the hidden, or myself and others, with objectification understood as alienation, is not infinite or fatal. Can humanity constitute itself in its infinite dialectic without objectification or reciprocal alienation, i.e., without the dialectic of master and slave? Can the victory over objectification be radical even though it is not possible for man to conquer death, and even though the dialectic of the hidden and the revealed remains invincible? Even if it remains invincible, we must not identify error with the hidden, since the hidden, even if it makes error possible, is not itself error. Furthermore, we must not confuse truth with its revelations. Truth can never be degraded to the level of its revelations, precisely because it is infinite and gives a meaning to its revelations. The above questions, however, have a more precise meaning. Can humanity overcome the situation of objectification and alienation, i.e., the master-slave situation? Is the crisis, as alienation, fatal, or is it conquerable? For Husserl, it is beyond doubt that *the crisis can be overcome.* At most, what Husserl does not mention is that the overcoming of scientific alienation coincides with the overcoming of war and social exploitation.

There is an implicit dialectic in phenomenology that Husserl has not had time to investigate. Yet he has indicated the paradoxes that generate its most important problems. The paradoxes lead precisely to a still uninvestigated dialectic.

Let us examine another aspect of the problem. Concerning the third paradox, Husserl speaks of individual facticity. Facts are what they are. Science can describe them only as they are or as they are presented. The "natural" sciences assert that, given certain facts, there must be other facts. So understood, laws express only factual regularities, and the world to which they refer is the world of facticity (*Tatsächlichkeit*).[14] An individual object, however, is not something ephemeral: it has certain "essential predicables."[15] Phenomenology studies the essences which characterize every individual fact, since many individuals can have a common essence. The individuals that participate in the same essences can be constituted by regions or categories of individuals. Every individual sound has the essence of sound in general. The presence of the essence of sound in any particular sound means that, along with all other sounds, it participates in some typical category which constitutes the sound "region" studied by acoustics. Acoustics indicates a material region or a material ontology. In its concreteness, every individual fact participates in always-broader material ontologies, and ultimately participates in formal ontologies. By "formal ontology" Husserl means the a priori theory of objects in general, or the general conditions that apply to the thinking of an object as "something." The "conditions of thought" are the "conditions of the possibility of a science in general."[16]

14. See the *Tatsächlichkeit* spoken of in E. Husserl, *Ideas: General Introduction to Pure Phenomenology,* trans. W. R. Boyce Gibson (New York: Humanities Press, 1931), p. 53.
15. *Ibid.*
16. E. Husserl, *Logical Investigations,* trans. J. N. Findlay (New York: Humanities Press, 1970), I, 232.

[25]   *Husserl's Scientific Ideal*
       from the Prolegomena
       to the Formal and Transcendental Logic.
       Resumption of Such an Ideal in the Crisis
       and the Problem of
       Phenomenological Psychology

IN THE FIRST VOLUME OF THE *Logical Investigations*
(the *Prolegomena*), Husserl says that, generally speaking, science must be normatively disinterested.[17] As Husserl will discover later, this means that every praxis must be oriented according to the horizon of truth.

The unity of science should follow from general laws that
are based on fundamental laws. To the extent that a science is
based on the fundamental laws, it appears as an ideally closed
unity of laws which rests on one basic law. Science, then, is the
unity of a systematically perfect theory which brings together
fundamental, homogeneous laws. General theories of this kind
are general arithmetic, geometry, analytical mechanics, and
mathematical astronomy. To the extent that they are theories,
these sciences are theories of individual manifolds brought together in a unique type of explanation. For example, arithmetic
draws the manifold of numerical propositions into a unity of
essence, and analytical mechanics unites the multiplicity of mechanical facts. These are Husserl's examples.[18] In them, however, Husserl does not distinguish between material and formal
ontologies, but hints at the distinction when he distinguishes
between concrete and abstract sciences. Concrete sciences are
geography, history, astronomy, and anatomy. He says, for example: "The truths of geography are united by their relation to
the earth."[19] Such a point will be developed by Husserl later in
the manuscripts D 17 and D 18.[20]

17. *Ibid.*, p. 86.
18. *Ibid.*, pp. 228–29.
19. *Ibid.*, p. 230.
20. The first one has been published in Marvin Farber, ed.,
Philosophical Essays in Memory of Edmund Husserl (Cambridge,
Mass.: Harvard University Press, 1940); and the second by Alfred
Schutz in *Philosophy and Phenomenological Research*, VI (1945–
46), 323–43.

When Husserl wrote the *Prolegomena,* he thought that the unity of the concrete sciences is not essential. For this reason he saw that the concrete sciences are dependent upon the abstract sciences of essences and not upon individual facts. From this viewpoint,

> The single individual thing and the empirical connection do not count intrinsically, or they count only as a methodological point of passage in the construction of a general theory. The theoretical natural scientist, or the natural scientist in the context of purely theoretic or mathematicizing discussion, sees the earth or the stars, quite differently from the geographer and the astronomer. They are to him *per se* indifferent and count merely as examples of gravitating masses in general.[21]

In the example we still find the appeal to the general character of a manifold considered from the viewpoint of one of its typical essences. But Husserl seeks a formal and highly general theory. He arrives at the formal precisely by seeking the ideal conditions of possibility of the science of every possible science in general. The ideal conditions of possibility do not concern the general aspect of either this or that science, or the science which draws together this or that type of manifold into a unity of the same type. The connections of the truth of such a science are deductive. It is therefore a matter of clarifying the conditions of possibility of a deductive unity in general. For Husserl, this "presupposes" that all the operations "yielding" knowledge [22] can be performed by the psychological subjects, or, as he later put it, by the operations of the concrete monads. Ideal conditions concern the a priori laws of the theory or its essence. However, they are closely related to those real operations which are considered to be psychological in the *Philosophie der Arithmetik.* Husserl insists on the fact that the ideal meaning does not depend on real psychological operations (which may also be called "factual"). As we shall see, he does not mean that these are not originative. The criticism of psychologism thus rests on the demand to clarify the essential character of science. But the essences are not Platonic realities opposed to facts. They simply indicate the sense of scientific truth that psychologism failed to grasp. The polemic against psychologism follows from the rejection of the reduction of the intentional meaning of truth to the factual psychic phenomenon as understood by naturalistic

21. *Logical Investigations,* I, 231.
22. *Ibid.,* p. 232.

psychology. On the other hand, as happens in the *Crisis,* Husserl comes to see the precategorial origin of every theory in the non-naturalized psychological operation. This, however, occurs after the *Lebenswelt* has been discovered and the mundane is no longer naturalized. These non-naturalized psychological operations are the operations of the *Lebenswelt* in which transcendental subjectivity functions (the same is said in *Erfahrung und Urteil*). Thus, the fact can be considered to contain implicitly the essence that the theory explicates. From this viewpoint, the *Crisis* seems to rework the psychological dimension. Phenomenology, then, appears as the science of essences. However, it is the science of the essences implicit in real operations. This is a viewpoint anticipated in the *Philosophie der Arithmetik.* In Husserl's thought, phenomenology as the science of the *Lebenswelt* is connected to the problem of psychology and the idea of a non-naturalistic psychology, i.e., to an intentional psychology. This is a central problem in Husserl, and it is closely connected to the problem of the transcendental foundation of logic as presented in the *Formal and Transcendental Logic.* To found logic transcendentally means to capture "the living intention of logicians."[23] In the mundane we face sciences and logic that have forgotten their intentional meaning.[24] Husserl pointed this out as early as 1929. The historical-phenomenological investigation must rediscover the occluded and hidden meaning. This meaning must be connected to the teleological meaning of the science of the *Lebenswelt,* to time, and to history.[25] This is tantamount to revealing the profundity which has remained hidden in mathematical thought.[26] On the other hand, the teleological meaning is immanent in concrete historical life—in the intermonadic community of concrete men. The already historically constituted sciences have a hidden intentionality. We can rediscover this hidden meaning, since we belong to the human, historical, and scientific community: we belong to the community of reciprocal interpenetration[27] according to a teleological direction, i.e., according to an intentional, teleological meaning. In the *Formal and Transcendental Logic* we already notice that, for Husserl, the European sciences have lost their teleological and philo-

---

23. E. Husserl, *Formal and Transcendental Logic,* trans. Dorion Cairns (The Hague: Nijhoff, 1969), p. 10.

24. *Ibid.,* p. 2.

25. *Ibid.,* p. 4.

26. *Ibid.,* p. 8.

27. *Ibid.*

sophical intentionality. Their situation thus requires a "completely radical" theory converging on the tragic character of modern scientific culture, in which "logic has been pleased to let itself be guided by the de facto sciences, particularly the much-admired natural sciences." [28] Here it is clear that the "factual" is that which has been hidden and fetishized. It is subsequently pointed out in the *Crisis* that what leads to this loss of meaning is the occlusion of the precategorial origin of the categorial. Authentic factuality, the unhidden but unveiled factuality, is the precategorial life of the *Lebenswelt*, to which logic and all the sciences must ultimately return.

There is an undeniable development from the *Philosophie der Arithmetik* to the *Crisis*. Through his investigations, Husserl has had an opportunity to try many diverse paths and to change in unpredictable forms. At first sight, the relationship between phenomenology and psychology appears as one of these unpredictable forms. In the *Philosophie der Arithmetik*, Husserl seems to be seeking the psychological foundations of arithmetic, but, in fact, even if he believes the contrary, he investigates precategorial and subjective operations. He does this more explicitly in the *Formal and Transcendental Logic*, *Erfahrung und Urteil*, and the *Crisis*. In the *Philosophie der Arithmetik* he speaks of a "unifying observer" and "internal experience." [29] At this point Husserl is not aware of the path that he will have to tread, but his later analyses will depart precisely from the subjective operations already discovered in the *Philosophie der Arithmetik*.[30] As has been pointed out, in the *Philosophie der Arithmetik*,

> Husserl makes us understand that the simplest procedures of conscious activity are in such a correlation that, through the thematization of the logical object, it is possible to get back to the corresponding subjective act.[31]

In the *Prolegomena* the criticism of psychologism, i.e., of naturalistic psychologism, is very bitter. However, it cannot be said

28. *Ibid.*, p. 3.
29. E. Husserl, *Philosophie der Arithmetik* (Halle: Pfeffer, 1891), p. 79.
30. *Ibid.*, p. 81.
31. See F. Bosio, "Psicologia e Logica della Fenomenologia di Husserl," *Aut-Aut*, no. 68 (1962), p. 138.

that Husserl is simply a pure logician, a mere theoretician of "logical objects." [This "mere theoretician of logical objects" is precisely what J. N. Findlay wishes to make of Husserl, in order to assimilate him to "Anglo-Saxon philosophers." See Findlay's Introduction to Husserl's *Logical Investigations*, especially pp. 2–3. Findlay's interest is partisan, while Paci's is scholarly and philosophical.] Under the influence of Natorp, he poses the whole problem in a new cast: he seeks something antecedent to both naturalistic psychology and formal logic. What he seeks is presented as *phenomenology* in the introduction to the second volume of the *Logical Investigations*. The difficulties of logic and psychology are traced back to an antecedent level which is precisely the phenomenological level that, in the *Crisis*, will appear as the precategorial *Lebenswelt* and subjective operation. "The difficulties of clearing up the basic concepts of logic are a natural consequence of the extraordinary difficulties of strict phenomenological analysis." [32] The description must be the "immanent description of mental acts," [33] and eventually becomes "intentional description."

The logical contents, the categories themselves, must not be abstractly constructed but directly experienced and "lived." For this reason, Husserl speaks of the logical that is lived.[34] These premises lead directly to the problem of the flesh-and-blood intuition of all categories, the central problem in the sixth of the *Logical Investigations*. There Husserl asks: How is it possible to experience directly the categories in flesh and blood? This problem torments him and leads him to rewrite this section. It also leads him to pose, all together and in a rather confused manner, the future problems of phenomenology, including the precategorial and subjective (or, rather, intersubjective) foundation of the sciences. It can be argued that the problems of the *Crisis* arise from the crisis in which Husserl found himself when facing the problem of the foundation of the categories,[35] i.e., when he sought the meaning of the categorial operations as founded operations.

32. *Logical Investigations*, II, 9.
33. *Ibid.*, p. 10.
34. *Ibid.*, pp. 12 ff.
35. *Ibid.*, pp. 128–29.

[26]   *A Reconsideration of Husserl's*
        Scientific Ideal. Fact and Essence.
        Personal Individuality as a Conquest
        and Teleological Task

To FOUND LOGIC TRANSCENDENTALLY means to found it upon transcendental subjectivity; however, at the same time, it also means to found it upon precategorial life. Therefore, the transcendental reduction and the reduction to the *Lebenswelt* are closely connected in the *Formal and Transcendental Logic*. Similarly, both reductions depend on the reduction of fetishized and naturalized facts to their essences. They thus depend on the eidetic reduction, as seen in the first section of *Ideas*, and particularly the first chapter, "Fact and Essence." [36]

The eidetic reduction becomes clarified in the dialectical relationship of the bare and individual fact immersed in the relativity of the Heraclitean flux. Here, the fact appears as singularity *hic et nunc*, which does not allow for science because science is always general in the sense that it deals with essences. This principle has always been upheld by Husserl. However, the factual is not simply the individual. If the fact does not allow for an essential and teleological science (as a science of the intentionality of meanings), this is because historically (and, in this sense, factually) the sciences are *already constituted*. Having lost the awareness of their origin in the *Lebenswelt*, they have lost their intentionality. The phenomenological, genetic, and historical reconstruction once again allows us to find the *Lebenswelt* by rediscovering the occluded origin. To do so is to "ground transcendentally," i.e., to ground both logic and the sciences upon transcendental subjectivity. Therefore, it is necessary to distinguish between individual facticity, which does not seem to be amenable to scientific treatment, and the facticity disoccluded in the analysis of the *Lebenswelt*. The first is not scientific because it is not essential, and the second is not scientific because it has lost the transcendental and precategorial origin. In Husserl, these two meanings are sometimes confused. The facticity which prevents the discovery of the original meaning-structure must be freed from mundane fetishization and occlusion. If we free it

36. *Ideas*, pp. 51–80.

from occlusion, we will be able to capture and to clarify the intentional life and the always-functioning world upon which all the sciences depend. The essences are implicit in this world. They are the various types or common traits of the concrete precategorial acts. It is a "relative" world of individual facts, but not of objectified facts. It is a world of live subjective facts, reciprocally interrelated in intermonadic life and intentional meaning.

When Husserl says that a science of the single individual fact is possible only to the extent that the individual has an essence,[37] he means that there is no isolated, individual fact, because facts are related in intermonadic life, in the relativity of such a life, and in the *Lebenswelt*. Essence is *typicality* and *relation*, the connection of every individuality, of every monad with other monads. To participate in the essence means that we find in the *Lebenswelt* an intermonadic connection according to various types, the most general and abstract of which are the formal ones expressed in a theory of the possibility of the connections of objects in general. It is a theory of all possible theories and, in its most abstract form, can be said to be a general ontology. It offers the formal connections of objects, i.e., the laws of formal connection of all concrete monads. Formal logic, arithmetic, and pure analysis all depend upon it. Formal ontology becomes specified in material ontologies. For instance, among all possible objects we can single out natural objects constituting the ontology of the region "nature," or the objects of consciousness constituting the ontology of the region "consciousness." It is clear that we proceed to the concrete individual by proceeding from the formal to the material. From the viewpoint of generality, all sciences depend upon a universal-formal theory, i.e., on the theory of the possibility of all objects in general. Broadly speaking, logic appears as the science under which all the other sciences must be subsumed.

In terms of specificity and concreteness, the sciences depend upon the way concrete life appears in the first person, upon perceptual evidence, precategorial life, and the *Lebenswelt*. Each moment of the *Lebenswelt* or intermonadic life contains the essential relations binding it to other moments. To explicate such relations as essences is to overcome the closed fact in its own singularity and to connect it to the essences and predicates constituting it. These predicates are already the essential relations between concrete monads in the first person and all other mon-

<hr />

37. E. Husserl, "Philosophie als strenge Wissenschaft," *Logos*, I (1910–11), 218.

ads. The fact is closed in its singularity when it is not revealed in universal correlation. This occurs when one does not take into account that every fact is what it is because it is bound to others, because it is essentially determined by others and lives in the intentional life of all intermonadic relationships aiming at a *telos*. Even if only implicitly, every fact as a part contains the whole intermonadic life in its teleological intentionality. Unless it is discovered by reflection, the life of the whole in the part remains hidden. Phenomenology "aims" at discovering and revealing all the ties connecting individual entities. This is what seeing *the essence in the individual fact* means.

Here, the science of facts is the science of functioning intersubjectivity: facts are hidden to the degree to which reflection does not discover them as reciprocally interrelated. Essential relations and eidetic regions are living forms of the intermonadic life of subjectivity that every subjective monad can discover by reflection. It thus discovers the forms of relations with other monads within itself. This discovery is possible because of the transcendental reduction and reflection, as they gradually reveal the forms of connections. Although it is the reflection of a concrete ego, it is also a progressive specification which proceeds from formal connections to concrete specifications. The ego departs from itself and rediscovers itself. But it rediscovers itself in scientific and essential relationships. Subjectivity has bracketed its own mundane facticity and has been reduced to its own transcendental life, to its own evidence as perception in the first person: to living presence. What I have bracketed in me is my mundane, factual individuality—my closed singularity. By discovering my relational and transcendental life, I undertake the revelation of all the relations that constitute me even as a subjectivity which is formally identical to every other subjectivity. Little by little I reconstitute, or constitute, those connections which specify purely formal relationships. By so doing, I approach concreteness. Finally, I try to reconstruct and to ground as true my concrete individuality, which I have negated as mundane but whose meaning I can discover in the intermonadic connection and its teleology. What is discovered here is that the individual for whom I am looking, the ego as I myself am, is a teleological task closely bound to the teleological task of universal intersubjectivity. It is in this intersubjectivity that I must acquire the meaning of my life in harmony with the life of all other past, present, and future individualities.

The concrete ego is both the original point of departure and the teleological task. It is the ideal of an individuality, or a fulfilled and mature personality. I bracket my fetishized and isolated individuality in order to live, while at the same time conquering my own concreteness in universal, intermonadic life. By reflecting in this life, I ground phenomenology and constitute the sciences. By constituting the sciences, I rediscover my individuality —no longer bracketed and isolated, but as an individuality with a role in the teleological history of intersubjectivity. This is the meaning of the *contraposition* of essence to fact. It means both to discover what is hidden in functioning, intentional life and to discover all that is covered, occluded, and objectified. It means reconstructing a phenomenological history of the sciences and their origin in the life-world. Furthermore, it entails the rejection of myself as I have been preconstituted, because I was born and find myself in the mundane facticity of the world. I must constitute myself in terms of universal intersubjectivity and its meaning. Although already made, my individuality must develop according to an "interest" which is also the interest of humanity in general. This universal interest is teleological and requires a separation from mundane and partial interests. The reduction is therefore an exercise of disinterestedness (in relation to the mundane), and it is disinterested knowledge. But the exercise of a disinterested knowledge is detachment from mundane and closed interest, since detachment permits us to live in teleological, intersubjective, and historical interest which is the interest of truth and the true meaning of being. My mundane individuality exercises the transcendental reduction in order to become receptive to the interest which allows me to conquer a meaning of my individuality in relation to all other individualities. This disinterestedness in the mundane (which leads to the superior, teleological, and intentional interest) is what makes the discovery of the highest function of the sciences possible. Therefore, when, in the *Logical Investigations,* Husserl makes the normative sciences depend on the theoretical and nomological sciences, he wants to arrive at the intentional meaning of the truth immanent in history. This is a meaning that phenomenology must progressively reveal and remove from objectification. This fact is understandable in its essential connections, because it is an index of universal correlations characterizing the teleological meaning of the life of the world and history. The relation of fact and essence that characterizes phenomenology as a whole is understandable in its most profound meaning through what we have said. The relation of fact and essence, however, does not exhaust phenomenology, but rather necessitates new phenomenological analyses.

[27] *Individuation and the Ideal of a Rational Society*

PHENOMENOLOGY AS THE SCIENCE OF THE *Lebenswelt* is a science of that which is essential in every individual fact. But to reveal the essential implicit in the individual means to negate the already made, objectified, and hidden individuality, in order to conquer a true individuality. Individuality is true only as a community of individuals whereby individuals are truly such as to give a meaning of truth to their own continually developing individualization. From this viewpoint, to individuate oneself means to discover the essential relationships constituting oneself and others. To discover the essential relations in the constitution of the eidetic sciences means, for us and others, to progressively constitute an increasingly more rational and more individuated society. What is important is that, once again, intersubjectivity and society *are not conceived as abstractions vis-à-vis the individual.* Husserl suggests that there is no authentic sociality other than in progressive individuation. There is no individuation other than in the progressive self-constitution of a social life of the community according to a rational meaning—according to an infinite, teleological idea of rationality. The connection of the essential and the factual, the formal and the concrete, the general and the individual, can and should be considered in terms of this perspective.

The true meaning of the general does not negate the individual: the essence is the individual's life and the individual truly lives only in essential relations. For this reason, the most formal theory (the theory of all theories) is necessary for the most concrete factual life, and vice versa. The individual is generalized, and the general is individualized. The science of precategorial life, of the *Lebenswelt*, corresponds to the most formal science, and the latter is implicit in the former. Here we rediscover the symmetry of the reduction of the *Lebenswelt* and the transcendental reduction. Ultimately, the most formal ego coincides with the most fetishized ego, if the former is separated from transcendental life. The extreme limit of the concrete is as inconceivable as the extreme limit of the abstract. The most formal theory is the theory of all possible individualities. In their pure and fetishized individuality *hic et nunc*, these reveal themselves in their most abstract form and not in their utmost concreteness. Extreme individuality coincides with extreme universality. Reduced to a pure form, I coincide with my fetishized, abstract individuality, and vice versa.

The above points are general; deeper study of them requires extreme caution. Such study involves in all of its aspects the problem of individuation, which is one of the greatest problems in phenomenology. The individual is an individual to the extent that he is the concrete case of an essential relation, while the essence is always implicit in a concrete case. What is involved, however, is the very problem of subjectivity. The relationship of reflection and intentionality can also appear as a continuous clarification and specification of functioning life, which from this viewpoint can be said to be undetermined. Reflection clarifies, specifies, and individualizes. Reflection is a matter of *a* profile, of *a* perspective which can, and therefore must, be investigated. Reflection can specify because it is temporal and renders possible a relationship between the occluded, functioning life within me, and that which, within me, as a live person in the evidence, constitutes itself as a concrete consciousness. It is a concrete monad with its own history, its own beginning, and its own function in the intermonadic community. Reflection is subjective life perceived and known as the temporal presence that the passing present retains and extends toward the future. Bringing the present that has passed to the present, remembering the forgotten, reliving it, and previewing the future—these are modifications of the temporal presence in which reflection is rooted. The monad is constituted in reflection as an individuality with a history. "Constituting" here means transcendental self-constitution within subjectivity, and not in objectification. Constitution is possible only because I reject my mundane facticity and renew myself. I constitute myself only in the sense of intentional phenomenological awareness, or phenomenological life which becomes self-conscious. If I am in the mundane, I discover my functioning life by means of the reduction. By becoming self-conscious as transcendental reflection, this functioning life is constituted as a general form that is increasingly individualized in intentional life and in the meaning of truth of the intermonadic community. I am transcendental, subjective life, a transcendental subject, and I can begin from myself precisely because I am life in the first person and living presence. Individuality is finite, yet it contains the infinite. It is a nucleus (*Kern*). Individuation is linked to the dialectic of functional life and reflection, the hidden and the revealed. The self-constituting of individuality in intermonadic life is possible in the dialectic of center and periphery. On the other hand, not only can individuality be hidden, but it can also be alienated, fetishized, and objectified. It is objectification that gives rise to the dialectical conflict of the subjects and the attempt of one subject to negate another.

That my individuality can appear to me as a teleological ideal does not mean that it can obtain as something definitive. I-myself as an individual have the truth within myself, but I have it as the index of an infinite explication according to the meaning of universal correlation. For this reason, my individuality does not give me a definitive science, but, in the phenomenological investigation, it must be considered as an index, as the point of departure of phenomenological explication. This means that if the cosmos (*Weltall*) is within each individual, truth (the meaning of truth) is never a singular revelation within me; it is the index of all other possible revelations. Therefore, truth turns out to be connected to a system of universal relationships. The attempt to make truth coincide with its index is to attempt to identify the hidden with the revealed, and therefore is the negation of the task of phenomenology. In this sense, Husserl denies the possibility of a science of separated individuals, the singular, or atomic, entities separate from relations.

Because of the impossibility of a science of separated individuals, in relation to the third paradox presented in section 52 of the *Crisis*, Husserl claims that there is no science of individual singularity, and that the individual fact, in terms of phenomenological analysis and the science of the *Lebenswelt*, can appear only as an index of essential connections (pp. 203–5).

6 / The Extreme Paradox
of Phenomenology

[28]   *The Original Ego*

OUR RECONSTRUCTION OF THE *Crisis* has led us to sections 54 and 55, which are very difficult and troublesome. In them Husserl faces decisive problems which remain obscure to him and are essentially unresolved. In fact, this state of affairs lends support to the claim that these paragraphs document the failure of Husserlian research. This, however, would be not only a harsh conclusion, but also a false one. It seems that Husserl, like Goethe's sorcerer's apprentice, cannot control all the forces he has unleashed.

It is important to remember that the ego that Husserl discusses should not be transformed into a theory or mythological and philosophical construct. This becomes clearer in the many unpublished manuscripts now being published, where Husserl investigates more thoroughly the problem of the unique functioning ego (which is both my concrete ego and intersubjectivity) as if it were a categorial and intellectualistic construction.

The "general" tendency of the two paragraphs is clear. Husserl is striving toward transcendental intersubjectivity and real, intentional human society. The problem is still intersubjectivity. But Husserl wants to forewarn us against dogmatic, naïve, and naturalistic conclusions like Comte's religion of humanity. We are also forewarned against anthropological solutions wherein man is considered the center of the universe, without one's suspecting that this position is not at all obvious and that it often becomes humanistic in the rhetorical sense. Husserl also forewarns us against philosophies which negate the human subject in the name of being and a new ontology. This last observation refers particularly to Heidegger who, in a private unpublished letter, is accused by Husserl of an "ingenious lack of scientificity." From this viewpoint Husserl remains consistent: he does not give up but pursues the task in the phenomenological sense indicated in "Philosophie als strenge Wissenschaft."

Husserl does not intend to be an idealist in the traditional sense. But in the face of Heidegger's *being*, which Husserl considers a reversion to one of the highest forms of naturalism, Husserl considers himself an idealist in the same sense as Ernst Cassirer. Hence, with regard to Heidegger, Husserl vindicates his special brand of idealism, which cannot correctly be interpreted traditionally. Husserl does so in his preface to the English translation of *Ideas*.[1] According to Husserl, Heidegger is guilty of the most serious misunderstanding, insofar as he forgets the subjectivity which is simultaneously concrete man and transcendental function. Given this occlusion of the meaning and the foundation (the occlusion fought throughout the *Crisis* as the occlusion of the precategorial), Heidegger's position actually falls into naturalistic anthropologism, notwithstanding the fact that he talks about being. This is precisely what Heidegger seeks to avoid in his *Letters on Humanism*. In Heidegger, man is no longer in the first person. This Husserlian position vis-à-vis Heidegger probably originates in the recently published texts entitled *Phänomenologische Psychologie*.[2]

According to Husserl, Heidegger's philosophy is based on an unfounded ontologism which naturalizes man. This is summed up well in the note Husserl wrote on the margin of page 62 of his copy of *Being and Time*: "All this is my own theory, only here it lacks a profound basis."[3]

1. E. Husserl, *Ideas: General Introduction to Pure Phenomenology*, trans. W. R. Boyce Gibson (New York: Humanities Press, 1931), pp. 11–30. For the remainder of the idealistic position understood in the indicated sense, see E. Husserl, *Erfahrung und Urteil*, 3d ed. (Hamburg: Claassen, 1964), pp. 48–50.

2. See E. Husserl, *Phänomenologische Psychologie* (The Hague: Nijhoff, 1962), especially pp. 5–20, 354–64.

3. See Husserl's notes in the margins of his personal copy of *Sein und Zeit* in Alwin Diemer, *Edmund Husserl: Versuch einer systematischen Darstellung seiner Phänomenologie* (Meisenheim am Glan: A. Hain, 1956), p. 30. For the way in which Husserl reacts not only to ontologism but anthropologism as well, see "Phenomenology and Anthropology," in *Realism and the Background of Phenomenology*, ed. R. M. Chisholm (Glencoe, Ill.: Free Press, 1961), pp. 129–42.

Those who conclude, on the basis of the above observations, that Husserl's philosophy can be reduced to idealism are confronted by an immediate denial:

> There can be no stronger realism than this, if by this word nothing more is meant than: "I am certain of being a human being who lives in this world, etc., and I doubt it not in the least." But the great problem is precisely to understand what is here so "obvious." [P. 187]

It can be said that phenomenology is the crossing-point, the reciprocal foundation of idealism and realism. However, the weakness of doing so has already been indicated: it is the weakness of the position which ultimately conceives phenomenology as a philosophical theory combining two other philosophical theories. It is the mistake that Merleau-Ponty sometimes makes, a mistake which can be avoided by realizing that phenomenology is not a theory or a system and that it does not "constitute" anything.

It seems that Husserl has already anticipated and criticized such positions by criticizing the categorial theories of the ego and intersubjectivity. (Here, "categorial" means *without basis.*) He says that the philosopher should not forget himself in his own books. As philosophers, we should not forget that we are men who, as men, act according to transcendental functions. The stress of my concreteness in the first person is, at the same time, a stress of the only original ego that I am myself, as others are in the same way as *I am.* We should not talk naïvely about ourselves, the unique original ego, and intersubjectivity. As indicated, we start from that ego which we already are, not for theoretical reasons but because it is impossible to do otherwise. It is possible to read the *Crisis* and fail to understand this, as has constantly been stressed in this commentary. Husserl, however, often failed to do the same for his readers. This is one of the fundamental reasons why the *Crisis* needs a commentary and reconstruction.

Husserl writes:

> Our naïve procedure was not quite correct, and this is because we have forgotten ourselves, the philosophizers; or, to put it more distinctly: *I* am the one who performs the epochē, and, even if there are others, and even if they practice the epochē in direct community with me, [they and] all other human beings with their entire act-life are included, for me, within my epochē, in the world-phenomenon which, in my epochē, is exclusively mine. The

epochē creates a unique sort of philosophical solitude which is the fundamental methodical requirement for a truly radical philosophy. In this solitude I am not a single individual who has somehow willfully cut himself off from the society of mankind, perhaps even for theoretical reasons, or who is cut off by accident, as in a shipwreck, but who nevertheless knows that he still belongs to that society. I am not *an* ego, who still has his *you*, his *we*, his total community of cosubjects in natural validity. All of mankind, and the whole distinction and ordering of the personal pronouns, has become a phenomenon within my epochē; and so has the privilege of I-the-man among other men. The "I" that I attain in the epochē, which would be the same as the "ego" within a critical reinterpretation and correction of the Cartesian conception, is actually called "I" only by equivocation—though it is an essential equivocation since, when I name it in reflection, I can say nothing other than: it is I who practice the epochē, I who interrogate, as phenomenon, the world which is now valid for me according to its being and being-such, with all its human beings, of whom I am so fully conscious; it is I who stand above all natural existence that has meaning for me, who am the ego-pole of this transcendental life, in which, at first, the world has meaning for me purely as world; it is I who, taken in full concreteness, encompass all that. This does not mean that our earlier insights, already expressed as transcendental ones, were illusions and that it is not justifiable to speak, in spite of the above, of a transcendental intersubjectivity constituting the world as "world for all," in which I again appear, this time as "one" transcendental "I" among others, whereby "we all" are taken as functioning transcendentally.

But it was wrong, methodically, to jump immediately into transcendental intersubjectivity and to leap over the primal "I," the ego of my epochē, which can never lose its uniqueness and personal indeclinability. [Pp. 184–85]

Let us pause: "*I* am the one who performs the epochē . . . even if there are others . . . with me." To stress the ego in the first person, in flesh and blood, does not amount to returning to a theory of the ego or to the category "ego." It is the return to the unique functioning ego that only I am, even if all others are *similar to me*. Without this premise, phenomenology fails. This is why Husserl insists upon it. "It is I who practice the epochē." We can arrive at this through the Cartesian *cogito*. But the Cartesian *cogito* is not a theory: it is Descartes himself. This is Husserl's fundamental criticism of Descartes, which parallels Husserl's criticism of Kant. It is not necessary that I, along with my live reality, become a category, a word, a myth. It is true that by talking I can say only "this I is I," i.e., utter a tautology, just as when

I speak of evidence I can speak about it only tautologically. However, in my concrete life I am unrelinquishable reality and not a tautology. The reduction of my "concreteness" to a category, a word, or a tautology is, in the most negative sense, the primary form of *alienation*.

Philosophical solitude is therefore not a whim; like *freedom*, it is a human *necessity*. I do not wish to estrange myself from the community: whether I wish it or not, *fundamentally* and above everything else, I am the only ego which is in the first person for me. Before anyone denies this he should try to see himself as completely uprooted from his own experiencing and living in the first person. He will not be able to do it: the first person is a *fact*, a reality which cannot be altered by any theory or argument. From this follows something which at first sight appears paradoxical, i.e., that Husserl's *absolute subjectivism* is *absolute realism*. This is not the ambiguity of realism and idealism as Merleau-Ponty thought. It is the *radicalism* of the subject as a fact. It is the basis for the return to the things themselves. As Marx used to say, for man the root is man himself: "To be radical is to grasp things by the root. But for man the root is man himself." [4]

Now, Husserl says that I cannot jump into society and intersubjectivity from that root that is I-for-myself. Naturally, Husserl does not deny intersubjectivity. Yet he does not want the jump to contrapose intersubjectivity or society to the concrete individual. Insofar as I am concrete and not an abstract category, insofar as I am the root, I am the first person and unrelinquishingly so. The society which makes me abstract, and uses technology and the sciences to make me abstract, is itself an abstract society. Even worse, it is a society that contraposes itself to individuals, fetishizes them, and makes them abstract.

Therefore, I cannot leap into Heidegger's intersubjectivity of the *Mit-sein* by passing over the subject, the radical and original subject. If the original ego (*Ur-Ich*) is removed, intersubjectivity is also removed. "Being," or the community understood in a naturalistic sense, destroys both real individuality and the unrelinquishable person.

This, however, is not enough. Many other things are said in the cited passage. Since I am the original, real, and radical

---

4. Karl Marx, "Toward the Critique of Hegel's *Philosophy of Law:* Introduction," in *Writings of the Young Marx on Philosophy and Society*, trans. and ed. Loyd D. Easton and Kurt H. Guddat (Garden City, N.Y.: Doubleday, 1967), p. 257.

ego, I am not the man of naïve realism or of naturalistic anthropology. In this sense, says Husserl, "it is I who stand above natural existence that has meaning for me." With my primary concreteness, with my individuality, I am also in its transcendental functions: "I . . . who am the ego-pole of this transcendental life, in which, at first, the world has meaning." It is in this full concreteness that I "intend" that the others and the world "have meaning" for me to the extent that I am also transcendental. The reader should not forget that it is a matter of "having meaning."

Now, the world and the others have meaning for my concrete-transcendental ego to the extent that they *reveal themselves* and thus become *phenomena*. In fact, as Husserl says, "the whole of humanity," the very I-man, the world which is "such and such," become phenomena and can be investigated. Does this mean that the world and the others exist only to the extent that they appear to me as appearances, as the product of my imagining, thinking, and theorizing activity? This is *phenomenalism* and not phenomenology. Phenomenology is precisely the opposite of any form of phenomenalism. To realize this is a main and perhaps fundamental step toward understanding and experiencing phenomenology.

However, it can still be asked: How can I, concrete and in the first person, consider the world, myself as man, and all others, at the level of *phenomena,* if I, the others, and the world are both concrete and real at the same time? How can I say that I am a subject of a world which is a mere *phenomenon* of my consciousness, and also that I am concrete in the same way that others and the world are concrete? At this point we have reached the *extreme paradox* of phenomenology mentioned in section 53 of the *Crisis,* which is misleadingly entitled: "The paradox of human subjectivity: being a subject for the world and at the same time being an object in the world." Paradoxically, here we must remind Husserl of his own admonitions; we must remove Husserl from his own self-oblivion.

[29] *Primary Meaning of the Paradox*

THIS PARADOX HAS AT LEAST TWO MEANINGS. Let us begin with the first. Phenomenology aims at resolving the whole of the world into intersubjectivity, and, by so doing, transforming the whole world into a phenomenon. But "universal inter-subjectivity, into which all objectivity, everything that exists at all, is resolved, can obviously be nothing other than mankind" (p. 179). It is the same problem of the whole and the parts that has tormented Husserl ever since the third of the *Logical Investigations*. Let us try to explain this in more familiar terms. Man is the subject and the world is the object. Man is part of the world as a whole. Yet the world, to the extent that it obtains only for the man who experiences it, is contained in man who is still part of the world. In other words, man is internal while the world is external. However, the internal man is within the external world, while the external world is within the internal man. If the paradox of section 53 is posed in these terms, Husserl does not solve it as he claims in section 54 to have done. Different and occasionally contradictory solutions are offered in the unpublished manuscripts. Yet, viewed in its most profound sense, the problem posed by the paradox remains unsolved. Not only does it say that man is both a concrete subject and a transcendental ego, but it also says this: man is both internal and external.

Unacquainted with these Husserlian positions, Sartre attempted to solve the problem by noting that man is the *interiorization* of the world, and that the world is the *exteriorization* of man. But what must be stressed is that man is, *at the same time,* both interiorization and exteriorization.

Let us suggest an interpretation on the basis of the indicated developments. We suggest that the *problem of materialism* is hidden within the extreme paradox of phenomenology. Materialism is itself linked to the problem of the thing and to the decisive and fundamental problem of time.

With due reason, common consciousness thinks that both matter and the world of geological eras existed before man, and that they are not merely phenomena for man. Husserl acknowledges this in many manuscripts. But he forgets it in section 53. This is one of the reasons why we have said that the task of this commentary is to rescue Husserl from self-oblivion.

It does not follow that we intend to contrapose metaphysical materialism to Husserlian subjectivism. The starting point for both Husserl and ourselves is always the subject in its actual presence. However, when I constitute the past as past within the actual present, this past is not an illusion, and I discover that it has actually existed and has preceded me. Phenomenology cannot accept geology as already accomplished: it must discover those operations whereby the geologist recognizes the eras that have preceded man, and these operations must constitute the geological past as absolutely real. It has preceded me just as my very parents have. Without it I would not have been here. It has preceded me and continues to permeate me as if the planet Earth and the entire universe were the inorganic body of my individual, concrete, and transcendental ego. It permeates me as my material, organic, and animated individuality: as the body of intersubjective humanity, animals, plants, and the very minerals as material bodies (in Whitehead's terminology, as *prehensions*). Inert matter is mine but I am also inert matter, the inert universe. As a part, I unknowingly contain the whole universe, in the same way that I am not aware of my own bones unless I fracture them, or of the air that I breathe until it is lacking. Inert matter is *subjective* in its own way. Materialism is not a substantialism extraneous to the subject: I am the world, the whole world. If this is true—and Husserl suggests it when he discusses parts and wholes—then the universal, material whole is within me even if I am not aware of it. It is in me as hidden, operative, and material life. How are we then to interpret the original ego (the *Ur-Ich*)? In at least three ways: (1) the *Ur-Ich* is the actual presence from which I must necessarily begin; (2) the *Ur-Ich* is the infinite, cosmic, and geological past which, departing from the actual, I know to be real even if it constantly operates unconsciously; and (3) the *Ur-Ich* is the future because, in the present, the hidden past is revealed and transformed in my life-task and in the task of the whole of humanity. It is transformed in the *telos* of humanity that is in each and every concrete subject as the unique functioning ego and as universal intersubjectivity.

I begin from reflection, from consciousness. Here the ego is understood, in the purest Husserlian sense, as primordial. It is man, but man in his transcendental functions aiming at constituting a pure humanity without making the transcendental ego into a substance or myth. The *Ur-Ich* seems to be more than merely human: it is more than man as he is. It is an *Ur-Ich* as a teleological ideal, as a direction toward an intersubjective humanity in which every alienation should have disappeared and in which the individual and humanity should be integrated. However, this humanity already lives in the present and in actual humanity—at least as a guide and ideal. It already lived unconsciously and latently in the past as the direction of the evolutionary process of man. In its three meanings, the *Ur-Ich* is always in time. In fact, the dimensions of time (past, present, and future) are stasis-points of the *Ur-Ich* which, in this sense and only in this sense, can be said to be omnitemporal. This omni-temporality is a characteristic of the transcendental ego that lives in every man. However, it is also the present omnitemporal-ity in the temporal finitude of every concrete life which is born and dies. It is the whole, but it is also the part. It is the part, but it is also the whole. The part which is I, mortal and *irreversible,* is the omnitemporality which, *precisely because it lives only once, lives forever.* Man is the universe and the universe is man. Teilhard de Chardin asked: "Y-aurait-il un homme sans la terre?" [5] Although he does not take into account the unrelinquish-able meaning of the subject, as a geologist and anthropologist Teilhard de Chardin has had to start from his present ego (from his actual *Ur-Ich*) in order to discover that pre-life and the pre-human past are as meaningful as the future. It is man who *gives sense* both to nature and to history: "l'homme donnant son sens à l'histoire." [6] But, at this point, man no longer obtains as either the entity or the man of naturalistic anthropology. He becomes the ego in the first person who discovers, in the evidence and in the presence, the nucleus *of the meaning of truth of time.* At this point, phenomenology is fully rediscovered.

This interpretation of Husserl should not be considered meta-physical in the traditional sense. Husserl rejects materialistic, ontological, and teleological metaphysics. For him, God is not an entity and does not have reality. God reduces to the *meaning* of truth beyond that idolatry which transforms him into a being. If phenomenology contains a religion, it is the religion of the meaning of truth.

When Husserl first mentions the paradox, he knows that it can be resolved with a metaphysics or positive religion. However, his religion is phenomenology as the new science.

> As scientists, can we content ourselves with the view that God created the world and human beings within it, that he endowed the latter with consciousness and reason, that is, with the capacity for knowledge, the highest instance of which is scientific knowl-edge? For the naïveté that belongs to the essence of positive re-ligion this may be undoubted truth and remain a truth forever, even though the philosophers cannot be content with such naïveté. The enigma of the creation and that of God himself are essential component parts of positive religion. For the philosopher, how-ever, this, and also the juxtaposition "subjectivity *in* the world as

5. See Pierre Teilhard de Chardin, *Le Groupe zoologique humain* (Paris: A. Michel, 1956), p. 24.
6. *Ibid.,* p. 9.

object" and at the same time "conscious subject *for* the world," contain a necessary theoretical question, that of understanding how this is possible. The epochē, in giving us the attitude *above* the subject-object correlation which belongs to the world and thus the attitude of focus upon the *transcendental subject-object correlation,* leads us to recognize, in self-reflection, that the world that exists for us, that is, our world in its being and being-such, takes its ontic meaning entirely from our intentional life. [Pp. 180–81]

That which guides us toward the meaning of truth is the intentional life that also gives meaning both to us and to the world. With this we move from the first to the second meaning of the paradox.

[30]   *The Second Meaning of the Paradox*

THE SECOND MEANING is inherent in intentionality. Here the problem is no longer only that I am simultaneously internal and external. Nor is it that I am part of a world which is the whole, while I am also a whole containing the world. The paradox is resolved if I and the world are no longer considered as obvious closed data in a material or spiritual being of their own. We are a self-transcending correlation. In other words—using momentarily the young Sartre's terminology—we can say that intentionality is an annihilating operation: a negation of either being or the world. To "intentionalize" means to be directed toward certain meanings. The subject transforms the world into a phenomenon insofar as it catches its essential truths. It is the essence of man or an ideal intersubjectivity. It does not negate being if being is the concreteness of man and the world. It negates the mundane. It transforms the world into the revelation of the truth or a phenomenon. Intentionality grasps the scientific and essential meaning of the world and men. In fact, it constitutes the scientificity of the world and history by departing from actual concrete man in his transcendental functions. Truths are hidden in the mundane. Intentionality reveals them, and phenomenology as science progressively discovers the truth of the meaning of the world and men that has been and is transformed in the present and will be realized in the future.

As such, the paradox becomes the contradiction between what is but has no meaning, and what will reveal and subsequently become the meaning of the future as well as the meaning of what has been. As intentional operators that constitute meanings, we are not mere object-men or naturalistic-men. Rather, as Husserl puts it, we are operative and active "subjects" (p. 182).

We must distinguish two aspects of the preceding. As functioning subjects, we can function both consciously and unconsciously. The *profound functioning of the ego* can be either conscious or unconscious. In this situation, the *Ur-Ich* can be either anonymous latency and unconscious presence within me of the past geological universe whence I come, or actual individuation and humanity. Insofar as actual humanity aims at self-constitution as true and meaningful, this aiming is transcendental intersubjectivity while it remains material and real humanity. These observations are relevant to the problem of intersubjectivity. Every ego is within intersubjectivity, and every ego is the only functioning ego. Every man is concrete and is also the expression of the intentionality of meaning and truth. In this context, Husserl says that every man becomes "an objectification of the transcendental ego," i.e., the *intentional tension* that lives in him, in others, and in the world. But the transcendental ego (or the only functioning ego) does not become an activity or a separate substance because of this. We can say, however, that the functioning ego is unique because it lives in every subject and is simultaneously transcendental intersubjectivity. For this reason, we must always begin with that unique, functioning ego which is each one of us. We must begin from that ego in the first person from which intersubjective constitution alone can depart. Husserl writes:

> Only by starting from the ego and the system of its transcendental functions and accomplishments can we methodically exhibit transcendental subjectivity and its transcendental communalization through which, in the functioning system of ego-poles, the "world for all," and for each subject *as* world for all, is constituted. Only in this way, in an essential system of forward steps, can we gain an ultimate comprehension of the fact that each transcendental "I" within intersubjectivity (as constituting the world in the way indicated) must necessarily be constituted in the world as a human being; in other words, that each human being "bears within himself a transcendental 'I.' " [Pp. 185–86]

What is relevant, therefore, when it is fully understood, is that every transcendental ego *necessarily* turns out to be a concrete ego: man's ego or a man in the world. This clarifies the first phase of phenomenology. By negating the mundane, phenomenology arrives at the transcendental subject. By analyzing the transcendental subject, however, phenomenology finds that the transcendental subject is *necessarily* the man who lives in the world, i.e., myself. Conversely, I-myself in flesh and blood turn out to be the transcendental ego. Husserl moves within the two indicated poles. For this reason I can constitute intersubjectivity by necessarily departing from the ego which I am to myself in the first person and which contains the transcendental ego of every other ego. In turn, intersubjectivity can always be found within the unique functioning ego.

7 / Psychology and the Unity of the Sciences

[31]   *The Crisis of Psychology
and the Crisis of the Sciences*

THE PROBLEM THAT HUSSERL attempts to pose in the first section of the third part of the *Crisis* (pp. 103–89) concerns "a really scientific philosophy." The fundamental characteristics of this philosophy are briefly but clearly indicated in the second section, dedicated to the path that must lead to phenomenology by departing from psychology. Husserl writes that, in order to be scientific, phenomenological, rigorous, and new, a philosophy must proceed from the bottom to the top according to the evidence of every step that it takes (p. 192). This can only be a philosophy that is based upon the most fundamental basis, i.e., upon the transcendental ego. It is a philosophy of the "spirit of finality" (but not a concluded and definitive philosophy). From now on, every objectivistic philosophy will be regarded as naïve.

With Descartes and Kant, the history of modern thought has arrived at transcendental philosophy. Yet the discovery of the transcendental has been occluded by the metaphysical "in-itself" (p. 192) which is connected to the dualism of *res cogitans* and *res extensa* and, therefore, to the mind-body dualism. With this dualism that renders body and mind two separate substances, we enter the field of psychology that must now be investigated. Objectivism splits into two objects, one corporeal and the other psychic. Thus, we obtain psychophysics and the occlusion of what Brentano used to indicate as peculiar to psychic phenomena, namely, intentionality. With the objectification of the psychic level, philosophy cannot develop as phenomenology. It cannot develop as the science of subjective intentional life which is the foundation of all the sciences and their domains. Objectivism loses the philosophical momentum. The sciences are separated from one another precisely because they are separated from philosophy. Art and technology are substituted for science.

> But art is not science, whose origin and intention, which can never be sacrificed, is to attain, through clarification of the ultimate sources of meaning, a knowledge of what actually is and thus to understand it in its ultimate sense. [Pp. 194–95]

In other words, art and technology do not disocclude. It is not possible to reduce philosophy to theoretical technology (p. 195). Notwithstanding the efforts of Schuppe, Avenarius, and the neo-Kantians, transcendental philosophy after Kant and Hegel becomes dispersed and confused. Philosophy—and here Husserl reiterates the polemic of "Philosophie als strenge Wissenschaft"—becomes the history of philosophy (historiography), or else it loses its own "scientificity" in personal philosophies as *Weltanschauungen.* As the first and unique science, philosophy is in crisis and, with it, so are the sciences. Husserl points out that it is important to understand that what has failed is the intention of founding a *philosophia perennis* (p. 197). It should be noted that it is intentionality, and not the enclosure, that gives a meaning to the *philosophia perennis.* Husserl's task consists in contraposing the "idea of philosophy as the ultimately grounding and universal science" (p. 197) both to romantic philosophy and to philosophy degraded to a tool.

Transcendental philosophy has lost its momentum because it has not been constituted in the genuine "transcendental reduction." Without the reduction, Kantian transcendentalism appears as a "construction" and not as a return to precategorial life (the *Lebenswelt*). Now, as we know, for Husserl phenomenology cannot and must not be a construction. Instead, it must be a progressive unveiling of the occluded. It is based not on an artificial metaphysics but on intuition and evidence (p. 200). If Fichte and Hegel have failed in their attempt to found a transcendental philosophy, it is because they have constituted "mythical concept-constructions and . . . world interpretations based on obscure metaphysical anticipations" (p. 201), instead of reflecting upon transcendental subjectivity.

Subjectivity leads us to psychology, since, as *transcendental* subjectivity, it must constitute psychology. Transcendental subjectivity is not empirical, yet it cannot be different from empirical subjectivity. The transcendental ego is constitutive but is also the soul of the concrete man. Fichte's transcendental ego is not different from the ego of the man Fichte. It is the failure to recognize this paradox that has prevented the further elaboration of transcendental philosophy (p. 202). The paradox has bound the destiny of transcendental philosophy to the destiny of psychology. Fichte's transcendental ego needs a psychology of the soul of the man Fichte—of the "empirical subject" Fichte. However, objectivistic psychology could say nothing about the soul of the man Fichte, since it had to turn that soul into an object of psychophysics. It is precisely objectification, i.e., the bankruptcy of psychology, that has led to the failure of transcendental philosophy, which is possible only if psychology is constituted as the science of subjective life. Unless psychology frees itself of objectivism, transcendental philosophy and phenomenology become impossible, since transcendental philosophy demands a psychology of the subject and subjects. This must be a psychology that does not reduce the psyche and man to fetishized objects. Husserl thinks that, as such, psychology appears as the central point of the crisis. The history of psychology is a history of continual crises, and the results of this situation also extend to transcendental philosophy.

Transcendental philosophy and authentic psychology are possible only through a return to the prescientific, precategorial dimension, to the *Lebenswelt*. The objectified bodies of the natural sciences and the objectified souls of naturalistic psychologies are unacceptable and incomprehensible to transcendental philosophy. It is not possible to accept bodies and souls as mundane facts. Psychic life, along with corporeal life, must be transcendentally constituted, i.e., it must be connected with the precategorial world in which we always live and in which everything is constituted by concrete, transcendental, and human subjectivity. If Fichte's transcendental ego is also Fichte's body and mind, psychology falls within transcendental phenomenology, within the science of the *Lebenswelt*. Although all the sciences must be constituted within their specific fields, like psychology they must become phenomenology. They have to be founded precategorially, since they are nothing more than branches of transcendental philosophy understood as rigorous science, first science, and new science.

> Psychic being, accordingly, and objective spirit of every sort (such as human societies, cultures), and in the same manner psychology itself, are among the transcendental problems. [P. 204]

This means that all sciences must be brought back to the constituted and constitutive historical life of which phenomenology is the science and, as we put it, the new science. It must be pointed out that this new science, different from all others yet the beginning and end of all of them, is not the naturalistic historiographical science of history [*storiografismo*]. It is scientific and rational life that aims at liberation from occlusion and fetishization. It is the life in which all the sciences live, including historiography. It is the constitutive operation (*Leistung*). It is the operation and praxis in which being is freed from its own fetishization and occlusion by constituting its meaning as the meaning of truth, i.e., the meaning of time and history. Phenomenologically operating being is awakening being that emerges from the somnolent background. It carries out a self-revelation in the first person as that unique transcendental subjectivity within which are constituted as centers all cooperative subjects, all "psychic beings," "objective being of any sort," "human societies," and "culture." If psychology becomes the science of subjects, then all the sciences become sciences of subjects, i.e., sciences of human society and culture, branches of the unique science within which humanity is constituted. The first section of the third part of the *Crisis* leads to the second section, to psychology; but psychology must lead to the clarification of the intentional and teleological function of all the sciences (*Geisteswissenschaften* and *Naturwissenschaften*). In turn, this teleological function will have to reveal itself as the teleological function of the meaning of being, temporally constituted as "awake" or as the meaning of truth.

[32]   *The* Crisis *and* Ideen II

MY INDIVIDUAL EGO which is evident to myself is the first apodictic principle. It is both lived evidence and a transcendental principle. Fichte's individual ego contains transcendental self-consciousness. "I am transcendental, but I am this man. I am apodictic." [1] "My human life transcendentally contains my transcendental egological life of constitutive and operative consciousness." [2]

1. A V 20, p. 23.
2. *Ibid.*, pp. 25–26.

The transcendental life that lives "within" my human self-consciousness is intersubjective. "The consciousness of inter-subjectivity, then, must become a transcendental problem" (p. 202). The problem of psychology is therefore closely connected to the problem of the relationship of solipsism and intersubjectivity. How is it possible that others are within me if I am solipsistic and individuated? The problem is insoluble if man as a subject is a "naturalistic" object, a naturalistically localized substance. If I am an object in the naturalistic sense, it is impossible for me to be within others and for others to be within me. In order to render this possible, that is, in order to make possible the posing of the fundamental problem of psychology, it is necessary that I the man be evident to myself as a man. It is necessary that the evidence reveal to me *the essence of man* and of every possible man as a subject containing transcendental consciousness constitutive of myself and others. Because of this, psychology cannot resolve its own problems except by becoming transcendental psychology, i.e., by discovering its own foundation in transcendental phenomenology.

On the other hand, transcendental phenomenology has been blocked in its development by the fact that psychology has captured the problems of the subject and subjects in such a way as to occlude the transcendental problem immanent in them. If we consider the rough drafts beginning with Hobbes and Locke to be "scientific" psychology, it could not participate "in the theoretical accomplishments . . . which are the task of transcendental philosophy" (p. 204), precisely because it was occlusive. In moving from psychology to phenomenology, Husserl finds himself faced with the problem of the occlusion of the *Lebenswelt*.

Psychology wanted to be the "science of psychophysical realities, of men and animals as unitary beings" (p. 204). It seemed natural for psychology to be posited as the science of souls as objects, in the same way that physics is the science of bodies. The world is thus bifurcated into bodies and souls. And this is how the world appears in its mundane obviousness. But this mundane obviousness is all but obvious: to phenomenology it appears as an enigma and ultimately is revealed as the pre-categorial world of the *Lebenswelt* constituted by transcendental subjectivity. It is the *Lebenswelt* that is necessary to all the sciences to the extent to which all the sciences are grounded in it. Then, it will be in the *Lebenswelt* that the "scientificity" of scientific psychology will have to be grounded in order to have meaning. This goes for every "category" of psychology as a science. Categories will have to arise out of the precategorial *Lebenswelt,* i.e., they will have to be founded by the science of the *Lebenswelt* in the same way that, in *Erfahrung und Urteil,* the categories of logic turn out to be founded by the science of the *Lebenswelt.* Is there a categorial level of psychology? Is it borrowed from physics? Will there be an ontology of psychology founded upon the ontology of the *Lebenswelt,* or will the *Lebenswelt* absorb the ontology of psychology? The ontology of the *Lebenswelt* as the science of the precategorial seems to be the science upon which all the sciences must be founded. This is equivalent to saying that all the sciences must be founded upon transcendental subjectivity. On the other hand, in the relation between latent life and its evident revelation, in the relation between somnolent and waking life, transcendental subjectivity is also constituted as the psychological relation between the individual and the universality of the transcendental and, therefore, as the relation between the various concrete subjects that contain transcendental life. It is in the precategorial life where we always live that the transcendental lives in the first person, in the concreteness of all the monads, one within the other. The two themes of the *Lebenswelt* and psychology are inextricably connected. Based on the science of the *Lebenswelt,* however, this conjunction must render psychology possible as a bounded science (as a science in the new sense, as intentional psychology), in the same way that, always in the intentional sense, it must render possible the constitution of all other sciences. How is it possible to determine the science of psychic life, "psychic being," "objective spirit of every sort," which is but the science of every type of "human society" and "culture" (p. 204)?

It is important to notice how, in terms of what has been said, the problem of psychology gradually appears as the problem of the sciences of the spirit, in terms of what Hegel meant by "subjective spirit" and "objective spirit" (human communities, cultures). Like the sciences of nature, the sciences of the spirit must be brought back to the *Lebenswelt.* The *Lebenswelt* is therefore the common root of both the sciences of nature and the sciences of the spirit. This means that the two types of science must be constituted by transcendental subjectivity.

The problems that Husserl faces here have their origin in those problems treated in *Ideen II:* the transcendental consciousness brought to light in *Ideas* must appear in the operations that constitute material nature as it is lived and constituted by the ego, as it appears and becomes aware in the ego.[3] The whole first section of *Ideen II* undertakes anew the problem of the *Dingvorlesung* of 1907, and appears as the "constitution of material nature" that requires aesthetic constitution, i.e., the transcendental aesthetic discussed in the first section of the third part of the *Crisis*. More precisely, in the first chapter of the first section of *Ideen II*, that which is analyzed is "nature" in general as the sphere of pure things that are constituted in terms of sensible perceptions and are distinguishable from "phantasms." The problem of "phantasms" is fully dealt with in many of the unpublished manuscripts D.[4]

In its active and passive life, nature here is not mundane. Rather, it is the nature constituted after the reduction of the mundane to transcendental consciousness.[5]

We can immediately observe that the natural sciences presuppose the transcendental aesthetic and the constitution of the pure material thing. In the *Crisis* it is emphasized that the constitution of the material thing is based, in turn, upon the *Lebenswelt*, as is also true of "animated matter."[6] The constitution of animated matter is discussed in the second section of *Ideen II*.[7] The life of the aesthetic living body with its problems of normality and abnormality is also founded upon the *Lebenswelt*.[8] If the region of material bodies and things renders physics possible, the region of aesthetic living bodies and their kinesthesis will have to become the base of biology. The problem of the foundation of the latter is also dealt with in Beilage XXIII of the *Crisis*.[9] It is through the living body and its constitution that it is possible to analyze the psychic life of the soul in *Ideen II*.[10] Here we have the regional ontology of a psychology that Hegel assigned to subjective spirit. It is important to notice the analogy between the problems treated by Husserl and those treated by Hegel in the *Encyclopedia* and, more precisely, in the first part of the *Phenomenology of Mind*, i.e., in the section on subjective spirit with its three

3. E. Husserl, *Ideen II* (The Hague: Nijhoff, 1952), p. 1.
4. *Ibid.*, pp. 21–27.
5. *Ibid.*, pp. 11–13.
6. *Ibid.*, pp. 27, 32.
7. *Ibid.*, pp. 90 ff.
8. *Ibid.*, pp. 55 ff.
9. E. Husserl, *Die Krisis der europäischen Wissenschaften und die transzendentale Phänomenologie: Eine Einleitung in die phänomenologische Philosophie*, ed. Walter Biemel (1954; 2d printing, The Hague: Nijhoff, 1962), pp. 482 ff.
10. *Ideen II*, pp. 143 ff.

subdivisions of anthropology, phenomenology (as the science of consciousness), and psychology (theoretical spirit, practical spirit, and free spirit). If the analogy to Hegel is maintained, the problem of the *Leib* appears in Hegel in the last part of the third section of the philosophy of nature (still in the *Encyclopedia*) devoted to animal organisms.

The third section of *Ideen II* [11] is devoted to the constitution of the spiritual world. However, it must be noted that the passage to the phenomenology of spirit is possible in Husserl only through the problem of intersubjectivity which is constituted through empathy (*Einfühlung*).[12] We thus obtain an idea of the breadth and complexity of the problem of intentional psychology that goes from the transcendental aesthetic to the phenomenology of communities and cultures in "objective spirit," thus laying the foundations for the "sciences of the spirit." It is absolutely vital to emphasize the fact that, by undertaking anew in the *Crisis* what is treated in *Ideen II*, and by bringing it back to the *Lebenswelt*, to a transcendental foundation which is more flexible and concrete than the one indicated in *Ideas*, Husserl lays the foundation for the resolution of the dualism of "nature" and "spirit." Both the nature of the natural sciences and the spirit of the social sciences must be transcendentally founded.

Yet one cannot fail to observe that, in the *Crisis*, Husserl seems to forget some of the fundamental conclusions of *Ideen II*.

In overcoming the classical Cartesian dualism (*res extensa–res cogitans*), the "critical phenomenological" viewpoint allows a critical reading of the Hegelian *Encyclopedia* according to the Husserlian principle whereby phenomenology is not a systematic mythological construction but is the foundation as the return to the "things-themselves," i.e., to the evidence, to the *Lebenswelt* and transcendental and operative-reflective life. In a Husserlian reading of Hegel's *Phenomenology of Mind* we discover the path leading to spirit by departing from the precategorial. It is a problem that the young Hegel treats unconsciously. Husserl, on the other hand, does not realize that he is re-treading Hegel's path in a new way, thus unknowingly opening the way for a phenomenological interpretation of Hegelian and post-Hegelian philosophy.

11. *Ibid.*, pp. 177 ff.
12. *Ibid.*, pp. 167 ff.

[33] *Problems of the Constitution of Psychology as Science*

As A PHILOSOPHER, I continually reflect upon the functioning ego which becomes conscious of the world and is, at the same time, intentional and operating life. In reflection, I become aware of the fact that every objectivity is the result of a transcendental constituting operation and, therefore, that the whole psychological world is constituted by transcendental consciousness. Transcendental consciousness is operative before reflection, but the ego is not aware of its constitutive function. Transcendental life functions and operates, yet it remains "anonymous" and "hidden" (p. 205). I am a transcendental ego but I am not aware of it. Thus my interests are "naturalistic" and are not connected to the transcendental finality. Reflection leads me to the teleological level of a task of an infinite scientific explication. Before, I did not know that my human entelechy demanded a transcendental explication. Now I know that I have a transcendental task. In terms of psychology, I am a man in his material and psychic reality. Within me, as a man aware of being transcendental, the material and psychic reality acquires a meaning in the horizon of transcendental finality. What connects psychology and transcendental phenomenology, then, is the relation of the ego-man and the transcendental ego. As a psychological man, I perceive the world. It is given to me according to psychological modalities. I perceive it to the extent that I perceive myself according to those subjective modes of givenness whereby I perceive the world. Thus, I "have" the world even if I do not reflect upon how I have it. I can describe my psychological mode of living the world and my mode of perception without reflecting that the world is constituted in my functioning subjectivity. However, I can reflect upon my functioning subjectivity and then realize that the transcendental ego operates in my perceiving. The psychology of the perception of the world contains transcendental subjectivity even if I only retrospectively discover my psychological-perceptive life. Similarly, I can depart from psychological-perceptive life in order to arrive at the transcendental ego.

That which is revealed in transcendental philosophy is a consciousness that lives in psychology, and psychology includes a consciousness that is resolved in transcendental philosophy. In the ultimate analysis, psychology is founded when transcendental philosophy retrospectively discovers the antecedent moment when the ego lived as the psychological ego in the field of psychology. Departing from present and clear consciousness, the retrospective function of consciousness discovers within itself the level of psychology as the level of the transcendental genesis. It is the retrospective function that re-presents its genetic moment. It re-presents it by recognizing it as the specific field of psychology. I discover within myself the human psychological world as the genesis of the transcendental. But I discover it in terms of transcendental philosophy, even if I know that the latter is revealed as such through the disocclusion of its genesis.

In a certain sense, the genetic-psychological level is a modality of present transcendental consciousness that discovers within itself its own operative psychological life, which is recognized transcendentally but is always revealed as the sphere of psychological functioning. Psychology does not abandon this occluded functioning. It seeks its characteristics and the modalities of its givenness as functioning. Thus, operative psychological life is continually constituted in terms of transcendental reflection that recognizes it as functioning within itself. This constitution is none other than the constitution of psychology as a transcendentally founded science. If a science of the *Lebenswelt* is possible, so is a science as the self-recognition of psychological functioning as a world or an ontology, which is in itself recognizable only within transcendental consciousness. The transcendental recognizes its own human psyche within itself, but recognizes it as its continual genesis discovered retrospectively. Taken by itself, this is the level of psychology. On the transcendental level, I recognize the sphere in which the world is constituted as the "human world-picture." It is the lived world: lived as real in psychological life as the object "of being my psychic life and that of other human beings—the life in which everyone has his world-representations, finds himself as existing, representing, acting according to purposes in the world" (p. 207).

Therefore, I depart from a mundane psychological life in which I am a man lost in the world. I perform the epoché on the mundane psychological life along with its interests enclosed in the mundane. I reach transcendental consciousness, and in it I discover the transcendental ego which is lived as occluded in the mundane psychological life. This discovery allows a new meaning to be given to the way whereby I "have the world" in my psychological life. Mundane psychological life is now characterized in a particular way whereby the transcendental ego operates in it—something that I know now but did not know before. The essential structures of the mode whereby the world is psychologically given to me turn out to be the structures of operative psychological life as such. Functioning continually reveals itself in its structure. Psychological life is revealed in its structure and thus allows for psychology as the science of a special region of transcendental life. The vast transcendental horizon comes to be determined as psychological life and thus constitutes psychology as a science to the extent that it establishes the essential region of those essential typical operations of transcendental consciousness which we can call psychological. Husserl seeks to clarify a situation in which the sphere of psychology, although always rooted in transcendental subjectivity, can yet be considered as an ontology in itself. "Ontology" here means a typical region which is internal to transcendental consciousness and can be investigated and described in its internal structures.

It is important to note that transcendental subjectivity is precategorial to the extent that it is in the *Lebenswelt.* Consequently, psychology has its origins in the *Lebenswelt,* since it originates in it. However, it is a science determined according to those typical structures that characterize psychology as a transcendentally founded science. Here, we must discover what those modalities of the self-giving of the world are, according to which it appears not as the world of material things or living bodies but as that of *animated living bodies* organized according to the "soul." The problem appears in all of its complexity when one realizes that even the mode whereby I live material things in passive and active sensation is "psychological." The same can be said of the mode whereby I live organic bodies of the "lived" world of biology. If transcendental life is determined as psychological life containing the *Erlebnis* of living bodies or biological life as human life (as anthropology in the broad sense), then biological life contains the life of sensations, i.e., the *Erlebnis* of material bodies. The functioning precategorial life, which I discover as a whole in reflective consciousness and in subjective transcendental life, recognizes itself retrospectively, i.e., in the constituting subjectivities, as having originated from anthropological life—from the psychology of all the "animated" beings, from biological life, and, finally, from the life of material things. Thus, phenomenological reflection allows the constitution of the essential structures of that precategorial way of living that has become the science of the *Lebenswelt,* which subsequently becomes intentional psychology, intentional anthropology, intentional biology, and intentional material life. Only in terms of transcendental consciousness do I know that transcendental consciousness is functioning in matter, in biological, psychological, and anthropological life, and, ultimately, in myself as a man (as an *Ich-Mensch*). In order to discover myself as such, I must limit the regional ontologies upon which all the sciences can be constituted within the general ontology of the *Lebenswelt.* Then they will result as transcendentally founded, i.e., as essential structures of that unique science which is phenomenology: as branches of the first philosophy. From this it follows that psychology is necessarily the first transcendentally constituted science, departing from transcendental subjectivity. By revealing operative subjectivity to itself, this grounds the science of the *Lebenswelt* as the general ontology —the first and broadest branch of which is psychology.

So founded, psychology and the other sciences are no longer mundane, since they are connected to their foundation, to their "meaning-structure [*Sinngebung*]." Thus connected, they acquire a teleological character. They are functions of the rationalization of the whole operative life. This life is revealed in aiming toward self-perfection and idealization, and toward the end that, hidden in the cosmos and history, appears as a task. This task is to transform the cosmos and history according to an infinite and rational process of perfecting. The sciences are *functions* of this process of perfecting, and consequently they are not self-exhaustive means, pure techniques in which subjectivity (intentional historical life) is objectivized and fetishized. The ontologies appear as ideal, as essential visions that, in their domain, determine an infinite perfecting of all the essential structures of reality whereby the first science, the ontology of the *Lebenswelt,* appears as the teleological-rational ideal of the concordance of all the sciences. It is the ideal cosmic-teleological horizon of the history of nature and spirit, the horizon of universal teleology.

[34]   *Psychology and History.*
         The Intentionality of Regional Ontologies

THEREFORE, THE COMPLEX PROBLEM of the relation of psychology and phenomenology implies the whole program of

Husserl's philosophy. We must always remember this when reading the part of the *Crisis* which is devoted to psychology. The problem of psychology entails the problem of the constitution of all the sciences, in terms of their precategorial origin, and in terms of the unity of their historical-universal teleology where science is not objectification but the intentional horizon of humanity. The second section of the third part of the *Crisis* was never completed. However, with the first section devoted to the *Lebenswelt*, the meaning of the foundation of the sciences based upon philosophy is clarified. The sciences are based upon the *Lebenswelt* and the transcendental reduction. From this viewpoint, the third part of the *Crisis* again deals in a unitary form with the two themes that, in the introduction to *Ideas*, Husserl had programmatically assigned to *Ideen II* and *Ideen III*. The problem of first philosophy (developed in *Erste Philosophie* and the *Cartesian Meditations*) appears in the *Crisis* as connected to the problem of the *Lebenswelt* and the historical genesis, i.e., to the problem of the occlusion of the *Lebenswelt* and the fall of philosophical intentionality. The idea of philosophy that *Ideen III* was to have treated is resolved in the relation between the reason innate in history and the teleological horizon. On the other hand, the *Crisis* again takes up the theme that was to have been dealt with in *Ideen II*, while *Ideen III* was never written as originally planned. The problem of *Ideen II* was essentially that of the constitution and transcendental foundation of all the sciences, both the natural and the social sciences. The fundamental nexus of transcendental philosophy and the sciences was the problem of psychology, which becomes central for Husserl in 1924 and 1925, at the time of the lectures now published in the ninth volume of *Husserliana* under the title *Phänomenologische Psychologie*.[13] (This book contains the article on "Phenomenology" which was prepared for the *Encyclopaedia Britannica*.) The problem of the foundation of the regional ontologies, and subsequently of the intentional sciences (among which, besides psychology, anthropology is very important), turned out to be the problem of the precategorial foundation in connection with the transcendental foundation and the problem of history vis-à-vis its teleological horizon. Husserl probably would have taken up the whole question again in the fourth part of the *Crisis*—which he never wrote, but which we know was to be devoted to "the idea

13. E. Husserl, *Phänomenologische Psychologie* (The Hague: Nijhoff, 1962), pp. 64 ff.

of all sciences being taken back into the unity of transcendental philosophy" (p. 400).

Even if only in its own domain, psychology has universal subjectivity in its unity as its theme. As such, it is a decisive science for the relation between transcendental philosophy and the sciences. This is why Husserl asserts that psychology is the truly decisive field (p. 208). It is the road that must lead to transcendental philosophy. This means that it is possible to ground psychology transcendentally and, subsequently, to ground all the sciences in terms of philosophy.

Unrecognized transcendental subjectivity operates in psychology. That is, it is present even in psychology understood as an occluded, anonymous, and naturalistic science. The world of psychology is produced by transcendental activity. I and other men, in reciprocal perception and self-perception, live in a flowing process that has its foundation in constitutive transcendental operations. We live in the flux of human and psychological life and, in general, in history. The human and psychological flux is not a mundane flux but, in the ultimate analysis, derives from transcendental historicity that remains to be investigated (pp. 208–9). Here, mundane psychology and mundane history, naturalistic psychologism and naturalistic historicism, appear on the same level. If the foundation of psychology is connected to the foundation of all the sciences, it is also connected to that altogether peculiar science which is the science of history. In the same way that psychology, in becoming naturalized, finds itself in the field of naïve obviousness whereby the problem of its own foundation and meaning is not raised, so history, which contains the psychological histories of men and the history of intersubjectivity, can fail to raise the problem of its own transcendental foundation and therefore the problem of its own meaning, which is but the teleological meaning of phenomenology as a new science. The concrete monad has its own genesis binding it to an intersubjective history founded upon the temporalization of transcendental subjectivity. It has its own genesis to the extent that this transcendental subjectivity is real, individuated, and embodied in spatiotemporal monads and spatially localized and temporally determined historical monads. We can say that, embodied in spatiotemporal historicity, transcendental subjectivity forgets itself. It forgets that the historical individuations are the products of a unique functioning subjectivity. This activity functions but is occluded. To disocclude it is to discover that naturalistic psychology is founded upon precategorial life. To clarify this life means to bring to light that which operates in it. This is to discover the functioning in the reflection of transcendental consciousness, when the transformation of transcendental consciousness into science takes place. It is the transformation of the anonymous life of the functioning into phenomena. It is to discover in consciousness its own anonymous and occluded genesis by departing from the *lebendige Gegenwart* of consciousness. It is to discover it in the modalities of the present of consciousness which disocclude and presentify the past as past.

The relation of the genetic precategorial world and transcendental consciousness is the relation of the conscious (reflecting) transcendental ego and the not-yet-aware ego. This relation is the immanence, in the present, of the hidden functioning and revealed, evident, and apodictic life from which phenomenology departs. Without extending itself from present consciousness in its modalities, the immanence of apodictic life is not possible as a relation. In turn, this extending is the transcendental foundation of history as it is the transcendental foundation of intersubjectivity. One can naïvely assume intersubjectivity individuated in local-temporal things of material nature which are organic and animated bodies, psychological life in general, and the "spiritual" life of cultures and civilizations. But then the sciences that deal with it are naturalistic. If, instead, I consider natural history and the spatiotemporal psyche as a product of transcendental life (*lebendige Gegenwart*) or as a product of functional life illuminated by reflection and discovered by consciousness from within, then the revelation of this functional life, which is but the explication of the transcendental field belonging to the *cogito* (discussed in the second of the *Cartesian Meditations*), is the revelation that takes place in the present and its modalities, and therefore within internal time-consciousness. This is the time in which the relation between the anonymous and the revealed is possible as a transcendental relation, as the temporal transcendental life in which the ego functions and reveals its own functioning to itself. This temporal transcendental life is the foundation of history or transcendental historicity which, with its temporal modalities and its stasis-points [*estasi*], is the permanent structure of the relativity of the *Lebenswelt* and its flowing. It is, therefore, the transcendental structure of historicity.

The foundation of psychology leads psychology, along with the other sciences, back to transcendental historicity. The latter always operates as the permanent structure of life in which we always live, and it reveals itself to philosophy as the fundamental structure characterizing the ontology of the *Lebenswelt* and, therefore, history. History so understood is the total field of phenomenology which then appears as the phenomenology of history and, therefore, in the form we have indicated, as "new science." This is the profound sense whereby, in terms of the "path departing from psychology" and by analyzing the "re-orientation of the psychological attitude into the transcendental attitude," Husserl goes from the investigation of "hidden" to the investigation of the "transcendental historical dimension, from which the meaning and validity-accomplishment of these apperceptions ultimately stems" (p. 209). Without doubt, here the *Lebenswelt* is the history in which we always live and in which a permanent law allowing an ontology and a science is always functional as the fundamental structure of the *Lebenswelt*. This law is temporal life in its modalities which are discovered, departing from the present consciousness of its own life in the first person, as modes of the presence, i.e., as its intentional and teleological meaning. The disocclusion of the naïve flowing, the self-revelation of consciousness according to the very forms of conscious presence, the transcendental foundation of history departing from philosophy, and, therefore, the relevance of the precategorial structure of the genesis and its teleological character—all of these are, at the same time, seeing in anonymous life its essential structures according to an idea of teleological concordance or rationality. Seeing the essential structures according to a teleology is the disocclusion of reason innate in history, so that from being passive it becomes active. Seeing the essential structures according to a teleology is to conceive and to live history rationally and, therefore, according to the essential structure of its *telos* within which all the structures of life and the essential structures of all sciences (all the regional ontologies) agree with each other. Then the sciences are no longer naturalistic. They are the very structures that make possible the rationalization and progressive action of teleological reason in history. For Husserl, this is how the sciences are given back their *historical function*. This historical function consists in constituting permanent and perfectible values for the entire *Lebenswelt*. We must constitute being according to truth by overcoming every fetishization of being and every ontologism without meaning, intentionality, and *telos*. We must clarify the fact that the field of phenomenology is the field of truth which gives meaning to being. It is no longer possible to speak of being as the foundation, since being must always be constituted according to intentional truth. The regional ontologies become functions of the general ontology (in Husserl's sense), i.e., of the philosophy that constitutes being in time according to truth, yet is never identified with constituted being. This means that life is intentional, and that any limitation and essential structure is possible within it. The same applies to ontological regions, to localizations, to determinations of life and matter, and to every form of psychophysical life. Psychology has its roots in transcendental life. Only by departing from transcendental life in its continuous self-transcending toward truth, i.e., by departing from intentional life, can we constitute historical being and explain the dialectic of history, its struggle, the falling-short of intentional consciousness, the pauses of wakeful consciousness, sedimentations, fetishizations, tiredness, and death. Husserl's point of departure is life, the lived evidence, and, therefore, the activity that intends a horizon which it has never had before, even if the horizon has been intuited. This horizon is describable, representable, picturable, and reachable in the essential intuition and in the teleological essences which allow the compartmentalization of the ontological regions. Within such compartmentalizations, the sciences can develop according to an infinite ideal of truth which is the ideal of the teleological-rational unity of all theories. So understood, the sciences themselves bring to light the hidden, the anonymous, the occluded, and they struggle against the fetishization which remains in spite of the disocclusion and the vision of the rational *telos* that gives meaning to the world and history. All this means that the ontologies express innate and hidden reason and posit it as the ideal of rational, ethical, and scientific perfecting. The ontologies are intentional and their meaning, which is the very meaning of the *Lebenswelt,* of history that becomes the science of life by becoming self-conscious, is the intentional meaning of the horizon of truth.

The Husserlian ontologism is the negation of the philosophy that considers being as if it were already constituted, fetishized, and dead. It is the resolution of *ens* in the life of *verum* that lives to the extent that it is always beyond the given being, and always lives intentionally in the world in which we all live: in the *Lebenswelt.* If the sciences have been possible, it is by virtue of the functioning of intentional life. To make the sciences aware of the functioning and their forgotten intentionality is to ground the sciences transcendentally and lead them back to their rational and teleological function. As such, they appear as branches of one science, of philosophy understood as the "new science," of which we have here "thematized the transcendental historicity" in relation to science.

"Intentional" psychology can therefore be thematized in terms of its fundamental historicity. "Psychology, all humanistic disciplines, all human history" can remain in a state of unfounded naïveté (p. 210) and can appear as an already given reality. Yet this reality is always produced by functioning intentionality, or else it is one of its sedimentations. History is objectivity and can remain such. Transcendentally, what counts is that objectivity be precisely an objective pole constituted by the pole of transcendental subjectivity, the pole of constitutive historical subjectivity.

I am always in objective history and mundane historicity. What I ignore if I am lost in it is that such objectivity is constituted by transcendental historical subjectivity. Similarly, I am always in the objective world where I live with others. But if I am lost in objectivity, for me the *Lebenswelt* becomes identified with constituted mundane life and not with the precategorial transcendental life which operates in the *Lebenswelt*. It is the latter that allows the foundation of that science of the *Lebenswelt* that alone can make the constitution of the other sciences possible. Psychology is bound to the domain of the mundane. It is bound to mundane psychological life whose various aspects can be expressed in the language of a given "linguistic community." But as an intentional and nonmundane science, psychology must discover that the mundane is transcendental life revealed in the phenomenology of the *Lebenswelt*. Thus, psychology itself is not mundane but intentional. The mundane must be resolved into the precategorial and its science, i.e., into the science of the transcendental structures that live in the *Lebenswelt* (p. 210).

Once the mundane is revealed as the *Lebenswelt,* it acquires another meaning. If I return to the mundane after the transcendental reduction, I find that the world has changed. The actions that I used to perform when I was lost in the world acquire an intentional and teleological meaning. They become moments of the life of truth. As a man in the mundane psychic life, I am always a man after the transcendental foundation, but I am no longer mundane. I am an *Ich-Mensch* who has discovered in his own psychic life the transcendental life, which in turn is ordered according to essential structures and regional essences which are revealed in psychology as the science of intentional psychic life. This is a life that wants to realize itself "scientifically," i.e., wants to live psychologically according to truth. Here science is no longer separated from life, and psychology is not a field separated from psychological life. By revealing the essence and the *telos* of psychological life, intentional psychology becomes the norm of perfection: an infinite ideal. Therefore, Husserl's nonobjectified scientificity (phenomenological scientificity, or the "new" scientificity) does not leave historical life in a nonscientific, nonrational, uncivilized, barbaric situation. Science is not abstract study. It is a function of the rationality of life according to that reason which, while passive, "not awakened," and occluded, can support an irrational civilization. Nevertheless, when it is disoccluded and awakened, it becomes conscious in the responsibility of philosophy as the *Selbstbesinnung* of humanity. It becomes the guide and norm of history in the intentional unity of all of the sciences. The sciences are in crisis precisely because they live in an irrational human society which uses rational means, i.e., scientificity reduced to pure instrumentality.

Psychology is not an abstract research technique. As a science it is praxis which, by bringing to light the essence and the meaning of psychological life, transforms it from irrational into rational psychological life. Psychology transforms psychological life from a senseless to a sensible psychological life, from a self-oblivious psychological life to one that becomes self-conscious of its own transcendental and historical function, from an anormal to a normal life in which an individual psychic life has, along with other psychic lives, a teleological function. This is how psychology reacquires its own meaning-structure that had been lost with psychologism: with mundane and naturalistic psychology. "Experimental" psychology is not negated, but it is connected to its function in the totality of natural, physiological, biological, psychic, cultural, spiritual, and historical life. The results of the transcendental foundation of psychology and phenomenological analysis transform the sciences and life in rationally oriented "paths." The whole experimental world of the sciences is transformed and reopened to the *Lebenswelt*. It is undertaken anew in its teleological functions. All the sciences become sciences of life and reabsorb in themselves the results of the work of phenomenology. This is the meaning of the problem of the reabsorption (*Problem des*

Einströmens) of the results of phenomenology. I-myself as a man reabsorb in myself, in my humanity, the phenomenological work, i.e, I intentionally transform my humanity (p. 211).

Psychology as it has been up to now must be transformed, and this can be done only through the *Einströmen* of the results of phenomenology. The absorption of the transcendental on the part of psychic life, and therefore on the part of psychology as a science, must open the way for the new intentional psychology (p. 211). Therefore, if psychology has hitherto failed it is because it has not reabsorbed the transcendental-subjective dimension (p. 211). It has remained naturalistic and categorial and has not gone back to its meaning-structure, to its foundation in transcendental subjectivity operating in the *Lebenswelt*. How are the "souls" given to us in the *Lebenswelt*? To discover the meaning-structure of the souls we need to carry out the same work of disocclusion as for the bodies of mathematical physics. We must investigate how the souls are given in the *Lebenswelt* before they are transformed into the objectified souls of naturalistic psychology. We must see how the souls "animate" the bodies. However, these bodies are not those of mathematical physics or objectified biology, but living bodies or bodies-"proper." To comprehend bodies as living bodies amounts to seeing how the souls are spatiotemporally localized in live bodies: how every soul, by localizing itself in the *Leib*, psychically lives the world that is presented to it in the body-proper, in the organs, and in the lived system of its own organs (p. 211). The soul moves such a system. It is, therefore, in an almost Aristotelian sense, the principle of movement of the body-proper. "Principle" here means the animating and organizing life of the movement of the body according to the way the body lives spatiotemporally in the world and functions in it with respect to corporeal things and other bodies-proper in all of the modalities of spatiotemporal movement. The soul lives in the spatiotemporality of the world through its organic body-proper (its *Leib*). Each soul has a typical manner of living, governing, moving, and animating its own body-proper. Each soul can say, in the first person, that it animates its own body and that it is the only soul of its body-proper, upon which it acts directly and immediately, and that it is not the soul of other bodies. The soul is the psychic element of the *Lebenswelt*. As such, it is not a psychic object, in the same way that it is not a bodily object, even if it is the principle of living movement. This is not objectified movement which is reduced, for instance, to the movements of the bodies of mathematical physics. Psychology has not clarified this point and, thus, by remaining bound to Cartesianism, has conceived the soul to be real in the sense in which the objectified bodies of mathematical physics are real.

[35]   *The* Leib *as the Meeting Point
of the Internal and the External*

FOR PHENOMENOLOGY, there is a normative ideal im-
plicit in every science and regional ontology that characterizes it.
This ideal becomes explicit only in the transcendental foundation
of the sciences, in their common origin in the *Lebenswelt,* and in
their self-constitution as the ideal of truth and the *telos* of history. Husserl emphasizes this ideal in the following way:

> We can speak of science as such only where, within the indestruct-
> ible whole of universal philosophy, a branch of the universal task
> causes a particular science, unitary in itself, to grow up, in whose
> particular task, as a branch, the universal task works itself out in
> an originally vital grounding of the system. Not every empirical
> inquiry that can be pursued freely by itself is in this sense already
> a science, no matter how much practical utility it may have, no
> matter how much confirmed, methodical technique may reign in
> it. Now this applies to psychology. [P. 213]

Science has, therefore, its own restricted ontology. However,
this ontology has a meaning in the working out of a universal
philosophy and can be developed even within its limited domain.
What unites all these limited ontologies is an idea that, although
specifically determined, indicates a universal task in specific
tasks. This is so to the extent that all ontologies are founded upon
the *Lebenswelt,* i.e., are founded by phenomenology as first science and are, therefore, critically founded. Unless a science appears with these characteristics it becomes objectified.

A science without these characteristics becomes fetishized as a technology which is passively endured even if it is successful. But this is not scientific. It is not a progressive realization, in the historical totality, of the idea of reason that gives meaning to history. Husserl stresses the tension that develops between the science which is science *simpliciter,* and the isolated, unrelated empirical procedure. "Professional" psychology, disengaged from the indicated tension, does not realize its "meaning as a science," its "philosophical" scientificity. The task that it abdicates thus falls to the philosophers (p. 214). The realization of the scientific meaning requires the overcoming of the dualism between psychology as the science of souls conceived as *res* and physicalistic psychology. Scientific meaning requires that psychology be founded upon inner experience, which is but "the psychologist's primordial inner experience of the subjectivity of his own self" and the intersubjectivity comprised in it. This last requirement demands the overcoming of nature, understood in the physicalist sense of the natural sciences, and the return to the *Lebenswelt* (p. 214). Only then is it possible to investigate the world of the soul, the ontology of psychology. This is a world which is not bound by the "causal laws" which hold together the "exact" world of Galilean physics (p. 215).

Mathematical physics is to be brought back to the bodies in the same way that the latter, as plena, are lived in the *Lebenswelt.* At this precategorial level, we can observe a structure of the *Lebenswelt* which is the foundation of Galilean physics, post-Galilean physics, and, potentially, every future physics. Physics as a science is founded only to the extent that its regional ontology is revealed. Within this ontology, physics is a closed science that can be developed to infinity according to an idea of itself that appears as an articulation of the general science of the *Lebenswelt* and its transcendental meaning. Analogously, psychology has to be returned to the way in which the living bodies, and not the plena, are lived in the *Lebenswelt.* In addition, psychology must be brought back to the way in which the souls embodied as forms of animation, of coordination of the proper organic body, and of the organs of sense, are lived in the living bodies. Now, the laws that determine the ontology of physical and material bodies (the plena)—that is, the precategorial laws of the ontology of the "region of nature"—are not the laws that govern lived biological bodies as bodies-proper. The same can be said of those laws governing the whole body-proper and soul

(*Leib-Seele*), the world of persons, the world of the intersubjective formation of "objective spirit," and the world of "cultures."

In general, we can say that the structural relations of the ontology of the natural region are characterized as causal relations. For Husserl, ontology is a typical essential relational character of a structure of the *Lebenswelt*. It consists of typical operations of transcendental life in the *Lebenswelt* that are essentially interrelated and eidetically revealed. Therefore, "lived" causality is precategorial. That is, the category of cause, as Husserl had clearly seen in the sixth of the *Logical Investigations*, can be grasped intuitively and allows for a categorial intuition. This indicates that its foundation is in the way it is experienced and lived in the *Lebenswelt*. This experiencing is occluded: it is the task of phenomenology as the science of the *Lebenswelt* to disocclude it. This means that we must discover the precategorial origin of the category of cause in order to become aware that causality is a way in which nature is given to me as material nature. Causality is, therefore, a typical mode of the object-pole in its self-resolution in a form of givenness to the subject-pole. Nature is here lived as "materiality," as a particular spatiotemporal causality that determines "things" through their surroundings and their "circumstances" (*Umstände*), and it determines them as "substances" in substance-cause correlations.[1] "A thing is what it is in relation to 'circumstances.'. . . Reality-proper that we call materiality is not merely a sensible scheme,"[2] i.e., it in fact lives in a concrete reality. Precisely because of this, the law of things, as things of the region of nature, is not an abstract categorial law but is full of hyletic content. This content is given in a lived causal connection in which the thing is "circumstantiated" by the things that determine and cause it, and vice versa. Ultimately, causality is not categorial, but precategorial and hyletic. Matter is given to me as matter in its impenetrability, opacity, passivity, and resistance. It provokes me, conditions me, and makes me experience what has not been done by me: being as such (*Sosein*), or matters of fact. The *Sosein* can be reduced to a lived modality. It is reducible to an *Erlebnis* that can be characterized as the *Erlebnis* of passivity of the hardness of "things" that, in terms of the activity of the ego, can appear enigmatic, ex-

1. E. Husserl, *Ideas: General Introduction to Pure Phenomenology*, trans. W. R. Boyce Gibson (New York: Humanities Press, 1931), p. 85.
2. E. Husserl, *Ideen II* (The Hague: Nijhoff, 1952), p. 41.

ternal, contraposed, oppressive, fatal, unexplainable, necessitated and determining, and "metaphysical." All of this (and there is more) gives an idea of the precategorial causality that I live in that *Erlebnis* of the *Lebenswelt* that permits an ontology of the region of nature. This *Erlebnis* constitutes the typicality of such an ontology, and the science founded upon it has a "scientific" meaning precisely because it is founded upon an ontology and, therefore, upon the precategorial dimension or transcendental subjectivity.

The ontology of organic and animated nature is different from the ontology of material nature, and it is founded upon the precategorial experience of the *Leib* and the *Seele*. The first is characterized by causality and the second by conditioning (*Konditionalität*).[3] The constitution of animated nature has a dual reality, represented by the concrete unity of *Leib* and *Seele* that characterizes the animal and the human subject.[4] The *Leib* lives as an organon in its own organs of sense. There it is constituted as the field of localization (*Lokalizationsfeld*). Thus, the *Leib* is both a physical thing—first and original thing (*Ursache*), and therefore in a "causal" circumstantiated place—and also the field of sensible organization, the modality of feeling, and the organic center of all sensations and perceptions.[5] The *Leib*, which subjectively is directly experienced as one's own body, as my body, experiences the materiality of the thing. Hence it contains the constitution of things, the ontological level of "material" things among which the *Leib* moves, feels, and feels itself moving [6] with its conditioned and at the same time autonomous kinesthesis. To the extent that the *Leib* is active and activates receptions and sensations, it is my subjective *Leib*, the body through which I feel and experience matter. Here, causal spatiality is lived by the *Leib* as the first center of reference.[7] In relation to it, embodied spatiality (*leibliche Räumlichkeit*) is constituted as lived in the forms by which it is given to the senses, to touch, hearing, and sight. Thus, the *Leib* appears as the first point of orientation around which lived-space is ordered. In the *Leib*, the "there's" are ordered around the "here." What is distant is ordered around what is near. Consequently, my *Leib* is the zero-point (*Null-*

3. *Ibid.*, p. 65.
4. *Ibid.*, p. 139.
5. E. Husserl, *Ideen III* (The Hague: Nijhoff, 1952), pp. 9, 111–21; also see *Ideen II*, p. 153.
6. *Ideen III*, p. 120.
7. *Ideen II*, p. 65.

punkt) of every orientation. It is the only "material thing" and "body" that can be experienced here and now in its immediate subjective self-givenness [8] as mine, as the body that "I can" move, as the body that gives me certain possibilities and faculties.

The *Leib* is thus a physical thing, but it also has its "psychic" autonomy. This is because it is, in a certain sense, a physical thing given as self-physicality [*autofisicità*], self-sensation, and the principle of self-perception. In this sense, it is dependent upon circumstantiated causality and is at the same time an autonomous principle. Its law is not mere causality but a psychophysical causality (*psychophysische Kausalität*). It is the meeting point of the physical and the psychic, the identity of the "external" and the "internal." There, the perception of activity is also apperception of the property. The perception of the other is apperception of the other in my body. Thus, I apperceive my "subjectivity" in the other *Leib*, and I picture to myself the live principle that moves it: the soul (*Seele*) is born out of the reciprocal feeling of solipsistic live bodies in a bodily "copresence": I touch and am touched, I see and am seen, I hear and am heard.[9] Analogous to the way which I feel one of my hands with the other, I am both the feeler and the felt, I can feel the other *Leib* not only as a feeler, but as felt in me, and my *Leib* as felt by the other feeler.[10] The other's sensibility is thus experienced in one's own sensibility, through the corporeal living and reciprocal sensibility of the sexual act in which my "touching" the other body is connected with "being touched."

Undoubtedly, we are on the level here of a bodily, sensible life that follows laws which are more active than those obtaining for the surrounding "material things" in their precategorial causality. We are no longer in the region of material nature; we are in a region which is both physical and psychic. This is the region that Husserl considers dominated by *Konditionalität*. It has for its subjective center a physical living thing: the solipsistic *Leib* which, in its solipsism, feels the bodily living intersubjectivity of others. Therefore, we are already on the level of psychology. It is by now clear that psychology, considered in its categorial operations, can follow neither the "circumstantiated" causal laws nor the naturalistic laws of a psychology that studies psychic life as

8. *Ibid.*, p. 158.
9. *Ibid.*, p. 161.
10. Sartre's criticism of Husserl in *Being and Nothingness* was possible because Sartre was not familiar with *Ideen II*, which was still unpublished at the time his book was written.

res, as a body in the physicalistic sense. The *Leib* is a meeting point. It is a point of transformation and reciprocal insertion (*Umschlagspunkt*) of the internal and the external, the passive and the active, and the perceptive and the apperceptive.[11] It is localization in causal spatiotemporality even if it is itself localized. It is both a moved body and the principle of kinesthetic motion. Although it is a thing among causal things, it is a willing organ and the "carrier" of autonomous movements.[12] By discovering itself as proper autonomous life, it discovers its own animated life as it relates to the animated life of others. Every animal is a causal body, a subjective body-proper that discovers its own solipsistic character in relation to the solipsistic character of others. The animated being perceives and apperceives the other. It perceives and apperceives with the other. Each animal is *Urpräsenz* and *Appräsenz* that becomes *Kompräsenz*.[13]

In the reciprocity of the copresence and of the *Einfühlung*, the *Leib* is revealed to me as soul, the "embodied" principle of autonomy in a living body. By discovering its own *Seele*, it discovers that the souls of others are also embodied, and that *Seele* and *Leib* are strictly connected. If we abstractly consider the *Leib* without the *Seele*, we notice that every *Leib* is localized even if it is the center of localization. If we consider *Leib* and *Seele* in their unity, each *Leib* turns out to have its animating center in the *Seele*. This is not simply the center of its own sensible systematic character or all its organs of sense; it is also a center that functions as the living principle of development. At the very moment in which the *Leib* reveals itself by discovering its own causality, it discovers itself not only as circumstantiated substance but as the autonomy of kinesthetic movement. It discovers, with increasing clarity, its own individuation which, in man, will reach its peak only in the person. The united *Leib-Seele* reveals the concrete animal monad in its development, its genesis, and its history. History becomes effective individuated historicity in the man-monad—in the person.

In the complex movement of Husserl's thought, the ultimate principle, the *telos* hidden by all the degrees of psychic life, appears as an innate principle that comes to light with man and by means of the man who discovers reason within himself. This enlightenment takes place by passing from causal spatiotemporality to conditionality, and from the latter to the "development" of

11. *Ideen II*, p. 161.
12. *Ibid.*, pp. 151–52.
13. *Ibid.*, pp. 162–66.

the lived, precategorial, psychophysical spatiotemporality that characterizes the *Seele,* and from this, once again, to the person. The ultimate principle is a historical principle. It is the sense of universal teleology. It is transcendental historicity.

Through the *Seele* and the intersubjectivity of every *Leib-Seele* and every human monad, the *Leib* becomes the organ of spirit (*Geist*). If causal spatiotemporality is the terrain, the monadic animal unity of *Leib-Seele* becomes the hinge of intersubjective life. It becomes the hinge of the life of the couplings (*Paarungen*) among animated beings (of the couplings as genetic centers, as centers of erotic and procreative life). It becomes the terrain (*Boden*) upon which individual lives are generated and developed in their genetic connection.

The person is *Mitglied der sozialen Welt,*[14] the social community of cultures and, consequently, he is the organ of "objective spirit." He is the organ of the forms of progressive realization and the struggle for the realization of the *telos* in history. Thus psychology passes from the *Seele* to the *Geist.* The law of the *Geist,* of the social life and spiritual community of persons which is bound to causality and conditioning, is the living law of a new ontology. This is the law which Husserl calls *motivation.*[15]

[36]   *The Agreement of the Ontologies*
         and the Teleological Idea of History

THE SCIENTIFICO-NATURALISTIC and objectified conception of body and soul is different from what we actually experience in the *Lebenswelt.* It is different from "actual experience [*wirkliche Erfahrung*] . . . prior to the theoretical superstructures" (p. 215) from which it is necessary to go back to "pure experience" (Husserl places *"reine Erfahrung"* between quotation marks and is surely thinking of Avenarius).

If we return to the pure experience of the *Lebenswelt,* we find the spatiotemporality of real and material nature in which the bodies first live in spatial extension and temporal succession. Now, the psychic level is not precategorially lived in the spatiotemporality that characterizes material bodies. In pure experience, the psychic level is not experienced as something bodily, as something which participates directly in the body. Husserl

14. *Ibid.,* p. 175.
15. *Ibid.,* pp. 189, 220 ff.

says that this is true of the souls as well as of the forms of "objective spirit" or all kinds of "spiritual objects," e.g., works of art. The "spiritual formations" are not immediately corporeal; rather, we can say that they "have a corporeality" and that, in this sense, they indirectly participate in corporeality. In their psychic or spiritual meaning, they have a way of their own, they have the modality of having a body and being "embodied." In terms of spiritual formations, spatial extension, as a material region of nature and the way it is precategorially lived, is something "inauthentic" (*uneigentliche*).[16]

Everyone experiences the embodiment of souls in original fashion only in his own case. What properly and essentially makes up the character of a living body I experience only in my own living body, namely, in my constant and immediate holding-sway [over my surroundings] through this physical body alone. Only it is given to me originally and meaningfully as "organ" and as articulated into particular organs; each of its bodily members has its own features, such that I can hold sway immediately through it in a particular way—seeing with the eyes, touching with the fingers, etc.—that is, such that I can hold sway in a particular perception in just the ways peculiar to these functions. Obviously it is only in this way that I have perceptions and, beyond this, other experiences of objects in the world. All other types of holding-sway, and in general all relatedness of the ego to the world, are mediated through this. Through bodily "holding-sway" in the form of striking, lifting, resisting, and the like, I act as ego across distances, primarily on the corporeal aspects of objects in the world. It is only *my* being-as-ego, as holding sway, that I actually experience as itself, in its own essence; and each person experiences only his own. All such holding-sway occurs in modes of "movement," but the "I-move" in holding-sway (I move my hands, touching or pushing something) is not in itself [merely] the spatial movement of a physical body, which as such could be perceived by everyone. My body—in particular, say, the bodily part "hand"—moves in space; [but] the activity of holding sway, "kinesthesis," which is embodied together with the body's movement, is not itself in space as a spatial movement but is only indirectly colocalized in that movement. [P. 217]

Here, Husserl resumes the work of many years: again we find what we can read today in *Ideen II* or *Ideen III*. We also find a

16. E. Husserl, *Die Krisis der europäischen Wissenschaften und die transzendentale Phänomenologie: Eine Einleitung in die phänomenologische Philosophie*, ed. Walter Biemel (1954; 2d printing, The Hague: Nijhoff, 1962), p. 220.

great many of the problems of transcendental aesthetics which are dealt with in the manuscripts of Group D. However, it is important to notice that what has already been said stems primarily from the viewpoint of the *Lebenswelt,* upon which depend the three great ontological regions: material nature, animal nature, and spiritual world. (They are discussed in the three parts of *Ideen II* and synthetically outlined at the beginning of *Ideen III,* where material things, the *Leib* and the *Seele,* are explicitly indicated as the foundations of physics,[17] somatology or the science of the *Leib,*[18] and psychology in general [19] in its relations with phenomenology.[20]) The material a priori of the *Lebenswelt* that is thematized in the *Crisis* is the precategorial dimension as the functioning subjective dimension. It is the original dimension, the pretheoretical a priori to which psychology and all the other sciences must return. The "regions" are the modalities of subjective and intersubjective functioning that must be pointed out by an ontology of the *Lebenswelt.* This ontology enlightens the essence of material bodies, i.e., it lets us see how they are "lived" in pure experience. The *Leib* and the *Seele* must also return to the *Lebenswelt.* Therefore, the general ontology of the *Lebenswelt* "is articulated" in the regional ontologies. Similarly, the sciences must be founded upon these regional ontologies. On the level of ontological regions, the a priori of the *Lebenswelt* becomes the point of origin. It reveals itself as the original source of the ontologies: "Das a priori im Sinne der Region ist der Quellpunkt der Ontologien." [21]

It is to be noticed that the regions are inserted and, we can say, "packed" into one another. The nature of material spatio-temporality, i.e., the nature of the material bodies, is inserted and internal to the *Leib.* And the *Leib* is strictly inserted into the *Seele* in the same way that the latter is inserted into the person. Furthermore, the person inserts himself into other persons, in spiritual intersubjectivity, in "objective" spirit, or in the *Geist.* In the *Lebenswelt* I live and precategorially experience all these strata to the extent that the functioning *Ur-Ich* lives in all of them. The *Lebenswelt* reveals itself in the reflections of the ego upon its own functioning, in the self-determination of the originality of the ego, in its essential forms, and in its regions. It ap-

17. *Ideen III,* pp. 1–5.
18. *Ibid.,* pp. 7 ff.
19. *Ibid.,* pp. 19 ff.
20. *Ibid.,* pp. 21 ff.
21. *Ibid.,* p. 36.

pears as all the modes of givenness, as the articulation of the subjective modalities with which the objects are intended and experienced in the forms of their universal correlation.

The modalities of the *Lebenswelt* correspond to the modalities of the ego. Ultimately, through the various degrees of reciprocal insertion, these are the functioning modalities of the ego that becomes aware in its functioning and comes to be revealed phenomenologically. If we find a material nature at the base it is because the *hyle* appears at the foundation of subjectivity and in the way the ego lives matter in its passive and active aspects. The *Leib* is the body-proper. But it is also the material thing. It is the central and original thing. It is the center of sensations and perception and is the organ of the organs of sense. The spatio-temporality of material things is internal to the *Leib* as the center of orientation. In its spatiotemporality, material nature is clarified and determined precisely by reinsertion into the *Leib*. However, when I speak of the *Leib* as the organ of sensations, perceptions, power, doing, and willing, I am already at a higher dimension with respect to which the *Leib* is an organ. I am in the domain of the *Seele*. With its surrounding world (*Umwelt*), the *Seele* leads me to the level of the person, where all the preceding strata are further clarified and determined. Here the various ontologies appear as products of intersubjectivity. Similarly, the sciences, the forms of "objective spirit," and the cultures are intersubjective. They are products of the various human communities, and their "scientific objectivity" is conditioned by the common work of scientists as men and as members of a historical society and culture. Thus, it can be said that the "person" is presupposed in the clarification of the meaning of the region of nature where the person as soul becomes localized through the *Leib*.[22]

What has been said is relevant to the problem of time. The time of material things inheres in the time of the *Leib*. The latter, through all its strata, traces back to original time (*lebendige Gegenwart*) in which the *Ur-Ich* becomes temporalized, and in which the functioning ego is revealed in that particular type of temporalization which is reflection. The functioning ego thus appears as its own functioning. It does so to the extent that it lives in the modalities of the presence, in the freeing of the unique, original, and reflecting ego that discovers itself in the modalities of the presence. These modalities constitute the funda-

22. *Ideen II*, pp. 175 ff.

mental structure and ontology of the *Lebenswelt,* as well as the ontologies of all the sciences. Again, all this leads us back to history made within the modalities of the presence in which the ultimate and teleological sense of intersubjectivity is constituted. Ultimately, it leads us to universal teleology. The *telos* appears here as the progressive "subjectification," the progressive disocclusion and integration of an intersubjective agreement of persons and their worlds (*Umwelten*). This is the integration of material things according to the notion of the agreement of all their sides. As such, it always proceeds from the thing to the *Leib,* and from the *Leib-Seele* to persons, cultures, societies, and civilizations. The teleological idea of history concerns the agreement of all ontologies, and therefore of all transcendentally founded sciences. It is the same idea that, on the formal level, appears as the theory of the multiplicity of all theories and, on the level of material sciences, as the "ideal of a system of all ontologies." [23] This system is the ideal system of all the essences and their regions. Therefore, it is an ideal system that can guide the *Lebenswelt* in its historical temporality. It is the teleological idea of historical temporality. It is the teleological idea of historical reason that, in the *Selbstbesinnung* of humanity made possible by philosophy, appears as the task of constituting a rational humanity. This task appears as the intuitive-intentional horizon which we have indicated as the new science and which is evident in its teleological role.

[37]   *The Phenomenological Analysis of Matter.*
        External Nature, Otherness,
        and the Unconscious

PHENOMENOLOGICAL EXPERIENCE obtains in a continual tension that goes from the "mundane" toward subjectivity and intersubjectivity. The initial material thing, as in Hegel's *Phenomenology of Mind,* is still poor and indeterminate. Its constitution is guided by the Kantian idea of the progressive constitution of the thing. The same can be said of the *Leib,* the concrete monad *Leib-Seele,* persons, communities, and cultures. Progressive constitution is always a matter of a process of subjectifica-

23. *Ideen III,* p. 104.

tion, rational self-consciousness, self-normativity, and scientifico-historical self-responsibility. Subjectification is the continual struggle against fetishization and occlusion. It consists of aiming at the awakening, awakened living, and it is the bringing to the surface of that which is vague in the background. It is the tendency to presentification and re-presentation: the tendency to let the past live once again in the present in order to renew the present and constitute that present that has now passed. It is an effort to let occluded and forgotten meaning-structures, cultures and civilizations, and dead persons live once again. It is the tendency to let the initial moment, the creative beginning of a history and a period of history, come alive once again for the monads, or the persons. Broadly speaking, it is the tendency of reliving the procreation from which all of us have been born in an original *Paarung*, and in an intersubjectivity of genetic and historical concatenations. It is the tendency to the re-presentation and recognition of one's own origin from which, after procreation, our first ego emerges in the initial act of birth. However, this first ego remains unknown and unre-presentable, and, ultimately, it is felt as something extraneous or improper, or as an extraneous *Paarung* within which all of us have been born. Even if it is unknown, it is our *Paarung*. But it is also foreign to us. It is a beginning of our history that we do not learn directly, in the direct evidence in the first person, but from others, the "documents" of the history of our ego and intersubjectivity. In reality, the return to the *Ur* of the past, to the unrecognizable historical source, reverses to the *telos*. Similarly, it is in the *telos*, in my future, that the longing for the "internal of procreation"—for the *Paarung* from which I have been born—becomes the constitution of a new *Paarung* and the birth of offspring. But, as has been said, the original *Paarung* is a genetic chain of monads. It is a historical monadology.

Historical recollection re-presents the meaning of the past present in the actual present (the *lebendige Gegenwart*). It does this for the *telos* of the future, the teleological ideal of history, and the intentional horizon of nature, living bodies, persons, civilizations, and humanity.

This is one of the ways in which the sense of progressive subjectification appears in Husserl. We must not forget that such a meaning obtains on all levels, in all regions, in every subjective modality of experience, and in every original givenness of the *Lebenswelt*.

In the ways in which it is given, the relativity of the *Lebens-*

welt is the active being of the phenomenon. This active being is for him who concentrates on what appears to the ego or its subjectivity. Husserl calls it "the entity itself" (*das Seiende selbst*) (p. 220). Notice here that there is no being [*essere*] prior to active being [*essente*]. That is, there is no presupposed being prior to revelation, the phenomenon, subjective givenness, the life of transcendental subjectivity and its functioning, and, therefore, the *Lebenswelt*. The functioning ego is broader than what is revealed in the evidence. The evidence, in fact, is surrounded by various degrees of evidence (*Abschattungen*). The functioning of the ego is hidden, forgotten, or occluded subjectivity—but is subjectivity nonetheless. What now obtains for me here is my *Leib*. It is in the penumbra, or it remains in the background, but it is potentially in me and can become actual if I move or if I change the position of my *Leib* which is the center of orientation. Through these changes, that which was in the penumbra can come to light, and that which was in the light can become obscure. However, all of this does not mean that the revelation and the obscurity are part of being (*Sein*), or that being is the foundation of active being (*Seiende*). Even the background in the penumbra is part of functioning subjectivity. It is a modality of functioning that my ego or my *Leib* can experience passively, while another *Leib* experiences it actively. The nonidentification of my body and the other's, my monad and the other monad, my person and the other person, is due to the fact that every *Leib* is a center of orientation with all of its *Abschattungen*. Every *Leib* has a central role.[24] (Every *Leib* is *Leib-Kern*.) All of the *Leiber* are centers, but the zero-point of departure for the orientation is different for each of them. This implies that what is clear and what is obscure for me, in a certain center of orientation, change their relations if I change my center of orientation. They change if, as a material thing, I shift in the world of material things, since the *Leib* is also a material thing (*Ursache*).

The *Leib* is the "here" whence every "there" originates. Everything is arranged around me as the center. For instance, everything is to my right or to my left, up or down with respect to my bodily *Leib* that I can move by means of my kinesthetic movements. By shifting as the center of orientation, I produce variations in the perspectives whereby the world is represented, given, and revealed to me. What is passive and what is active also vary accordingly. The whole world for me is "in the kinesthetic hori-

24. Manuscript C 6, p. 7.

zon" of my *Leib*.[25] For the other *Leib*, the whole world is in his kinesthetic horizon. The common matter within which both I-myself and the other *Leib* move is that which every one of us experiences as the material spatiotemporal corporeality, the world of things, and the hyletic background in which we are both rooted. This background is at the same time the hyletic root that I-myself and the other have within us and the materiality that we call external and spatiotemporal. This materiality limits our movements. For instance, it prevents me from being an observation point in a given location while at the same time being in another place. This impediment, which obtains for every *Leib*, is represented very well by the impenetrability of matter, its hardness, its resistance, its passivity, and my "enduring" materiality as something external, or my "experiencing materiality as such." What individuates myself and the other are the different observation points, the different ways in which we are embodied in material spatiotemporality, which is the hyletic root of corporeal subjectivity for both of us. "External" matter is a modality of experiencing the material base in which every *Leib* is rooted. This base is the matter of spatiotemporal nature. In the *Lebenswelt*, this matter is lived with all of the modalities with which materiality is presented.

The result of this attempt to pursue Husserl's analysis can be expressed by indicating that the "unconscious" appears as the external material world and as the otherness not yet consciously constituted in my *Umwelt*. In the limit, the unconscious seems to coincide with the materiality of things. It coincides with the obscurity and the impenetrability of "external" matter, the *Abschattungen* surrounding the *Leib-Kern,* and with the things surrounding the *Leib*. It seems to coincide with the "circumstances" among which the *Leib*, as a thing, is causally determined. This is so even if the *Leib*, as a center of orientation and movement, has the faculty of moving and is within the "conditioning" of causality. Here the "external" appears as a modality of the "internal." The "physical-material" appears as a modality of the immanent, preindividually functioning subjectivity of every individual *Leib*. When the various monads, in their own intersubjectivity and *Lebenswelt*, discover material nature as a common modality antecedent to their own individuality and their own personality, and constituted by the *Leib-Seele* unity and the surrounding environment, they discover a common way of experiencing material

25. Manuscript D 3, p. 17.

nature, and they can constitute its ontology—which is valid for all monads and persons. The material "objects" of this ontology, considered as the foundation of a science, will be the objects of the mathematical science of nature, i.e., the objects of physics. As Husserl explains in the *Cartesian Meditations*, the "objectivity" of a science is constituted on the intersubjective level. Therefore it has as its foundation the modalities according to which every monad experiences the *Lebenswelt* within what can generally be called the psychic level of bodies-proper, persons, and communities. (In the case of physics it will be a matter of the communities of men as students of physics, and each scientist in such a community represents all men, and all humanity.)

[38]   *The Problem of Materialism.*
The Foundation of the Sciences
and Phenomenology. Husserl and Dilthey.
The Psychic Phenomenon

ACCORDING TO WHAT HAS BEEN SAID, the ontology of material nature comes to be constituted within the ontology of psychic life, subjectivity, and intersubjectivity. "External" matter is a cluster of modalities by means of which bodies-proper feel materially as coordinating systems of sense-organs and perception. As the given of the *Lebenswelt*, matter seems to turn out to be perception understood as original modality. But perception is part of psychic life. This is why Husserl asked himself the following questions:

> Why does the whole flowing life-world not figure at the very beginning of psychology as something "psychic," indeed as the psychic realm which is primarily accessible, the first field in which immediately given psychic phenomena can be explicated according to types? And correlatively: why is the experience which actually, as experience, brings this life-world to givenness and, within it, especially in the primal mode of perception, presents mere bodily things—why is this experience not called psychological experience rather than "outer experience," supposedly by contrast to psychological experience? Naturally there are differences in the manner of life-world experience, depending on whether one experiences stones, rivers, mountains or, on the other hand, reflectively experiences one's experiencing of them or other ego-

activity, one's own or that of others, such as holding sway through the living body. This may be a significant difference for psychology and may lead to difficult problems. But does this change the fact that everything about the life-world is obviously "subjective"? Can psychology, as a universal science, have any other theme than the totality of the subjective? Is it not the lesson of a deeper and not naturalistically blinded reflection that everything subjective is part of an indivisible totality? [P. 220]

In this passage, Husserl, with his usual profundity, hints at "difficult problems" for psychology. Certainly, the analysis of these problems can lead us to increasingly more profound investigations. We can broach them by means of other questions: Is matter a subjective mode of experiencing? Is it a mode whereby the *Leib* experiences itself as *Ursache*, and therefore as an external body which is not living, material, and subject to the causal relations within the "circumstances" (*Umstände*)? And can the *Leib* move as *Leib-Kern* if it does not move in the material and circumstantiated nature lived in perception, but, however, does not thus cease to be material even if experienced as such in the psychic sphere? Ultimately, is this not the reason why the *Leiber* are differently localized in time and space, and the *Leib* is different for every monad and person? Is matter not a causal structure that conditions the monads and their history? But what do we really mean by matter, and, in the ultimate analysis, what is "materialism"? Even if it does not seem so, this may be one of the most difficult and most "profound" questions of philosophy: materialism is all but "obvious."

Moreover, if everything falls within the psychic sphere, are not all ontologies part of the ontology of psychology? And, in fact, does not matter, resolved in the modalities of perception (and therefore the ontology of the region of the physical science of nature), fall within the ontology of psychology? And if everything is part of the ontology of the psychic sphere, will it also include the ontology of the *Lebenswelt*? And phenomenology also? Then what is the relationship between psychology and phenomenology? These last questions make it quite clear that "the path" departing from the problem of psychology as a science leads to transcendental phenomenology. But this path raises difficult new problems which we can merely mention here. Can we also say (always as hints): Does not the path departing from the problem of the constitution not only of psychology, but of any science, lead to phenomenology? Does not this fact mean that phenomenology absorbs all of the sciences, *even if it must consti-*

tute them in their articulation? Are there, therefore, different ways? But is there a "life of all the paths"? And what would be its meaning? Is there a unique path in the "totality," as Husserl indicates at the end of section 63, that renders the articulation of the various paths possible without identifying with any of them, without dogmatically considering any of them absolute, without being fetishized in the objectivity of the particular paths in which this path, the path of paths, is articulated, without denying to each path its meaning, without annihilating it in the unity? How can we explicate what remains implicit in these questions?

Husserl once again reiterates that the nature of exact science is not nature as it is actually experienced. It is not the nature of the *Lebenswelt*. The nature of exact science is "hypothetical." It derives from the *Lebenswelt*, but substitutes itself for lived and intuited nature (p. 221). Exact idealized nature appears as "external" in relation to the lived and intuited nature of transcendental subjectivity. Thus, it is not considered to fall into the region of psychology, which seems to be characterized by "internal" experience. However, if we think not of "exact" nature but of the lived nature of the *Lebenswelt*, we become aware of the fact that even external and material nature is internal to the extent that it is life experienced by transcendental subjectivity. Thus, the "mind" and the "body" are not contraposed, since they are two different ways of experiencing the same subjectivity, and it becomes impossible even to think of a parallelism of "mind" and "body." The two modalities of experiencing, the bodily and the psychic, are two regions constituted by the same transcendental experience. Phenomenological analysis reveals the two regions to us. It grounds their diversity in the unity of the ego, which is both body and mind. This means that the two regions (or the two ontologies) are different. The exact sciences of nature and psychology, even if understood in the broader sense of social science (*Geisteswissenschaft*), are, as such, different in their methods. They are different even if they are both grounded in the *Lebenswelt* and, therefore, in the same transcendental life. The natural and the social sciences are thus two articulations of the same transcendental experience in which the external and the internal are two modalities of experiencing corresponding to two diverse ways of subjective functioning. The social and the natural sciences have a similar origin. It is transcendental life that "is given" in the evidence, and is founded and "rigorous" only to the extent that it has a foundation in the evidence. For

Husserl, rigor does not mean the exactness of the natural sciences or mathematics. It is, rather, the intuitive foundation given in the *Lebenswelt* that renders possible the various ontologies and sciences. It does this in terms of the various degrees of givenness and evidence. The foundation of the two types of science (natural and social) is a unique precategorial rigorousness. Therefore, it is not possible to transpose the categorial exactness of the natural sciences to the level of the social sciences (*Geisteswissenschaften*).

If, in "Philosophie als strenge Wissenschaft," Husserl criticizes Dilthey, or rather, as he says later, Dilthey's school, it is partly because he thinks that in the *Introduction to the Sciences of the Spirit* (1883) Dilthey has conceded too much to the positivistic or naturalistic ideal, i.e., to the temptation of founding the social sciences upon "categories analogous to naturalistic categories" or, at any rate, upon a categorial and not precategorial "method." This critique of Dilthey is not altogether justified, as Husserl himself eventually admits in the lectures on phenomenological psychology of 1925. During this period (1925–26), Husserl seems to radically reconsider the problem of psychology that also forces him to reexamine the history of modern psychology in connection with the preparation of the article on "Phenomenology" for the *Encyclopaedia Britannica*.[26] Heidegger is deeply involved in the preparation of the article, for in these years he actively collaborates with the master. An echo of this involvement can be found in paragraph 77 of *Being and Time*, which is devoted to Dilthey and Paul Yorck von Wartenburg. Yorck stresses the fact that the guiding principle of Dilthey's analytical psychology is "subjective" or, better, "intersubjective." In fact, he suggests that Dilthey assume a more critical attitude toward "constituted" psychology which is not founded upon *Erlebnis* or, in Husserl's words, "not founded upon precategorial evidence" and transcendental subjectivity.

We must remember that in 1907 Husserl already has a clear idea of the transcendental reduction, as can be seen from the *Idea of Phenomenology*—the five introductory lectures to a course concerning the problem of the "constitution of things" (*Dingvorlesung*).[27] It is in this writing that he begins to introduce the dimension of the precategorial: the *Erfahrungswelt* that was

26. E. Husserl, *Phänomenologische Psychologie* (The Hague: Nijhoff, 1962), pp. 237 ff.
27. E. Husserl, *Die Idee der Phänomenologie* (The Hague: Nijhoff, 1950), p. x.

later to become the *Lebenswelt*. In the *Dingvorlesung*,[28] Husserl
says that science depends on prescientific experiencing. The
antecedence of the subjective experiencing of the *Lebenswelt*
with respect to science (the *Vorgegebenheit der Erfahrungswelt*)
is a very early theme in Husserl. He inherits it from Avenarius'
work, *The Human Concept of the World*,[29] where the *Lebenswelt*
appears as *reine Erfahrung*. There, the precategorial as a return
to the human and natural concept of the world [30] (natural and
not naturalistic) is contraposed to the Kantian "categorial."
Therefore, we must maintain that, in Husserl, the return to
transcendental subjectivity has always been connected to the
return to the *Lebenswelt* and a non-naturalistic psychology. This
is a new intuitive and descriptive psychology which is based upon
the evidence and in which the description is not naturalistic but
"phenomenological." All of this is already clear in the second
volume of the *Logical Investigations*. When Husserl criticizes
psychology in the first volume of this work, he is thinking of
naturalistic psychology. He is not talking about that psychology
which can be called descriptive in the phenomenological sense,
since it is based upon transcendental subjectivity. When he wrote
the *Philosophie der Arithmetik* and the *Prolegomena*, Husserl had
not clarified or yet arrived at the transcendental reduction. This
led him to regard the method that he used in the *Philosophie der
Arithmetik* as the old psychological approach. In fact, in this
work we find the phenomenological method already employed to
a great extent.

In Husserl, the problem of phenomenology is always connected to the problem of psychology. What is important for him
is that psychology leads to the *Lebenswelt* and transcendental
subjectivity and, therefore, to a precategorial and transcendental
foundation of the natural as well as the social sciences (*Geisteswissenschaften*), i.e., a foundation based upon the rigor of the
evidence. The suspicion that Dilthey's psychology was not aiming
in this direction led Husserl to criticize Dilthey, or, rather, the
"atmosphere" of "historicism." Husserl doubted Dilthey's rigorousness with respect to the givenness of the evidence of inten-

28. *Vorwissenschaftliche Erfahrung*, in manuscript F I 13. Also
see Walter Biemel, "Die entscheidenden Phasen in Husserls Philosophie," in *Zeitschriften für philosophische Forschung*, II (1959),
204–5.
29. R. Avenarius, *Der menschliche Weltbegriff* (Leipzig:
Reisland, 1927).
30. *Ibid.*, pp. 25 ff., 63 ff.

tional life, and suspected that "historicism" remained categorial and failed to ground itself in the first certainty of evidence and the *Sinngebung*. Thus, it ended in skeptical relativism. In the correspondence between Husserl and Dilthey after the publication of "Philosophie als strenge Wissenschaft," the positions of the two philosophers came closer together. In fact, in a letter dated July 5–6, 1911, Husserl observes that "there are no serious differences" [31] between his and Dilthey's philosophies. In 1911, Husserl announces the fundamental principle of the *Crisis:* the principle of the *Lebenswelt* according to which (precategorial) bodily nature is "a priori a sphere of relativity." Phenomenology as the science of essences, i.e., the essential structures in which the relativity of the *Lebenswelt* lives, is first science or, as Husserl puts it here, "metaphysics." He does not mean metaphysics in the traditional sense, which he rejects in agreement with Dilthey,[32] since he rejects a metaphysics of being where one does not perform an epochē of being, but allows it to appear acritically and dogmatically outside of the transcendental reduction to the *Lebenswelt*. In this case, being is necessarily a category or the objectification of a category.

These short remarks obviously do not exhaust the problem concerning the relations between Husserl and Dilthey. They are necessary, however, since in section 64 of the *Crisis* Husserl invites us to reconsider the problem of the relations between the natural and the social sciences. This is a problem which is at the core of Dilthey's thought and at the source of the distinction between "descriptive" (*Erklärung*) and "explicative" (*Verstehen*) science. Dilthey proposed a psychology that was criticized by Windelband, Rickert, and Ebbinghaus. According to Husserl, Dilthey was excessively influenced by these criticisms.[33]

On the other hand, in the *Crisis,* Husserl himself faces the expression "descriptive psychology" and substitutes for it the term "phenomenological psychology," or "phenomenology." The core of the question lies in the fact that it is necessary to investigate what is excessively obvious in the two terms "descriptive" and "explicative." What is important for Husserl is that description be the description of the original givenness of the

31. See Walter Biemel, "Correspondencia entre Dilthey y Husserl," *Revue de Filosofia de la Universidad de Costa Rica,* II (1959), 114.

32. *Ibid.,* p. 117.

33. *Ibid.,* p. 103.

Lebenswelt. This is a description which is subsequently the true explication and explanation to the extent that it implies the transcendental foundation and reflection upon functioning life which becomes explicit in the stress on its modalities, essential structures, and regions.

9 / Phenomenological Psychology and the Foundation of Psychology as a Science

[39] *The Interruption of the Crisis*

IN THE PREVIOUS CHAPTERS we have attempted not only to comment on and reconstruct but also to complete the Husserlian position concerning the relation of phenomenology and psychology. In our reconstruction and attempted development we have not been able to restrict ourselves solely to the text of the *Crisis*. It seems that Husserl has not had the opportunity to outline such a synthesis. In fact, in Husserl the relation of phenomenology and psychology has always been difficult and dramatic. We may say that the two have always been flowing and in a state of crisis. A document relevant to this relation is to be found today in the *Phänomenologische Psychologie*. The fundamental problems there are, on one hand, the unity of the sciences, and, on the other, the unity of man with his environment and the world. Neither problem can be resolved in the way Heidegger eventually attempted in *Being and Time*, a solution that may have originated in Heidegger's collaboration on the article "Phenomenology" that Husserl wrote for the *Encyclopaedia Britannica*. Now, the sections of the *Crisis* dedicated to "the way into phenomenological transcendental philosophy from psychology" still reflect the fluid and problematic relation which, in Husserl, has always existed between psychology and phenomenology. The solution is to be found only in the unity of man and his transcendental functions, and in the relation between internal and external experience. As we have seen, the unity of man and his transcendental functions is exposed much more clearly in *Ideen II* than in the *Crisis*.

The unity of the sciences is founded upon the unity of man, who is at the same time material, biological, psychic, and spiritual. Phenomenology then appears as the science of the whole man, or as *radical humanism*. If this humanism is not naturalism it is because man, although he is material and external, is at the same time real and transcendental.

This problem is central and can be considered from a viewpoint that Husserl himself never used. As a material and living being, man has needs. The relation between man and matter is also a relation between the subject who needs goods and the goods that satisfy his needs. On the precategorial level, this means that a phenomenology of the living needs of the subject in the first person can constitute the basis of *political economy* as a science. Intentionality itself, then, takes on a new meaning. It appears not only as *consciousness* of something but also as *dependence on something*. On the precategorial economic level, my subjectivity may turn out to be the need of something that conditions life. The crisis of the sciences appears precategorially as an economic crisis and appears categorially as the crisis of political economy. Also, political economy becomes the "truly decisive field"—to use Husserl's expression for psychology. In terms of economics, man is not simply an object of study, i.e., an abstract object or abstract producer. The same applies in physical anthropology: man is not solely the cultural object of Malinowski's naturalistic anthropology. Man is the agent of history. In order to be truly scientific, economics and anthropology will have to become historical, intentional, and oriented. They cannot hide behind the mask of a mythological neutrality. Husserl has never dealt with these topics, yet these topics can permit a *correction and a renovation of phenomenology*.

What remains is the great Husserlian teaching: all the sciences, without any distinction between the natural and the social sciences, must be founded upon the transcendental subjectivity that unites the life-world and intersubjective experience, matter and spirit, and the external and the internal. There are, however, many sciences. They have their regions or, in Husserl's words, their regional ontologies. These ontologies are distinct in the vocational work of the various scientists, but they all agree to the extent that every scientist is a human and transcendental subject, a whole man. The regions and the scientific operations are correlative to the operations of the total ego which is simultaneously humanity and nature. Therefore, every scientific operation aims toward the idea of the agreement of all ontologies and toward sciences that are transcendentally founded. This idea can and must guide the history of humanity in the becoming-conscious which imposes upon philosophy the task of constituting a rational humanity. The problems of the unity of the sciences and the relation of psychology and phenomenology lead us to the last section of the *Crisis,* which deals with the theme of "philosophy as mankind's self-reflection; the self-realization of reason" (p. 335 [This section appears as Appendix IV of the English edition, and as the summary (*Schlusswort*) of the German.]). Actually, the *Crisis* ends in the preceding section. Section 73 belongs to manuscript K III 6, and it has been added as a conclusion by the editors of *Husserliana* in an attempt to remedy the interruption of the text. But the interruption remains, and so do the problems of the entirety of man and of the unity of the sciences, precisely those problems that we have sought to reconstruct and to develop in the two previous chapters.

[40] *The Fundamental Themes of Husserl's*
Last Psychological Investigation,
and Contemporary Psychology

HUSSERL'S WAVERING concerning the relations of psychology and phenomenology is to be found particularly in sections 65 through 72 of the *Crisis,* where many different problems cross and become confused.

The first theme deals with the return of psychology to the subject and the operations of the psychologist. This theme is important not only for psychology but also for all the rest of the sciences. Husserl criticizes objectivistic naturalism, psychophysical parallelism, behaviorism, and even *Gestaltpsychologie* and psychoanalysis. In many respects, Husserl's approach has been developed by Merleau-Ponty's *Phenomenology of Perception.* This is particularly true for Husserl's remarks on perception, and for the meaning of the term "behavior" (pp. 237–46).

However, this is not the central point. What is crucial is that the psychologist depart from his own subjectivity in the first person from which perceptions and precategorial psychological life originate. "The psychologist will naturally have to carry out the epochē and reduction from his own vantage point and first of all upon himself; he must begin with his original self-experience and his own original world-consciousness, i.e., the self-apperception of himself" (p. 253). Thus, the psychologist will no longer start out from sense-data psychology because these sense-data are not original perceptions but abstractions and constructions (p. 242). The reduction required of the psychologist is therefore the reduction to *himself*. It is a psychological-transcendental reduction to the *Lebenswelt*, since it leads not to the discovery of the theory of psychic experience but to precategorial psychic experience.

The psychologist who returns to the subject in the first person discovers his own psychic life, which also comprises that of other subjects. This is the second theme:

> Each soul also stands in community with others which are intentionally interrelated, that is, in a purely intentional, internally and essentially closed nexus, that of intersubjectivity. [P. 238]

The psychologist must begin by

> proceeding from his own life, those others who also live, and their life, whereby each life with its own intentionality reaches intentionally into the life of every other, and all are interwoven in different, closer, or more distant ways in an association of life. [P. 240]

These observations are broadened when Husserl writes that "a priori, self-consciousness and consciousness of others are inseparable" (p. 253). Here we find the conception of the unique functioning ego and intersubjectivity operating perfectly, even for psychology. Husserl also adds: "All souls make up a single unity of intentionality with the reciprocal implication of the life-fluxes of the individual subjects, a unity that can be unfolded systematically through phenomenology" (p. 257). The unity of the souls is expressed in every form of empathy (*Einfühlung;* see the fifth of the *Cartesian Meditations*). At this point, the problems of the "universal community" reappear, i.e., the problems of the "family, people, community of peoples, and then as essential structures of human historicity" (p. 259). Here psychology passes into non-naturalistically understood anthropology and history. This means that the psychologist departs both from his own subjectivity and from the historical presence of his time that he lives in the first person. The necessity of departure is what is meant when we say that it is necessary to depart from *contemporaneity*, i.e., from actual presence. The actual presence, however, never presents simply a world of souls to me. This is the *abstraction* of psychology. Husserl writes: "Psychology, the universal science of the pure souls in general—therein consists its abstraction" (p. 252). From this viewpoint, psychology is purely descriptive. Its peculiar epochē is not the reduction of the unique functioning and intersubjective ego, but what, in a psychological context, Husserl calls "the *phenomenological-psychological reduction*" (p. 236). This, however, does not succeed in remaining as solely what it is.

> Thus we see with surprise, I think, that in the pure development of the idea of a descriptive psychology, which seeks to bring to expression what is essentially proper to souls, there necessarily occurs a transformation of the psychological-phenomenological epochē and reduction into the *transcendental*. [P. 256]

> There is only a transcendental psychology, which is identical with transcendental philosophy. [P. 257]

These statements illuminate the path that leads from psychology to transcendental phenomenology, but they do not help us understand the field peculiar to psychology. It must arise out of a peculiar experience of the life-world that produces a particular region. Husserl has clarified the precategorial origin of arithmetic and formal logic; he has clarified the origin of mathematical physics; but the previous statements do not clarify the origin of psychology. Psychology becomes confused with transcendental phenomenology. Arithmetic and physics are precategorially founded by transcendental phenomenology, but they do not become identified with it. What is precategorial experience? And what are these operations typical of the subject in the intersubjective relation that are the basis for the regional ontology of psychology as a science?

Before answering, we must point out that the sciences' ontologies are not to be separated as if they were categorial theories or metaphysical ontologies. Their various precategorial structures and the operations constituting them are interconnected. The nature from which physics arises is precategorially lived as materiality, and its causal nexuses are precategorially lived (and not as scientific laws) in the *circumstantiality* that determines those nexuses. The bodies held by this original causality are not phantasms, categories, or ideas; they are real bodies. For the Husserl of *Ideen II*, this is what distinguishes real things from phantasms. Therefore, precategorial *causality* is the typical structure of material things, and even of that material thing which is my body. On the other hand, animated nature is held together by conditioning. My body is *conditioned* by its genesis and environment, although it is a spatiotemporal point of departure and a principle of movement. In its relations with other bodies my body feels and is felt by departing from itself. This is how the coupling of reciprocal empathy (*Einfühlung*) comes about. From this basic relation follow the familiar communities, peoples, and actual human historicity from which I always depart as a scientist and philosopher. But historical presence is not an isolated ontology. It is the ontology of all ontologies. Thus, we enter the region that Hegel called "objective spirit," which not only is dependent upon the causality of precategorial nature and conditioned by the environment, but lives according to conscious *motivations* and projects. Therefore, the specific field of psychology is the field of conditionings, of what conditions me in relations with others, my motivations, and my projects. This field, on one hand, depends on material nature and its causality, and, on the other, it is oriented according to the motivations and goals of "objective spirit," i.e., according to the meaning of the community and history. The psychological reduction thus reenters the field of transcendental phenomenology, but, at the same time, it remains separate from it. Psychology as a science does not study the causal law of inorganic bodies. Rather, it studies environmental conditioning and natural causality that determine animated life (which biology will study as its region). These motivations are of interest to anthropology, social psychology, and the psychology of cultural operations in general. Husserl, who has dealt with all of this in *Ideen II*, is not able to bring it to the level of the *Crisis*.

The above is in need of further clarification, and this clarification constitutes the third theme. If psychology deals with the intersubjective level, with respect to the meetings and clashes of persons and groups on the dialectical level, one always encounters the experience of matter (the exteriority that I find in myself and others), need, instinct, and impulse. When, in the fifth of the *Cartesian Meditations*, Husserl grounds intersubjectivity, he must pass through the distinction between one's own body and an extraneous body. When I as a subject deal with another subject and the other deals with me, the other and I-myself are not only *cogito* or *cogitata*, but also *concrete monads* and concrete men. This does not prevent me from also seeing the other as an image, an essence, a phantasm, or an ideal. The ideal human society becomes the *telos* of history in the reciprocal intersubjective constitution. If in the first case the intentional objects are men, in the second the intentional object is the *meaning of truth of humanity*. This meaning of truth includes, unifies, and transforms the meanings of truth of all the sciences into an intentional task. Here, the spirit of scientificity of mathematical logic and the eidetic structures of every science unite the truths discovered and yet to be discovered. The man who has been able to ground mathematics and physics can and must found a rational society which can unify the essential structures of all the sciences and realize man's universal goal. Ultimately, this is an ideal. But it is an ideal immanent in the structure of the world. If we see the eidetic side of this ideal, we can say that, although men die, the idea of humanity never does. Husserl here reiterates what he had said in *Ideas:* "One can say of a simple tree that it burns up, but a perceived tree 'as such' cannot burn up" (p. 242). This is true if the tree is a phantasm (a vision), but it is not true if the tree is in precategorial nature. Three trees can burn, but the *number* three does not burn. But the number three is constituted by the precategorial activity that says "one, two, three," and Husserl has already clarified this in *Philosophie der Arithmetik.* Ultimately, the trees and I-myself are precategorial, material, and real, unlike abstractions, which are categorial. Precisely because they permit abstractions, the ego and things are not themselves abstractions. On the other hand, things, and I, as a material body, are already precategorially bound by qualitative relationships. It is precisely because of this that mathematics has its origin in quantitative precategorial nature and can be applied to nature even if it can be spaced beyond its original nucleus in formal infinite operations. As Husserl put it: "Nature is in itself what it is, and is in itself mathematical, no matter how much we know or do not know of mathematics" (pp. 264–65). Therefore, there is a factual precategorial world, even if I cannot deduce nature from mathematics. The latter would mean an a priori knowledge of reality, i.e., of every possible factual world. The same, continues Husserl, is true of psychology: "For the realm of souls there is in principle no such ontology, no science corresponding to the physicalistic-mathematical ideal, although psychic being is investigatable in transcendental universality, in a fully systematic way" (p. 265).

Nature is mathematical even if I do not realize that it is. It follows the laws of physics, chemistry, and biology, even if I do not know that it does. Therefore, we believe that there is an unconscious experience of mathematical, physical, chemical, and biological precategorial reality. There is an unconscious experience of material nature. As we have seen, the problem of the unconscious in psychology can be connected with the problem of materialism and externality. Freud himself is aware of all this when, in *Beyond the Pleasure Principle,* he seeks to connect the death-instinct (which, as an instinct, belongs to psychology) to the "silent" wearing of the body, to aging, consumption, the irreversibility of time, and entropy.[1] However, in the lived and precategorial sense, entropy and irreversibility are none other than the disequilibrium of need. For Freud, the final satisfaction aims at peace, according to the principle that Barbara Low calls the nirvana principle, a view not too well received by contemporary psychoanalysts.[2] In reality, all this indicates the yet to be investigated connection between the unconscious and the external world, between failing—or the falling-short of consciousness (sleep and death)—and nature. For me as a subject, death is the extreme form of externalization. But I always carry externalization with me (Freud would say I carry it as an instinct). In order to live, I must satisfy needs with goods. Without the satisfaction of needs I die. In the intersubjective dialectic this appears on the level of master and slave. I can be dominated by another subject because the other can control me by controlling the goods necessary for my life. Thus, *psychology leads us back to the elementary precategorial structure of political economy.*

If psychology has its own field in relation to others, it is clear that, even if it is at the center of transcendental phenomenology, it has its specific place. If the connections with the material world and externality are necessary to psychology, it becomes easy to understand why psychology, without being fetishized or reducing psychic operations to the bodies of mathematical physics, can also study behavior, in the sense of behaviorism, and forms, in the sense of *Gestaltpsychologie.* What is important is not to transform behavior and forms into metaphysical substances or false concreteness (according to Whitehead's principle of misplaced concreteness). At any rate, it is necessary to discover the precategorial foundations and disocclude the operations which are constitutive of the various currents of contemporary psychology.

Husserl writes: "Reflecting upon myself in my self-consciousness, I find myself to be living in the world" (p. 251). Certainly,

1. See Sigmund Freud, *Beyond the Pleasure Principle,* trans. James Strachey (London: Hogarth Press, 1961), pp. 12–13, 51–52.
2. See Ernest Jones, *Life and Work of Sigmund Freud,* Vol. III, *The Last Phase, 1919–1939* (London: Hogarth Press, 1957), p. 289.

I must not consider my consciousness as a *tabula rasa* since, were this the case, this table would be conscious of itself. We have seen, however, that self-consciousness and the consciousness of estrangement are a priori inseparable. Now, estrangement can take the form of other subjects, but also of the estrangement of nature (external matter). The world is where I as a subject express, realize, and "estrange myself." Here the term "estrangement" does not have the negative connotation that it sometimes has in Hegel (and in some cases the very term "alienation" appears in Husserl). It means "my very reflection tells me that I live in the world," and it becomes, as a psychic act, a mode of behavior in the world. This is the fourth theme, and it is here that the investigations ranging from Minkowski to Binswanger's *Daseinsanalyse* find their place. If the subject is in the world, every psychic act is also a way of behaving in the world and with respect to others. Here it is important to analyze how, in relation to others, every subject represents the world to himself and moves in it. Binswanger has developed his ideas by departing from Heidegger's *Dasein*. But if we consider that Husserl's subject is always in the world and lives in the *Lebenswelt* before he lives in the world of the sciences, we can say that he can develop anomalous ways of perceiving space and time, of feeling needs and satisfactions, past and future, and, consequently, he can develop anomalous ways of recalling and anticipating, of nostalgia and hope, of remorse and desperation. This is not the place to analyze the work of *Daseinsanalyse*. What is interesting, rather, is to indicate the possibility of correcting and reconstructing *Daseinsanalyse* according to the precategorial and transcendental foundation of psychic life as living-in-the-world. Binswanger analyzes the world of the "we" (*Wirheit*). What is lacking is the point of departure from subjectivity in the first person or, as Husserl would put it, the foundation. It is not possible to "jump" from the subject to intersubjectivity. Our mode of being in the world is also the mode whereby, in each one of us, intersubjectivity dialectically constitutes itself by departing from our functioning ego.[3] This method may enable us to understand the sense in which objectification and the crisis of the sciences are bound to alienation understood in the psychiatric sense, and how the latter is related to the reduction of man to thing, i.e., to social alienation understood as *Verdinglichung*.

3. Concerning Binswanger, see my paper, "Indicazioni elementari sull analisi esistenziale," *Aut-Aut*, no. 60 (1960), pp. 403–10.

[41]   *The Vocational Epochē*
       and the Transcendental Unity of Man

IN SECTION 72 where the *Crisis* is interrupted, Husserl conceives of "the relation of transcendental psychology to transcendental phenomenology as the proper access to pure self-knowledge," and reiterates that by beginning anew from transcendental phenomenology we can always return to "the natural and mundane attitude." Pure psychology, as any other science and vocation, has its vocational times and their epochē (pp. 257–58).

Here we can give an additional Husserlian interpretation of the term "epochē." As a professional, I suspend all judgments concerning every activity and work which is not mine. It is a matter of specialization and division of labor. However, Husserl always stressed that, although he was a scientist, he never ceased to be a man. If I do physics, my biological, precategorial, and psychological life is not thereby interrupted. I can say only that biological and psychological life are not themes of my investigation at that time. The time of my work can be the time in which I work in a factory or teach. But I remain a whole man in either case. Both cases are abstractions, but they are abstractions of an altogether special nature. They are categorial abstractions. They are working abstractions. The problem here is the following: can I, as a man and as a subject precategorially performing all of my operations from which the sciences originate, identify myself with my vocations, i.e., reduce myself to only the operations of a worker or professor? If I did that I would become an abstraction. I would be a strange abstraction because I would be an abstraction in flesh and blood that lives as if it were real.

In an ideal society I would be a professor and a worker by remaining a man. Therefore, I would never have to lose my precategorial integrity and I could maintain it in every phase of my vocation. This depends on me, but also on the society in which I live. As Marx says, society cannot force me to become an *abstract worker*, i.e., a concrete man who is forced to live as if he were abstract. From this viewpoint the concrete man is transcendental; it is the man who never becomes an instrument or an object for another man or society. When science and technology are considered as mere instruments, they lose their intentionality unless they are engaged in the constitution of a rational human society in which all men are subjects and not objects. Thus, both science and technology become objectified, i.e., they turn man into an *object*. But science and technology become the means of realization of the human *telos* when, in their specific fields, they multiply human possibilities, free man from slavery, and adapt themselves to the causality of nature in order to dominate it, in order to turn it into a body that man and humanity can use as their own. The planet Earth is this body-proper of humanity that Husserl has indicated in the manuscripts D 17 and D 18.

Humanity free from wars and with the help of a technology which is its own, i.e., in a situation in which, for each man, his own work is his path to self-realization, is a concrete, rational, living, and transcendental humanity.

Therefore, the struggle against objectification is a struggle to bring technology back to man in order to free technology from alienation and return it to its foundation and intentionality or, in a word, its transcendental subjectivity. This implies in principle and in essence a *positive evaluation of technology* that coincides with the meanings of truth of the life of man and his task in history. Technology is not in itself negative; it is negative only in the historical situation typified by the atomic bomb. It is because of this that we are in crisis and need a radical transformation of man according to the spirit of philosophical radicalism that Husserl defended.

[42]   *The Struggle against the*
        Alienated Use of the Sciences
        in Order to Regain the Meaning of Man

ALTHOUGH THE VIENNA LECTURE OF MAY, 1935 ("Philosophy and the Crisis of European Humanity") is the best-known text included in *The Crisis of European Sciences,* it is neither the clearest nor the most fundamental. The lecture was only the pretext that led Husserl to write the true *Crisis,* the one that we have tried to analyze and reconstruct from the beginning, i.e., the part that develops the Prague lecture of November, 1935 ("The Crisis of European Sciences and Psychology"). Immediately after writing the two lectures, Husserl began to elaborate and rewrite the two texts, thus giving birth to the work which he never finished. The main problem bothering Husserl can be expressed as follows: how is it that all the universal operations that constitute the sciences and form philosophy are born in a particular place at a determined time, i.e., in ancient Greece, to develop subsequently into the sciences and European philosophy? It is a question of a historical *matter of fact.*

Here Husserl faces historical factuality. To the extent that he is rational, man is essentially universal and transcendental, and rational humanity is subjective insofar as it is transcendental. Yet man is a physical and circumstantial object in the world. This is a paradox. Carried to its extreme consequences, it is the paradox mentioned in section 53 of the *Crisis* that reappears in the problematic relations of psychology and phenomenology and, subsequently, in the relations of psychology and the sciences. The radical character of the paradox, which is only indicated in the Vienna and Prague lectures, has led us to reconstruct and develop the *Crisis,* and to seek to fill in the fourth part of the work that was never written. We do this to indicate our own solutions regarding the unity of the sciences. These are solutions which pose the problem of the foundation of political economy and the possibility of a human society where every man is a subject. In such a society the alienation that reduces man to a thing (*Verdinglichung*) has been overcome. It thus becomes a society *which has the planet Earth as its own body.* Consequently, Husserl's "objectification" becomes alienation. It becomes connected to the socioeconomic historical situation and demands a change of man that would lead him to the level of a radical, universal—and therefore intentional—humanism.

The proposed solution is not exactly what Husserl had in mind. What is important for us, however, is that it seems to be required by the internal coherence of his thought, by the elaboration and development of the internal problems of phenomenology. Yet, as we have attempted to show, it would be wrong to say that Husserl has given us no indications of the path we have attempted to tread.

For example, it is true that Husserl speaks of a teleology which is properly European (p. 274 [The Vienna lecture is translated as Appendix I of the English edition of *Crisis*]). But it is also true that, for him, European teleology, the goal attainable only through the constitution of a rational human society, is an implicit goal of all humanity. When Husserl fights naturalism, he wants to fight a biological or zoological conception of history. Husserl writes that "there is, for essential reasons, no zoology of peoples" (p. 275). Thus he is led to stress the "spiritual" value of Europe which is, however, also the spiritual value of a rational humanity, i.e., the spiritual value of the sciences that have lost their intentionality and the value of philosophy.

Certainly, we must depart from ourselves and from "our nation," but "the historical continuity leads us further and further from our nation to neighboring nations, and thus from nation to nation, from one time to the next" (p. 274). "Ourselves" means us-as-men, as transcendental humanity, and as humanity divided into nations. In fact, there is a dialectic among nations and there has been a dialectic of master and slave. We must ask Husserl: Is this dialectic permanent or temporary? There is no doubt that he would answer that it is temporary. This is why he speaks of a crisis and of the possibility of overcoming it. The crisis "is not an obscure fate, an impenetrable destiny; rather, it becomes understandable and transparent against the background of the *teleology of European history* that can be discovered philosophically" (p. 299). What kind of enlightenment is it? What is involved is understanding that Europe is not a zoological or naturalistic fact. It is not anthropological in the naturalistic sense. In addition to being a fact, it is a *concept*.

> In order to be able to comprehend the disarray of the present "crisis," we had to work out the *concept of Europe as the historical teleology of the infinite goals of reason;* we had to show how the European "world" was born out of ideas of reason, i.e., out of the spirit of philosophy. The "crisis" could then become distinguishable as the *apparent failure of rationalism.* The reason for the failure of a rational culture, however, as we said, lies not in the essence of rationalism itself but solely in its being rendered superficial, in its entanglement in "naturalism" and "objectivism." [P. 299]

Objectivism is the degradation of the subject to the level of the object, the *reversal of the subjective into the objective.* In this sense, it is the alienation of man, and we shall see that this is how alienation appears in Marx. Within Husserl's limitations, however, the paradox is this: while Europe had the rational mission of constituting a subjective society, not only has Europe in fact forgotten its task, but it has ended up by doing the opposite. In fact, Europe is not simply a renouncer: it is "sick" (p. 270). Why? The answer Husserl offers in the *Crisis* is this: Europe has used the sciences and philosophy for ends other than those for which they were meant. The sciences and technology have become instruments for naturalizing man, for rendering man into an objectified thing. We can elaborate Husserl's thought as follows: the sciences and technology have been used by Europe for the exploitation of man and for world domination, while they were intended—in terms of their essence—to liberate humanity and to pursue "infinite rational goals" according to the teleology immanent in the meaning of truth of men and the history of man.

Since the sciences have been misused to dominate man, it has been possible to believe in the failure of the sciences and philosophy, *that is,* in the failure of *rationalism.* But it is not rationalism that has failed. The failure consists in the *misuse of the sciences,* i.e., the naturalism that renders man into a thing and an object. This is the true crisis of the sciences, which is subsequently the crisis of human existence. The crisis must be fought by returning his subjectivity, his rational intentionality, and, therefore, the proper use of the sciences, to man. Because of this, all of the *Crisis* can be interpreted as a struggle against naturalism understood as the alienated use of the sciences. This is a struggle that wants to give man back his meaning. The true title of the *Crisis* should have been: *The Struggle against the Alienated Use of the Sciences in Order to Regain the Meaning of Man, His Society, and His History.*

[43]   *The Style of Temporal Causality and Historicism*

To pose the spiritual problem of Europe, Husserl has had to face the problem of the historical genesis of the sciences and philosophy, and of the relation of the natural and social sciences. This explains the themes of the two dissertations of 1928 and 1930 which have the respective titles, "Idealization and the Science of Reality—The Mathematization of Nature," and "The Attitude of Natural Science and the Attitude of Humanistic Science, Naturalism, Dualism, and Psychophysical Psychology."

In the manuscripts, Husserl has gone over the themes of these two dissertations many times, and sometimes in very different, if not altogether opposed, ways. We see these themes in a new guise in the Vienna lecture and, ultimately, in the *Crisis* itself. But we know that such a line leads to the problem of the unity of the sciences and the unity of man, a theme that can be investigated through a reading of *Ideen II* inspired by the investigations of the *Crisis*. The relation of the natural and the social sciences is encountered with the problem of psychology and, in our reconstruction and development of the themes of the *Crisis*, leads to the problem of the foundation of political economy. Yet Husserl speaks of pure "spirituality" in the Vienna lecture. It is important to note that "the human spirit, after all, is grounded on the human *physis*" (p. 271), and that Husserl stresses the fact that culture, if it is not naturalized, remains bound to the precategorial environment. In other words, we must not study culture in the same way that we study biology and zoology. Because of this, Husserl also stresses the specific character of the social sciences (*Geisteswissenschaften*). However, this does not mean that the various cultures are not bound to nature, or that scientific theories of nature are not bound to the historical process (p. 354). Spirituality cannot be studied as if it were a body of mathematical physics. Yet, as we have seen in *Ideen II* and as Husserl repeats, the psychic and spiritual animated life is not only conditioned, but is determined, by the precategorial causality of matter. "For animal spirituality, that of human and animal 'souls,' to which all other spirituality must be traced back, is individually, *causally* founded in corporeity" (p. 271; emphasis added).

Precategorial causality is the fundamental theme of *Ideen II*, and it continually reappears in Husserl's manuscripts. It is a problem connected with many others and, at times, is treated with extraordinary clarity. In some manuscripts the analysis is derailed by a sudden obfuscation of the investigation and, in extreme cases, there is a storm in which Husserl himself is lost.

The manuscript K III 13, published as Beilage I of the *Crisis*, is very important. In it we find good examples of Husserl's extraordinary ability to interconnect various themes. Thus, we read: "Physical corporeality is always causally and inductively interwoven in its surrounding-world givenness as a concrete living thing, as the body of men and animals, and as plant organisms." [1] Things, animals, and men are typical, even if new types can come about: they are therefore knowable in their typical existence. This is the theme of the analysis of the essences and eidetic phenomenology. However, the essences are not things, and things are real precisely because they are bound to a causal necessity.

Precategorial causality is "lived" and extends itself in time. For Husserl, it has "a historical style." Reality bound by causes, time, and historical style is also togetherness and agreement. Men and things live in a reciprocal nexus. The exact categorial causality of the sciences arises from lived precategorial causality.

1. E. Husserl, *Die Krisis der europäischen Wissenschaften und die transzendentale Phänomenologie: Eine Einleitung in die phänomenologische Philosophie*, ed. Walter Biemel (1954; 2d printing, The Hague: Nijhoff, 1962), p. 349. [Henceforth we shall refer to both the Beilagen of the German edition and the appendixes of the English edition of the *Crisis*. As not all the Beilagen have been translated into English, and insofar as Professor Paci frequently refers to these, we shall have occasion to refer the reader to the original German text. We would like at this point to acknowledge Professor Wilhelm Halbfass for the invaluable aid he has given us in clarifying Husserl's frequently obscure German.]

Psychology wants to be constituted according to the exact causality of physics. But, as such, it forgets the causality of the *Lebenswelt*. It runs the risk of forgetting that there are not only causal dependences and conditionings, but also motivations. Are human relationships only causal relationships among things? "Nature is purely for itself a universe of real causality," but psychic life is not just an immediate relation of cause and effect. Causality "does not produce direct action in spatiotemporal distance." [2] Yet animated bodies influence each other even at a distance: e.g., with meaningful signs, or through language.

Furthermore, when I see something, I experience a whole series of visions and *phantasms* of the thing. Obviously, these phantasms are physical facts (light or sound waves), but they are also a mode of communication at a distance between myself and things. By themselves, phantasms are not reality, but I can use sounds and real gestures as signs, as means of communication. Causal facts become meaningful and man can express himself through phantasms, visual gestures, and heard sounds. Thus, a language comes about wherein my recollections, my experiences, and my human and scientific operations can be sedimented. At this point we are on the level of the psychic sphere whence it is possible to pass to the spiritual level.

History is time, but it uses signs in time. Passing history leaves its tracks and documents in which living persons who have lived in the past and whom I can re-present, reconstruct, and relive have been sedimented.

Causal reality, phantasms, time, communication, language, the community of present men, and the community and communion of actual men with those who have lived already—all of this becomes a problem. It is the problem of the psychological relation among men in time, and the problem of the structure of causal time. The problem of time also has a style and reveals itself as the structure of historical time in the connection of present, past, and future, between the forgotten and the awakening, and between the awaited and the projected. This temporal style of historical becoming gives us the permanent structures of becoming according to which becoming becomes or, as Husserl puts it in Appendix V, gives us the historical a priori.

2. *Ibid.*, p. 352.

Every fact occurs according to this a priori, and every a priori presupposes historical facts: Husserl explicitly mentions this paradox (p. 350). But he also resolves it: we can investigate the permanent structures of becoming even if these structures appear as facts. We are ourselves *facts*. But we can continually investigate ourselves and bring to light the structure of our person and all of its modifications. And we can do it because, for us, our being a fact is subjective life which departs from the clarity of the evidence and is ultimately constituted as intersubjective life. Thus, even though I have only direct access to documents and not the subjects that have left them, it is possible for me to understand and reconstruct the historical fact. I can do this by departing from the historical fact that I am for myself. Here, I am a fact that, in relation to the historical community and natural causality, I must continually clarify to myself.

In essence, man as subject is the possibility of historical clarification. Man is the being who is able to comprehend himself historically. This is part of his nature and the *nature of the world* in which the men of the past have also lived. "It must be shown, then, indeed as something belonging to the individual essence of man and thus to the world, that in mankind this capacity can never cease, can never be completely absent, even if it remains undeveloped for factual reasons" (p. 350).

Let us note that, by departing from the problem of real precategorial causality and following its thematizations, we have reached the problem of historicism and its foundation. Husserl says: It is the first time that this happens to me. That is, it is the first time that the problems that we have sought to clarify, including the problems of the essences, the phantasms, the sedimentation of signs and documents, appear to Husserl to be necessarily connected to the problem of history (p. 351). But, as we know, we can deal with this even in relation to the *Lebenswelt* and psychology. Consequently, given the nexuses submitted to a phenomenological analysis, it must be said that all of the preceding conditions are the problem of spirit. Spirit appears in its radical and essential communion with historical time and the meaning of historical time, and, therefore, with the meaning of man in history.

Already in Brentano, intentionality characterized the psychic phenomenon. Now it turns out to be the human ability to grasp essential structures and the connection of typical essences. Spirit becomes the possibility and ability to clarify and enlighten the factual, and transform it in terms of the clarification.

Perception understands itself in action by orienting itself toward a unity, allowing an agreement that appears as *telos* and meaning. For Husserl, this orientation is a *spiritual operation* that departs from precategorial causality and perception. The spiritual operation even gives a positive meaning to scientific idealization. But it finds its base in real things, in their phantasms, in their appearances. It "has its material in the 'thing-appearances,' the 'thing-representations'" (p. 348). In action, through the flux that aims toward unity, I am oriented toward an "ontically valid unity" (p. 349). In Husserl's language, this means "toward a meaning of truth." This is what man and the world already aim at in perception itself, and it is connected to the whole of the temporal flux. Now, in the same way that we still have the ability of historical self-understanding, we also have the ability of self-orientation toward a meaning of history, notwithstanding the crisis. Rather, the crisis reveals the meaning of history as the need for a radical historical change: as the regaining of intentionality against alienation. For Husserl, intentionality so conceived is the infinite movement of spirit whose goal is *truth*. In man, the evidence indicates his intentional ability and the inalienable possibility of regaining himself by departing from his own subjective presence in the first person. In this sense, intentionality is constitutive, infinite, and perennial. Husserl thinks that being is not immortal. What is immortal is the movement in the name of which being is negated as already given, already made, and as already constituted. Paradoxically, as meaning, the goal is a *negation* of being.

Seen in this context, and only in this context, Sartre's interpretation of intentionality appears very close to Husserl's spirit. Subjectivity is unavoidable. We must, therefore, necessarily depart from ourselves, and not do so by choice. We find subjectivity as a fact in ourselves. There we find the paradox of a subjective factuality in the first person. Subjective factuality is the center of clarification of every factuality. But the clarification is the negation of preconstituted and mundane being. Therefore, subjectivity is the negation of the mundane being of the mundane in favor of the meaning of truth. This negation appears to Husserl as the perennial structure of the intentional movement that is not being, but is self-transcendence for the meaning of being.

[44]   *The Meaning of the Immortality*
        of the Spirit. Phenomenology
        as the Religion of Truth

IN THE 1930 DISSERTATION, Husserl tries to see in
what sense the natural sciences fall within the social sciences
(*Geisteswissenschaften*), and he hints at the idea that the first
fall into the second to the extent that the latter are historical
sciences. As we know, what is historical for Husserl is based
upon the actual historical presence—upon present intersubjectivity. The point of departure is always we "who carry out the
universal consideration of persons, drawing into it the universal
consideration of the surrounding world" (p. 334). We are European, but we go beyond ourselves. Europe should have gone beyond itself by transcending itself and intending, as idea, the
meaning of a rational humanity. We again find history and intentionality connected here. The intentionality of meaning certainly has a theoretical character (p. 282). However, theory
must not be separated from practical life: it must give an ideal
direction to humanity, to the humanity

> which, in its concrete existence, lives first and always in the
> natural sphere. This occurs in the form of a new sort of praxis,
> that of the universal critique of all life and all life-goals, all cul-
> tural products and systems that have already arisen out of the life
> of man; and thus it also becomes a critique of mankind itself and
> of the values which guide it explicitly or implicitly. Further, it is a
> praxis whose aim is to elevate mankind through universal scien-
> tific reason, according to norms of truth of all forms, to transform
> it from the bottom up into a new humanity. [P. 283]

For Husserl, praxis must radically change humanity. But in
this change it must be guided by "universal scientific reason,"
i.e., by the idea of reason, the meaning of truth. The crisis originates in a contradiction and, therefore, in a *dialectical* situation.
This dialectical situation is changeable if the sciences do not
objectify man and if they once again find their intentionality.
This intentionality must aim not only at understanding history,
but also at changing it according to the idea of a rational society
and truth that must guide humanity.

In the previous considerations, the religious tone of phenom-

enology reappears. It is a tone in which scientificity and faith
coincide. From this viewpoint, "rational" religion is a criticism of
traditional religions and mythologies, in the same way that it is,
in general, a critique of all "cultural products and systems that
have already arisen out of the life of man." The relation between
renovation and tradition is dialectical: phenomenology inherits
the philosophies of the past, but it inherits them by criticizing
and renovating them. The various religions seek to arrive at a
sole truth felt in the many paths leading to it. The traditional
God becomes "the bearer of the absolute *logos*." From this viewpoint, the *logos* generates a critique of the "national Gods
[which are] . . . there without question, as real facts in the
surrounding world" (pp. 288–89).

For Husserl, God ultimately turns out to be the idea and the
life of truth. It has no reality in itself. If man and humanity
transcend themselves in a rational idea, this is ultimately a
limiting idea and not a reality. Here, we once again find intentionality as "consciousness of something" essential but not real
(recall the tree that does not burn). The final truth is not a
being and is not conquerable. It is the meaning of the world and
being, but it is not being. It gives life to being, but it gives the
life of truth and not mundane life. Truth lives in intentional
life, i.e., in the self-overcoming, and it is the principle and the
unreal point of arrival of intentionality in which the world goes
beyond itself. To the extent that it has a meaning, Husserl's position here is paradoxical. It should be noted that what is important for Husserl is the prevention of the reduction of the final
truth into real mundane being. Again, his struggle is a struggle
against fetishization and *idolatry*. In essence, man can exhaust
neither God nor truth. If phenomenology is a science of being-
existing-for-truth, a science of the *cogito* which always surpasses
itself in the *cogitatum,* the idea that allows phenomenology to
comprehend the existence that always surpasses itself in truth
is analogous to the idea of God. It is the "pure idea of divinity,"
or, better yet, divinity as pure idea.[3] Although Husserl is not
clear in his rare considerations about the theological problem, it
seems that for him God turns out to be the *intentionality of the
meaning that gives meaning to being*. Essentially, since truth as
the meaningful direction of being can never be possessed, intentionality is infinite and its goal is unreachable. The goal has
always been, is, and always will be present as a demand in the

3. Manuscript F 1 14, p. 43.

world; but it is not the world. It is the meaning of truth that is inexhaustible in the world. The inexhaustible demand is such that the movement is perennial and the *becoming immortal*. This is why Husserl writes that "only spirit is immortal." Spirit is the infinity of the movement by which the world transcends itself toward its meaning of truth, toward the intentional ideal of scientificity. This position cannot be called spiritualistic, since truth is precisely the truth of man, the world, and matter. Conversely, it cannot be said to be materialistic, since, in Husserl, even matter continually surpasses itself.

In reality, both materialism and spiritualism are theories, while phenomenology is not a theory but an original experience without which no theory would be possible. The foundation itself as religious intentionality is always in us, in our subjectivity, in the actuality of our presence in which the other subjects are constituted. In addition, history is constituted by departing from the actuality of our presence.

11 / The Dialectic of Language and the Foundation of History

[45]   *Linguistic Sedimentation,*
the Living Body of Language (Sprachleib),
and Technology

WE HAVE SEEN THAT, if it is true that animated bodies
are bound to a causal style, then they can also communicate at
a distance by using, for example, visual perceptions as signs.
This and similar behavior make language possible, along with
the sedimentation of the actual presence in a permanent physi-
cal-causal reality and the fixation of this presence in a document.
This fixation is somewhat similar to the consolidation of the
past in us. It is in its becoming sedimented life in our organism
from which we can illuminate and render presence once again.
But this is a presence that now lives as a memory. Considerations of this kind are already familiar to Husserl in 1904 in the
period of the lectures on internal time-consciousness. Along with
the phenomenological analyses of 1907, they reveal an unpublished phenomenology which is present (although perhaps unrecognizable) in the main works which Husserl published in his
lifetime. In explicating the *Crisis,* we have kept in mind this
usually ignored phenomenology. But the very development of the
Crisis, as it was prepared for publication, allows for various deviations and for the development of themes that have remained
implicit. The whole theme of the origin of mathematical physics
in Galileo, and that of the precategorial origins of geometry,
could have been treated in a different fashion in order to illuminate unsuspected aspects of the problem, e.g., those regarding language and technology. Good examples of this may be

found in the essay on the "Origin of Geometry," published as Appendix VI of the *Crisis*.

The thematization is complex. Here, the problem of the *Crisis* is seen from a new angle, as in the analysis of the "thing" that appears differently as a function of vicinity and distance, and the movements and temporal modifications (the thing that I have seen yesterday, that I have forgotten, that I remember, that I am looking forward to seeing tomorrow, as identical or changed, according to a different consideration of what surrounds and determines it in a complex *circumstantiality*).

What always remains present in the background is the major theme of phenomenology: time.

The problem of the origin of geometry is a general historical-temporal problem. Yet geometry is here, in my world and cultural environment. It has been founded by certain human operations. It has been *transmitted* to me. An operation that was presence while being performed is still here, but no longer as a present operation. Rather, it is here as a complex of signs and techniques in which it has been sedimented in order to be repeated an infinite number of times, even if we have forgotten the original operations. A presence can therefore become fixed and reach me in this fashion. It can be repeated in the techniques that reproduce it without losing any result—even if the original operations have been forgotten. Now, in order to grasp the meaning of geometry, and maybe even new meanings, I must rediscover the original operations and make them once again present and living. However, it is also true that the presence that was once alive and founded must reach me and be transmitted. In order to do so, it must become sedimented and be repeatable as if it were embodied in me.

Technology is an embodiment of the founding operations: they become "automatic." I no longer need to found and discover them as in the first time. Paradoxically, automation, which is repetition, is also the possibility of turning constitutive subjective operations into "natural" ones. Husserl discovers the function of sedimentation and technology and, what is more important, the function of the complex and yet natural operations which we repeat every day when we talk. The problem of the foundation of the sciences appears to be closely connected to the problem of the language which is transmitted and repeated through linguistic sedimentations and which I live as present, as actual, as if it were mine. The relation between physical signs (sedimentation) and living language seems to be analogous to the relation between the causal style and active psychic life, between real things and the subjective life of my body, between the chain of conditioning and spontaneity, and between matter and spirit.

As we know, all these relations are inevitably in the temporal flux, in intersubjective relations, and in the relations between subjectivity and things. Language is a complex of signs that involves a life. This life has been present and is now imprisoned in language. Nevertheless, it can always be freed and become present once again, since, with the signs, it is given to us by tradition. Language becomes sedimented and is transformed into a dead body which, however, can be revitalized into what it was when it was presence. All of this occurs through the continual sedimentations and the continual awakening, even though it is changed and renewed. This is because it is I as a subject who do all of this. Language becomes my own body which is preserved and transcended. It becomes my *own linguistic body (Sprachleib)*.

Husserl vaguely indicates that this problem is bound to the problem of technology. In order to understand the connection, we must point out that in technology I face something which is not mine but which I must appropriate in the same way that I face and appropriate an already established language. For instance, I contain "nature" and I must make myself nature in order to make it mine, so that it will no longer be foreign to me and I can dominate it. I must become nature myself and subsequently transform nature into my own body, through a technology that extends my body and, by means of instruments, gives it new perceptions, new visions, new faculties, and new abilities.

In the same way that language transforms physical signs into meaningful signs, the transmitted language into my own language and into the language of actual intersubjectivity, so technology gradually transforms nature into an extension of my organic-inorganic body. Ultimately, it transforms nature into an intersubjectivity whereby technology is a means used not to reduce other subjects into objects but into a rational society of subjects. It is the whole of the planet Earth which, through technology, becomes the body-proper (*Leib*) of humanity. We shall see that Marx speaks of nature as the inorganic body of man in precisely this sense. This entails technology's positive function, its active life, and its intentionality. At the same time, this entails repetition and the mechanical transmission that contraposes human technology to man, as when the language that we speak is radically misunderstood and what I say is immediately reduced to what is already established. Consequently, I-myself, as a concrete and living man, become reduced to a state where I can no longer talk. Language becomes external to me as if my body no longer belonged to me and were to become the property of a fixed and immutable tradition constituted once and for all. The struggle against the misuse of science is also the struggle against the misuse of technology. Furthermore, the struggle against the misuse of technology is also the struggle against the misuse of language: it is the struggle against objectified and alienated language.

Language's temporal, intersubjective, and historical problem is a *dialectical* one, and we already find it in the Marx of the *German Ideology*. The problem of technology also turns out to be dialectical. The appropriation of technology to prevent subjects from being expropriated in their work and to make sure that technology once again becomes the property of the living subjects, e.g., to ensure that the means of communication and exchange, such as commodities, do not become fetishized crystallizations of subjective operations—this is the struggle for the regaining of intentionality of technology, science, and human activity. Even for technology it is a return to the root, to the things-themselves—and for man, the root is man himself.

[46]   *The Evidence of the Functional Result.*
         Language as Intersubjective Life in Action
         and as the Sprachleib *of Humanity*

FOR HUSSERL, to pose the problem of the origin of geometry means to inquire "into the submerged original beginnings of geometry" (p. 354). It is important to go back to the origin by departing from the established geometry which we know and which has been transmitted to us. "Our human existence moves within innumerable traditions" (p. 354), and each tradition "is open . . . to continued inquiry" (p. 355). There must have been a first productive act (by now assimilated and forgotten) from which the present living culture has arisen. From that first act, geometry comes down to us, proceeding in its own way in a continual synthesis toward the future. There must have been a first spiritual operation. The term "spiritual" here indicates a concrete operation which "proceeding from its first project to its execution is present for the first time in the self-evidence of actual success" (p. 356). For example, the linguistic-spiritual operation originally "creates" the language by making it its living body and by identifying the physical operation—the sound—with what the sound indicates. The spirit is in its linguistic body (*Sprachleib*). The forthcoming realization is evident precisely in its coming forth, and here Husserl gives an operational definition of evidence as *evidence of the result*. "Successful realization of a project is, for the acting subject, self-evidence; in this self-evidence, what has been realized is there, *originaliter*, as itself" (p. 356).

This evidence of the result of an operation can always be repeated if the same operation is performed anew in different times and by different subjects. In this sense, the result is an intersubjective operation that constitutes an objective world (the geometric world), since it is valid for everyone. This objective world can be obtained again by all possible subjects that make geometrical space their "own" by making their "own body" the specifically spatial existence of geometry. The existence of geometrical forms as idealizations is obtained through operations which are precategorial precisely because they lead to categorial abstractions. Husserl forgets to clarify some important points that he has mentioned in the *Crisis* and various manuscripts. The operating subjects are concrete monads precategorially existing in space and time where they perform their operations. Thus, the surveyor who uses idealized figures to measure the field that has now become an exact figure, or that has been divided into exact figures, already exists in the *Lebenswelt* and its spatiotemporal causal nexuses. These nexuses are given to him before the idealization as figures which are not yet exact but are susceptible to idealization. The field is not exactly divided into perfect squares. By surveying and measuring its surface, I perform the operations that lead me to squares that "correspond" to the field. These squares give me the size of the field precisely because I have performed my operations on the field and in the whole precategorial world in which I live. By themselves, the squares are the products of a spiritual operation. Yet I have performed this spiritual operation by walking with my body on the Earth. The result is idealized because I have thematized only space by departing from precategorial causal spatiotemporality.

If I look at the result I will have an "ideal objectivity." If I relive the operations, this objectivity will once again have its original body as its own body, my measuring actions, and the Earth. The square that I have discovered is an ideal square. The operations that have founded it have been real the first time and will be real every time that they are performed again. Husserl himself notices this and, in a different context, speaks of "actual, original activity" (p. 365).

Once founded, the ideal square has the property of being always self-identical. I can fix it in a physical sign and draw it. As an idealized object it will always be the same square. Language fixes and sediments the result which can be transmitted even if the operations that have founded it are forgotten. Yet, by discovering these operations, I can perform them again, thus giving back to the sedimented ideal result its concrete body in the operations that have constituted it. Geometry "is identically the same in the 'original language' of Euclid and in all 'translations'; and within each language it is again the same, no matter how many times it has been sensibly uttered" (p. 357). The manifestations are always signs, and they exist in the world as physical bodily facts: but it is the same ideal form expressed in the various bodily facts. The same is true of all the words of a language. They are derived from an original operation that I no longer need to perform when I repeat the same words. But how can the subjective operation of ideality, e.g., of a square, be expressed in such a way as to fix its ideality, thus giving it its body, i.e., the body of an ideal result? This body comes about through the operations. However, the result is sensibly expressed in the idealized figure of the field that I can draw on paper.

The gesture whereby for the first time I indicate a thing, the *gesture for that thing*, the sound that expresses the thing not once but an infinite number of times by always expressing the same thing, expresses an idealization. The word "lion" obtains for all lions. In its self-repetition, it is the expression of a class of animals, i.e., of an ideality. Here the word appears as the linguistic sedimentation of the first subjective operation and of the correlative idea intended by that operation. Each time the idealization is expressed, it refers precisely to the real lion: the idea is filled by *its* body, and it is pronounced by *my* body. Although ideal, the idealization refers to a reality, even if the lion is not in front of me right now and it is the lion that someone else has originally seen. The first vision has been sedimented. It is transmitted as such, and each time that I pronounce the words again the sedimentation is awakened, the language becomes alive; it becomes the linguistic body-proper. This linguistic body allows a specific communication among subjects removed in space and time. It allows the communication because a man has first spoken to another man, and the latter has understood him, whereby both the first and the second will henceforth use the same words. Language therefore proves that a relation with the other not only is possible, but *has already happened:* the language that I speak is the result of a coupling, of an *Einfühlung* which has already taken place, has been fixed and sedimented. I can learn the language because I pronounce the *Einfühlung,* because I make the language into *my* words, thus making them into my *Sprachleib.*

All of this is connected with the themes of the chain of generations and the theme of my living again the first *Einfühlung* [1] with the mother. Language is connected with the constitution of the other and my self-constituting *in* the other. It is my mother who speaks to me and transforms the *given* transmitted *langue* into a language that I pronounce for the first time. In de Saussure's terms, here we have the transition between the collective language and my subjective language, between the *langue* and the *parole.* [2] The language is transmitted in the concatenation of generations and it transmits to us the life of those who have used it, since the *parole,* through the *langue,* once again becomes *parole* in me. "In this sense civilization is, for every man whose we-horizon it is, a community of those who can reciprocally express themselves" (p. 359). "Thus men as men, fellow men, world—the world of which men, of which we, always talk and can talk—and, on the other hand, language, are inseparably intertwined; and one is always certain of their inseparable relational unity" (p. 359).

For Husserl, language *is not the word of being but the word of subjects* who always live in the world, experience the world, and communicate with one another precisely in terms of the subjective foundation which transcends itself in the truth of words, in their embodiment in the *Sprachleib,* in their sedimentation and awakening: in the continual passage between *langue* and *parole.*

The linguistic community, "the empathic community," can always found the language anew in each of its subjects. What has been alive in me and is now forgotten can be recalled and represented. What has been alive for him who has left me a writing of his, the sedimentation of his living language, becomes alive for me once again if, departing from the idealized words, from the sedimented language of a poem, I can go back to the operations that have produced that poem and make them mine,

1. Manuscript K III 11; also see my *Diario Fenomenologico* (Milan: Il Saggiatore, 1961), p. 106.
2. Ferdinand de Saussure, *Course in General Linguistics,* trans. Wade Baskin (New York: McGraw-Hill, 1966), pp. 13–14, 19.

in the same way that the author of the poem could say that they
were his, or as if they had been mine and I had forgotten them
and now I have remembered them anew, thus removing them
from oblivion.

Husserl is interested in language as intersubjective experience
in action. What I say when I talk is not only mine; it belongs to
each subject who, like myself, speaks my language. If I fix the
word in a sign, each subject will be able to turn this sign into his
word. He must do so if he wants to understand the documents of
the past and make them his own. Ultimately, language is the
Sprachleib of all those who have spoken it, speak it, and will
speak it. On a more profound level, each language goes back to a
gesture, to a sound, or to a *phoneme*. This is what makes translations possible between all of the languages of the planet Earth.
In its primordial origin, the *Sprachleib* belongs to the whole of
humanity precisely because each *langue* is originally *parole;* a
subjective operation. To translate and comprehend means to rediscover the common founding operations, the humanity of every
language, the operative unity of the very act of talking. On the
phenomenological level, here we encounter Wilhelm von Humboldt's great insights. The origin is, historically, the first operation. Yet, in each subject, the origin is always *his* actual origin.
To rediscover the first operation that has been transmitted, to
question the tradition that I have within me, means, paradoxically, to discover myself. In myself I discover those who have
been and who have spoken, transmitted, and renovated the language in the same way that I, precisely when I receive it, make it
mine and renew it. In linguistic commerce, sedimentation is
what permits discourse and the exchange of words. But words
are not fetishized commodities. They are the living products of
living men. They are processed and produced by subjectivity: in
expressing them, every individual makes them words of all of
humanity.

[47]   *Language and the Precategorial*
        Foundation of the Economy.
        Technology and Human Emancipation

LANGUAGE HAS A HISTORICAL ORIGIN. It has become
sedimented. However, it can exist a second time as origin. I rediscover the origin of the past by reliving in myself the *langue* as

parole, by reliving the collective codified language as the language that is born and originates in me. The first and the second origin are historically removed. What separates them is the forgetting of language and its present rediscovery. There have been interruptions, in the same way that my life is interrupted by sleep and the life of humanity is interrupted by individual deaths. The awakening of the forgotten language is a special mode of communication between me and those who lived before. It is a coupling and a communion between myself and the dead, rendered possible by sedimentation, by the self-fixing of evidence in a technique, and by the reactivation of the evidence that allows other subjects to live through me. Even prior to my coming into being, I was present as a receiver for those who spoke and expressed themselves in subsequently sedimented expressions. In order to become alive once again, these expressions presuppose that I today perform the operations transmitted from a faraway world to the world in which I live. This is what renders possible permanence and becoming, the transmission of an exact expression and its renewal. Sleep and death separate me from the past, along with the matter which embodies the spiritual operations that I subsequently relive. Matter, signs, phantasms, and visions make possible communication at a distance, the overcoming of solipsism, the perennial and always-new life of intersubjectivity among subjects. Sedimentation takes place in matter: expressive life becomes inert. But the opaque inertia which, like sleep and death, separates me from those who have been and those who will be, is also what unites me to them. What is once again coming to the fore is the problem of materialism and the positive function of sedimentation and technology that Husserl should have stressed more than he did. Relations between man and man, and between man and precategorial nature, are impossible without technology. An intersubjective society cannot be constituted without technology. Man can reject the function of the intersubjective foundation made possible by technology. In this case, however, communication would absorb man, and technology would alienate him from himself. The other positive side of technology, however, is that only through matter and sedimentation in matter can all men constitute a unique intersubjectivity.

In order to talk to the child, the mother must come down to its level: she must reduce the *langue* to a gesture or sound. In order to work with matter, the worker must use his own body as an instrument. In order to be transmitted and progress, science must become embodied in precise formulae in the same way that poetry becomes embodied in words, rhythms, and unchanging accents. In order to constitute a free society of subjects, man must work and extend himself through his technical instruments. He must substitute the subjective ownership of the means of work and production for the work of slaves in which man is objectivized and alienated from man. Reduced to itself, technology takes life and meaning away from man when it annihilates the goal and is used to produce alienation. Used intentionally, technology becomes a means of human emancipation and can become an expression of man's personality. As praxis, sedimentation and technology are activities that do something today in order to obtain something else tomorrow. The peasant tills the land in order to nourish himself with the goods that it produces. We are in the domain of precategorial economic operations, upon which political economy as a science can be founded. A kind of intentionality operates in this domain: the intentionality *for something* that will be there tomorrow if I work for it today as a means to an end, to reach according to a causal-historical style that leads man back to nature and frees him from nature through labor and causal precategorial necessity. Ultimately, technology and labor will have to stop being means and become the satisfaction of a need. The problem of sedimentation implies the relation between subjects in space and time: the problem of the communion of subjects in history. Language is a sedimented praxis that renders reactivation possible. The renovation of meaning implies not only the problem of the body-proper but also that of material nature, technology, and labor. These in turn imply the problem of the precategorial economic structure of the *Lebenswelt*, and the problem of the subjective and intersubjective founding economic operations according to fundamental structural modalities that Husserl never investigated. This new phenomenological clarification reveals that the precategorial causal structure is also a precategorial economic structure constituted according to the relation "if I do *A* now, I will obtain *B* later." It implies the complex relation between means and ends, the possibility that the means are means for the ends, and the possibility of the alienation or annihilation of the end by the means. Along with science, technology must rediscover its own historical intentionality, its own function as a means of emancipation for the foundation of a society of subjects in the renewal of intersubjective relations. Even if he did not deal with technology and labor, Husserl discovered the original problem as the problem of the his-

torical foundation by studying the problem of the origin of geometry and language.

[48] *Evidence as Historical Operations and the Concrete Historical A Priori*

THE INVESTIGATION concerning the origin of geometry
leads Husserl to the original historical foundation. In the present,
I discover the past origin within me. In fact, I do not choose to do
so but must always begin from the present. The present discovers
within itself, now, the real past that has preceded it, and in the
actual origin it recognizes and re-presents the past origin. What is
original and primordial is myself, the concrete unavoidable subject. The evidence, relived and refounded, is discovered as the
evidence of the present that has now passed, in the evidence of
the actual present. The *synchronic* intersubjectivity of the present
finds within itself the real preceding *diachronic* structures that
have permitted the synchronic presence. In the case of the
sciences, the evidence appears in a long chain of sedimented
evidences and in the actual evidence that it contains and rediscovers. Evidence turns out to be not only temporal *qua* presence,
but also essentially "historical" (p. 369).

In its most precise sense, genetic phenomenology is historical.
The problems, the investigations aiming at clarification, the
evident intuitions of principle, are everywhere historical. We are
in the horizon of the humanity within which we now live. This
living horizon is constantly present to our consciousness: as a
temporal horizon, it is implicit in each of our present horizons.

> To the one human civilization there corresponds essentially the
> one cultural world as the surrounding life-world with its [peculiar]
> manner of being; this world, for every historical period and civili-
> zation, has its particular features and is precisely the tradition.
> We stand, then, within the historical horizon in which everything
> is historical, even though we may know very little about it in a
> definite way. But it has its essential structure that can be revealed
> through methodical inquiry. [P. 369]

I begin with myself as the unique operating subject and with
other cooperating subjects, but I rediscover the past.

> The whole of the cultural present, understood as a totality, "im-
> plies" the whole of the cultural past in an undetermined but

structurally determined generality. To put it more precisely, it
implies a continuity of pasts which imply one another, each in
itself being a past cultural present. And this whole continuity is
a *unity* of traditionalization up to the present, which is our present
as [a process of] traditionalizing itself in a flowing-static vitality.
[P. 371]

We must remember that it is in the present that I find the real
past that has preceded me. Similarly, it is in the present that the
unity becomes a multiplicity: the unique operative ego as intersubjectivity. What all this means is that original experience
becoming permanent in history is precategorial life that makes
itself historical by departing each time from the present. It ultimately refers to the intersubjective foundation that has its own
structure and can investigate it: it is the problem that Husserl
indicates as the *concrete historical a priori* (p. 372). History is
not categorial historiography, and history is always founded by
the subjects in the nexus of matter, nature, work, language, and
real communicative commerce. Since history is so founded, it has
an intentionality and meaning. The fact was, is, and becomes
meaningful. Fact and meaning are extended in the dialectic of
time and truth, and their fundamental structural modalities are
sedimentation and awakening, tradition and renovation.

"We can also say now that history is from the start nothing
other than the vital movement of the coexistence and the inter-
weaving of original formations and sedimentations of meaning"
(p. 371). In other words, history is the subjective concrete functioning in its intersubjective communication and exchange. It is
the value of human functioning. It is not the degeneration of
labor to exchangeable objectifications, i.e., to the level of *commodities*. We, the concrete and transcendental functioning subjects, are at the base. Each and every one of us as men is a
transcendentally functioning subject who can reciprocally alienate or radically transform himself in becoming conscious of the
crisis obtaining in praxis by living in the world according to the
historical meaning of truth. Philosophy, science, culture, and institutions are all human products: they should not be extraneous
objects turned against men. We are the subjects of historicity, the
persons who create culture and function in the totality: the personal functioning humanity. We are the active men that transmit
and renew ourselves dialectically in our own structures, which
are also cultural, anthropological, and social structures in the
same way that language is sign and meaning, real operation and

intentional direction, sedimentation and living linguistic body, i.e., the *Sprachleib* of humanity.

We are in the world because we are subjects, and we give an orientation to anthropology, sociology, and history. Past and present cultures obtain through living intersubjectivity. The magic world of the primitives functions like European rationality. (In these years, 1935–36, Husserl reads Lévy-Bruhl and becomes interested in the problem of primitives.) In Husserl there is an indubitable connection between the problems of language, anthropology, and sociology. The problem of the genesis that, in turn, is the problem of physical matter and of living matter and, in general, the problem of nature, is at the base of this connection. All the indicated precategorial structures are part of the *Lebenswelt*. The regional ontologies of anthropology, sociology, and linguistics, and even those of physics, biology, etc., derive from the *Lebenswelt*. The problem of language turns out to be a formulation of the problem of the unity of the sciences—the unity rooted in the evidence considered as historical operations and as the subjective foundation which is constitutive of the structure of the universal historical a priori.

In our reconstruction we have attempted to show the internal coherence of Husserl's analysis in order to indicate the fundamental reasons why the analysis of language becomes transformed into the problem of the subjective foundation, the problem of the presence, and the concrete and individual *parole* of the precategorial and intentional-historical structure. Here, "structure" means: living-subjective and intersubjective experience, the natural and historical reality of subjects which contain the world within themselves and experience it along with its causal style, and the meaning of truth of humanity that lives and is temporally constituted.

[49]   *The Phenomenological Foundation
        of Linguistics and the Connection
        between Linguistics and Anthropology*

THE FUNDAMENTAL REASONS why the problem of language leads necessarily to the problem of concrete men living in the natural and historical world—the problem which explicates the relation between the unique functioning ego and intersubjectivity—constitute, and have constituted for some time, the basis of linguistics. As indicated, the Husserlian treatment of the problem of language as the relation between the operating ego and intersubjectivity is reminiscent of Wilhelm von Humboldt, who perfectly well understood the nature of the relation between the speaking subject and the language constituted in tradition— what reappears in de Saussure, with different intentions, as the relation between *parole* and *langue*.

In his major essay "On the Differences in Human Linguistic Structure and Their Influence on the Spiritual Development of the Human Race," von Humboldt writes: "Language is deeply enmeshed in the spiritual development of mankind. It accompanies it at every level of its current progress or lag." [3] To the extent that they are subjective and individual, languages are free, but "bound to and dependent on the national groups which speak them." [4] Language has an internal and an external aspect: "The production of language is an inner need of mankind, not merely an external vehicle for the maintenance of communication, but an indispensable one which lies in human nature." [5] Let us recall for a moment the problem of intersubjectivity and the problem of linguistic commerce. Von Humboldt's "human nature" is, in Husserl, the concrete and transcendental subject: it is the *Ich-Mensch* and, as an unavoidable subjectivity, the physical reality and the intentional meaning of language. Von Humboldt does not stop with a naïve dualism of the internal and the external, but intuits what in *Ideen II* appears as the point of trans-

3. Wilhelm von Humboldt, "On the Differences in Human Linguistic Structure and Their Influence on the Spiritual Development of the Human Race," in *Humanist without Portfolio: An Anthology of the Writings of Wilhelm von Humboldt,* trans. Marianne Cowan (Detroit: Wayne State University Press, 1963), p. 254. It is likely that Husserl had read von Humboldt, given the suggestions found in A. Marty, *Über den Ursprung der Sprach* (Würzburg: A. Stuber, 1875). [Professor Paci refers to the Italian translation of this paper, in Wilhelm von Humboldt, *Scritti di Estetica,* trans. Marcovaldi (Florence: G. C. Sansoni, 1934). The English text cited here contains only a partial translation of von Humboldt's essay. For the complete original, see Wilhelm von Humboldt, *Gesammelte Schriften,* 17 vols. (Berlin: Deutsche Akademie der Wissenschaften, 1903–25), "Über die Verschiedenheiten des menschlichen Sprachbaues und ihren Einfluss auf die geistige Entwicklung des Menschengeschlechts," in VII, 1–344.]

4. Von Humboldt, "On the Differences," p. 255.

5. *Ibid.,* p. 258.

formation and reciprocal insertion of the internal and the external (*Umschlagspunkt*). This is the point of insertion localized in the *Leib* which in turn is founded in real precategorial causality. Von Humboldt even anticipates the problematic of the internal and the external, including Sartre's problematic of interiorization and exteriorization: "The everlasting goal of humanity is therefore the blending of inward independent creativity with all the outward givens of the world." [6] For von Humboldt, language presupposes both history and the foundation of the other on the part of the subject: talking implies that one is being listened to, and that the speaker constitutes the alter ego in the ego:

> consummate spiritual development, even in the loneliest abstractedness of a single soul, is no less dependent on language, and language demands to be addressed to an outer, other being who understands it. Articulated sound wrenches itself loose from the breast, in order to awaken in the other an echo leading back to the ear. Simultaneously, man thus discovers that there are other creatures with similar inner needs, capable of meeting the diverse yearnings present in his own inward sentiments. [7]

In Sartre's language: when I speak, I have already recognized the other and the other knows that I have recognized him and that I know this of him. In Husserl, the problem ultimately brings us back to the genetic concatenation, to the mother from whom the child learns the language with the first *Einfühlung*. [8] The language becomes the individual language of the child by passing through the tradition received by the mother: thus, says Husserl, the child enters history. [9]

In the child, history begins in the same way that Descartes's philosophy begins anew. When we rediscover von Humboldt's problems in Husserl, we rediscover them as well founded. I begin from myself, from my actual presence: this is the origin. But the origin is also my birth, which in turn is connected to the chain of generations. Ultimately, this not only connects history and nature, my psychic life and matter, but also connects the finite monads between *birth* and *death*, and therefore connects the intersubjective temporality of history which is transmitted and renewed, departing from each concrete and singular subjectivity.

6. *Ibid.*, p. 261.
7. *Ibid.*, p. 271.
8. Manuscript K III 11 (July, 1935).
9. See my *Diario*, p. 7.

It has been said that the intersubjective foundation presupposes matter and the animated body: the physical reality of the signs and the *Sprachleib* of language. Von Humboldt is aware of this when he says that thought is connected with sound.[10] What is true of the subjects and intersubjectivity is also true of culture. Von Humboldt becomes aware of the positive value of the multiplication of languages and cultures precisely when he stresses the unitary character of language and the individuality of the speaker. The unitary character of the language and the individuality of the speaker pose the problem of the relation between the individual and the species, and between species and species. They do so with a movement of thought similar to Hegel's and Marx's notions of the *process of the species* that is bound to the sexual relation indicated by von Humboldt in the essay of 1795 ("On Masculine and Feminine Form"). For Marx, this is a process whereby the human species lives in the individual and the individual, as a part, can contain the human species within himself, according to a typical Marxian dialectical relation. But the dialectic must not be objectified: the structure implies the subject, and the subject the structure. A categorial dialectic without the real precategorial structure's being founded upon the continual relation between the concrete subjects and the groups is impossible. In the same way, it is impossible to have an origin which is only in the past whence the present is born, or only in the isolated present that does not rediscover the past as its real past by departing from its actual presence, i.e., from founding subjectivity. Individual and mankind do not become identified: the very reality of historical becoming, temporal reality, becomes possible because of this difference. Yet, on the other hand, it is always humanity that lives in each of its individuations. According to von Humboldt:

The effectiveness of an individual's effort is always fragmentary. But it seems to share, and up to a certain point it truly does share, a certain similarity of direction with that of the entire human race. For every individual's direction is conditioned by and in turn helps to condition the intrinsic connectedness of the course of time, past, present, and future. From another and profounder point of view, however, the direction of any individual diverges from that of the race, these two types of movement, crossing and recrossing and tangling with each other, constituting the web of world history insofar as it is connected with inward man. The

10. Von Humboldt, "On the Differences," pp. 280–81.

divergence is readily seen by the fact that the fate of the human race seems to proceed, and, so far as we can judge, proceed with increasing perfectibility, quite independently of the ever-recurring disappearance of one generation of men after another, whereas the single individual has to depart from the scene . . . suddenly and often in the midst of his most significant contributions.[11]

In the first part of the quoted passage von Humboldt speaks of an "intrinsic connectedness of the course of time, past, present, and future." In the second part he speaks of the finitude of the individual who suddenly departs from the uninterrupted continuity of history. What is implicit here is the problem of birth and death, which is bound to concrete individuation. Both problems reappear in Hegel's anthropology (in the *Encyclopedia*) and in the anthropology of Feuerbach's real man. But the ego as a man—as a real man of flesh and blood who contains the world and yet constitutes it and who contains the past and yet founds it, the individual ego born from intersubjectivity and yet constitutive of intersubjectivity, the ego which is individuated between birth and death and in the connection between the living and the dead in history and culture, the ego so alive, functioning, and reflective—this ego is the real precategorial foundation of phenomenology. This dialectic embraces every real unavoidable individuality and every structure. Furthermore, the structure makes no sense unless it is founded by the ego in the same way so that it cannot fail to contain the structure, although it is the first principle from which it must depart. This problematic is essential to phenomenology as well as to anthropology and linguistics.

The preceding observation is of particular interest to de Saussure and to the paradox implicit in the *Course in General Linguistics*. In brief, we can say that it is impossible to discuss the individual *parole* without founding it on the concrete individual, i.e., on Husserl's real and transcendental subject. Given the previously attempted connections and clarifications, this means that if it is possible to speak of synchronic structure as an objectified system without discussing the subject and constituting subjects, it is also impossible to speak of a structure independent of real historical time and dialectic. In fact, de Saussure occludes the foundation. The categorial and naturalistic system (in Husserl's sense) is to be brought back to the *Lebenswelt*, to living subjective and intersubjective language. As has been seen, the actual

11. *Ibid.*, p. 267.

presence, the very evidence, is historical. According to Hjemslev, the essence of de Saussure's theory is the distinction between word and language.

> The whole of the theory can be logically deduced from these primordial theses. . . . F. de Saussure discovers language; at the same time there is the awareness of the fact that the linguistics of the epoch had only been interested in the word [parole] and that up to that time linguistics had overlooked its "unique and true object." [12]

This passage indicates the mentioned paradox: linguistics without the *parole*, i.e., without the talking subjects, is not founded, and if structuralism is possible, this is because it performs an abstraction of which it is not aware, thus forgetting the real precategorial operations. Langauge can be studied if it is founded upon real subjects and moves within the intentionality of the *Sprachleib* of humanity, and, therefore, within historical intentionality. On the other hand, the phenomenological foundation can recognize in structuralism and phonetics all their "scientific" value and the value of the investigation of the Circles of Prague and Copenhagen. Pos insists upon the "return to the talking subject," upon the problem of the foundation, and he poses such a problem of principle, and it does not imply the denial of phonetics and structuralism, in the same way that the problem of the origin of geometry does not deny geometry. [13]

De Saussure has juxtaposed the talking subject, understood as *parole*, to the object of the study of linguistics, understood as *langue*. [14] Merleau-Ponty develops the problem in the dialectic between the talking subject and the linguistic tradition, between the synchronic and the diachronic. This proposal must be connected to the physical reality of the signs and, to use Merleau-Ponty's term, to the "corporeality of the signifying." [15] Furthermore, as Merleau-Ponty indicates, [16] these themes are closely connected with the problem of sedimentation and its reactivation. In this respect, Merleau-Ponty rightly stresses the return to the

12. Louis Hjemslev, "Langue et parole" (1943), in *Essais Linguistiques* (Copenhagen: Nordisk, 1959), p. 69.
13. See H. J. Pos, in H. L. van Breda, ed., *Problèmes actuels de la phénoménologie* (Brussels: Desclée de Brouwer, 1952).
14. Maurice Merleau-Ponty, "On the Phenomenology of Language," in *Signs*, trans. Richard C. McCleary (Evanston: Northwestern University Press, 1964), p. 86.
15. *Ibid.*, p. 88.
16. *Ibid.*, pp. 89–93.

Lebenswelt and intersubjectivity. He thus concludes: "When I speak or understand, I experience that presence of others in myself or of myself in others . . . and I finally understand what is meant by Husserl's enigmatic statement, 'Transcendental subjectivity is intersubjectivity.' " [17] What we have attempted to show is that the Husserl statement mentioned by Merleau-Ponty is the very foundation of phenomenology. The deepening of the theme of sedimentation leads us to understand the function of sedimentation and technology, of the precategorial foundation of political economy, within the domain of the problem of the unity of the sciences.

Lévi-Strauss has attempted to connect structuralism, phonetics, and anthropology. If phonetics is the study of the precategorial structure of the sounds that make a language possible, then we have seen that this problem is present in Husserl in all of the investigations of the transcendental aesthetic. It is present in the conception of body as the organ of the organs of sense, in phantasms, and in signs and communication at a distance. There is no doubt that at the base of these investigations we find a real physical man in the same way that the transcendental subject is physical and real. Lévi-Strauss discovers the problem of phonetics and linguistic structures by studying the relations between linguistic connections and kinship relations. Yet he tends to objectify the human subjects, thus reducing them to scientific *objects* of study. Thus, he forgets the intersubjective and precategorial foundation and, with it, the dialectic. Anthropology as a science makes constructions, but it must not forget the operations through which it makes the necessary ones. If it occludes them it loses its intentionality and, with it, the orientation of anthropology according to a *telos*. The anthropologist and the linguist need abstractions, but the subject who is speaking and the man whom I study are not just abstractions. As we have seen, the structure is not separable from the subject and intersubjectivity, because of fundamental phenomenological and historical reasons.

Lévi-Strauss suggests that structure can function as the basic principle of all the human sciences, starting with sociology and anthropology. For Lévi-Strauss it is a matter of categorial structure, since his structure does not refer to empirical reality but to the models constructed in order to explain it. "Models" are complex formations which are valid only so long as we do not forget

17. *Ibid.*, p. 97.

the base upon which they have been constructed. This base is natural, precategorial, and historical in the sense described. A phenomenological analysis of the "model" will probably discover hidden problems and would certainly be very fertile. What is important, however, is not to use the model as an abstraction transformed into reality. Phenomenologically, the concrete and individual ego is both typical and transcendental. Thus, it can become a model or a type without losing its concreteness. The typical structures of the *Lebenswelt* are real only if they are precategorial and subjective. Subjective operations are both real and intentional and, given the connection between historical and temporal style and the meaning of history, they are always oriented. We have a real dialectical structure because we have a subjective and precategorial foundation. Methodological abstractions are useful in terms of such a dialectical structure. Abstract thought, in its origin from the *Lebenswelt,* is concrete temporal reflection. This is the problem that Lévi-Strauss poses in *The Savage Mind* (1962). But when Lévi-Strauss writes that although, in terms of empirical reality, the social structure is a model, and, as such, is not empirical, he finds himself faced with the problem of the precategorial foundation of sociology as a science (and the same is true of anthropology).[18] This problem, as already indicated, leads back to the evidence understood as a historical operation, and to the universal historical a priori. Thus, even recent linguistic investigations and their connection with anthropology reintroduce the problem of intersubjectivity and historical meaning.

The problem of intersubjectivity appears here in all its breadth, i.e., as the problem of the relations between civilization and culture. There is also an *Einfühlung* between civilization and civilization and, in relation to the constitution of an authentic humanity of subjects, all civilizations have their function, including so-called primitive civilizations. All civilizations are cooperative with respect to the *telos* of humanity. Technology as a means of emancipation can and must belong to all. But this is possible only if the techniques and the means that render them possible are not the property of this or that group, of this or that nation, but of all the men of the planet Earth.

18. Claude Lévi-Strauss, *Structural Anthropology,* trans. Claire Jacobson and Brooke Grundfest Schoepf (New York: Basic Books, 1963), pp. 277–78.

12 / The Phenomenological Foundation of the History of Philosophy

[50] *History of Philosophy and Teleological Genesis*

THE PROBLEMS THAT THE READER FACES toward the end of the *Crisis* are the problem of history and the problem of the history of philosophy. From the investigation of the origin of geometry and physics, their promulgation, sedimentation, and reactivation, Husserl proceeds to the problem of the continuity and renovation of philosophical thought. He goes back to the philosophers whom he knows best and who have contributed the most to the constitution of phenomenology: the largest part of manuscripts K concerns a reexamination of the thought of Descartes, Locke, Hume, and Kant. Phenomenology is the heir of preceding philosophies. But how must this heredity be conceived? Husserl's preferences become a problem that implies some of the fundamental phenomenological themes.

From the very beginning one is amazed to find that in the manuscripts K Husserl once again returns to an examination of the philosophers of whom he has always spoken and whose study would seem to have been exhausted. A sufficiently complete attempt was already given in the lectures published as *Erste Philosophie*. But Husserl feels that this study is always renewable and must be renewed along with the meaning of the philosophical tradition. The philosophers of the present relive and renew the philosophers of the past. This is a historical position which contains a philosophy, i.e., phenomenology. Husserl's preference for Descartes has a specific reason. It is related both with the subjective, human, and transcendental foundation, and with the problem of intersubjectivity. This latter problem must be understood in a broad sense as including the living and the dead, and, therefore, continuity, the interruptions of continuity, and the intention and realization of the past philosophies. Precisely because its foundation is precategorial and human, philosophical reflection is not uninterrupted: it always begins anew and in different ways. This is unavoidable if it always leads us back to man, and if man does not passively accept a constituted tradition.

The transcendental subject does not give us an uninterrupted philosophy precisely because the transcendental subject is also human. *In fact,* the subject is human before being transcendental. Philosophy is bound to the interruptions, to the generative chain, to the *birth* and *death* of the concrete monads. The philosophers who have preceded us are our fathers, and we are the fathers of our sons. Here the return to the subject coincides with the return to the concrete individual who is born and dies. Philosophical continuity is conditioned by this fact, and, therefore, by the various ways in which philosophers and cultures elaborate and reelaborate philosophy. The tradition must necessarily be undertaken anew each time by the concrete and founding subject who constitutes it, relives it, and corrects it. Basically, the relationship between different philosophies is the intersubjective relationship between diverse men and cultures. If geometry must go back to its past and present origin, it is because geometry is founded by man. This leads back to the human foundation and refoundation of philosophy, whose task is the foundation and unity of the sciences. The philosophical tradition has a unity. Yet it begins anew in each philosopher and in each man. Thus, our relation with the tradition is a relation with dead philosophers and with our fathers. The problem of the history of philosophy and the basic reason for Husserl's preference for Descartes appears at this level, which contains the problem of continuity and the renewal of generations and cultures.

Here we must emphasize the relationship of the continuity and renewal of philosophy—and thus of the history of philosophy—with the problem of generation and universal teleology dealt with primarily in manuscripts E. Universal teleology is connected to anthropology. Like Hegel and Feuerbach, Husserl also finds himself faced with the problems of eros,[1] sleep, the unconscious, wakefulness, the interruptions of consciousness and its renovation, the individual, the species and the genus, and the universal connection between animated beings among all of the "creatures," plants, and physical bodies. In turn, all this leads us to the investigation of the different types of plants, animals, and men.

The sequence in which these problems appear in the manuscript K III 4 (1934–35) is typical. If psychic experience is bound to the body, this connection roots it in the world and in the biological-genetic context of all living nature. The investigation of generation, birth and death, and the various species of animated beings turns out to be explicitly connected to universal teleology.[2] Husserl poses the problem of the precategorial origin and classification of natural history, and of the meaning of psychic and animal life within the totality of nature and, finally, in the dialectic.[3] What is the meaning of evolution? In what sense do species succeed each other and coexist? The problem of birth and death is at the root of all universal teleology. In the same manuscripts, Husserl also stresses the problem of birth.[4] Seen in the diachronic dimension, whose origin is birth, universal teleology ends up with the philosopher's becoming conscious of his responsibility, with philosophy's being conceived as humanity's self-reflection and as the reflection of reason—the theme subsequently dealt with in Appendix IV and Beilagen XXVI, XXVII, and XXVIII (manuscripts K III 6, pp. 16–99; and K III 4, pp. 44–47, 59–67). Therefore, the contents of the Appendexes and Beilagen become integrated with the problems of birth and death mentioned in connection with pages 48–56 of manuscript K III 4, which has not been published in either the German or the English edition of the *Crisis*. We have mentioned them because they indicate a fundamental connection between the philosopher that begins anew, and *man*, the concrete monad who lives and dies in time. For the same reason, we have hinted at manuscripts E, where the tradition and its renewal are connected very closely with the problem of human generations and, in general, with the problem of evolution. Man's *new beginning* is based upon the

1. See my *Tempo e Verità Nella Fenomenologia di Husserl* (Bari: Laterza, 1961), pp. 245 ff.
2. K II 4, pp. 48–55.
3. K III 4, p. 56.
4. *Ibid.*, p. 17.

relation between sons and parents, on the first *Einfühlung* with
the mother, on the fact that every man recapitulates the evolution that has preceded him, according to what Husserl calls the
ontogenesis-phylogenesis relation.[5]

We are now able to understand one of the main reasons for
Husserl's reconsideration of the history of philosophy as part of
the intersubjective relation between the living and the dead, between sons and fathers. In hereditary forms, every son ontologically recapitulates the phylogenesis in a new way. Man as a
philosopher occludes and rediscovers new avenues. By always
reconstituting the past according to new lines, he discovers both
occluded and new meanings.

We can now read the beginning of Beilage V by noticing the
meaning that the expression "philosophical fathers" comes to
assume:

> In reflecting historically upon our philosophical fathers, we come
> to Descartes. As we know, Descartes has the history of philosophy
> behind himself, a community of philosophers that goes back to
> Thales. But Descartes "begins anew." "We philosophers of the
> present," of this philosophical present, thus begin anew and reflect
> upon the motives of the philosophical dissatisfaction with this
> present, upon the dissatisfaction of present mankind with our
> philosophies, and upon our own dissatisfaction in the face of an
> immensely increasing multiplicity of philosophies that is repug-
> nant to the meaning of philosophy. This dissatisfaction contains
> motives that can lead us to enter into the historical reflection, and
> motives to consider our philosophical present as a philosophy-
> historical one, and to awaken the historical recollection of our
> philosophical forefathers. Our generation is derivative; this char-
> acter can be traced through a chain of generations, in the par-
> ticular case of philosophical generativity, up to those whom we
> call our primogenitors, the originative founders of our thought-
> intentions and spiritual formations which, regarding the meaning
> and validity they continue to have for us, derive from the origina-
> tive intentions and archetypes of those primogenitors. In this man-
> ner of historically recollecting re-presentation, to the extent that
> we are able to perform it, we presentify the self-reflections, namely
> of the former philosophers; but this historically recollecting awak-
> ening of past philosophers and their philosophies that we under-
> stood by a subsequent understanding as products of thought, in-
> tentions, intents, and realizations of the intents of those awakened
> philosophers, reveals the philosophers and their philosophies in
> the derivativeness from each other in diverse ways: as heirs, they

5. E III 5, in *Tempo e Verità*, p. 249.

sometimes collect their heredity, and, as disciples, interpret and develop it at best, while at other times they reject the heredity, partially or totally critically, especially with regard to the multiplicity of past philosophies that are ready for being inherited, be it with entire and total rejection—as, e.g., we reject the whole of Scholasticism since we consider it altogether useless—or we can recognize in it some positive elements and yet reject it as an already concluded heredity.[6]

We must point out that Husserl here returns to the phenomenology of time worked out in 1904 (because of the use of the expression "recollecting re-presentation"). Also, the phenomenology of time becomes connected, as has been repeatedly observed, with the problem of the ego and the other (in the fifth of the *Cartesian Meditations*), up to the limiting case in which I not only rediscover my past ego in time, but, in terms of this modality, I proceed to constitute all other egos, living and dead.

[51]   *Praxis, Dialectic,*
        Return to the Subject

IN BEILAGE XXVI, Husserl clearly discusses original generative historicity.

Original, generative historicity, the unity of spiritual life, the life of a total community of human persons generatively connected, who, in their singular communified activities, in which all single persons participate, reshape a surrounding unitary world which is theirs into a surrounding cultural world, into a world which has arisen and continues to arise out of their activity; and this in a double sense. The surrounding world of cultural objects [*Kultur-Sachen-Umwelt*] is the world of handed-down products, of the acquisitions of past activities, and of the handed-down forms of acting meaningfully. All this is included in the process of cultural objects. But correlatively, the persons and the entire personal total horizon belong to the surrounding world of each person, and they are in it with the personal spirituality which has shaped itself in and out of acting (it is also in the acting as its spiritual-hereditary

6. E. Husserl, *Die Krisis der europäischen Wissenschaften und die transzendentale Phänomenologie: Eine Einleitung in die phänomenologische Philosophie*, ed. Walter Biemel (1954, 2d printing, The Hague: Nijhoff, 1962), p. 392.

factors that determines its essence) and which continues to shape itself in that acting which is now actual.[7]

It is important to pay attention to the preceding passage, which in many respects is the result of many yet to be edited pages.

The "unity of spiritual life" is the intentional-historical meaning which is maintained in the totality of human persons, in the tradition and the renewal, and in the relation between the living and the dead. This totality is the totality of real men who in their dialectic tend toward an open meaningful totality, toward the meaning of truth that dialectically develops in the clashes and encounters of men and cultures. So understood, the *intentional totality* is the reality and unreality of meaning, intentional movement, and the *telos* of truth of such a movement. The totality, always in a stage of dialectical transformation, is founded upon material and generative evolution. It is activity, the praxis of the community of persons and of the various societies and cultures. In this sense, Husserl sees the very world in which men have acted and still act as the "field of every praxis." [8] The various subjects are united in "common" activities according to various historical situations: each "I can" is a "practical possibility." [9] As Husserl has put it more than once, reflection itself is in time. It must be considered as a practical experience and, in this sense, empirical,[10] bound to the interests of "collectivized" subjects.[11]

Husserl stresses these themes in the manuscript A VII 13 (begun in 1921 and reworked in 1930). In the second part of the manuscript, these problems are connected to the problem of nature understood as "the universe of pregivenness," as the pregiven world.[12] Nature is the domain of our subjective operations. Human praxis and nature constitute the *subjektiv-vorgegebene Welt*. This is how man appears in the unity of instinct and of need (and, we would add, of work) with reflection, which is then the unity of the intentionality of historical persons with the al-

7. *Ibid.,* p. 502.
8. "'Feld' aller Praxis," in A VII 13, p. 178. For an analysis of the problem of praxis in Husserl, see G. Pedrolini, "Realtà e prassi in Husserl," in *Omaggio a Husserl,* ed. Enzo Paci (Milan: Il Saggiatore, 1960), pp. 195–211.
9. A VII 13, p. 20.
10. *Ibid.,* pp. 7–10.
11. *Ibid.*
12. *Ibid.,* pp. 122, 127, 179.

ready given world of nature, the unity of body and consciousness. Since the *Leib* is also a person, this unity is part of the
life of the world (*Weltleben*) in its natural and personal generative unity, according to the "constitutive process of the genesis" [13]
and the dialectic of subjects and cultures.

In the manuscript A VII 14 (1930–32), the same themes are
related to the problem of birth and death, and Husserl insists
upon the "continuity of the human doing." [14] There is a continuity of the praxis of humanity, notwithstanding the interruptions of birth and death, and the separation between and dialectic
of the various cultures. Perception itself is praxis. Thus, the
world emerges as the horizon of possibility of every "I can." The
horizon of the human world finds praxis at its base as its fundamental structure.

We can understand why Husserl says in Beilage XXVI that
persons "reshape" the world according to their activity, and why
he says:

> The persons and the entire personal total horizon belong to the
> surrounding world of each person, and they are in it with the
> personal spirituality which has shaped itself in and out of action
> . . . and which continues to shape itself in that action which is
> now actual.

In this passage one can still notice the distinction between
the "surrounding world" (*Umwelt*), the "surrounding cultural
world" (*Kulturumwelt*), and the "surrounding world of cultural
objects" (*Kultur-Sachen-Umwelt*). We live in an *Umwelt*, in an
already given precategorial natural environment. We transform
this environment by praxis into a "cultural environment." The
result of our labor is such that in the world we rediscover not
only natural objects, but "cultural objects" produced by work,
technology, art, and philosophy, and by the results of the philosophically oriented praxis.

All structures are present in the historical world. Consequently, Husserl continues, in Beilage XXVI:

> This renders human existence, and, correlatively, the human sur-
> rounding world, as the surrounding world of objects and persons,
> into a historical one; human existence is always historical in this
> broadest sense, something inferior, more primitive, or superior,
> with a miserly or very rich spiritual form, whose wealth is based

13. *Ibid.*, p. 46.
14. A VII 14, p. 57.

upon a tradition that continues to be worthy but is sedimented and continually transformed; this is so with humanity, even that of primitives, which lives according to ends, forms of work, and activity of an inferior degree, or [has its tradition in] rich, differentiated, high-level [forms of work and activity], in which manifold levels of inferior finalities are interwoven.[15]

It is important to notice the decisive interest in the primitives, the recognition that their praxis can also be of a high level and that it continues, even when it is inferior, in the superior activities in which, by tradition, "manifold levels of inferior finalities are interwoven." In other words, primitive activities obtain even in nonprimitives. In this sense, mythical thought becomes a problem: see the manuscript K III 3 (1934–35), and the manuscript K III 7 (1935).

Thus, the Husserlian "totality" is to be understood not as concluded but as intentionally oriented. The final idea is not an established reality: it is infinite and teleological. Its meaning is constituted in praxis. It is praxis that becomes enlightened, and the act of becoming conscious that becomes praxis. Thus, Husserl can write: "The whole is a unity of meaning-fullness in the meaning-structure and the meaning itself as form, which has not a priori been defined by men as a final meaning." This latter would be fetishization and idolatry: "Men are not the functionaries of a finality, who have wanted and realized this total humanity, i.e., this surrounding world." [16] This means that men are not the functionaries of an already constituted final idea in terms of which they have created the world. Then the world is already given. Man is already in it, in the base, as nature: hence his praxis. Had it been otherwise, there would be no praxis and there would not even be history and the world. I am, with the world and in the world, a *fact*, and I cannot do other than begin from myself. For Husserl, the creation of the world is not a problem. Were there such a problem, phenomenology would not be possible. Hence, along with Descartes, we begin from the subject. We free ourselves from biases in order to begin in that world in which the subject is and has always been: a world to make and constitute.

Here we find again the necessity to begin anew. In my presence with which I begin there is always the past, and I rediscover it by departing from myself. I rediscover it as it has been and as

15. *Krisis*, p. 502.
16. *Ibid.*, pp. 502–3.

it is. But precisely because I begin anew, I can transform the world and history. My praxis indicates and realizes new finalities: it reconstitutes the world, remakes culture, and transforms history. *The dialectic is inconceivable except as the return to the subject:* there is no already made and constituted dialectic. At the center of the dialectic there is man who is already made and who remakes himself. There is the world which is already made and which, in history, makes itself anew and transforms itself departing from man, from human praxis, from man who begins anew.

[52]   *The Specter of Categorial Philosophy
          and the Meaning of the Dream
          of a Philosophy as a Rigorous Science*

HUSSERL WRITES THAT IF LIFE IS HISTORY, "it can arise in single men," and, naturally, through intersubjective constitution, it can arise in groups.

> But on the other hand, if there already is historical life, then there can arise in and from single men a new final life, and this is admirable, a new final life arises that not only adjusts itself to the historical totality: correlatively, when these final formations of a new kind come to insert themselves into the multiplicity of the already typically valid formations of meaning, they weave a new thread in the order of culture, a new figure in the multiplicity of figures. This end and acquisition of a new kind transfers something from its meaning to the already existing ends and acquisitions. And correlatively: in the development of organic historicity, from those single persons that create the new final meaning emanates the reshaping of the entire humanity, of the total association of generativity (of the historical unity), that little by little creates a new humanity, which has as its correlate a culture of a new kind that is not only organic but that has also drawn a total meaning of a new type from the creative actions of the single persons.[17]

Although they are in the generational and evolutionary chain, to the extent that they begin anew, men can always indicate a new direction from the beginning, confronting the culture and confronting the situation of the already made world. The move-

17. *Ibid.,* p. 503.

ment of a new culture that allows the *total reshaping* of a new humanity can arise from the impulse of the individual. This impulse departs from actual presence and the act of becoming-conscious which, ultimately, is philosophy itself. From this viewpoint, Husserl will insist, even excessively, on the "community of philosophers." However, his conviction remains that philosophy, at its root, is the actual self-reflection of humanity in order to arrive—and this is all the more necessary in a situation of crisis—at a reshaping, or, rather, at a transformation of actual humanity.

The solution of the ongoing crisis demands that philosophical consciousness which is made possible by phenomenology. It is a matter of a "scientific" act of becoming conscious, i.e., of a precategorial science *sui generis*, which we have already indicated as the new science, or as the science of history in the sense that this term is understood in phenomenology. Here, the dialectic is not an objectivized naturalistic dialectic ("philosophy of nature in-itself" or "philosophy of history in-itself"); it is the dialectic inherent in the temporal and pregiven structure. This dialectic originates in the founding subject. The actual genesis is part of the genesis in the evolutionary sense, and rediscovers the past as the reality that had led to the present from which the philosopher (i.e., the phenomenologist) always departs in order both to reactivate the sedimentation of the tradition and to elaborate new directions and reshape humanity. We see here all the complex implications of "beginning anew" and of Husserl's preference for Descartes. Clearly, this preference makes sense only if the *cogito* is not pure consciousness isolated from human generational capacity and its dialectic, but only if the *cogito, instead of being posed* as an axiom, *is posed as man in his physical and historical concreteness* and in his transcendental intentionality, which appears here as the becoming-conscious of the historical situation and the possibility of transforming it.

Husserl has only partially seen these extreme consequences. If philosophy must always return to man, there is no transmission between philosophies as a continuous and uninterrupted philosophical self-development in the history of philosophy. The history of philosophy does not exist separately from the history of culture, from human praxis, from men in their concreteness and historical individuality. At the base of the history of philosophy, there is man who reflects and the concrete dialectic among men in the world. Husserl is well aware of all this, even if he has not fully developed his analyses. Yet he feels that something threatens his research. We could call this threat the *specter of categorial philosophy* and its reflections in the history of philosophy. From this viewpoint, phenomenology itself must be submitted to a phenomenological analysis—and Husserl has often said this. This is what we have attempted to do and will continue doing throughout this work.

What can "categorial philosophy" mean? Philosophy is categorial if it is not founded on subjectivity and the *Lebenswelt*. To the extent that it is founded, phenomenology is the only precategorial philosophy. It is so to the extent that it is a return to man and the things-themselves. It is the science of the *Lebenswelt* and the new science of history that leads to the actual becoming-conscious of the crisis and of the need to reshape and transform man and the world. If this is the case, the transmission of philosophy takes place through men to the extent that every man returns to that original root of things which for man is man himself. This transforms the meaning of the history of philosophy. Therefore, if philosophy is precategorial, it is *first philosophy* [18] in the Husserlian sense, and transforms the meaning of the history of culture and science.

The historical life of philosophy is different from the historical life of science in a special way. For philosophy, the transposition and the reactivating are different from what they are for the sciences. In Beilage XXVII, Husserl writes:

Scientific propositions are formed by individual scientists and founded as scientific truths—but being and the verification of being are claims only as long as other scientists can put forth opposing reasons, and as long as these are inconfutable. This means that the realization of the cognitive purpose of the individual scientist is authentically scientific only if he has taken into account the universal horizon of coscientists as real and possible coworkers. Since this horizon is an open infinity, this can only mean that the working individual scientist has present to him an ideal total horizon of other coworking scientists. It can only mean that he a priori takes into account, at least in his method, the ideal possibility of the other theoretical subjects and ideal possible standpoints, possible truths, and verifications which would be relative to these persons and standpoints. The validity which he gains for his own insight must be a universal validity for whomever is in a theoretical attitude and for whomever is in relation to the same cognitive theme; it must not be a standpoint-truth, a situational

18. See E. Husserl, *Erste Philosophie* (The Hague: Nijhoff, 1958), essays I and II.

truth which implies those situational presuppositions which do not exist for any other conceivable scientific fellow men. Everyone and every group always lives in certain individual and particular situations—and for everyone there is a situational truth or falsity, that of prescientific everydayness [Alltäglichkeit]. Scientific knowledge surveys [Übersicht] all situations and yet wants to do justice to all of them. Its aim is the knowledge of *objective truth* which permeates the relativity of all possible situations, a truth which can be construed by anyone in his own situation. It must be scientific knowledge that permits the practically sufficient deduction of these relative truths which are valid for all possible situations, and for the objective truth-meaning for all practice.[19]

Moreover, "every scientific proposition is an end, an achievement, but at the same time it is material . . . for science as a unity of sense that is livingly-becoming. Evidently, the correlate of this unity is the unity of the scientists." [20]

The unity of scientists is possible for the actual and possible unity of the working field of the unity of the sciences. In history, scientists form a great unique community:

> Each scientist is as such necessarily conscious of himself researching in an open community of coscientists [Mitwissenschaftlern], and of taking over, situating in himself, their own doings and horizon of activity.[21]

These passages seem to force us to "recall" the origins of Husserlian phenomenology. One involuntarily thinks of the young Husserl as Weierstrass' assistant in Berlin (1883–84). At that time Husserl considered science alone, and, specifically, mathematics, to be important. This admiration never ceased and we find it again in the quoted passages, where Husserl seems to propose science as a model for philosophy. In Vienna (1884–86), Brentano awakened in Husserl the hope that philosophy too could be treated scientifically, and this is why Husserl decided to dedicate his life to philosophy. In the *Philosophie der Arithmetik* he already tried, within an apparently psychological framework —and this is how Husserl regarded it—to analyze the constitutive operations of arithmetic. Primarily in relation to the foundations of logic, the first volume of the *Logical Investigations* (*Prolegomena*) seems to return, with its bitter criticism of psychologism, to the scientific ideal which, in the cited passages,

19. *Krisis*, p. 506.
20. *Ibid.*, p. 507.
21. *Ibid.*

appears as the ideal of *objective truth*. Subsequently, the second volume of the *Logical Investigations* seemed to indicate that Husserl was returning to the presumed psychologism of the *Philosophie der Arithmetik*. In reality, Husserl was providing the basis of phenomenology as a new kind of science. He did this primarily by developing the concept of intentionality as the *consciousness of something*. Actually, this already presupposed the return to subjectivity, which in turn implied the problem of time and therefore of history (1904–5). The first clear idea of the need to return to the subject goes back to the summer of 1905 and can be found in the five lectures now published in the *Idea of Phenomenology* (1907). The distinction between descriptive psychology and transcendental phenomenology appears in the manuscripts B II 1 and B II 2 (1907–8). By now, Husserl understands that phenomenology can be a science of subjective and precategorial operations without thereby falling back on psychologism. Consciousness becomes constituting subjectivity. But at the same time he poses the problem of the "thing" that in *Ideen II* leads him to analyze the real causal and precategorial world and the foundation of changeability and, finally, to elaborate all the problems that we have attempted to clarify.

The *Dingvorlesung* of 1907, an attempt at a phenomenology of thingness and pregivenness, was not understood by his students. Yet Husserl knew that such an investigation reveals some of the decisive problems of phenomenology and, first and foremost, the problems of space, parallel to the problems of time dealt with in the 1904 lectures on internal time-consciousness. All these problems, and others that cannot be discussed here, were preparations for the famous essay on "Philosophie als strenge Wissenschaft" (1910–11), in which he expounded the idea of the scientificity of philosophy. This is not the scientificity of mathematics or the natural sciences. Yet something of the youthful ideal inspired by Weierstrass and Brentano has remained in this famous essay, and it remains in the background of all of Husserl's works.

Certainly, phenomenology is rigorous. But we know that it is so only on the basis of evidence, actual presence, and the actual subjective and intersubjective point of departure. This is the starting point of the philosopher who wants to begin anew. It is an origin in which we can once again find the origin of man. Therefore, the origin of the man who philosophizes is an origin, in the precategorial world, of the precategorial operations that ground and constitute the sciences. Precisely because of this, the history of philosophy is not uninterrupted and continuous. Yet philosophy is scientific in the sense of the new science that we have attempted to clarify.

The scientific ideal remains, and we have seen it in the final passage of the *Crisis*. But the scientific ideal is possible only because it is founded on subjective precategorial operations and on all that has come to light through the work that Husserl has carried out in the *Crisis*. Philosophy can realize the scientific ideal only by returning to the concrete subject, e.g., by bringing the history of philosophy back to the history of man in all its wealth—for the same reason that the idealized bodies of physics have their foundation in concrete bodies, in the precategorial plena.

Therefore, unlike the exact sciences, philosophy cannot realize that continuity whereby "every scientific proposition is an end, an achievement, but at the same time is material for further scientific work, for which each scientist is codestined." For philosophy, as for the scientists, the concept of generation cannot be understood in a particular and figurative sense.[22] The scientists themselves are men, and the generation, the precategorial historical evolutionary chain, is real. Every man dies, other men are born, and the philosopher, at his root, is a man. Yet philosophy must be scientific, and almost all that Husserl says about science in the long quoted passage must be applicable to philosophy—even if the philosopher begins anew. Philosophy is rigorous because of its beginning-anew and because of its continuous return to the factual and transcendental apodicticity of the human subject. It is factual because I am already in it and cannot deny being in it in the first person—and this is unassailable even if all my *cogitata* were dreams or fantasies. It is transcendental because within me there is the cosmos (*Weltall*). I can constitute it after the epochē and, by so doing, I accept the tradition while at the same time, in becoming-conscious, I renew it in order to reshape the world.

Philosophy is, therefore, *dialectical*. Through the dialectic, and therefore also through the variety and contraposition of philosophies—which is but the contraposition of social structures and cultures—philosophy aims at the meaning of truth. Also, in time it continually reshapes the world for the horizon of truths and according to the teleological meaning of history. There are different philosophies because each man begins anew,

22. *Ibid.*

rediscovering his path in order to arrive at philosophy and the meaning of historical truth. These different paths confront each other and are corrected and self-correcting. Their scientificity consists in their point of departure from the subject, from the concrete man. As such, the criterion of truth becomes the pre-categorial and subjective foundation which can clarify, in the diverse philosophies, the way in which the foundation has been pursued and forgotten, ignored and prepared, investigated or occluded, and negated or distorted in theoretical or intellectualistic constructions. Here it is appropriate to reiterate that we have insisted upon the fact that *phenomenology constructs nothing.*

The failure to understand this is one of the causes of the crisis. Since philosophy has not become rational and scientific like a science, it is claimed that philosophy cannot be rational and scientific. In reality, when this claim is made, what is misunderstood is the way and the sense in which philosophy is scientific.

Faced with this situation, Husserl himself seems to recall his youthful ideal of philosophy as a rigorous science, the ideal of Weierstrass' time and of his first encounter with Brentano. And he seems to ask himself: Why is it that philosophy cannot be as rigorous as the exact sciences? He knows what answer to give. It is his age that does not know how to give such an answer. If the youthful ideal of a philosophy as rigorous as mathematics were a dream, he has dreamed such a dream, and he stresses the fact that he has done so in the face of a philosophy that renounces scientificity (p. 389). The youthful dream returns in the guise of the specter of a pure philosophy as rigorous as mathematics. It returns as the specter of a philosophy that has no need of returning to the subject, to man, and therefore to the dialectic. This is the specter of categorial philosophy, of a tired philosophy that accepts objectification (or alienation), accepts naturalism, *renounces the exigency of transforming humanity,* and loses philosophical intentionality and, along with it, the intentionality of the sciences. It is precisely the pretense of a philosophy as rigorous as mathematics—and rigor in this sense is reserved only for mathematics—that provokes the opposite reaction: skepticism, relativism, the philosophy of "world-views" [*Weltanschauungen*] that Husserl already criticized in "Philosophie als strenge Wissenschaft." If applied to philosophy, rationalism in the scientistic sense is correlative to irrationalism. For phenomenology, rationalism is not a dogmatic rationalism, and em-

piricism is not an abstract construction. It is because of this that
the old Husserl, in his attempt to go over the history of philosophy once again, reconsiders Locke and Hume and their confrontation with Descartes and Kant—a confrontation that can
be grasped by comprehending the meaning of the fundamental
relationship between rationalism and empiricism. But in re-
thinking all this, he rethinks the trodden path, the youthful
dream of a philosophy as rigorous as mathematics, the first encounter with Brentano. It is a youthful dream that has been
realized in a founded philosophy that returns to apodictic subjectivity which is, as such, serious and rigorous. But this philosophy, which is phenomenology, has remained misunderstood
even by Husserl's closest students, and it remains misunderstood if the meaning of the return to subjectivity is not grasped.
This meaning should be easy to grasp, since its evidence is what
is closest to us and it is within ourselves in the same way that
we are the world and experience the world.

The scientificity of phenomenology, i.e., the task to which
Husserl has dedicated his life, runs the risk of remaining a
dream while he writes the *Crisis*. Phenomenology, Husserl used
to say, is unfortunately only *mine*. He thinks of his students'
misunderstandings, of which we have some documentation,
even in Beilage XIII (which was to be the preface to the third
part of the *Crisis*), and he believes that "philosophy is in danger."
Thoughts of this kind have led Husserl to write the famous
phrase that is found at the beginning of Appendix IX: "Philosophy as science, as serious, rigorous, indeed apodictically rigorous, science—*the dream is over*" (p. 389). It is a dream that I
have dreamed in my youth. Considering that phenomenology is
mine only and *I have remained alone*, it remains a dream now
that I have discovered the meaning of phenomenological scientificity.

[53]   *The Analysis of World-Views.*
        The Unitary Intentional Orientation.
        Meaning and Function
        of Original Philological Operations

MUST WE, THEREFORE, SURRENDER to personal philosophies, to philosophies as "world-views" or as "subjective" phi-

losophies, not in the sense of phenomenological subjectivity, but in the relativistic sense? Husserl does not think so, but he feels that the world-views must be explained. It is necessary to know how it is that they exist and how they come about. Husserl would have some means for this explanation: a world-view is not true and founded in the sense of a phenomenological analysis. But fantasies have their truth as fantasies and their function for both the individual and the community. "Phantasms" are possible, and it is necessary to understand their modality in the same way that it is necessary to understand the modality and function of dreams, myths, and, finally, art. Once again, this investigation would have to take into account the manuscripts D, which are dedicated to the transcendental aesthetic and to the problems of the phenomenology of language.

In this sense, the relationships among philosophies could also be studied. Even if it corrects Descartes, and Husserl has subjected him to an engaging critique, phenomenology has preferences for Descartes, and we have seen why this is not an arbitrary choice. Obviously, phenomenology also has other preferences: Locke, Leibniz, Berkeley, Kant, Brentano. But it finds itself in opposition to many philosophical currents, e.g., positivism as naturalism in the Husserlian sense of objectivism, and psychologism. We must explain these oppositions even more than Husserl himself has done. Among other things, such an explanation would include the analyis of world-views and ideologies. Phenomenology is neither an ideology nor a world-view, but this does not exempt it from the analysis of its origin and its function as a world-view. The analysis is all the more necessary if each philosopher must begin anew. It is only with much difficulty that each philosopher can perform a total epochē of prejudices in order to free himself totally of personal inclinations, environmental influences, and the errors and hopes of his age.

Husserl feels that world-views must be analyzed along with the conflicts and animosities between philosophers; that personal interests and errors must be taken into account in order that one be able to recognize and overcome them. Like folly, he sees error and evil as deviations from normality. They are deviations that overrun the intentionality directed toward truth as a good. In a negative and dialectical sense, error and evil are understandable only in relation to intentionality oriented toward the truth. Therefore, they are permeated by intentionality even if they want to negate it. In our time and crisis, the evidence of the good has been weakened or occluded. The faith in philosophy—in truth and in the religion of truth—has itself been weakened. But "the man who has once tasted of the fruits of philosophy, has become acquainted with its systems, and has then unhesitatingly admired these as among the highest goods of culture can no longer let philosophy and philosophizing alone" (p. 389). It must, however, be recognized that, if its root is man, philosophy cannot develop according to a linear and categorial continuity. Nor will it fall into skepticism if man himself has, uneliminable from himself and from humanity, the possibility of founding the sciences, of using them for the constitution of a rational and subjective community according to the historical meaning of truth that is "innate" in every man and humanity. To the extent that he is his own norm and is normal, man can rediscover the others in himself. Each man can discover in each part, beginning from himself and his own apodicticity, the meaning of the whole. Finally, he can correct himself for the realization and reshaping of humanity and the world.

There have been and there are, in fact, world views. Their self- and reciprocal correction is permeated by intentionality. There have been and there are various histories of philosophy, various preferences. From its own viewpoint, phenomenology must also explain, directly or indirectly, positively or negatively, the preferences of other philosophies: in the process it will be able to clarify itself and study the continual transformation of the preferences. Phenomenology will be able to do so *scientifically* precisely by beginning anew in the very history of philosophy. The history of philosophy is not possible either as the *mere sum* of all philosophies or as just the explication of an individual viewpoint. At any rate, both these attitudes would be impossible. The first would fail, since the theory of the mere sum is already a philosophy, even if the sum is a sum of viewpoints which can neither be integrated nor added. The second would fail, since every individual as a man is the *type*-man for whom each individual experience, if unique, to the extent that it is lived only once and by an individuated man who is born and dies, is also *typical* and, as such, is both an individual and other individuals, the real transcendental man, the uniquely functioning ego and human intersubjectivity. Apodictic evidence is not a choice: I am in flesh and blood in the evidence. The typicity, the transcendental function, the universal relation understood in the sense of the *a priori of the correlation*, are immanent and implicit in the evidence. My reality, understood in the most empirical sense, i.e., in the apodictic sense that I cannot deny since it is I that is evident, and not in that of a constructed empiricism, is true along with other human realities, to the extent that it transcends itself in an intentional direction.

Hence, notwithstanding diversities and struggles, and precisely because it is brought back to man, the history of philosophy finds its unitary meaning even in world-views and errors. This is true even though philosophy, although it has clarity as its task, will never be wholly clear to itself and will always remain partially an enigma, since it cannot resolve the world in a definitive knowledge, and since its task is the reshaping of the world according to a truth which will never be owned once and for all. Thus Husserl concludes:

> I know, of course, what I am striving for under the title of philosophy, as the goal and field of my work. And yet I do not know. What autonomous thinker has ever been satisfied with this, his "knowledge"? For what autonomous thinker, in his philosophizing life, has "philosophy" ever ceased to be an enigma? Everyone has the sense of philosophy's end, to whose realization his life is devoted; everyone has certain formulae, expressed in definitions; but only secondary thinkers, who in truth should not be called philosophers, are consoled by their definitions, beating to death with their word-concepts the problematic *telos* of philosophizing. In that obscure "knowledge," and in the word-concepts of the formulae, the historical is concealed; it is, according to its own proper sense, the spiritual inheritance of him who philosophizes; and in the same way, obviously, he understands the others in whose company, in critical friendship and enmity, he philosophizes. And in philosophizing he is also in company with himself as he earlier understood and did philosophy; and he knows that, in the process, historical tradition, as he understood it and used it, entered into him in a motivating way and as a spiritual sediment. His historical picture, in part made by himself and in part taken over, his "poetic invention of the history of philosophy," has not and does not remain fixed—that he knows; and yet every "invention" serves him and can serve him in understanding himself and his aim, and his own aim in relation to that of others and their "inventions," their aims, and finally what it is that is common to all, which makes up philosophy "as such" as a unitary *telos* and makes the systems attempts at its fulfillment for us all, for us [who are] at the same time in company with the philosophers of the past (in the various ways we have been able to invent them for ourselves). [Pp. 394–95]

This passage must be read carefully. Evidently, the *poem* is a *critical* limit. Also, the historian's function presupposes philological work. We must reactivate the sedimentations. But it is necessary that they be there to be sought, discovered, and chosen. Naturally, they must be established in their reality. Here too, as in Beilage IV, the sedimentation becomes a proving ground of the function of technology: in this case, of philological technology and its intentionality.

Philological technology is a condition of historiography to the extent that historiography is the *opening of the past*. The historiographer must reconstruct the facts in their "objectivity" (in the sense whereby the term is contraposed to relativism and arbitrariness). He must establish the "past present" as such, and do so through the sedimentations and documents. What is needed here is an elaborate phenomenological analysis of philological operations, not only in the sense of sedimentations and their reactivations, but also in the sense indicated in relation to language, the precise form of the text, its variations, and its "fortune." Ultimately, this philological operation presupposes the connections among nature and history, man, and precategorial causal environment. It presupposes the man who, in his concreteness, roots himself with his very body (the *Leib*) in the history of nature and in the history of evolution, i.e., in the genesis.

The sedimentation in the text is a sedimentation in matter, and it is a means of transmitting the living presence through time. Therefore, it is a condition of human intersubjectivity and its historical meaning of truth. From this viewpoint, the original philological operation is that which everyone performs in his present: it is that which we too perform, in our actual presence, when we leave sedimentations for the future. It follows here that historiography, already in the present, is the *opening of the future*. We write *for* and *with* the *purpose of*. At the root of our writing we can discover a need, the need of that which is outside of us, of others, the need for living, for not dying, for procreating. And here we again encounter the precategorial structure that remained obscure and unknown to Husserl: political economy as a science, as the structure which, as a historical-economic structure, the historiographer rediscovers in his praxis, not only as an investigator and narrator, but also as a technician of the investigation, the reconstruction, the choice, and the reactivation of the documents and the texts.

13 / Experience and Reason

The Empirical Aspect of Phenomenology

THE PREVIOUS CHAPTER has brought us to the relation between philosophy and the history of philosophy. An important instance of this can be found in the way Husserl investigates the relations between empiricism and rationalism in Beilage XIV. The contraposition of empiricism and rationalism is not that the first "asserts that the foundation of knowledge rests on experience, while the latter disavows it." [1] For rationalism, too, natural science presupposes experience and, above all, perception. What distinguishes empiricism is its antimetaphysical tendency.[2] Locke and Hume were not scientists or mathematicians.

> In Hume, the theoretical interest certainly prevails over the political and practical interest in general, but the proper field [*eigentliche Feld*] of his scientific interests is the sociohistorical world, and the individual man as a theme is man in this world, the man of the manifold life who is acting in the world.[3]

As we know, Galileo's and Newton's physics cover the "original ground of the prescientific life-world." [4] But for practical empiricists like Hume, science does not deal just with

---

1. E. Husserl, *Die Krisis der europäischen Wissenschaften und die transzendentale Phänomenologie: Eine Einleitung in die phänomenologische Philosophie*, ed. Walter Biemel (1954; 2d printing, The Hague: Nijhoff, 1962), p. 446.
2. *Ibid.*, p. 447.
3. *Ibid.*
4. *Ibid.*, p. 448.

physical bodies. Empiricism does not aim toward the categorial but toward the precategorial world. "Thus . . . in empiricism is entrusted the tendency of a scientific discovery of the life-world with which we are familiar in everyday life, but which is the scientifically unknown life-world . . . the historically relevant [one]." [5] This is the first function of empiricism *"in the historical development* or, more trenchantly, in *historical teleology."* [6]

In addition to this first function, however, we find a second, represented by an interest in cognitive psychology. This leads empiricism to deal with sensations and perceptions—without, however, understanding the true sense of subjectivity that Descartes had discovered. What empiricism needed was "the Cartesian discovery," [7] which would have taken empiricism to a deeper understanding of the relationships between the problems of knowing, based on the human and transcendental subject, and the problems of the life-world, of the world of praxis, and of the historical world. Beilage XIV is very important, because in it Husserl clarifies the connection between the precategorial and subjective foundation of knowledge, and the historical and practical world.

In historical teleology, empiricism needs the *cogito*. But the *cogito* appears as operating in the life-world understood as the practical and historical world. Therefore, we should expect Husserl to attribute to the *cogito* a task that Descartes has not discovered. In fact, Husserl always stresses the *cogito* and criticizes Descartes's erroneous way of interpreting and developing his discovery. Empiricism needs a critically analyzed Cartesianism. What must be criticized is what Descartes believes he can derive from the *cogito* considered as an axiom. The Cartesian *cogito* is simply a thinking *cogito* and does not live in the world. The Cartesian ego is not self-transcendent. It is not aware of containing the world after the mundane has been eliminated by means of radical doubt. Hence, unlike Husserl, Descartes poses the problem of an external world (*res extensa*), rather than analyzing the spatial and temporal concreteness of the ego. In Beilage X of the *Crisis*, Husserl writes that, in order to resolve the problem, Descartes falls back on "the service of the proof of the existence of God." [8] Here lies his empiricism: he is an empiricist to the

5. *Ibid.*, p. 449.
6. *Ibid.*, p. 447.
7. *Ibid.*, p. 450.
8. *Ibid.*, p. 422.

extent that empiricism is directed toward the life-world in which the ego always is and remains, with the methodic doubt which appears as necessarily complementary to Cartesianism.

Kant reopens the Cartesian problem but loses the Cartesian radicalism, i.e., the problem of the foundation and the need to transform man and world after having become conscious of philosophical self-responsibility. "In him one does not find this radicalism of philosophical self-justification," [9] even though Kant grasps the sense of the responsibility of philosophy *qua* philosophy.[10] However, to the extent that he poses the problem of transcendental subjectivity, Kant is a pioneer. The Kantian transcendental ego, however, is not the real ego, the subject in flesh and blood, the subject who lives and functions in the pre-categorial world. It is thus coherent for Husserl to scold Kant for having occluded the life-world which renders the foundation of the sciences possible. As we know, Kant develops the foundation by contraposing Hume's skepticism to the a priori of the forms of intuition of space and time, and to the categories. Husserl doubts Kant's understanding of Hume's empirical radicalism, although Kantian subjectivism is very important for phenomenology, as can be seen in Beilage XVI. This leads Husserl to vindicate Hume against Kant. But this also leads him to criticize Hume in, e.g., Beilagen XI and XII.

In fact, Hume's importance for phenomenology has been decisive from the very beginning. Only Natorp's criticisms forced Husserl to reexamine Kantianism to the point of considering phenomenology as a total critique of theoretical and practical reason that necessitated the return to the subject. But only in the *Crisis* does Husserl seem to give his final answer to Marburg's neo-Kantianism. It is fine to return to the subject. The subject, however, is not Kant's ego: it is the ego rooted in the empirical life-world where it performs all its operations. These are the operations of social and historical praxis upon which science and philosophy are based. Phenomenology has taken over the task that Descartes and Hume have not been able to carry out: the task of the foundation. Hume and Descartes are associated, joined, separated, and criticized. Their intentions and programs are sublated in the new intentions and programs of phenomenology: "In Hume there is a hidden intention of departing from what in Descartes had remained neglected, and of bringing the

9. *Ibid.*, p. 423.
10. *Ibid.*, p. 428.

original Cartesian intention to self-understanding." [11] This, which is in many respects Kant's task, is undertaken anew, but not fully, by Husserl. (One need only think of the teleology of the *Critique of Judgment*.) Husserl discusses classical German idealism only briefly. Strangely enough, he has left us no critique of Leibniz, whom he credits with having founded monadology. And he certainly has not taken Hegel fully into account. But the problems of Hegelianism and the Hegelian left live their hidden and unrecognized life within the turbulent elaboration of Husserlian phenomenology.

[55]   *The Rational Aspect of Phenomenology*

THE RELATION BETWEEN EMPIRICISM AND RATIONALISM can also appear as the relation between the ego-man of the life-world and its transcendental functions. I am both the real empirical ego in the Husserlian sense and the transcendental ego. As Husserl put it in Beilage XVI,[12] I am a "human being in experience" but I am also a self-reflecting ego. Here we encounter two attitudes. For the first, all the operations of the ego are in the real man. For the second, the ego is the reflecting ego which appears as "the pure ego, i.e., the ego for which the world in general and, with it, mankind and my being a man, are objects for consciousness." [13]

It is clear that Husserl here does not mean to reintroduce a dualism of the ego-man and the reflecting ego which has man as the object of its reflection. The two egos are not contraposed as *res extensa* and *res cogitans*. It is always the same ego, i.e., the concrete man who reflects and, in the reflection, is conscious of being a man. At the moment when it studies itself as a man, the reflecting ego can be said to be nonhuman. However, this does not mean that there is an ego-entity, e.g., God, which is pure reflection, even if we have to say that reflection transcends the real man in operating transcendentally. According to the Kantian definition of the transcendental, this is a way of operating that obtains only within the limits of experience. What reappears here is the theme of the relationship of empiricism and rationalism. The pure reflecting ego is and reflects in the first

11. *Ibid.*, pp. 437–38.
12. *Ibid.*, p. 456.
13. *Ibid.*, p. 457.

person. In a certain sense, reflection detaches itself from me in order to enable me to look at myself. Thus, it leads me not only to recognize that I am a man, but also to see what *obtains* for man, obtains for reflection or self-consciousness. Therefore, what obtains for me obtains as the intentional direction toward truth.

By reflecting upon human operations, the pure reflecting ego discovers their meaning of truth. If we consider the function of this pure reflecting ego, we notice that reflection which reveals truth to us and, in history, man's self-responsibility to truth. As mentioned, this truth is not a being but a meaning. Meanings are revealed to the pure reflecting ego who expresses himself according to meanings, thus continually negating his own given human reality for the meaning of truth. The very act of expression is already an intentional act. It is the proof that I am not only being but also the possibility of negating being for its worth and intentional meaning. In Sartre, an ego behaving in this fashion is the intentional negation of being. In this self-negation as a given man as such, the ego in the first person is the pure ego, which is free to negate itself in terms of truth. In the actual living presence, Husserl's pure ego negates itself in order to plunge toward the future and the possibility of truth in the future. Husserl says that this self-negating ego is the ultimate ego which, by going beyond itself, "realizes the validity of the world." [14]

Husserl's position is certainly paradoxical. The paradox, however, is inherent in the very structure of phenomenology. It is essentially characterized by the intentional movement and, in the ultimate analysis, by the dialectic. This dialectic does not obtain outside the subject in a preconstituted philosophy of history, but is centered on the subject and its possibility of going beyond, of *negating the negation* and transcending. The self-transcending ego is the pure intentional ego. It is the very operation of transcendence. For phenomenology, it is important that intentional operations are possible through reflection and that they are not mechanical and irrational. Thus, in a new form, rationalism returns to phenomenological empiricism. This is why the spirit of phenomenology is not that of Sartre's *Being and Nothingness*. Man's goal is not to become God and thus necessarily fail, but to operate for truth. From this viewpoint, *Being and Nothingness* is a *phenomenology of an impure consciousness* which refuses truth as irremediably conflicting with freedom. In this sense it makes a contribution to phenomenological research. In Husserl,

14. *Ibid.*

freedom passes through necessity, since man can reflect only because, before reflecting, he is a man in the world, born in the world, and conditioned and caused by the precategorial level. Hence, freedom coincides with the negation of the given as such and with the intentional movement toward the *telos*. It coincides with the intentional movement toward truth. In his own way, Sartre deals with this without founding it phenomenologically when, in the *Critique de la raison dialectique,* he talks about freedom's passing through necessity and about a horizon of truth.

To reflect means to understand that the responsibility of the validity of the world falls to the ego, which can, and therefore must, reflect. Husserl says that in the mundane-natural attitude this ego remains *anonymous.* It is the task of phenomenology to clarify what is anonymous and obscure, to render it a clear *phenomenon,* and to bring it to the level of reflection and responsibility. Also, it must not be forgotten that reflection is a temporal act. It is temporalization. It is the moment when the living person gives himself the meaning of his own praxis, or, if one prefers, it is not praxis for its own sake but is guided by reason and the meaning of historical truth. What reappears once more here is the function of rationalism as philosophical self-responsibility.

[56]   *Critique of Abstract Dualism.*
       Concreteness of the Subject
       and the Epochē

IN APPENDIX VII OF THE *Crisis,* Husserl says that we are constantly interested in the life-world as the world of praxis and factual operating, i.e., the "world of labor" (*Werk-Welt*). But we must connect all our actions to the meaning of truth of a totality in the process of *becoming-for-truth.* This is why we need the epochē. The daily truth demands a broader meaning of what is true and what is false than that of the anonymous, unconscious, and irresponsible (p. 379). This is why the life-world must not remain hidden and must become a theme of study, reflection, and science. Phenomenology is a new and intentional science of the life-world. Life has a goal, an end which is revealed in reflection as the "infinite horizon of a certain 'totality' "

(p. 381). Through the phenomenological analysis, the life-world becomes valid with respect to a "universal end" (p. 382). Our profession and this end cannot be separated. We must not become, and others must not force us into becoming, pure means, abstract professionals, or, to use Marx's expression, "abstract workers." We are conditioned, but we can change ourselves and the world. The possibility of change requires a realm of necessity as its foundation, while at the same time remaining free for the truth.

In Beilage XVIII of the *Crisis*, Husserl decisively asserts that truth and freedom are possible "for the new meaning of science and, first of all, a science of the life-world." [15] The new science "in the universality of its tasks that constitute its peculiar scientificity, eventually embraces all meaningful problems regarding being and the knowledge of truth." [16] Here we see a new aspect of the relation between experience and reason. Experience and the idea of truth are connected. "Experience is verified through further experience, through an active pursuit of experience, and through the continuation of the ongoing verification of what was with and preintended in experience." [17] In other words, experience is guided by the idea of truth, i.e., by intentionality directed toward truth. The same can be said of induction as part of experience. Experience is that which always verifies anew the intentional movement toward truth.

Verification must always be perfected, rectified, and corrected. The life-world does not leap once and for all from *doxa* to science. Ultimately, the science of the life-world is the science of the "*doxa* which has traditionally been treated with so much disdain." [18] Science makes discoveries by departing from the world of *doxa*. Once again, it is easy to notice the significance of the empirical component of phenomenology. "Objective" science, "no matter how paradoxical this might seem," is founded on the life-world, i.e., on the *doxa*, even if it follows the guiding idea of a rational truth in an infinite process. Here we find the rationalistic component. The guiding idea changes, perfects, and reshapes history. This can take place precisely because all science is founded on *doxa*. In phenomenology, it becomes increasingly more difficult to separate a well-understood empiricism from a well-understood rationalism. Essentially, phenomenology does

15. *Ibid.*, p. 463.
16. *Ibid.*
17. *Ibid.*, p. 464.
18. *Ibid.*, p. 465.

not allow this separation and appears not as the sum of the two moments, or as their ambiguity, but as their concrete synthesis. This synthesis is historical life oriented toward the truth, and it exposes *the dualism between experience and reason* for what it is: the symptom of a crisis.

As Husserl clarifies in Beilage XIX, the same must be said of the *abstract contraposition of the scientific world and the life-world*. Scientists

> are themselves men in the life-world—among the rest of men. The life-world is a world for all, and so are the sciences (which are first of all the world of the scientists) there for all men as ours, and as the actualized result (propositions, theories). They are here for all, subjectively-relatively, in the same way that the life-world is.[19]

The life-world itself has a "scientific" meaning and can be rationally lived according to the guiding idea of truth. Furthermore, it is the epochē that allows the progressive rationalization of the life-world. The world obtains for all and can be transformed for all. My freedom from prejudices reveals to me the human responsibility of living in the world. "I turn to look at myself, to the extent that I am that ego who is certain of himself as a man among men in the world, and I propose to question this certainty of the world . . . with all its contents." [20] Ultimately, the questioning leads to a praxis that transforms the world—a praxis that wants to be and must be rational.

> *The transcendental epochē is thus the total turning of the ego* that lives constantly in the life of its acts, in which turning the ego of the straightforward life, on the basis of the world, conceives a new world. Instead of continuing to live in terms of what it has already included as the amount of the will in its having, and wanting further and new havings on the basis of already acquired having —further activity which creates new having—and instead of wanting to be active, *the ego conceives* the will to know itself in all of its preceding being, and outlined on this base as a future one.[21]

Here the epochē becomes a temporal operation inserted between conditioning and freedom. Furthermore, the will is possible only to the extent that subjectivity is essentially intentional in all its

19. *Ibid.*, p. 466.
20. *Ibid.*, p. 470.
21. *Ibid.*, p. 472.

modalities. In this insertion of the will into history, i.e., into the relationship between necessity and freedom, the epochē appears both as a condition of knowing and as a condition of willing. Before performing the epochē, man may not know what he wants, and not want what he knows as true, as the meaning of his life and of the life of others and history. In the "mundane" situation, knowledge and will are contraposed. Because of this, man is led to negate this situation by means of the epochē. To the extent that he is not a prisoner of the mundane, he can comprehend and desire the meaning of the truth of life. The epochē departs from the actual presence and appears as the possibility of self-detachment, of becoming aware of oneself and the world. Reflection and responsibility become joined in the simple principle of intentionality which is always *consciousness of something* and which always departs from the presence even when it wants to recall the past and bring the unconscious to light, as Fink correctly notes in Beilage XXI.

The unconscious is closely connected with nature and internal nature and precedes us in time and space. In order to know it, however, I must depart from consciousness. Even the antithesis between consciousness and unconsciousness appears abstract and categorial if one realizes that every operation is not that of a part or of a faculty, or of a spiritual form of the subject. Rather, it is the operation of the total subject who contains the world—even that world he does not knowingly contain and the past that he ignores.

14 / Science, Morality, and Economic Reality in the Struggle of Philosophy for the Meaning of Man

[57]   *The Person.*
Precategorial Biological Experience.
Structural Conditioning and Freedom.
The Function of the Sciences
for the Constitution
of a Society of Subjects

FOR HUSSERL, sociohistorical reality is temporal, dialectical, and intersubjective. The concrete monads are persons insofar as they live in the cultural world. The person is always a unity of body and soul or, as Husserl occasionally prefers to put it, a psychophysical unity. Furthermore, the person is also rooted in the precategorial material world of causal connections. To the extent that the person lives in his own animated body and is localized in it, he is *conditioned* by genetic development. On the other hand, to the extent that he is part of the cultural world, he acts according to *motivations*. The possibility of wanting and acting intentionally reveals that the person is the repository of possibilities, or, as Husserl puts it, the "substratum of decisions." [1] The intentionality of the praxis, to the extent that it is the intentionality of persons, is the intentionality that appears as possibility and liberty and, as we have seen, as the will of truth while *passing through necessity*, precategorial causality, and conditioning. According to Husserl, there is a *material structure* that binds the person to an animated nature that conditions him. In-

1. E. Husserl, *Ideen II* (The Hague: Nijhoff, 1952), p. 331.

serted in causality and conditioning, however, we also find the
will and freedom. The deterministic precategorial structure of
the base does not exclude free will. Rather, it makes free will
concretely possible to the extent that subjectivity, although
caused and conditioned, can motivate its own praxis and act
according to the human and historical meaning of truth. Hence,
psychology cannot study the soul, i.e., the concrete person, except by renouncing the attempt to apply the causal laws of
physics to persons. Man always lives in the spatiotemporal world
and his "soul" is the spatiotemporally determined animation of
the body. The "soul" is always "individuated," even though
individuation cannot be reduced to localization and temporalization.

The soul is the animating principle of one's own body (Leib).
This body is always lived in the first person and cannot be reduced to the physical or biological level. As Husserl puts it in
Beilage XXII of the Crisis, my body and the body of each animated subject are "in the bodily universe of physical nature," [2]
but do not reduce, and must not be so reduced in a free and
humane society, to biological and physical bodies. As Marx puts
it, man must not be reduced to the level of a thing or work-
animal. Since men are concrete monads who can motivate and
illuminate their own praxis by means of reason and are not
reducible to mere biological and physical bodies, they "constitute
a 'living organism' bearing a spiritual reality with itself." [3] The
subjects are caused and spatiotemporally determined. Nevertheless, they can go beyond their own physical localization and
physical temporality to broader spatialities and temporalities. I
can recall the past and extend myself toward the future in the
same way in which, with my localization in my own body, I can
move and look beyond the space within which I move.

If persons are not just physical bodies, it is impossible to
have a psychology that studies animated beings in the same way
that physics does. In other words, a psychophysical psychology
is impossible.[4]

It is foolish to demand a psychophysical "causal explanation" for
the spiritual peculiarities of a man as necessary, singularly scien-

2. E. Husserl, *Die Krisis der europäischen Wissenschaften und
die transzendentale Phänomenologie: Eine Einleitung in die
phänomenologische Philosophie*, ed. Walter Biemel (1954; 2d printing, The Hague: Nijhoff, 1962), p. 476.

3. *Ibid.*, p. 477.

4. *Ibid.*, p. 478.

tifically necessary, to achieve what in the physical sphere is achieved by natural explanation. It would be like wanting to learn to know a man by way of that experience which penetrates bodily being, wanting to know him scientifically through physiology and, in general, through biophysics (in a broad sense). One can, of course, be face to face with a man as a person in immediate experience, which we also designate as the perception of a man, in such a way as to see his own body [*Leib*], and, in general, so that one has this body in the modes of sensible appearance, in his field of perception, as any other body of this field.

Apprehension as a body is there. But this does not also imply that, in order to learn to know the person in the experience, I must actualize the apprehension of the body as experience, experiencing acquaintance.[5]

This passage can be misleading.

First of all, in intersubjective constitution I know the other only by passing through visions and perceptions of his body in my own. We must therefore understand the passage as a critique of the pretense to the ability of reducing intersubjective relations to physical laws. However, this does not entail a negation of the necessary passage of the body of the other through my body as a precondition of my knowing the other.

Second, if subjects as persons are not reducible to things and animated bodies, as concrete monads they remain animated bodies and things and, in addition to being motivated and free, they are conditioned and caused. We must always remember circumstantial precategorial causality, i.e., the analyses of *Ideen II*. The person is always embodied and is also a thing like other things. For instance, he has weight and extension like any inanimate body. Because he is a person, however, we can consider his bodily movements and physiognomy as expressions of his state of mind and his projects. When he speaks, we can consider his words as expressions of his thoughts, his desires, and whatever he wants to tell us (or hide from us). In this sense, "the body which appears in the perceptive field functions for me as an 'expression'; it gives itself to me as an expressive system." "In nature, there never occurs my own [physiognomic] play, a turning of the eyes to environmental things, a blushing, a 'frightened start,' and similar occurrences." [6]

Animated bodies, and man specifically, are not only material or physical beings, but are always *also* physical beings: the word

5. *Ibid.*, p. 479.
6. *Ibid.*, p. 480.

"expression" implies the problem of language and its origin in gestures. Language is not just a physical sign or collection of phonemes; it is also a system and structure of phonemes.

The indicated problems seem to contain a certain *constitutive order* which has repeatedly been noted in the history of philosophy, beginning with Aristotle. A biological body is not *just* a physical body. It is *also* a physical body which, in order to be biological, must first be a physical body. A psychic body must also be biological. A person, and the historical societies of persons, are more than just physical and biological organisms. A physical body can change into a biological and psychic body, even if only as an infinitesimal biological and psychic body. This thesis has an illustrious philosophical tradition, albeit confused and never clearly specified. According to the Leibnizian principle that *natura non facit saltum*, nature may have to be considered as a living body, sleeping or unconscious. So expressed, however, this thesis is a hypothesis or construction, and, in principle, phenomenology cannot construct or hypothesize. However, it can arrive at an analogous analysis by posing the problem concerning the relation between the unconscious and external world.

In the phenomenological analysis of these problems, we must never lose sight of the precategorial foundation. This is particularly important for biology, which Husserl discusses in Beilage XXIII. To the extent that it must be founded precategorially, biology leads us back to our biological experiences which are lived in the first person. Hunger, thirst, sleep, and weariness are all "lived" moments with their typical and eidetic modalities. Psychic experiences are rooted in biological experiences and are never lived separately from the former, even if they are never reducible to them. Furthermore, "lived" biological experience is based on intersubjective experience and the constitution of the other (see the fifth of the *Cartesian Meditations*). In this context one need only consider the sexual relation.

Biological-precategorial experience makes possible precategorial biological *evidence* such as weight and need, since I feel hungry and sleepy in the first person. This parallels precategorial physical evidence, i.e., my contact with the hardness and heaviness of bodies, which I discover first when I must transport or work with matter. Husserl tends to forget all this. Yet, in speaking of biology, he says that "its nearness to the sources of evidence gives it in return such a nearness to the profundity of the things themselves that the path to transcendental philosophy must be most easy for it." [7] Hidden beyond this, we find Husserl's interest in the works of Du Boys-Reymond, Liebig, and, most of all, Hans Driesch.[8] However, if the problems of the "philosophy of biology" are reduced to the problem of transcendental philosophy, this reduction is based on the precategorial foundation of lived experience (*Erlebnis*), instincts, impulses, and needs. All of this is connected with intersubjective psychic experience and, therefore, with the problems of the modalities through which we psychologically experience the world according to our character or our neuroses and psychoses.

In general, for Husserl, each person has his own world and his personal way of experiencing it. This is true both in the normal cases and in the abnormal ones studied by *Daseinsanalyse*. "As a person I am what I am (and each other person is what he is) as a subject of a surrounding world." [9] For instance, I have my personal way of communicating, eating, sleeping, hearing sounds, seeing colors, and "living" the foreground and the background, the forms and the perspective. This way is influenced by others and by education departing from the first and most fundamental education that my mother has given me. The personal *Umwelt* is both subjective and intersubjective, because each subject, in intersubjective relations, constitutes the *Umwelt,* community, culture, and civilization. This also applies to the study of the *Umwelt* of animals, as Jakob von Uexküll has indicated.[10]

The preceding allows some important considerations. First, the intersubjective world of the historical persons is certainly not ruled by causal or deterministic laws such as those of physics. Second, there is no preconstituted dialectic of persons, groups, and societies, i.e., there is no "scientific" dialectic in the sense of physics. On the other hand, and for the same reasons, there is no preconstituted dialectic of nature. Yet persons, communities, and societies have a material physical reality necessitated by

7. *Ibid.*, p. 483.
8. Driesch has used phenomenology in his own way. In order fully to understand the problems in question, see Ernst Cassirer, *The Problem of Knowledge: Philosophy, Science, and History since Hegel,* trans. William H. Woglom and Charles W. Hendel (New Haven: Yale University Press, 1950), pp. 195 ff.
9. *Ideen II*, p. 185.
10. See Jakob von Uexküll, *Streifzüge durch die Umwelten von Tieren und Menschen* (Hamburg: Rowohlt, 1956). For a bibliography of his work, see pp. 171–73 of this text. For a bibliography of the works in this field of studies, see pp. 174–77 of the same text.

precategorial causality and are conditioned by instincts and biological needs. Persons thus have a causal structure as well as a structure of needs. The determining and conditioning material structure is undeniable precisely because it is the subjective structure of the life-world which grounds the sciences. However, there are no deterministic laws which regulate human relationships. Although human beings live in a conditioning environment, or, better, because they do, they are the "substratum of decisions" and the concrete principle of freedom, e.g., the freedom to transform the natural and social world. The transformation follows the principle whereby concrete freedom passes through necessity. The person experiences his world, and, collectively, persons experience their world, in the various communities, cultures, and civilizations. However, Husserl should have insisted that the freedom of persons and communities is rendered possible precisely by the preliminary satisfaction of necessity. The person emerges from necessity but cannot dispense with it. Although human history is not *just* nature, it must include it. We begin from the present and rediscover our past. However, this rediscovery forces us to recognize a permanent natural past within us, since we are unconsciously constituted by "external" physical nature. This is how Husserl deals with what he calls the "pre-past." [11] which is the origin. Thus, history is also nature. I and each community are conditioned by a deterministic precategorial structure, and we can become free precisely because of this structure.

Groups and communities are personal. Husserl writes:

> Each monad has, within itself and in community with the monads constituted for it in the world, its personal genesis, as the genesis of a concrete monadic ego, which develops its faculties and its habits and forms its personal being. This is also the case for each monadic multiplicity which is socially connected.[12]

Communities are conditioned by precategorial matter and by needs, but their dialectical relations do not follow a preconstituted law. Hence it is not possible to apply a scientific dialectic to history.

Husserl allows us to reassert the necessity and the conditioning of the material structure and the structure of needs on the

11. See Giovanni Piana, "L'Inedito Husserliano C 81," *Aut-Aut*, no. 70 (1962), p. 290.

12. C 16 VII, in Giovanni Piana, "Accomunemento, Storicitá, Tradizione Nello Husserl Inedito," *Aut-Aut*, no. 68 (1962), p. 121.

historical-human praxis. However, at the same time he prevents us from applying the scientific laws of physics and biology to history. Thus it is possible to find the meaning of the paradoxical relation between the conditioning necessity of the structure and the freedom of persons and communities rooted in the structure. In fact, they are free to transform the structure in given conditions precisely because of this paradoxical relation.

The transformation demands that man form and transform nature with his labor. It demands that man, through labor and science, pass from structural necessity to social freedom. In order to work, man uses nature and himself as nature. However, in labor he does not become a mere material object (as when he dies). Man becomes a thing in order to stop being a thing: he works in order to be free. A free society will be one in which the fact that man becomes a thing in labor is not exploited to turn man permanently into a thing or work-animal. But this amounts to saying, with Husserl, that men in history "constitute a living organism bearing a spiritual reality." Such a reality and spiritual freedom are not and must not be pure abstractions, for persons are not pure abstractions and they are rooted and conditioned in precategorial matter. Rather, it is the crossing-point of nature and history, necessity and freedom, "the external" and "the internal." Taken in itself, spirit is an abstraction. Life and freedom condition the structure by means of labor, technology, and science. As in the case of sedimentation and language, we here rediscover the positive function of technology and science as technology.

For Husserl, physics and the natural sciences in general are not needed to understand human and cultural relations, since it is impossible to apply physical laws to history. However, it does not follow that mathematics and physics cannot be used by history, sociology, or anthropology, even if none of these sciences are scientific in the sense of mathematical-natural science.

In order to explain a historical fact or a person, I can use, wherever possible, mathematics, physics, biology, psychology, sociology, and anthropology, since the whole life-world is present in communities and persons. What is important is not to occlude the precategorial foundation and reduce *subjects to objects*. The sciences can be used by man and united by phenomenology as the science of the precategorial foundation, precisely because Husserl has freed them from objectification and alienation. Precategorially founded sciences can comprehend the person precisely because they are rooted in experience in the first person and in the unity of the human person, i.e., the foundation of all science. In this sense, phenomenology can be seen as first philosophy, with all other sciences as its parts. As first philosophy, phenomenology is a science of subjects and not objects. On the human-historical level, it is the science that makes possible the constitution of free persons, upon the foundation of precategorial conditioning, by passing through necessity. Phenomenology is the causal, conditioned, motivated, and free science of the life-world. It is the becoming-conscious of a praxis oriented toward subjectivity and toward the constitution of a subjective and rational society. For the same reason, the phenomenologically founded sciences become the praxis and constituting elements of a human society which is free from exploitation and where no subject is an object for anyone else. These phenomenologically founded sciences are no longer fetishized, neutral, and alienated; they are oriented according to the idea of a true world and true society that constitutes the meaning of the world and human history. The crisis of the sciences can be overcome. Phenomenology gives the sciences their authentic function by giving them their categorial foundation, and gives them unity by rooting them in the experience of man and the human community.

[58]   *The Unhappiness of the Ego.*
The Moral Epochē. Irreversibility
as the Basic Law of the Life-World.
The Temporal Structure of Morality
and Economics. The True Meaning
of the Laws of the Dialectic.
The Spiritualistic Blackmail

ALL EGOS, as persons with other persons, are the living intentionality that is directed toward the constitution of a society of subjects free from alienation, objectification, and exploitation. Taken to its limit, this society is an idea that constitutes the meaning of history, the world, and man.

With philosophy and phenomenology, the ego questions himself in reflection. He discovers and rediscovers his own meaning of truth in the act of becoming-conscious that guides his praxis. In Beilage XXIV, Husserl writes:

The question of self-consideration which the ego poses to himself involves that for which he, in this whole life as a totality of aspirations, and in each active realization, is striving. The possibility, or, better said, the continuing possibility of each such consideration appertains to the fundamental essence of man—where the word "man" is understood as it is always understood in active life. The result of this self-consideration is the unity of an anticipating representation.[13]

Here, the society of subjects appears as a task to be realized in the future. This simple consideration introduces into the history of human societies the complex Husserlian dialectic of time that obtains for the monad as well as for the society of monads. This is also a dialectic of positive and negative, truth and error, good and bad. In addition, it is a dialectic of instincts and reason, and needs and "spiritual reality" in the previously discussed sense. The ego can realize something "inferior" or "superior."

> In the struggle between an inferior and a superior life of value, the ego again and again finds itself in the situation of having to become conscious in the form of the most profound dissatisfaction that it must strive after what is finally repugnant to it, a mode of life and strivings that brings it into struggle with itself (in terms of sentiment, it oppresses one into falling into unhappiness).[14]

Intentionality toward truth is not fulfilled in any particular realization. This happens primarily when one considers a particular conquest as an absolute value. The ego's happiness cannot be secured by confusing relative with absolute goods, mundane reality with intentional truth, or being with its meaning—confusion which is precisely *idolatry* and *fetishization*. The ego's happiness consists in following the infinite path toward truth and being open to meaning, notwithstanding all fetishizations and objectifications. By its very essence, this infinite path characterizes phenomenology. Time has its meaning not in being but in truth. This is the profound and final meaning of self-transcendence and the structure of human and world history. I have already concluded this in *Tempo e Verità*, the title of which is already a program for the correction and the development of phenomenology in contraposition to *Being and Time*.[15] But the problem broached in Beilage XXIV is more profound. It is the

13. *Krisis*, p. 485.
14. *Ibid.*
15. *Tempo e Verità Nella Fenomenologia di Husserl* (Bari: Laterza, 1961), p. 253.

problem of error, guilt, and evil. This problem requires a phenomenological analysis, which was never carried out but only
hinted at in Husserl's works. A phenomenology of evil is made
possible only by departing from man's good even when it is
denied. To use Kierkegaard's terms, this would imply falling into
the *anxiety of evil* which has been done, or into the *anxiety of the
good*—an anxiety which wants good and truth not to exist.
Naturally, a phenomenology of guilt would require a phenomenology of reparation closely connected to a phenomenology of
will.[16]

The will cannot be immediately realized—and we have seen
that it anticipates the future.

> Every will that cannot realize itself immediately, that is not im-
> mediately in the living evidence of the purpose, undergoes a
> transformation into a particular form of impulse that in the best
> of cases, when "its time" comes, will be realized in a mode of
> release by *fiat*. Here, by virtue of the dearth of clarity of purpose,
> forgeries and frauds are possible, along with deviations. Every
> purpose, in particular that which intentionally implies a multi-
> plicity of mediations, requires a recurring consideration, a recur-
> rence as a renewal of the originality of the evidence in its own
> sense. This is all the more so for the will pointed toward the
> ultimate meaning of the totality of determinate being.[17]

Therefore, the evidence, or my own self-presence, contains the
intentional impulse that directs it not toward egoism, but toward
the ultimate meaning of the totality of existence. This is the ultimate meaning of the moral principle of considering the other as
a subject and as a person, and not, by alienating him, as a thing.
This is the predominant principle of the entire *Crisis*, and it is an
essential human principle—one which is, however, occluded by
the mundane. Thus, the epochē has a moral aspect [18] which, by
freeing us from the mundane, must allow us to rediscover the
"natural" direction of the will toward the good and the *evidence
of the will* "pointed toward the ultimate meaning of determinate
being [*Dasein*]." But Husserl emphasizes temporality and, therefore, the *mediations* through which the will directed toward the
rational end must pass. The error lies in confusing the mediations for the end. Such confusion is the idolatry of mediations

16. See my paper on "Die positive Bedeutung des Menschen in
Kierkegaard," *Schweizer Monatshefte*, no. 2 (1963), pp. 177–84.
17. *Krisis*, pp. 485–86.
18. See Alois Roth, *Edmund Husserls ethische Untersuchungen*
(The Hague: Nijhoff, 1960).

and means, and ultimately even involves the fetishization of science and technology. The mediations are temporally realized. Therefore, error and evil are possible in and because of time. This makes possible a whole phenomenology of the ethical meaning of the modifications of the presence. For instance, in the present I can have *remorse* about the past. The past bothers me. I can attempt to occlude or repair it in the present or in the future, even in the future of a community or of humanity, if it is a matter of the past of a community or of humanity.[19] If past evil is considered infinite, the future will also appear as infinite vindication. Here, morality is connected with religion. A phenomenological reading and correction of Kierkegaard's work might discover in it the *hidden* and yet unsuppressible positive meaning of man.[20] However, Husserl's account cannot be exhausted in this. He says that the ego struggles with itself because of the dialectic of inferior and superior values. In an intersubjective context, the struggle of the ego with itself extends to the struggle among subjects. For instance, it extends to the struggle for the domination of one subject over another subject, one group over another group, or one community over another community. This struggle implies the possibility of reciprocal objectification and alienation at various levels. Aggressiveness among subjects is the correlative of the subject's aggressiveness toward himself, and vice versa. A situation of conflict can obtain on the precategorial material level, on the level of biological impulses and needs, and on the level of cultural and philosophical values. All of these levels are interconnected and project the struggle to the "living" level of economy, psychology, and culture.

The concrete monad is rooted in the biological and material structure. He must satisfy needs and impulses in order to live. Yet it is precisely the body that allows man to perform material labor by binding him to nature.

In order to live, man must begin by satisfying the most elementary economic needs. The ego is dependent and conditioned by them. He can feel superior needs in different ways and situations only to the extent that he has satisfied the more elementary needs. Here we are confronted with the binding character of the precategorial economic structure which is lived in the first person. On the various levels, economic behavior *seems* to follow

19. For this point of view, see Ernesto De Martino, *La Terra del Rimorso* (Milan: Il Saggiatore, 1961), pp. 13–15.

20. See my "Die positive Bedeutung des Menschen in Kierkegaard," pp. 183–84.

the following modalities: "I now do this in order subsequently to obtain that. In this relation I satisfy more determinate needs in view of others that will come, and I do not satisfy some now in order to satisfy others in the future." Of course, there is a marginality of needs, a minimum that must be satisfied in order for the subject to live. The precategorial economic structure is thus rooted in the very possibility of life and the conditions that allow life. Death is unavoidable, because of consumption, temporal irreversibility, and biological and physical entropy. The precategorial economic structure indicates in the clearest way man's dependence on natural and physical life dominated by ubiquitous irreversibility and entropy. Man satisfies the needs necessary to life and answers in various ways the problem of death according to groups, communities, civilizations, and cultures. The dependence on biological life clarifies the meaning of consumption, tiredness, the need for rest and for sleep, and, for the life of the species in general, the death of the individual.

Irreversibility is the necessary basic modality of the life-world. Husserl has not elaborated this point, which, among other things, indicates the close connection between superior and inferior values. Had he done so in relation to precategorial material causality, he would also have discussed precategorial irreversibility and lived consumption as tiredness, failures, the ego's impoverishment, and, finally, the meaning of the inevitability of death. The principle of irreversibility is fundamental. It allows relationism to fill one of the most important lacunae of Husserl's thought. We cannot here explicate all the consequences that result from the development of relationism in phenomenology. This would entail a correction of phenomenology in terms of relationistic research. The meeting of relationism and phenomenology allows us, among other things, to clarify the problem of individuation and to reach a better understanding of the relations among nature, life, and culture.[21] Man's ability to postpone death in certain situations, his need to promulgate the life that binds him to other men and makes him desire to live through his sons and to leave something of his through his works and through language, his psychological need to answer the shock produced by natural death or by death endured or given through aggression—all these are themes con-

21. For an elaboration of relationism and temporal irreversibility, see my *Tempo e Relazione* (Turin: Taylor, 1954), and *Dall' Esistenzialismo al Relazionismo* (Messina-Florence: G. d'Anna, 1957).

nected with the "unhappiness of the ego" and his disjunction from himself. These themes reveal to us the complex structure of the concrete monad and the interconnection of his material, psychological, biological, and cultural levels. Without elaborating these themes, we cannot comprehend presence, culture, civilization, and history. The connection of these themes is the unity of the sciences and the interdependence of physics, biology, psychology, sociology, anthropology, culture, and history. In civilizations and cultures, the need to survive appears as the need to be immortal and to connect the living and the dead.

What must be emphasized here is the relation between the structure of needs and satisfactions, and the problem of inferior and superior values. The temporal structure dominates economic life, culture, and history, because the temporal structure characterizes the life-world in an essential way.

In dealing with economics, we can investigate the economic-temporal modifications of the actual presence from which we must always depart. Some elementary needs must be immediately satisfied if the subject wants to live and does not want to abandon himself to tiredness and death: they cannot wait. What we have here is *urgency* as a dimension of presence—something to be related to the temporal modifications already described by Husserl in 1904 in the lectures on internal time-consciousness.

Even if elementary needs are "inferior" in the temporal structure of the precategorial life-world, they are *urgent*. Elementary needs and their satisfaction place man in a relation of *dependence* on the natural environment. Intersubjectively, these needs can place man in a relation of dependency on other men, classes, groups, and dominating communities. Man can be subjugated by means of war or by controlling the means of satisfaction of elementary needs. If the elementary needs are not satisfied, they can lead to that maximum alienation which is death (which is also the maximum objectification and externalization). This is also the case in the psychological, cultural, and historical situation of man, in relation to death with which war is connected (recall the Hegelian dialectic of the slave and the master)—but it is particularly so with the elementary economic condition. To appropriate the means and products necessary for the satisfaction of man's economic needs is to place him in a relation of dependency. On the economic level, man can be reduced to the level of a thing or work-animal.

Within certain conditions, a community or dominating class

of subjects can give to another class of men only what is minimally required for them to work and survive. I can reduce the
free time of others. I can condition it with working time. I can
force them to have inferior needs and impulses, since the satisfaction of elementary needs conditions the very emergence of
superior ones. At any rate, if I allow a man what is necessary
if he is to live and work for me, he will also have the strength
to elaborate his own culture, a psychological defense-system,
and a series of considerations concerning his condition. Even
in the worst situations, this reflection can make man self-
conscious of the human essence and therefore of his rights and
his meaning. He becomes conscious of what must be unaliena-
ble in man *qua* man and as a participant of mankind and its
historical intentionality. Originally, philosophy appears precisely
as this type of becoming self-conscious. It is provoked by the
negation brought about by a group or a community, or nature
(natural death), or by the economic difficulties of the environment. It is a becoming-conscious of what cannot be denied in
man because it belongs to the human essence. Philosophy, science, and culture turn out to be the becoming-conscious of
negation, and the desire for a negation of the negation. To the
extent that it is unhappiness and the contradiction of man with
himself and humanity with itself, i.e., a dialectic of opposition,
the struggle among groups and communities is a dialectic of
negation that vindicates the satisfaction of needs. This allows
"superior" needs and satisfactions and, therefore, the transformation of "quantity into quality." Thus we rediscover Engels'
dialectical laws. But we rediscover them free of scientistic
naturalism, and founded on the level of the intersubjective
precategorial structure, i.e., on the phenomenological level.

In the organization of the relations of production, it is possible for a man to prevent another man from living "spiritually"
according to a "will pointed toward the ultimate meaning of the
totality of determinate being." I can use other men for my
advantage, so that their working time, and their internal life
of labor, procure for me, the master, the *otium* needed for
spiritual ends. It is a case of various types of slavery.[22] This is
not incompatible with the fact that slaves end up by partly
assimilating the culture of the master. They partly contrapose
themselves to it, thus giving it a new meaning and founding

22. See the various essays published in *Rivista Trimestrale*, no. 1
(March, 1962) and no. 2 (June, 1962).

a new philosophy based on the becoming-conscious of negation and alienation. Therefore, in intersubjective social relations I can negate the final meaning of the totality of existence, and force others to lose it or be forced myself to lose it. This does not mean that the final meaning is there, or that it is innate in man, and that, as such, it tries to express itself as much as possible. Because of the economic precategorial structure, when I am forced to produce or when I produce the loss of intentionality, what is threatened in the state of slavery is the meaning of life, of the world and human history. The lack of recognition of the causal-economic conditioning structures of the precategorial life-world and their dependence on the impulses and needs of the concrete monad makes the *spiritual blackmail* possible. In the name of superior values, this blackmail denies the humanity of those who are subjugated and slaves, after having done all that is possible to deny the slaves' superior needs and impulses. Since man is a totality, the slave cannot be oppressed if he must produce. Thus, the negation of his essence and human rights becomes the creation of a philosophy understood as the negation of the negation. Even in a rich and wealthy society, a dominating group can regulate the needs of its dependents. It can degrade them, fetishize them, in order to lower the value of life as much as possible. Thus, a dominating group can detach from life the meaning of truth and the will directed toward it as "to the ultimate meaning of the totality of determinate being." Phenomenology discovers in man the innate impulses and the need for truth, in addition to the natural, economic, social, and historical situations that bind the material and precategorial life and the philosophical becoming-conscious of the negation and the totality of subjects in the actual presence.

[59]   *The Husserlian Conception of Philosophy.*
        The Struggle for Philosophy
        as the Struggle for
        the Emancipation and Meaning of Man

WE HAVE ATTEMPTED TO UNDERSTAND the profound ethical and economic implications of objectifications by analyzing Husserl's hints in a way not developed by Husserl himself. Men are subjects and not facts. Phenomenology is the science of subjects. Developed in the indicated sense, it becomes science as the becoming-conscious and the rational will of the liberation of humanity from slavery.

Men live in communities, in civil societies, and in states. This brings the whole problem back to the problem of professionalism and the philosopher's vocation. Unlike the pure technicians, here the philosopher appears to Husserl as conscious of the historicity of humanity and each of its members.

> When the artisans, the overseers, and the laborers in the common professional labor of an industrial operation, an official at the service of the State, occasionally consider the "meaning" of their professional existence, they do not need for that purpose a historical consideration. Not so with the philosopher. *His existence as philosopher is historical in another sense, in an altogether particular sense,* different from that of every other profession and also from the totality of professions that inhere in the structure of a people's [*völkischen*] or statelike [*staatlichen*] existence.[23]

This passage must be explained and corrected, especially in relation to what Husserl often refers to as the "ruling function of the community of philosophers."[24] The philosopher's historical meaning is the historical meaning of humanity and historical truth which cannot be exhausted by any popular or state authority. States and institutions are at the service of humanity, and not vice versa. In every historical presence, and in the connection between tradition and renewal, philosophy is the becoming-conscious of historical meaning by humanity. It is the becoming-conscious of the negation and will of the negation of the negation. It becomes a project for the future and the reality of the transformation of the world for the constitution of a rational society.

The philosophical vocation gives no superior dignity to the philosopher. All men are philosophers because they become conscious of their own meaning and of the positive value of good and truth. When they do not recognize in themselves the evidence of truth "pointed toward the ultimate meaning of determinate being," they reassert it indirectly in the anguish of good and evil. (We have seen how a phenomenology of evil is made possible only by departing from the good that man essentially contains.) Essentially, man contains the meaning of

23. *Krisis*, pp. 487–88.
24. See, for instance, C 1, p. 5.

humanity in himself. This explains the moral character of the epochē.

When a man denies another man's human essence, he denies him his humanity and the ultimate meaning of existence. Even in this case, the man being denied his human meaning and value reacts to this negation by becoming-conscious and by wanting to negate the negation. He who negates the other functions for him as a transcendental or *radical* epochē. In wanting the negation of the negation, the suppressed or subjugated community vindicates the value of the human totality, even though it is just a part. The evidence of truth "pointed toward the ultimate meaning of determinate being" becomes embodied in the oppressed class or community. Since the oppressor also denies this evidence of truth, the liberation of the oppressed is indirectly also the liberation of the oppressor from self-alienation. These situations exhibit complex dialectical relations. Case by case, individuation by individuation, they require historical-phenomenological analyses that clarify the different types of situations and their past connection or future possibilities.

The dialectic of consciousness seems to move between two extremes. One is the extreme of philosophy as integration, enrichment, the perfection of man and humanity, and intentional direction toward a society of subjects. The other is philosophy as the negation of the negation of the essence and meaning of man, as the becoming-conscious of an oppressed community and man. Both extremes are conjoined in different forms in the various historical, social, and cultural situations. As a professional philosopher and man, the philosopher struggles *for philosophy* directly or indirectly. This is not a struggle for an abstraction, or for a philosophical science separate from real, precategorial, historical, and social man, as if philosophy were a *res cogitans* separate from men. The struggle for philosophy is the struggle for human emancipation and perfection. The same must be said of science and culture, to the extent that they enter in philosophy as *first science*. Every culture and civilization present the two extremes and their individuated mediations. Thus, even the most oppressed communities have their cultures. Culture is also necessary to the oppressors and their alienation. In every community, emancipation means the emancipation of man and is always an effort of self-transcendence. It is a tendency toward truth: intentionality directed toward "the ultimate meaning of determinate being." Within the historical and anthropological domain, this leads to the evaluation and immanent intentional dialectical accord of every culture and civilization as its meaning.

In the actual historical situation, the crisis is one of alienation, and everyone must become conscious of the necessity to abolish exploitation and war. The crisis of Europe is its self-alienation. It is the oppression and the alienation of the exploited European classes and the non-European populations. In wanting to negate the endured negation, these groups can free Europe from the crisis to the extent that it is possible to free all humanity on the planet Earth. The struggle for philosophy thus becomes the struggle for the emancipation of all men. The existence of the philosopher is historical to the extent that he pursues his vocation. Originally the philosopher is a man like other men who can become self-alienated and alienate other men. His very philosophy enters into a struggle with other philosophies, and must explain both their errors and their meaning of truth. In a more profound sense: if each man is a philosopher, and philosophy struggles for its own truth, it is the same human struggle for human emancipation and for the realization of a free man among free men and a society of subjects according to the limiting idea of truth. Culture fulfills the same function in every situation. Although limited and typical of a community, and historically individuated, every cultural expression is positive if it expresses, directly or indirectly, the meaning of humanity and its teleological idea. Religions also turn out to be religions of truth, and in each of its individuated and particular historical expressions, art expresses the final meaning of the world, history, and man.

Therefore, the historicity of the philosopher is ultimately human, social, and cultural. As Husserl himself put it, if the philosopher struggles for philosophy, he does so as a *functionary* of humanity. Yet, the philosopher must not distinguish himself from artisans and technicians, for, contrary to what Husserl says, he shares his historicity with them as men. This historicity is the liberation from fetishistic technology and is directed toward human emancipation and the constitution of a rational society. We have seen that in this struggle, because of the wholeness of the monad, economics, morality, the structure of material precategorial needs, and the necessity of their satisfaction in the complex fabric of temporal modifications become conjoined. Material reality, body-proper, feeling, reflection, and the act of becoming-conscious cannot be stratified by following the Cartesian dualism of *res cogitans* and *res extensa*. The struggle for the meaning of human truth extends to the economic and precategorial level, to individuation, and to the meaning of teleological intentionality inherent in every situation. The emancipation of a population is human emancipation and not just the emancipation of that population alone. The emancipation of the proletariat is the emancipation of the entire alienated humanity. "The *head* of this emancipation is *philosophy*, its heart is the *proletariat*. Philosophy cannot be actualized without the transcendence [*Aufhebung*] of the proletariat; the proletariat cannot be transcended without the actualization of philosophy." [25]

25. Karl Marx, "Toward the Critique of Hegel's *Philosophy of Law:* Introduction," in *Writings of the Young Marx on Philosophy and Society,* trans. and ed. Loyd D. Easton and Kurt H. Guddat (Garden City, N. Y.: Doubleday, 1967), p. 264. For Marx, the proletariat is the class that must suppress itself as a class and, in order to do so, must suppress every class difference. *Aufhebung* is here translated by taking its meaning under consideration. See the German text: "Die *Emanzipation des Deutschen* ist die *Emanzipation des Menschen.* Der *Kopf* dieser Emanzipation ist die *Philosophie,* ihr *Herz* das *Proletariat.* Die Philosophie kann sich nicht verwirklichen ohne die Aufhebung des Proletariats, das Proletariat kann sich nicht aufheben ohne die Verwirklichung der Philosophie." See Karl Marx and Friedrich Engels, *Werke* (Berlin, D.D.R.: Dietz, 1956–69), I, 391.

15 / Unity of Man and Philosophical Self-Understanding

[60]   *Dialectic and Logic.*
Philosophy and the Totality of the World
and History in Its Becoming

PHILOSOPHY IS INTEGRATED WITH HISTORY, culture, and science because it is the science of intentional precategorial life, the foundation of the sciences, and the becoming-conscious of the *telos* for the transformation of the world and man in the historical dialectic. There is a continuity of philosophical intentionality, through both harmony and discord, as philosophy becomes individuated in the various cultures, civilizations, groups, classes, communities, and historical periods, and in the diverse environmental and economic conditions which are generally called "geographic."

The dialectical function of the sciences and of philosophy as the science of history *sui generis* obtains in genetic-universal continuity and in its periods. In Beilage XXV of the *Crisis,* Husserl writes:

> The philosophic and scientific generation lives in a philosophico-historical connection, i.e., in this respect, in a particularly conscious nexus with the previous generations, thus exercising a documented critique, correction, covalidating the alterations, making explicit the one-sidedness, unlocking the horizons of problems which have always been important but that up to this point had not been considered, and, in all this, explicating indeterminacies, obscurities, and ambiguities (not just mere words), and, at the

[275]

same time, outlining new and precise concepts, and new work problems.[1]

What Husserl says, completed by the already mentioned dialectic, allows us to understand the continuity of scientific and philosophic intentionality and the philosophical struggle against common opinion, prejudices, objectification, and fetishization. Every philosopher is historically rooted to the extent that he departs from his actual presence. Every period and every community is in some way part of the historical and dialectical movement toward truth. Even though historically rooted, however, science and philosophy are always open to the future. Science is only temporarily concluded.

> Temporarily concluded science has, in its own and at every time, an open indeterminate horizon of unasked or, at least, unmatured questions, which it has not grasped in the obscure immaturity, and with reference to which it is important to notice the horizon of the future progress of science which, through its real labor and through the already attained truth, will create the motivation to pose new questions in a determinate way and, as such, new domains of truths that can now only be anticipated in a completely empty way.[2]

Therefore, in addition to historical individuation, there is also historical "maturation." This is true of philosophy as the act of becoming-conscious and as the praxis of the transformation of man and civilization.

Philosophy faces the horizon of the future and looks back at the horizon of the past. It is the self-reflection of the presence living in the present world, "as the continually present that continually transforms itself in the past and the future-present. The flowing present is but the present of the universally flowing past, and of the future of the world. The being of the world is a being in the modality of time." [3] Philosophy is a *praxis of philosophers in the society of scientists,"* but it is a praxis which unites philosophers "with practically struggling men and the human socialities *in the world."* [4]

1. E. Husserl, *Die Krisis der europäischen Wissenschaften und die transzendentale Phänomenologie: Eine Einleitung in die phänomenologische Philosophie*, ed. Walter Biemel (1954; 2d printing, The Hague: Nijhoff, 1962), p. 491.
2. *Ibid.*, p. 493.
3. *Ibid.*, p. 494.
4. *Ibid.*

Historically temporal life contains consciousness of historical temporality, as common-consciousness, which, understandably, is in every single philosopher as a personal consciousness, based upon his working-place, working-problem, his own results. Scientific life and the being of science of the present in its social livingness [*Lebendigkeit*] appear in all of them essentially as a nucleus [*Kern*] in virtue of the broader horizon that includes other scientists.[5]

Husserl uses the term *Kern* to indicate the luminous center of the actual presence. The *Kern* is surrounded by penumbrae and indeterminate perspectives, but it captures the totality of perspectives. It is a spatial and temporal center that changes in time and can shift so as to vary cognitive perspectives.[6] The present as the *Kern* is a nucleus of self-reflection and clarity. It is actual time and the becoming-conscious of the actual situation. But philosophy is not just the becoming-conscious in the historical-temporal dialectic. As *first philosophy*, it is the nucleus from which all sciences depart. As such, it becomes philosophical and scientific self-responsibility. The philosophers' praxis is human reflection. Here, Husserl is thinking not of the governing function of philosophy but of its self-consciousness as "praxis operating in human sociality, in the world." The living presence in which I find myself is "social vitality." Containing the working scientists in its horizon, philosophy is the "science of the present in its social livingness." Phenomenology as the new science of history appears here as the science of society in its actual presence. As such, it can ground and constitute sociology. Sociohistorical presence has its past and its future. Therefore, there will be modifications of sociohistorical presence corresponding to retention, protention, recollection, and memorative anticipation. Recollection (or memory) discovers the reality of past history, while anticipation presumes and projects the future. All of this is important for the *reshaping of* sociohistorical reality and the transformation of the world. Like every man and community living in the present, the philosopher becomes aware of praxis and of its meaning, which is oriented according to the meaning of truth. He lives in the dialectic, and the philosophy that "sketches the logos of the world" lives in the dialectic together with the sciences. The philosopher needs the

5. *Ibid.*, p. 495.
6. See my text, *Tempo e Verità Nella Fenomenologia di Husserl* (Bari: Laterza, 1961), pp. 105 ff.

history of philosophy and the history of the sciences as part of
the history of human societies. He does not merely seek a
categorial history. He must discover a precategorial history of
the life-world from which the sciences arise through subjective
operations. Present society needs the history of the past so that
it can rediscover and reactivate its genesis in it. This "diachronic"
genesis is connected to the "synchronic" principle from which it
is impossible not to depart. It is connected to the original presence, which discovers itself by rediscovering the past and by
holding and renewing the tradition by reengaging it and transforming it in the present for the future in a series of perma-
nences and dialectical transformations. The past "matures" the
transformations of the present, and the present "matures" those
of the future. Therefore, the logos of the world is rooted in the
dialectic. Yet the welded unity of the sciences is constituted in
the temporal dialectic, e.g., the patrimony of mathematics, the
structure of *formal logic*. If, for Husserl, logic did not have a
precategorial foundation, there could be a contradiction between
logic and dialectic. Yet, the very structures of the life-world,
although living in the temporal dialectic, ground the permanence of logic. This is the theme that Husserl broadly develops
in *Erfahrung und Urteil*, where judgment is founded upon sensible temporality and perceptive experience (recall in this connection the transcendental aesthetic of manuscripts D).

The precategorial operations that permit the constitution of
logic by departing from the temporal precategorial dialectic
allow a *genealogy of logic*. Here logic is not passively accepted
but is continually reactivated by rediscovering the operations
that have and still do constitute it. This uncovers the dialectical
dimensions of *passivity* and *activity*, of the implicit and the
explicit, of possibility and impossibility.[7]

In contemporary thought, *Erfahrung und Urteil* represents
the overcoming of the contradiction between logic and dialectic.
History and the world are lived in precategorial time where the
logos is constituted. Every judgment originates the world, and
the world is the horizon of all possible substrata of judgment.[8]
The dialectic does not prevent the self-constitution of the logos
of reality and the world.

But the logos cannot give us a closed world, precisely because
it is constituted in time. I experience only parts of the world

7. E. Husserl, *Erfahrung und Urteil*, 3d ed. (Hamburg: Claassen, 1964), pp. 91 ff.
8. *Ibid.*, pp. 36–37.

and never the totality. Yet these are parts of an open totality, i.e., the world. The world is a horizon inherent in perception as an intentional direction implying other perceptions. For me the world is something which is always pregiven. In this sense, it can appear as a transcendent reality in which I happen to be.[9] The world is the terrain that renders the connection possible. But it is also always *in a process* which can never be fully exhausted. In every stage and subject, the process implies an open totality which is continually reasserted. The dialectic of the parts is possible to the extent that every part potentially implies a meaning of the world and of history, even in the limitation and failure of the part, and in the failure and perishing of subjects and communities. The dialectic is a totalization in process whereby every part is an index of the logical meaning of the world and history. The authentic logos is rooted in the dialectic and in time. Contradictions and negations are negative proofs of the truth of logos, and, in fact, they provoke the negation of the negation. Every part contains the meaning of truth which, if negated, reasserts itself in another part. In this dialectic—which is in reality much more complex than our presentation indicates—the world appears as "the idea of the totality of all individualities and groups."[10] Formal logic constitutes the permanent formal logos, because of the judgment's temporal origin. If there are a formal logic and totality, there must be a totality of meaning of the dialectic and a direction of truth of all groups and struggling communities.

Thus, formal logic becomes the index of the possibility of a real agreement. As an idea, this agreement appears as infinite and it operates and functions as the intentional totality inherent in every part, in every individual, in every community, and in every civilization and culture meeting in the historical process. There is no rationality coinciding with the reality of the world and history. In the dialectic, the classes and communities negated by other classes and communities tend to negate the negation. This means that subjects, groups, and communities are formed in a praxis and cannot oppose the positive meaning of historical truth except by ultimately paying for that opposition with their own self-destruction.

The dialectic is essential to history and to the world because "the cosmos has its own way of being idea, of being always only

9. See Gerd Brand, *Mondo Io e Tempo* (Milan: V. Bompiani, 1960), p. 59.

10. *Krisis,* p. 497.

given 'one-sidedly,' always only in individual realities, groups, etc., with horizons of a possible self-offering experience containing the correlative ideality of precisely what exists intrinsically in them." [11] That is, every concrete monad has its own way of experiencing the world. The world is given to every monad in relation to his life, character, and history. But every monad is finite and experiences a finite world. Yet this finitude contains a typicality and an *eidos*, as does every perception. A *universal correlation* is implied in every part. All of this must be seen in the intermonadic connections. But no disagreement would be possible without an original agreement and without the intentional direction toward an infinite ideal agreement and an infinite harmony. There is a direction toward an agreement of ideas and a harmonious society of subjects implicit in the idea that every monad has of the world. This realizes a moment of the meaning of truth even if it obtains in different ways according to different situations.

Having reduced monads, things, and modes to formal indexes, the agreement appears as the perfecting of formal logic. Because of the precategorial life upon which logic is founded, the relation is dialectical. If the dialectic can have an intentional direction and a meaning of truth that continues to be valid even as an ethical principle and in its negation, the future can also appear as the redemption from error and evil. If error and evil are lived as if they were infinite, the appearance of the future as infinite may have an ethical meaning.

Finite and temporal monads are born and die. Subjects are tied to generative nature in the same way that they are tied to the precategorial economic structure. Hence, every civilization and culture faces the problem of finitude and death, and they themselves represent an answer to this problem. History inherits the good and bad actions of those who have been. Its rational process is one of continual self-correlation, reparation, and positive reactivation which, to the extent that it is positive, has its own typical and universal value. Philosophy as the act of becoming-conscious assumes the negativity in order to undertake a continual struggle for positivity. It is the science of the open totality existing and becoming in the world. It is the science of every typicality and universality constituted in the world. "Philosophy must be a universal science of the world, universal in a double sense—of the universals of the world and of all

11. *Ibid.*

that is in the world—to the extent that this has a good meaning." [12]

According to Husserl, in the historical process the philosopher carries on a dialogue with dead philosophers. But every man—and every reflecting man is a philosopher—contains all those who have lived and those who will live in the genetic connection and in universal teleology. Heir of all the past in the present, yet free to modify his present and his society, he can and must orient his praxis according to the meaning of truth. In our own time, a society of subjects free from the alienation of exploitation and war is finally possible. This would be a society "appropriate" for all men on the planet Earth.

[61]   *The Whole Man*
        and Philosophical Self-Understanding

THE POINT OF DEPARTURE of phenomenology is present subjectivity, i.e., that which is original and experienced in the first person. That which is original is the intersubjective ego to the extent that it is the living society in the world that experiences and becomes conscious of its own meaning in every determination and part, yet at the same time according to a common intentionality. As we know, it is not a matter of choice. I am always ready in the world and I perceive and experience as a subject.

If there is a dialectic, I participate in it as a causal component. The dialectic does not objectively unfold in front of me and in front of other subjects as a separate, preconstituted, and mechanical reality. The dialectic is inconceivable without subjects, and vice versa. Subjects cannot deny themselves or the world. The dialectic conceived as an objective unveiling, separate from the subjects living in it and conditioned by it, is an objectivistic myth. It would be a reality *in itself* of which we, the subjects that are *for it,* cannot say anything—much less intervene in it as active subjects.

For Husserl, an objectified dialectic is categorial. It is a dialectic of abstract concepts, ideas, and constructions that have occluded their genesis in the precategorial world and in the subjective and intersubjective operations. This is a criticism

12. *Ibid.*

that can be directed at Hegel, as has been done by the left Hegelians. However, this critique cannot be the contraposition of materialistic objectivism to subjectivism. The problem of materialism is complex, and the reduction to the subject or to subjects does not deny matter, nature, causal concatenations, and structural conditioning. What is connoted by the name *structure* is to be experienced and conceived precategorially. Matter and the life-world are not metaphysical concepts or constructions. In order to grasp them I must grasp the very precategorial, material, sensible, and aesthetic foundation of logic. Here we need only recall what we have said in connection with *Erfahrung und Urteil*. I must depart from the *evidence*, from the undeniable experiencing of the subject living in the world and in community with other subjects. The deriving rationality is not identical with reality, but it is a meaning of truth of the reality that combats what is occluded and covered, against the errors and the negation, in a continual and infinite self-correction and rectification.

Consequently, the science of the life-world is not knowledge of an objectified *object-in-itself*, but the act of becoming-conscious of the temporal and historical situation. It is the act of becoming-conscious which, in order to be fulfilled and actualized, must be expressed in the rectification, reshaping, and transformation of itself and the world. Therefore, the science of the life-world is essentially praxis precisely because it is the science of the precategorial and of the operations performed and being performed by the subjects. Here, *science* has a *new* meaning. It is no longer the verification of an objectivity in itself. Rather, it is the consciousness of praxis, its intentional direction, the positive meaning of truth, and the effort of actualizing this meaning in the epochē of the mundane, i.e., in the epochē of a truth coinciding with the given. What Hegel lacked was the epochē, i.e., the first reflective dialectical operation of the subject living in the world. This has also been lacking in the consciousness of the actual presence, of subjectivity, and of ourselves in our precategorial reality and in our transcendental reflection, i.e., in our act of becoming-conscious. Even in Hegel, the unveiling of the world is objectified as the unveiling of an absolute in-itself. *We*, the *for-itself*, is theorized, constructed, and invented. It is actually occluded. The identification with the absolute escapes in time and in the totality of history and the becoming of the world. Although it might sound strange, what is lacking in Hegelian idealism is precisely the subjective and precategorial point of departure. Since the subject is not knowledge of the already made world, but the beginning of its transformation *in* the world, the lack of the subjective point of departure is equivalent to a miscomprehension of praxis.[13] Idealism has faltered because of its failure to recognize the subject in flesh and blood. This is why Husserl writes:

> Idealism was always too quick with its theories and for the most part could not free itself from hidden objectivistic presuppositions; or else, as speculative idealism, it passed over the task of inter-rogating, concretely and analytically, actual subjectivity, i.e., subjectivity as having the actual phenomenal world in intuitive validity—which, properly understood, is nothing other than carry-ing out the phenomenological reduction. [P. 337]

Therefore, idealism has lost the concreteness of the subject. Ultimately, the subject of idealism turns out to be mundane or a mere speculative assertion. If we investigate the subjects and the world that lives and is lived by every one of them, we find the reality of the world not as an objectified fact but as our reality in its becoming and intentionality. We can construct neither ourselves nor the world. We are not already in the world as speculative constructions or inventions, in the same way that matter, precategorial causality, conditioning, and ani-mated life are not constructions. Similarly, we cannot contrapose to the idealistic subject, which is the misplaced concreteness of ourselves, a realism or a materialism as abstract as speculative idealism. By doing this one would remain on the same level of speculative idealism. It is not possible to ground idealism and realism as separate and subsequently reunited or implied by one another. When Merleau-Ponty tries to do so he reveals a failure to understand the epochē and the phenomenological reduction.

On the one hand, such a position forces one to accept ob-jectivism according to the ideal of the physicomathematical natural sciences, while, on the other, one must criticize, in the name of the subject, that very objectivism that one has already accepted. The phenomenological reduction, as the temporal act of becoming-conscious in the dialectic and in the totality of world-becoming, recognizes life as precategorial and real in the same sense that the uninhabited geological past is real. However,

13. See my paper on "Anthropology, Dialectics, and Phenomenol-ogy in Hegel," *Radical America*, IV, no. 6 (September–October, 1971), 33–53.

it does not recognize life by speculatively asserting the ego or by subsequently contraposing the world to it in a similarly speculative fashion. Life reveals its own meaning in the investigation of the subject who, in the temporal presence, rediscovers a reality that necessarily preceded the very subject that has (diachronically) originated and conditioned it. This subject recognizes reality within himself as real along with his presence and his past. In the presence, I recognize the present as having preceded the past. By transforming and reshaping the present, I can proceed toward the future according to a project that has come to light in the act of becoming-conscious.

Therefore, we must not follow the attitude of the natural sciences which presupposes something objective "in itself." We must not follow it "at least in the way that the objective is opposed in the exact sciences to the merely subjective, the latter being understood as that which merely indicates something objective or that in which something objective is supposed merely to appear" (p. 336). This does not mean that the natural sciences are not natural, or that they are not "objective" in the sense that their verifications must permit the overcoming of any individual and relative viewpoint. It does not even mean that logic is not exact. What is criticized is the contraposition of an objective to a subjective reality, the metaphysical crystallization presupposed by the dualism of *res extensa* and *res cogitans* in all of its variations. This dualism is a construction, while the scientific operations, along with phenomenology, must depart from concrete and grounding precategorial operations. Furthermore, phenomenology cannot transform the results of the operations into a metaphysical dimension to be contraposed to the subject, and vice versa. The analysis of the sciences reveals to us their grounding operations and their function. But operations and functions are incompatible with any implicit, if not explicit, dualistic metaphysics. Science becomes the logos and the meaning of truth in the temporal dialectic and in the constitutive operations that progressively reveal the meaning of the world and of history.

The universally, apodictically grounded and grounding science arises now as the necessarily highest function of mankind, as I said, namely, as making possible mankind's development into a personal autonomy and into an all-encompassing autonomy for mankind—the idea which represents the driving force of life for the highest stage of mankind. [P. 338]

A grounded science is empirically grounded if we understand "empiricism" as we have already indicated. True empiricism is not dualistically opposed to rationalism. Thus, Husserl can write:

> Philosophy is nothing other than [rationalism], through and through, but it is rationalism differentiated within itself according to the different stages of the movement of intention and fulfillment; it is *ratio in the constant movement of self-elucidation,* begun with the first breakthrough of philosophy into mankind. [P. 338]

This movement does not lack pauses, obscurities, and errors, i.e., it is a dialectical movement. "It is a struggle of the generations of philosophers, who are the bearers of this spiritual development, living and surviving in spiritual community" (p. 339).

The *telos* of this movement is

> the ultimate self-understanding of man as being responsible for his own human being. . . . [The man who becomes self-conscious] not only in abstractly practicing apodictic science in the usual sense but [as being mankind] which realizes its whole concrete being in apodictic freedom by becoming apodictic mankind in the whole active life of its reason—through which it is human; as I said, mankind understanding itself as rational, understanding that it is rational in seeking to be rational; that this signifies an infinity of living and striving toward reason; that reason is precisely that which man *qua* man, in his innermost being, is aiming for, that which alone can satisfy him, make him "blessed." [Pp. 340–41]

The meaning of this blessing is to be related to what has been said of the unhappy ego. Clearly, it is not a speculative or contemplative blessing, but one rooted in man, like the meaning of truth. Man is unhappy until he succeeds in finding the sense of the movement of himself, others, and the world. And he is much more unhappy when, in the dialectic, he is contraposed to the meaning of truth, thus feeling, in his very unhappiness, that alienation does not belong to his nature, and that the very fact that it is possible to speak about alienation presupposes subjectivity as the norm of freedom and truth. The unhappy man is split. But man must be able to rediscover himself as a whole, as the origin of all his operations and their result, and as the origin of all of his work and products.

The performed task must not be detached from the subject

who performs it. The critique of an objectivity in itself and of dualism is also the critique of every reality considered extraneous and removed from the precategorial human operations guided by the intentionality of reason. Reason itself is not something real and outside of man and the world. It is the continual movement toward the rationality that coincides with the recognition of the entirety of man and of all human society. Reason is the intentional meaning of the whole man and his life. Therefore, we must not contrapose to man a spiritual reality, just as we cannot contrapose, by abstractly absolutizing terms, "reason" to "will," praxis to the meaning of truth as something dead and not realized in praxis.

The unity of man and the progressive comprehension and realization of a community of subjects are not separable from the intentional *telos* of reason. "Reason allows for no differentiation into 'theoretical,' 'practical,' 'aesthetic,' or whatever; that being human is teleological being and an ought-to-be, and that this teleology holds sway in each and every activity and project of an ego; that through self-understanding in all this it can know the apodictic *telos*" (p. 341). Philosophy as the becoming-conscious in time and in the world is the science of universals. It rediscovers in every part that which, even if not actually in the part, implies, according to the *principle of universal correlation*, the horizon toward which every part aims in the totalization in process according to the meaning of truth. Husserl can therefore conclude by saying: "This knowing, the ultimate self-understanding, has no other form than self-understanding according to a priori principles as self-understanding in the form of philosophy" (p. 341).

PART III

Phenomenology and Marxism

16 / History and Nature

[62]   *Materialism and Naturalism*

ALTHOUGH HUSSERL was not directly interested in Marx
and Marxist problems, Marx's philosophy repeatedly appears in
Husserl's phenomenology. As we have indicated, Husserl's
thought leads to the same problem areas with which Marxism
deals. Furthermore, if we approach Marxism from a phenomenological perspective, we can expect a critical Marxism and
possibly a new reading of Marxist texts.

Phenomenology reintroduces the question of materialism in
all its complexity. Moreover, phenomenological research acquires
a particular new meaning if it focuses on the problem of political
economy as a science, i.e., the problem of the precategorial foundation of political economy. Husserl thinks that psychology is a
sort of testing ground for phenomenology, i.e., a *science of decisions*. The same could be more appropriately said of political
economy which, because of its precategorial foundations, extends into the causal world of the base, into the structure of
needs and their satisfaction. Husserl never dealt with the problem of relating the sphere of needs and satisfaction and the
conditioning, precategorial sphere, nor did he treat the phenomenology of needs experienced and lived in the first person.
However, he did emphasize the deterministic and conditioning
character of the structure of the base.

An analysis of the temporal modalities of needs is possible in
relation to the phenomenological analysis of time. The discovery
of the temporal structure of needs is, however, the discovery of
original temporal historicity: the relation of needs and satisfac-

tion. In turn, this relation is connected with the finite nature of individual monads and their individuation, periods, pauses, and interruptions of lived time (tiredness, sleep, death). In brief, the relation is connected to lived temporal irreversibility (consumption) which forces the monads to work, in order to replenish what has been consumed, in order to survive. These considerations are connected to the dialectic among groups, classes, and communities. In this dialectic, which is uncovered by phenomenological analysis, we rediscover the Engelsian laws of dialectic in unusual guises. Human reflection, or philosophy, appears, in the conception of the dialectic that can be developed by departing from Husserl, as the becoming-conscious of the negation endured by one man because of another man, or by one group because of another group.

In the one who endures it, alienation, or the negation, generates the will to negate the negation. Husserl has considered the opposition of subjects in relation to reciprocal comprehension and intellectual communion, even though he sometimes explicitly deals with contrasts and struggles among groups (e.g., in the fifth of the *Cartesian Meditations*). In the dialectic of "inferior" and "superior" needs, the negation of the negation permits the satisfaction of the needs which, once obtained, opens the way to qualitatively superior needs (and therefore to their satisfactions). This discussion reintroduces Engels' "laws," i.e., the law of the interpenetration of opposites, the law of the transformation of quantity into quality and vice versa, and the law of the negation of the negation.[1] We need not discuss such laws as "scientific," or as detached and independent. Rather, we must emphasize that, in terms of phenomenological analysis, dialectical modalities such as those presented as laws by Engels must necessarily begin with subjectivity, both as a point of departure and as living and operating presence. Subjectivity is also intersubjectivity which is determined within living social groups.

The fundamental points are the insertion of the dialectic into subjectivity and the penetration of subjectivity as a causal element into every dialectical modality. Since in my living present I find the past and recognize it as such (even as, e.g., the geological past that has preceded men), we cannot here speak of *subjectivism* in the sense of traditional *idealism*. If we could, the

1. See Friedrich Engels, *Dialectics of Nature*, trans. Clemens Dutt, 3d ed. (Moscow: Progress Publishers, 1964), p. 63.

usual criticism of subjectivism would be valid.[2] Even Husserl points out that the problem of the world as always pregiven is not a philosophical problem, and, as we know, he declares himself a realist in this respect. We could, however, pose the theme of the dialectic of nature and the related problem of the relation between logic and dialectic.

The problem of the dialectic of nature is not so absurd as it may appear. If by nature we also mean animals and plants, then for phenomenology part of the problem concerns the relationship between man and animals—the different ways whereby animal species experience and live their world in relation to us—and we must begin the analysis with us. This is the main theme of the fifth of the *Cartesian Meditations*. It deals with the constitution of the other as subject, i.e., as a monad in the first person such as I-myself, who constitutes me as I constitute him. This theme obtains even when the other subject is an animal.

All animated subjects experience the world, live in a natural environment, and have a certain relationship to that environment. Availing themselves of tools, men work on matter and, because of given necessities, become as passive as matter in order to mold it. If the connection with the other subject is empathy (*Einfühlung*), the connection with the material world is a unique form of adaptation and domination. If I must perform a series of operations to adapt to material things, I can discover a particular mode of the being of things, departing from my experience of them as they are reciprocally caused and determined by what surrounds them, including myself. Whitehead has spoken of *prehension* among things—even if he has not always been clear about how (and why) he was able to talk about them. Starting with my adaptation, my clashing with material things, we may speak of a reciprocal agreement and disagreement of precategorial material things, i.e., agreement and disagreement not yet accepted by science according to some relations or typicity. I should arrive at a dialectic of natural things, and not the dialectic of concepts or categories used by science.

These possible analyses are alien to Engels' investigation, but they must at least be pointed out if we are to give a phenome-

2. See Antonio Gramsci, *Il Materialismo Storico e la Filosofia di Benedetto Croce* (Turin: G. Einaudi, 1948), pp. 138 ff. [Selected passages from this text may be found in Antonio Gramsci, *The Modern Prince and Other Writings*, trans. Louis Marks (New York: International Publishers, 1967).]

nological foundation to Engelsian intuitions. It cannot be said absolutely that a dialectic of nature is impossible in principle. Sartre thinks that we know nothing about it. Phenomenology could perhaps tell us something about this by means of a very difficult analysis. Sartre writes: "In a word, if there is a dialectical materialism, it will have to be *historical* materialism, i.e., a materialism of the internal: it is the same to make and to bear it, to live and to know it." [3] For us, "of the internal" means that materialism can be rediscovered in its precategorial concreteness, starting from the subject. It is possible to rediscover it as external, realistically and not phantasmagorically (in the sense of Husserl's "phantasms"), starting with precategorial causal experience where, as we know, each monad is embodied: where we are rooted in the first person as subjects.

Among other matters, materialism raises the problem of the internal and external. This problem is connected with the fact that each concrete subject, and therefore each whole man, is a consciousness and psyche (a consciously reflecting psyche) not separable from the body-proper (*Leib*), the body that is "one's own" for each one of us. But the *Leib* is also a natural thing among other natural things. As such, it follows the deterministic and causal laws of inanimate things, even though it cannot become completely inanimate except in death.

Inanimate things are external to us because we are also things and can in different ways pose ourselves as external and become inert with respect to ourselves, e.g., in sleep. Similarly, Sartre talks about a practico-inert praxis when we, while at work, become partly nature in order to dominate it, as when the peasant utilizes the inert weight of his body to make the spade penetrate the earth.

The phenomenological basis of the foregoing can be rediscovered in the phenomenological analysis which reveals our organic bodies as the meeting point of transformation, as the reciprocal interpenetration of the internal and external (*Umschlagspunkt*).

However, man is never in an isolated relation to the Earth. His work is inserted into complex intersubjective, genetic, psychological, and social relations. What is interesting on this level is that a man, a group, or a class can be used by another man, if not as inert matter (though this is possible, e.g., in the use of

3. Jean-Paul Sartre, *Critique de la raison dialectique* (Paris: Gallimard, 1960), p. 129.

cadavers), then as men degraded as much as possible to the state of animals or, in a more general sense, degraded to things. And this is human alienation as the "reduction to thinghood" (*Verdinglichung*).

A man using his body to operate a tool is in *principle* different from a man being used by another man as a tool. The second instance is possible because man's nature also allows the first. But if, because of my human essence, I consume myself and in the end cannot avoid death, it is not the same as if another man, taking advantage of the fact that in order to live I consume myself and have to satisfy some needs, uses me as a man in the most degraded sense for *his own* ends and not mine (death plays an important part in Hegel's master-slave dialectic).

The reciprocal interpenetration of the internal and the external on the subjective level includes both man's unity (which is compromised when I am reduced to a slave, an animal, or a thing) and the precategorial structure of consumption and reparation, of needs and satisfaction, which binds me to precategorial causal nature and its determinism. There is no doubt that man is conditioned on this level. But the theoretical and practical reduction of man to the level of an economic structure actually appears as a form of alienation which involves the internal-external relation. It is interesting to notice that the phenomenological foundation of the problem can clarify misunderstandings that could otherwise obscure it.

I endure precategorial causality and its determinism even if I am not merely a passive being. Rather, I do so *precisely because I am not merely passive*. Even though the structure is a determining factor, it does not obstruct intentional will and freedom. The reduction of man to a causality which would entirely determine human subjectivity or the concrete monad is the projection of a situation bound by intersubjective and social relations to the character of a certain historical period, e.g., in terms of the industrial revolution, to capitalism. The same is true of a materialism which aims at reducing man to nature and which, in Husserl's terminology, is called *naturalism*.

Marxism's insistence on matter and on the determinism of the economic structure is a historical reaction to bourgeois ideology which hides man's reality in order to mask exploitation. In fact, by reducing man to a mere instrument or thing, capitalism denies in theory what it practices. Therefore, it regards the material and economic precategorial in man as insignificant, while considering the soul all-important, according to what we have elsewhere called *the spiritual blackmail*. But the materialist recognition of the realities of matter and the conditioning function of needs plays the capitalist game if it merely reduces man to a conditioned organic body: to a merely deterministic, exclusive, thinglike reality. Matter and structure are vindicated in order to negate the dualism imposed by bourgeois society which divides the *soul* from the *body*, the *res cogitans* from the *res extensa*, just as the feudal world reduced the serf to pure *res extensa*, reserving the soul to the *otium* of the lord. The aim of Marxist materialism is to vindicate the whole man, the concrete monad, or, simply, *man*, if we do not thereby reduce him naturalistically, as Feuerbach does.

The abolition of classes is entrusted to the exploited group. The proletariat *can will* and, in given situations and under certain conditions, grasp the possibility and therefore the freedom to fight for emancipation. (These conditions, however, can lead to a voluntary self-alienation, both in struggle and in labor.) This is the proof of the aforementioned impossibility of completely reducing man to a thing while leaving him alive, i.e., the proof of the wholeness of man's nature. The contradictions of capitalism appear here in two complementary perspectives. In one, capitalism reduces the exploited either to a mere material thing or to an instrument. In this case capitalism cannot survive, because men reduced to the level of mere things do not produce. Or else capitalism leaves to the exploited enough humanity, or psychic life, and therefore enough will and ability to become self-conscious, to make it possible for them to remain men. In the latter case, capitalism creates the movement which tends to destroy it.

[63] *Man and Class. Part and Whole.*
       Dualism and Its Overcoming

INSOFAR AS THE EXPLOITED CLASS fights for its own emancipation, it also fights for the wholeness of man. In the dualism of *res extensa* and *res cogitans*, the proletariat fights not only for itself, but for all. That is, in seeking its own emancipation and, as a *consequence* of the endured negation, to negate such a negation, it seeks to suppress itself as a class. Thus, it seeks the vindication of the *subject man,* and the denial of the claim that the historical category of *class* necessarily inheres in such a subject. But its own emancipation is also the emancipation of others. Consequently, the emancipation of the proletariat is the emancipation of man and the abolition of class differences. The same is true of the emancipation of a nation: if such an emancipation is nationalistic, it reproduces the dialectical struggle among nations. If the emancipation of man is in the emancipation of that nation, the former becomes the abolition of nations as the end of the dialectical struggle of reciprocal alienation. For this reason, when Marx said that "the *emancipation of the German* is the *emancipation of mankind*," [4] he meant to deny nationalism itself. The proletariat, then, does not fight just for itself, but for the *whole* of mankind. It is a part, but a part which, as a part, contains a whole. Therefore, in praxis it is a totalizing historical movement which tends to realize the wholeness of man to the extent that it seeks to negate the dualism of *res cogitans* and *res extensa*. Notice that dualism, in all its implications and consequences, is none other than the naturalism discussed by Husserl. Thus, it is important to note that we can speak of materialism, without speaking of naturalism, through a phenomenological analysis of the concrete monad and its rootedness in precategorial material causality. If this is true of everything which is related to the dialectic, it is necessary to return to the subject understood in the phenomenological sense. Phenomenology is simultaneously a *return to the subject* and a *return to the things-themselves*.

[64]   *The Wholeness of Man.*
        Universality and the Meaning of Truth.
        Scientific and Critical Marxism

WE MUST ALWAYS EMPHASIZE that the phenomenological subject is a *conscious* and therefore free subject. However, it would not be conscious without its animated body, i.e., its soul, or psyche, and its organic body which is rooted in causality. To return to the subject is to recognize in man the possibility of his becoming conscious of his situation of crisis (alienation), and of the reasons for the crisis and alienation. Individuated in a

4. Karl Marx, "Toward the Critique of Hegel's *Philosophy of Law:* Introduction, in *Writings of the Young Marx on Philosophy and Society*, trans. and ed. Loyd D. Easton and Kurt H. Guddat (Garden City, N. Y.: Doubleday, 1967), p. 264.

historical situation, man can become conscious of such a situation because the return to subjectivity is a return to the actual presence lived in the first person as an *inalienable* and original point of departure. Praxis is guided by this becoming-conscious and by its analyses of the historical situation, beginning from the present which recollects and reinterprets the past for the future. This is valid on subjective and intersubjective levels, according to subjective and intersubjective dialectical modalities. On the intersubjective level, when the proletariat becomes conscious of the situation of crisis and negation, in order to negate and overcome the situation, it stands out as *a part distinguished from the others because of the positive totalization* and universality of values which it contains. The bourgeoisie has fought for *itself* as a well-determined class. The proletariat fights and must fight for all, i.e., for the *telos* and meaning of human history—even if it must pass through capitalist conditioning and alienation. Here, the becoming-conscious, the will, and praxis are directed toward a *telos*. The subject, or groups of subjects, know and will according to a universal aim. They come out of their own closed reality and go beyond it according to a practical and cognitive horizon. Here the subject is a subject *that goes beyond.* In the situation of the proletariat, *becoming-conscious* is *becoming-conscious of something* distinctive and universal. Therefore, it is *intentional* and *distinctively universal* in Husserl's sense. Man or the subject *exists* in his actual presence. But he is not closed in it, since he transcends himself in a universality which is at the same time both consciousness striving toward truth and tension striving toward concrete human universality, i.e., toward the totalization of men as whole subjects. In this sense, it is "scientific," i.e., belonging to science, which, beginning from the presence, is also the becoming-conscious of the historical situation where philosophy becomes historical reflection in and for history. The totalization takes place on different levels and in different degrees, and its aim is economic unification of the planet Earth that will permit social exploitation to be abolished.

The direction toward truth—understood as a precategorial and well-founded science of subjects and things-themselves, i.e., as *first philosophy*—is always broader than any of its specific historical realizations. Yet it is the *meaning of truth* of every individuated and determined period. The single concrete individual is finite, but he is opened to the totality. The real is determined, but it is also oriented toward an end which transcends it. The subject is a concrete man in the first person, such as myself in my actual individuated presence. He is a subject who finds within himself a particularity and a universality, just as he finds them in everything that he experiences and knows in a well-founded way. Therefore, he is both reality in the first person (man-subject) and the Husserlian transcendental subject. The crisis breaks this unity and bifurcates the concrete man. It separates me from my transcendental ego. At the same time, the sciences lose their function: they are no longer directed. The *telos* and intentionality are lost.

The dialectic of the actual is connected with the dialectical movement of the whole. The dualism involves the whole man who works and thinks: his psyche and his body. Specifically, it involves man considered as the reciprocal interpenetration of the internal and the external. Thus, economic and social alienation is also psychological alienation. It is a negation to which we must react by negating the negation regarding the entire mode of experiencing and living the world. More accurately, given that a man lives the natural, social, and historical environment both consciously and unconsciously, economic alienation always involves the whole man. This leads him to react with a typical behavior and a certain praxis. Given the connection between consumption which creates the need for satisfaction and temporal irreversibility or entropy, the precategorial economic structure is not only rooted in precategorial nature but is also inextricably connected to the dynamism and reactions of the psyche. Here we rediscover the historicism of psychoanalysis and psychology. This is the meaning of the oriented and teleological character of psychology understood not as neutral science but as an intentional science like all the others, engaged in the constitution of a human society free from exploitation.

The last paragraph indicates how Sartre has been able to talk about the internalization of the external and the externalization of the internal. Phenomenology offers a rigorous and consequential foundation to Sartre's position. The dialectic of the internal and the external, in its various forms, must never appear as a recursive or *static activity*. It is an oriented dialectic. If we want to use Sartre's language, we must say that it is oriented toward a maximum of the internal and a minimum of the external, i.e., toward a minimization of dependence on the conditioning causal structure, and toward the maximization of the autonomy of each subject in a society of subjects. This entails a particular psychic attitude held by the struggling groups. In its totalizing function, the exploited group fights the exploiting group and must fight it until the end. But the proletariat fights in order to remove both the exploited and the exploiting group from opposition and contradiction. Psychologically, the exploited group cannot simply identify itself with the enemy. It cannot fight at the enemy's level because to do so would amount to playing the enemy's game and reproducing the contradiction to be negated within the very group which wants to remove it. In the struggle, the exploited group must not end up by negating the negation on one hand while reaffirming it on the other. What must characterize the proletariat is the awareness of its own task and *telos*. It must remain aware of its totalizing function and the unity of man, in whose name it struggles. Psychologically, this means that it must fight alienation in a situation of alienation, and fight dualism while enduring it.

This entails that the sciences redeem their own function to the extent that they do not lose their intentionality. They can do so if scientific operations are recognized as based on, and departing from, the man-subject and precategorial experience. It would be impossible, however, if the sciences lose the meaning of their operations. These operations are bound to the whole process of becoming-conscious, to philosophy as the act of becoming-conscious of history departing from the actual presence, and therefore to philosophy in the phenomenological sense. Philosophy here does not mean a system or construction, but a progressive self-realization according to the meaning of truth. The sciences that lose this meaning fall into objectivism, fetishism, and alienation. They objectify and transform the *whole* man into separate objects of various scientific domains by becoming instruments in the reduction of man to a pure technical operator. Then the alleged neutrality of the sciences becomes *technistic alienation*. What returns the sciences to their function is the rejection of the concept of so-called "neutral" instrumentalization, illustrated by, e.g., the physicist who claims that, as a scientist, he does not have to worry about the atom bomb. The meaning of truth which guides the sciences is authentic scientific "detachment." But this detachment, through which the scientist aims at the truth, coincides with the positive historical movement, human emancipation, and the constitution of society of subjects. Marxism *is scientific* in this sense, and not in the naturalistic one. Its scientific aspect must coincide with the struggle against technistic alienation, the vindication of scientific freedom and autonomy, and the vindication of every cultural activity, including art. Only in this way can it effectively fight the technistic-capitalistic alienation in an integrated revolutionary struggle.

The meaning of truth characterizes *critical Marxism* and distinguishes it from the dogmatic variety:

> Since it is assumed that the goal of scientific discussion is the search for truth and scientific progress, he who starts out with the viewpoint that the adversary can express something that must be incorporated, even as a subordinate moment, in his own constitution, shows himself as the more advanced of the two. To comprehend and realistically evaluate the position and the reasons of the adversary (and sometimes the whole past is the adversary), amounts precisely to being freed from the prisons of ideologies (in the previous sense of blind ideological fanaticism), i.e., to depart from a critical viewpoint, the only fertile one in scientific investigation.[5]

[65] *Dialectic of Nature*

In attacking naturalism, Husserl does not mean to deny nature or the world. Rather, he attacks scientific alienation and, therefore, the fall of intentionality and the loss of the function of the sciences vis-à-vis the meaning of man. Alienation, or scientistic objectification, arises out of the attempt to apply the laws of mathematical physics to the human subject, society, and history. Such laws concern man only to the extent that, as Husserl would say, he is an original thing (*Ursache*) or a physical body. (Even I, the man, as any other physical body, fall with the acceleration of thirty-two feet per second squared.) The reduction of man to a mere physical body is alienation (*Verdinglichung*). Mathematical physics, as it is conceived and as it must be conceived, is categorial, while real nature is precategorial. Furthermore, the first is *based on* the second. Precategorial nature has its temporality and its historicity. As a matter of fact, since it is possible to speak of a history of nature, we can think that there could be a dialectic of nature. This dialectic must be constituted *by us*, taking as its point of departure the actual presence wherein we discover that there has been a real past, antecedent to man, and that there can be a future without man. We are part of that same nature that existed in the past and can

5. Gramsci, *Il Materialismo*, p. 21.

persist and continue in the future without man, and of which we will soon cease to be a part as living men. It is the nature studied by mathematical physics, geology, botany, and the other sciences, including natural history. Completely separate from the subjects that study it and from every living being, nature is dead. It is also precategorial because it does not coincide with the categories of any science—not even those of astronomy or mathematical physics.

This can be readily ascertained if we develop the theme of death, not only of man but of all living beings including those which could be living on other planets. Even if it has actually occurred, from a biological or astronomical viewpoint, conscious life, studied as an event of the cosmos, is an extremely improbable fact. Since we are the evidence of this reality, we recognize nature as real and independent of us who talk about it and "constitute" it as real. Clearly, to constitute does not mean to create: phenomenology does not construct or create anything. Insofar as we perform extremely complex operations—most of which are yet to be investigated—we can talk about a dialectic of nature by departing from our concrete experience of nature, from the precategorial causality binding us to the environment, from needs and satisfactions, from our work, and from our technical operations. Having admitted a dialectic of nature, we could mistakenly believe that the dialectic of nature evolves through the same laws of the dialectic of life which is also nature, but *lived* nature, and, in animals, animated nature. We are rooted in material nature, but we are not just material nature. Since science establishes laws, e.g., the "law" of evolution, which is certainly not of the same kind as the law of gravity, there is the danger of *projecting* into nature, more or less consciously, the dialectic which is functioning in our actual historical presence. Here we face once again the problem of the relation between the unconscious and the external world. Or, having more or less established that the dialectic of the struggle for existence has operated in the history of the species and that this law is scientific and therefore universally valid for all living beings including man, we conclude that such a law, and therefore war, is unavoidable, i.e., that it will reappear in each and every situation just as *static activity* appears to alienated man.

This is precisely an instance of alienation caused by naturalism, i.e., the attempt to apply to human history a physico-mathematical or biological law. (Ultimately, the second should reduce to the first.) In a cosmos of this type, alienated man cannot but disappear and, consciously or unconsciously, use science and technology for his own destruction. Therefore, there is a relation between naturalistic and technistic alienation: between the loss of the function of the sciences and our "atomic age." Naturalism entails the application of naturalistic categories to man, and the reciprocal projection into nature of unfounded categories that stem from a historically rooted ideology, understood in Gramsci's sense, or as a veil of ideas (*Ideenkleid*) hiding reality. The ideology of the struggle for existence projects into nature the social situation of capitalism. Thus conceived, nature returns the projection into capitalism as an unbreakable scientific law. A similar projection occurs in economics when the economic structure of capitalist society appears as unalterable.

The problem of Marxism is precisely that of shattering, in human history, laws such as that of the struggle for existence. Therefore, *in terms of a coherent Marxism, the dialectic of nature must be non-naturalistic*, and it must not be a dialectic of history. Thus, we must talk about materialism and not about a philosophy of nature or history, constructed upon categorial and preconstituted forms, which would end up by misunderstanding both the complexity of nature and the complexity of history. Non-naturalistic materialism is necessary in order to prevent the disappearance of man—as can happen in the atomic age—which would be the inevitable result of naturalism brought to its ultimate consequences. What is important for Marxism is that man can overcome and break class warfare. This will never be possible if the dialectic does not pass through the subject as a causal element of the dialectic, and departing from whom history comes to be comprehended in order to be transformed.

The law of evolution, interpreted as the struggle for existence and as *bellum omnium contra omnes*, offers us a typical instance of naturalism. Its extension into history is precisely what Marxism wants to deny. It can be said that, if the struggle for existence is a dialectical law, another dialectic of nature must be possible. But subjectivity, with its becoming-conscious, unavoidably intervenes. Its will and possibility of breaking all preconstituted and constructed philosophies of nature and history introduces the possibility of breaking the *bellum omnium contra omnes*.

On the sociohistorical and human level, the negation of the negation follows an already undergone negation, including the

original negation that appears as need. We must recognize subjectivity as original, without denying the causal and precategorial
reality of matter.

Here, subjectivity in the phenomenological sense reappears
as the original point of departure and as the actual presence:
our presence here and now from which it is impossible not to
begin. Husserl's criticism of naturalism allows us to understand
man's ability to change the laws of the *bellum omnium contra
omnes*, his dependence on the natural environment, and his
fundamental structure. Even for Engels, the important thing
was that Darwinian naturalism was not valid on the social and
human level. The naturalistic laws of Darwinism are not laws of
human history, and when Marx wanted to dedicate *Capital* to
Darwin he certainly did not think that laws identical to those of
Darwinism regulate society and history. Marx's criticism of
political economy, according to which the economic laws of a
certain historical phase cannot be taken to be eternal, leads us to
think that the laws of Darwinism could not have been regarded
by him as extendable to human history and, as such, eternally
valid. In fact, we read in Engels:

> Until Darwin what was stressed by his present adherents was
> precisely the harmonious cooperative working of organic nature,
> how the plant kingdom supplies animals with nourishment and
> oxygen, and animals supply plants with manure, ammonia, and
> carbonic acid. Hardly was Darwin recognized before these same
> people saw everywhere nothing but *struggle*. Both views are justi-
> fied within narrow limits, but both are equally one-sided and
> prejudiced. The interaction of bodies in non-living nature includes
> both harmony and collisions, that of living bodies in conscious
> and unconscious cooperation as well as in conscious and uncon-
> scious struggle. Hence, even in regard to nature, it is not per-
> missible one-sidedly to inscribe only "struggle" on one's banners.
> But it is absolutely childish to desire to sum up the whole mani-
> fold wealth of historical evolution and complexity in the meagre
> and one-sided phrase "struggle for existence." That says less than
> nothing.
>
> The whole Darwinian theory of the struggle for existence is
> simply the transference from society to organic nature of Hobbes'
> theory of *bellum omnia contra omnes* and of the bourgeois theory
> of competition, as well as the Malthusian theory of population.[6]

6. Engels, *Dialectics of Nature*, p. 313.

What Engels criticizes here is the biological-naturalistic concept of life and human history. It is difficult to deny that in Engels, in Marx, and in Marxism, there are naturalistic tendencies. But it is also difficult to deny that Marxism must also apply to itself the principle of historical evolution and consider naturalism as transcended.

[66]   *Italian Marxism.*
        Man in Labriola and Gramsci

IT IS POSSIBLE TO FIND, in the tradition of Italian Marxism from Labriola to Gramsci, the insistent theme of humanism
and the criticism of what has been labeled naturalism. It is a
criticism presented as a refutation of dogmatic or "vulgar" materialism, mechanism, and the illicit application of the categories
of physical-mathematical science to human history.

Labriola did not consider man as a natural object and he insisted on will as an inalienable element of the dialectic. For him,
man is a product of nature, but he must *become* a product of the
will. This would be impossible if the dialectic were solely objectivistic and naturalistic. Historical materialism reconstitutes the
genesis of the history of humanity in the mind, i.e., in man or in
his actual presence. Blind evolutionism is rejected because of its
genetic method. The dialectic passes through human subjectivity,
which in turn becomes a causal element of it and functions in it.

Men, says Labriola, are the subjects and objects of history.
In terms of the way we have defined "objects," this means that
men are conditioned and "made" by history and historical situations, i.e., they are materially conditioned. Precisely because of
this, however, they are also subjects able to speak of "us" and
act as "we." This is not the "object" of positivistic science. Therefore, it is not the naturalistic objectification.

We voluntarily accept the epithet of scientific, provided we do not
thus confuse ourselves with the positivists, sometimes embarrass-

ing guests, who assume to themselves a monopoly of science; we do not seek to maintain an abstract and generic thesis like lawyers or sophists, and we do not plume ourselves on demonstrating the reasonableness of our aims. Our intentions are nothing less than the theoretical expression and practical explanation of the data offered us by the interpretation of the process which is being accomplished among us and about us and which has its whole existence in the objective relations of social life of which we are the subject and object, the cause and the effect.[1]

Therefore, we have *science*, but not objectified science. We have the historical science of a process which conditions us and is transformed by us in our praxis. It is not a matter of deducing or demonstrating a situation, or of treating the sociohistorical situation as the object of sociological study. The *intentions* are products of the same process which they overcome, to the extent to which they comprehend and transform it. Rationality is neither a world of abstractions nor one of categories; rather, it is a direction which can and must become *intentions*, or, as we would say, intentional praxis. The fundamental point is that the conditioning itself makes it possible for the proletariat to become the *subject of history* and to move in a positive direction toward the horizon of historical truth. "The modern proletariat exists, takes its stand, grows and develops contemporary history as the concrete subject, the positive force whose necessarily revolutionary action must find in communism its necessary outcome." [2]

Here, necessity is not a logical or scientific category, and to understand it as such would amount to using Marxist terms in a positivistic sense. Given a certain action which has developed according to the historical modalities of its genesis, of the presence of the past in the present, and in the direction of the present toward the future, "necessity" is historical if recognized as such by the theoretical consciousness of the genesis. To become conscious is to become aware of the route to follow. "But the perfect theoretical knowledge of socialism to-day, as before, and as it always will be, lies in the understanding of its historical necessity, that is to say, in the consciousness of the manner of its genesis." The *Manifesto* is "the scientific and reflected revelation of the way which our *civil society* is traversing." [3] It is a revela-

1. Antonio Labriola, *Essays on the Materialist Conception of History*, trans. Charles H. Kerr (1903; 2d printing, New York: Monthly Review Press, 1966), pp. 17–18.
2. *Ibid.*, p. 18.
3. *Ibid.*, pp. 26–27.

tion which, because of the ways in which it is expressed, assumes the decisive and almost sudden tone of him who enunciates, in the fact, the necessity of the fact itself. Here is Labriola's contribution to critical Marxism: the *scientific and meditated revelation*, i.e., there is a science which allows facts to reveal themselves as a consequence of meditation and reflection. This means that it is not scientific to believe that there are preconstituted laws which explain how facts appear. Facts appear to meditation in a "sudden" way. They cannot be reflected upon once and for all. They must be continually considered and reconsidered in reference to the given situation, by constantly taking into account their genesis, and by seeking the linearity and the possibility of development of that same situation. What is impressive in Labriola is a "style" which never allows him to remain a prisoner of categorial abstractions.

Labriola sees with absolute clarity the categorial error of economics as a science. As he put it:

> Insofar as it was a doctrine, it separated, distinguished and analyzed the elements and forms of the *processes* of circulation and of distribution and reduced them all into categories: money, capital-money, interest, profit, land-rent, wages, etc. . . . It started from two hypotheses which it did not take the trouble to justify since they appeared so evident; namely, that the social order which it illustrated was the natural order, and that private property in the means of production was one and the same thing with human liberty.[4]

In Labriola, we find a thoroughgoing critique of the categories and the evidence. In his terminology, this is a critique of the *obviousness* by which economics as a science claims that the "natural" society be that of its age, i.e., the one that economics studies by means of its scientific categories. *Naturalism* is precisely this alleged agreement of the categories with the historical life which they embalm and arrest in "scientific" immutability. The analysis becomes the absolutization of the categories and the misunderstanding of their human function. Subsequently, Labriola rejects the "analytic attempt which, taking separately and in a distinct fashion on the one side the economic forms and categories, and on the other, for example, law, legislation, politics, customs, proceeds to study the reciprocal influences of the different sides of life considered in an abstract fashion."[5] What

4. *Ibid.*, p. 80.
5. *Ibid.*, p. 85.

is important is that Labriola has captured the idea of *totality*, and that his criticism is directed to scientific separation and abstraction. Perhaps for the first time, and with full awareness, Labriola contraposes the intentional unity of man and knowledge, of praxis and truth, to the separate sciences or, as Marx put it, to the sciences at the service of capital, to the capitalistic sciences, to the sciences that have lost the unity of life and historical intentionality. Precisely this unity and intentionality give critical Marxism the sense of fullness and wholeness which constitute its foundation. Labriola knows very well that the separation itself, i.e., the abstract which becomes concrete, is what characterizes capitalism. Consequently, he sees in the analyses of *Capital* that the retention of the capitalist abstractions is inevitable if they are to be overcome. In other words, he sees that Marx starts from within capitalism in order to expose it. As such, *Capital* gives us a complete study of capitalism. Because of this, Marx fully understands in depth the capitalist masks, and discovers reality and the true image of man in the dialectical situation. Labriola sees in *Capital* not an abstract theory but a dialectic in action. He sums up what we have said in the following way:

> Ours is the organic conception of history. The totality of the unity of social life is the subject matter present to our minds. It is economics itself which dissolves in the course of one process, to reappear in as many morphological stages in each of which it serves as a substructure for all the rest. Finally, it is not our method to extend the so-called economic factor isolated in an abstract fashion over all the rest, as our adversaries imagine, but it is, before everything else, to form an historic conception of economics and to explain the other changes by means of its changes.

Therefore, by "economics" Labriola does not mean the independent science of economics. Prior to science there is the temporal, material, and historical ordering of facts. This ordering of facts is precategorial, while economics is *categorial*. Economics as a science is conditioned by the ordering of facts, and not vice versa. Furthermore, the ordering of facts appears in various morphological states. We have seen elsewhere how psychology, linguistics, history, and philosophy undergo these "morphological states." The error lies in confusing categorial and scientific economics with the precategorial ordering of facts. (This, of course, is also true in anthropology and sociology.)

Economics clarifies the meaning of the crisis of the sciences, of their abstraction, and leads us to understand how their function can be rescued.

Labriola continues:

> Therein lies our answer to all the criticisms which come to us from all the domains of learned ignorance, not excepting the socialists who are insufficiently grounded and who are sentimental or hysterical. And we explain our position thus as Marx has done in his *Capital,* not the first book of critical communism, but the last great book of bourgeois economics.[6]

These extremely modern analyses led Labriola to insist on the critique of abstraction and scientific objectification. Thus, he speaks of the "abstract categories of individual psychology"[7] to which he contraposes, "for lack of a better term, social psychology,"[8] i.e., psychology brought back to the ordering of facts, to the totality and to the "whole."[9] Labriola here anticipates Sartre. Historiography must be grounded. The knowledge of the past must be reactivated in the awareness of the present. This is a "new criticism of the sources in the realistic sense of the word, and not in the formal documentary sense. It is, in short, to make react upon the knowledge of past conditions the consciousness of which we are now capable, and thereby to reconstruct them anew."[10]

Labriola mentions naturalism and says that "history must be naturalized": "This expression . . . may be the occasion of the equivocations of which we have spoken,"[11] and the explanations of the ambiguities he offers do not allow his Marxism to be interpreted as a dogmatic, abstract, and mechanistic naturalism. "History is the work of man,"[12] and what interests Labriola is "the integral formation of man in his historical development."[13]

We rediscover Labriola's awareness in Gramsci, who returns to the third of Marx's "Theses on Feuerbach": "Circumstances are changed by men and . . . the educator must himself be educated." Very likely, the Gramscian locution of the "philosophy

6. *Ibid.,* p. 86.
7. *Ibid.,* p. 163.
8. *Ibid.,* p. 111.
9. *Ibid.,* p. 228.
10. *Ibid.,* p. 107.
11. *Ibid.,* p. 121.
12. *Ibid.,* p. 120.
13. *Ibid.,* p. 123.

of praxis" is not extraneous to the eighth and ninth "Theses": "All social life is essentially practical." A materialism that does not conceive of the sensible world as practical activity is the intuition of single individuals in bourgeois society. In bourgeois society, individuals are abstract. Hence, in the sixth thesis, it is stated that Feuerbach presupposes "an abstract—*isolated*—human individual." However, isolation is not the only attribute that must be stressed: abstraction is just as important. This means that in bourgeois society the individual is not concrete and whole, because the human being has come to be conceived naturalistically as belonging to a species that "unites the many individuals *naturally*." Society must not be naturalistic but, as is claimed in the tenth thesis, it must be "human." In the "Economic and Philosophic Manuscripts of 1844," Marx pointed out that the concrete and real individual belongs to mankind precisely because he is a concrete and not an abstract individual. Only this type of individual belongs to the species, and he is both particular and universal. What must be avoided are abstractly conceived individuals, and the notion that society appears "as an abstraction in front of the individual."

Therefore, the "philosophy of praxis" presupposes a precise conception of man as an active subject. Neither man nor society is a categorial abstraction or naturalistic concept. Philosophy is not categorial: it "is history in action, life itself." [14] It is clear that the term "life" is not used here as a biological category. It is a life which is aware of its actions. As Labriola would have said, it is a life which, although produced by nature and history, becomes consciousness and will. Therefore, it can consciously transform nature and history. Life and philosophy are not abstractions. Philosophy *is rooted* in life. It is not a *res cogitans* contraposed to a *res extensa*, and the same must be said of the relation between structure and superstructure.

Man is "an active reaction to the structure," [15] even if he is conditioned by it, and his action is not really separate from it. Therefore, man is in the natural and historical process. But he is an active principle in such a process. When philosophy is reduced to history, this active principle must not be forgotten.

14. Antonio Gramsci, *Il Materialismo Storico e la Filosofia di Benedetto Croce* (Turin: G. Einaudi, 1948), p. 32. Also, see Gramsci, *The Modern Prince and Other Writings* (New York: International Publishers, 1967), p. 81. [Where possible, we shall cite the English translation of the text quoted by Professor Paci.]

15. Gramsci, *Il Materialismo*, p. 231.

[67]   *The Problem of Subjectivism*
        and Objectivism in Gramsci

IT IS NOT POSSIBLE to know reality without passing through man: to think the contrary is to fall into metaphysical materialism.

> The concept of "objective" in metaphysical materialism appears to mean an objectivity which exists even outside of man, but to assert that reality would exist even if man did not exist is either to state a metaphor or to fall into a form of mysticism. We know reality only in its relations with man, and just as man is an historical process of becoming, so also knowledge and reality are a becoming, and objectivity is a becoming, etc.[16]

In the first part of the quoted passage it is stated that reality does not exist without man. But this is not to be interpreted in the sense of subjective idealism, in relation to which Gramsci quotes Varisco concerning Tolstoy's *Childhood, Boyhood and Youth:* "I skim the paper," writes Varisco, "to read the news; would you hold that I have created the news with the opening of the paper?"[17] If this is what is meant by subjectivism, we must recall that for Husserl the world is always pregiven (*vorgegebene Welt*).

Gramsci does not want to contrapose a naïve subjectivism to a similarly naïve objectivism. This is why he speaks of mysticism in regard to a reality, existing outside of man, which we could know without departing from ourselves as subjects. As a matter of fact, he writes of Bukharin:

> The point that must be made about the "Popular Study" is that it has presented the subjectivistic conception as it appears from the criticism of common sense and that it has taken up the conception of reality of the external world in its most trivial and a-critical form, without even suspecting that the charge of mysticism could be brought against it, as in fact was done.[18]

The viewpoint of an "external objectivity thus mechanically understood" cannot be accepted.[19] We must therefore return to

16. Gramsci, *The Modern Prince*, p. 107.
17. Gramsci, *Il Materialismo*, p. 140.
18. Gramsci, *The Modern Prince*, p. 106.
19. *Ibid.*

man a "historical becoming." "Objective always means *humanly objective,* what may correspond exactly to *historically subjective,* in other words objective would mean *universally subjective.*" [20] Therefore, objectivity is a result of the operations of various subjects: a result of *intersubjective operations.* All men, as men and as units of mankind, can carry out these operations. (Recall the relation between the individual and the species, in Marx's criticism of the abstract individual.) Therefore, that which is objectively valid is constituted by subjects in history. Gramsci does not conceive of his reality as objectified (to do so would be mystical and metaphysical), but as the product of subjective operations. As Husserl would say, history is humanity "collectivized," and historical intersubjectivity constitutes an objectivity which is *universally* valid for all subjects. Objectivity is *constituted* by subjectivity understood as intersubjectivity. Clearly, the society of subjects cannot be an abstraction, but rather must be a society of integral and concrete individuals or, as we would say, of "concrete monads." Abstractions cannot constitute anything. The humanly objective is grounded by the historically subjective, i.e., by the *universally subjective.* This constitutes the humanly objective, i.e., what is objective for *man.* Science gives us an example of "concretely objectivized and universalized subjectivity." [21]

Science is *objectified subjectivity.* If we forget that it is based upon concrete subjectivity (the precategorial: we men are not categories), then science will fall into objectification in Husserl's sense, i.e., alienation.

[68]   *Critique of Scientism and the
         Teleological Intentionality of History*

IN GRAMSCI'S THOUGHT, we find a sustained critique of scientific fetishism and a call for a return to the human foundation of the sciences, i.e., to their "meaning-structure" without which they lose their function in the history of humanity. Gramsci outlines this as a critique of *scientism.* Since the object is contraposed to man as something not having its foundation

20. *Ibid.;* emphasis added.
21. *Ibid.,* p. 107.

in human operations, this contraposition renders the foundations of objectivity incomprehensible. If the sciences reduce objects to objectifications of their particular fields, "to physical or biological bodies," and so forth, the sciences lose their true total objectivity, i.e., the objectivity of bodies understood as plena, in reference to Husserl's discussion of Galileo. Therefore, the sciences must be unified in a unique and totalizing science: the science of man who is at once individual and universal. This science—which for Husserl is philosophy as phenomenology and as the becoming-conscious of history—is historically in process: it aims at the unity of mankind and at a unitary cultural system which simultaneously demands a society of subjects free from exploitation. Furthermore, it aims at a society in which no subject makes an object of someone else. Gramsci has stressed not only the historical process but also its intentionality and *telos*. The sciences have a *function* insofar as they do not lose their intentionality and aim at the constitution of society and the unity of mankind. Only an objectively unified society will be the effective product of subjectivity and subjective operations. In Husserl, to return their subjective foundations to the sciences is to discover their functions for the constitution of a rational society in history, i.e., a human society free from alienation.

The unitary culture of which Gramsci speaks is the non-alienated culture where the sciences are parts of a totality and of that science which is the becoming-conscious of the historical process that departs from the actual presence: *historical science* as becoming-conscious, will, reflection, and praxis. The *telos* is the life of the spirit insofar as it appears as the goal and point of arrival. For Marx, communism is not exhausted in the achievement of economic abundance. Rather, it aims at constituting a harmonious social life where each individual can develop, with others, his faculties and personality. The concept of spirit is prominent in Gramsci. Spirit is conceived as a goal which gives meaning to the historical dialectic. Gramsci does not accept a superficial critique of subjectivism, just as he does not accept a superficial critique of teleology. Arguing against Bukharin, he recalls Kant's *Critique of Judgment*. Quoting Goethe, he observes:

In the conception of *historical mission* could we not discover a teleological root? In fact, in many instances it assumes an ambiguous and mystical meaning, but in others it has a meaning which in the fashion of the Kantian concept of teleology, can be maintained and justified in the philosophy of praxis.[22]

What Gramsci says of Kantian teleology applies even more to Husserl.

Thus, Gramsci interprets history and its meaning as the struggle for *objectivity*. This is a struggle for the realization of a society of subjects to whom the products of their operations and labor are no longer contraposed as something external (alienation as *Entfremdung*). *The struggle for objectivity is also a struggle for subjectivity:* for a subject who does not see his own work and products as enemies revolting against him and erasing him in contradictions. This is fundamental to Gramsci's thought. It is worthwhile to quote fully one of his pages, emphasizing that he develops what is most authentic and profound in all of Marx's thought, and not just the "Theses on Feuerbach." The adverb "historically" is and must be underscored. If, in conjunction with Gramsci, we mention *historicism,* we must not forget that the term "historicism" implies all the indicated problems. Thus, Gramsci writes:

> Man knows objectively in so far as his knowledge is real for the whole of mankind *historically* unified in a unitary cultural system; but this process of historical unification takes place with the disappearance of the internal contradictions which tear human society apart, contradictions which are the condition for the formations of groups and the emergence of ideologies which are not concretely universal but are rendered immediately short-lived by the practical origin of their substance. There is, therefore, a struggle towards objectivity (towards being free from partial and fallacious ideologies) and this struggle is itself the struggle for the cultural unification of mankind. What the idealists call "spirit" is not a point of departure but of arrival, the totality of superstructures in development towards unification which is concrete, objectively universal, and not just a unitary presupposition, etc.[23]

Contradictions are the cause of the foundation of groups and, therefore, of classes. It is clear that the proletariat will have to overcome the class struggle and posit itself as the constitutive part of totality, i.e., a classless society, cultural unification, and, ultimately, *spirit,* which is not a presupposition but a *telos.*

22. Gramsci, *Il Materialismo,* p. 165.
23. Gramsci, *The Modern Prince,* pp. 106–7.

Notice once again the critique of ideologies. They have a "practical" origin. (This is similar to Croce's concept of "error.") As such, they are false, nonuniversal, fallible, and partial. They engulf and cover reality. The movement toward the liberation from ideologies is the correction of error. Therefore, it is directed toward the *meaning of truth*. Therefore, Marxism is, in principle, not an ideology but a critique of ideologies. In Marx, the term "ideology" has this negative meaning. Gramsci considers even the sciences as "ideological" in their scientism and mechanism.[24] Ultimately, the sciences must be brought back to man and to the concrete structure from which they originate. In phenomenological language, the sciences must be brought back to the subject and to the world of precategorial life. Science must be *grounded* in a philosophy which is not an ideology. In terms of Gramsci's remarks concerning the relation of philosophy and life, the sciences have their foundations in life, and not vice versa. Here, life is not something irrational, but the structure of the *Lebenswelt* of which philosophy as phenomenology is the science that aims at a radical transformation of man and the world. Gramsci writes:

> To pose science as the basis of life, to make of science the conception of the world *par excellence*—which clears the eyes of every ideological illusion, which places man in front of reality as it is—amounts to falling back on the idea that the philosophy of *praxis* needs philosophical supports outside of itself. But in reality even science is a superstructure, an ideology.[25]

Further on he speaks of "scientific superstition."

We must not believe that Gramsci is thinking of a blind or purely voluntaristic praxis, or a *praxis for praxis* which would be as abstract as a *philosophy for philosophy*. "The philosophy of praxis" must be able to capture the ideological aspect of science in order to see what it hides. Once again, it is a matter of returning science and the sciences to their foundation and function in the history of mankind. Science is criticized as "superstition," and not in its function. The ideology is uncovered through a nonideological principle which could appear as a "positive ideology" but which is, in fact, philosophy as the becoming-conscious of history for its teleological transformation. Through this teleological-cultural unity, the sciences regain their function

---

24. Gramsci, *Il Materialismo*, pp. 7, 48–49, 50 ff.
25. *Ibid.*, p. 56.

and their meaning of truth starting from the actual historical situation. Praxis which is not founded by and for man, and not enlightened by the becoming-conscious, can be erroneous. It is clarified and rationally enlightened in the operations that constitute it. Therefore, it demands an analysis of the operations and their meaning. Such analyses require that the distinction be made between the effective operations and the way in which they do or should appear. At the root of the operations, we find the causal and precategorial material structure, and the economic needs which are not abstractly transformed by political economy. When Gramsci criticizes "vulgar" materialism and metaphysical objectivism, he does not deny the conditioning of the structure. Certainly, we can still talk of a reality existing without men, even if this reality is constituted by departing from man himself. Gramsci's criticisms of idealistic subjectivism and naïve objectivism lead us to believe that he had in mind a constituting subject and not a creator of the world: a subject becoming-conscious of the meaning of truth of the world and history. The subject is man, but not as a mere natural being. Rather, the subject is the man who transcends himself and, with other men, aims at the *telos* of a human and not naturalistic society. He aims at "spirit" conceived not as a presupposition but as an end and as the horizon and meaning of truth which gives meaning to the whole historical process. So considered, man is real and "transcendental." His praxis is *intentional*. It is life that gives a meaning to itself, even if in its task of unending transformation it never coincides with the truth.

[69]   *The Actual Situation and Subjectivity*

THEREFORE, IF SUBJECTIVISM IS NOT UNDERSTOOD in the trivial idealistic sense, the problem of subjectivity is resolved in the conception of the concrete subject: presence, evidence, and experience in the first person. Actually, we cannot discuss subjectivism or objectivism without investigating these terms in their noncategorial and nonmythological meaning. Precisely because it is "dangerous" to misunderstand the term "subjectivism," we must analyze it along with the problem of the subject in its various aspects. This is why phenomenology is important. The problem of subjectivity is not an isolated one; it is actual and urgent for the contemporary situation and philosophy.

This is not accidental. Man presently runs the risk of becoming "occluded," and with his occlusion the present crisis becomes the radical crisis of civilization. If Husserl's *Crisis* is important, it is precisely because it denounces the danger of man's occlusion. To criticize Husserl in the name of science is absurd: no philosopher has ever defended scientific rationality so vigorously as he did. If "science" is reduced to disciplines which are isolated in their own fields, they will not be able to resolve man's problems. If, on the other hand, we seek rationality and "scientificity" in the sciences, it is precisely because a "scientific" rationality is operative in all of them. This rationality is not reducible to any particular scientific method, and, therefore, it is not within the competence of any science as such. Rather, it pertains to philosophy understood as a new science *sui generis* or, if we wish, to ethics as the becoming-conscious of human and historical goals. To prevent degeneration to the level of an empty materialism, this ethics will have to be constituted in terms of an interpretation of actual humanity and the preceding history which conditions it. This interpretation must be a philosophical interpretation of the ongoing situation, of human praxis and its dialectic. The great teaching of science is that "rationality" cannot be divorced from the particular scientific methods but must deal with man and his history in their totality. If this is a scientific problem, rationality must not and cannot simply deal with method and separate scientific fields, but must become the principle and the end of history. It cannot be scientific research separate from the men that carry out this research. It must deal with the subjects, the meaning and the end of their actions, and the possibility of their constituting a rational humanity of subjects where no subject is a slave of another in the natural, cultural, and historical environment (*Umwelt*).

If it is to be valid as the meaning of the truth of human history, science must be posited as *the horizon of the truth of history*. Such a horizon of truth is not something which is contraposed to the subjects. It is the meaning of the life of humanity. The sciences are in crisis to the extent that they occlude this meaning and subsequently hide man. "Humanity" and "man" are not abstract objects of study. They are not just the men of physics or biology or physiology, although man increasingly needs these sciences and reflections upon them, not only instrumentally but also in order to know himself and the world he wants to construct according to reason. "Humanity" is not an abstract "collective." *We are* humanity. Humanity comprises the individuals and peoples of the whole world. We are active or passive in a progressing history that it is our task to direct in one sense rather than another. It is this *we* that is hidden. It is this *we* that constitutes and can use the sciences for atomic destruction or for the beginning of a new historical period. In the dialectic, *we* must bring about a *radical revolution* wherein each man and humanity deal with their own negativity while attempting to negate it (negation of the negation). In this revolution, quantitative operations must be transformed into qualitative ones. They must allow a *qualitative change*. They must permit a change of life's meanings and goals so that, ultimately, the paradoxes and contradictions become *functions* of a *totalizing and constructive synthesis* and do not become arrested in an insuperable antinomy which is accepted at face value. Such acceptance would be the surrender of man to his own negativity. It would amount to a recognition of the impossibility of constructing a rational society free from the exploitation of man by man, of class by class, or of one people by another. The possibility of radical change is bound to the recognition of the operating subjects and of the conditions within which they act. To reiterate: to return to subjectivity is to return to *us* as actual and concrete beings, and to our real problems. These problems concern the environment and *world-wide* interdependent structures.

The sciences are in a crisis to the extent that they remain within the abstract sphere of the intellect. The crisis is a crisis of humanity to the extent that the sciences do not recognize themselves as bound to the problems of the dialectic and history in action and to their totalizing movement. To raise the problem of subjectivity and the dialectic is not to raise the problem *of* history in an abstract form, as has been done by those historicists for whom history has become an undialectical novel. To raise the problem of subjectivity is to raise the problem of the meaning and truth of history *in* history which *we* make in accordance or conflict with others, by assuming *ourselves* our negation and by choosing our own actions. The end is not *any* indifferent end. It is the action for the realization of a rational society which overcomes war and exploitations, along with "naturalism," fetishism, and slavery. This is the *horizon of truth*, although it is not the horizon of truth of a philosophy understood as ideology or as a formal conciliation of the dialectic. It is the horizon of truth of a philosophy that is based on what men actually experience *as they experience it and within the limits in which they experience it,* according to which every man is required to work. In the ultimate analysis, this allows the recognition of the meaning of the totalizing historical movement of the history of humanity in the meaning of the life of each man. This is a philosophy which, in the manner of collectivity and society, inheres in each of us in *flesh and blood* and in the first person.

The occlusion of the subject is the occlusion of society, history, and truth. As Marx says: we "must not establish 'society' as an abstraction in front of the individual." The abstraction here is the occlusion of subjectivity and the subject's operations. It is the occlusion of truth which is present as *reason* (not as abstract intellect) in each meaningful human activity, daily action, social reaction, and cultural and artistic product. Art is also in a crisis because it occludes man and his reason. It believes that in the aesthetic work and its results the whole man does not present himself with his body, his soul, his history, and his total rationality. The art that has become identified with the self-destruction which it wanted to denounce is now dead and, *notwithstanding its successes,* prowls among us as a cadaver. Something radically new and extremely simple is beginning. We no longer demand the abstract "why" of the world; we demand the meaning of truth according to which man wants to live in order to be truly man. Hence, we are not interested in the "why"; it is the "how" that interests us: how to radically renew our humanity. This amounts to emphasizing the way, the meaning, and the end in which man expresses himself in the world and objectifies himself in his work, *without at the same time becoming occluded and lost in the objectification.* It is a matter of a new way of living the already given world in which we find ourselves. It is "a new meaning of human existence in the already spatiotemporally given world, the meaning of a self-objectification of subjectivity." It is the meaning of a humanity conceived as a rational humanity, a "humanity that understands its being as rational in wanting-to-be-rational, that understands this as meaning the infinity of life and efforts toward reason." This "reason is not fragmented into theoretical, practical, and ethical reason," because it is human reason, implicit in every human operation in the world and history according to the horizon of historical truth. Phenomenological reason is dialectical insofar as it recognizes the negation in order to negate it. It finds the meaning of history and its truth in the actual presence in which *we* live.

One of the most important results of phenomenological

experience is the rediscovery of the dialectic. Husserl knew that the crisis of the sciences was the crisis of humanity. He rediscovered the dialectic while denouncing the mythology of the Kantian transcendental ego in order to bring the ego back to the concrete monad. He brought the "past" back to the real world without transforming the latter into the arranged world of the categories of the intellect. To discover the concreteness of the monad is to discover the subject. To discover the subject is to discover man. But "man" must not be reduced to an abstraction. Man *for us* today is the man of the atomic age, of the age of developing and still autocratic communism, of neocapitalism, of the awakening of Africa and Asia, of the confrontation of cultures, and of the slow but continuous self-transformation of religions in faith and in truth, and in the crisis of this faith. These developments make man aware, as never before, of the need to radically transform human civilization. The shadow of self-destruction, which man himself has evoked, stimulates and seems to threaten him only from the outside. In reality, the atomic apparatus is the degenerate externalization of an inner will of radical change which still ignores itself and which we believe will be able to change the history of the world, as soon as it is recognized for what it is. The concrete man is not an abstraction. Is he the man in his world? The man studied by *anthropology*? And what is anthropology? A science or a philosophy? As a science, it is "the comparative study of man." Certainly, paleoanthropology and paleoethnology are human sciences similar to the study of the forms of the human body (Husserl used to call it *somology*). Once again, the human sciences are psychology, sociology, ethnology, and "cultural anthropology."

Obviously, for us the human sciences are fundamental; but is it possible to reduce man to a pure object of study of these particular sciences? Is it possible to consider him at the same level as any other object, as if we students of man were not men and subjects? In answer, these same sciences demand a philosophical reflection concerning them as sciences. It is not possible to eliminate them in the name of a relationless philosophy, just as it is not possible to eliminate philosophy in the name of science. Man is what he is to the extent that the world and history have made him what he is, among other men, in the present world. This world also contains the sciences and what man has learned or failed to learn from them. This is the world of nature and of real history as we experience it.

Furthermore, history is, first of all, our presence to ourselves in historical time. The history is not created by us. We have been "made" by it as *subjects that have become*—and we have become as a result of the subjects who have preceded us. All this is not immediately known. We come to know it little by little, from our infancy and through education in the society and environment in which we live. Often we know and learn it passively. But this is not the only way to know it. In fact, we truly know it only to the extent that we are active in our reflection and do not unreservedly accept tradition with its wealth and biases. We really begin *from ourselves,* verifying anew that which is valid by experiencing it and representing it as such.

The point of departure is our presence and our reflection upon the present situation. Reflection reveals us as being conditioned without our knowing it. It reveals to us the reality of a past which, even if forgotten, has nonetheless constituted and keeps constituting the present. We *begin from our present subjectivity.* But it is naïve to believe that our subjectivity is the abstractly considered "subjectivity," as when *we do not realize* that we have within ourselves the whole of the reality of our epoch and the entire reality of the world (as if subjectivity were not something in the world which has always molded us). It is similarly naïve to believe that the world is not within our subjectivity. If I begin from the subject it is precisely because I want to know what is always within me. I want to see how it has made and molded me, as it continues to be molded in myself and others, and how and toward which direction. I cannot immediately know everything. But if I want to know the meaning of my life in the world with others (rather, more precisely, *in others* which are in me and vice versa: Husserl's *Ineinander*), I must seek a totalization of the partial truths and operations and results of the particular sciences: I need a totalizing historical movement. Scientific results cannot be accepted as such. They must be verified so that their genesis and previous verification cannot be forgotten. We must not accept the biases with the truth, but must accept only verifiable experiences as valid, i.e., those that are always *presentifiable.* The rejection of biases allows the continuous correction and discovery of new aspects of truth. If to experience and to presentify is to verify without biases, the resulting verifications have at their basis the interest of truth, and not occlusion and bias. Here, truth is scientific in the full sense.

As philosophers and scientists we are searchers for truth

because we accept what we experience as "it is given to us" when we experience it, within the modalities in which we experience it, and because we search for truth independently of any authority, any "personal" interest, any category, or any caste or class. In this sense we are and must be *disinterested*. To believe that this means that philosophy and the sciences are not concrete facts, and that they are "pure contemplations," is the product of a strange precipitation. At any rate, knowing is a praxis. What characterizes scientific praxis is its basis of truth, its struggle against occlusion and oblivion, its requirement of clarifying the genesis and arriving at universally valid and re-presentable results, i.e., provable in each case and by all in the first person (and not, therefore, because asserted by another, by some second or third person, and, even less, by abstract authorities scientifically and philosophically nonexistent). Precisely because of this, "scientificity" is not reducible to isolated scientific results. It is the rational truth which is immanent in every research: it is reason as the *meaning of truth*. It is the principle of truth which is present and constituted by each subject, even if it is occluded and forgotten.

The very possibility of the particular sciences is entrusted to the movement of immanent reason as it appears in each and every human subjectivity. If man studies himself as an anthropological subject, as a subject of economics and a historical participant, he is necessary to the orientation of truth in each scientific research. Such studies are undertaken because man seeks rationality and because *he* wants to know and correct his own errors. *He* wants to realize himself in history as a rational being. The disinterested search is guided by the interest of reason, which is in the interest of truth. So understood, this interest is *active and operative* in *each particular scientific research*. The totalization and *intentionality* of reason in progress operates in each particular research, just as *the whole operates in each part*. Man is a totality even when he studies physics or geology. Similarly, the results of physics and geology are valid for the wholeness of man, for the ongoing totalization of the history of humanity, and, therefore, for the human subjects and their praxis.

The separation, the fetishized division of labor, is the crisis of the sciences. But, originally, it is not a matter of the crisis of the sciences. It is rather a matter of the crisis of existence, of the *crisis of human subjectivity*. Husserl knew this. And he knew that this is the crisis of human society in a given phase of its development. More precisely, it is the crisis of a society that wants to use the sciences while forgetting and occluding the constitution of a rational society. What Husserl did not know is that the crisis of the sciences, as the occluded use of the sciences that negate the subject, is the crisis of the capitalist use of the sciences, and, therefore, the crisis of human existence in capitalist society. On the basis of this knowledge, *phenomenology becomes the revelation of the capitalist occlusion of the subject and truth,* and the disocclusion of every ideology based on such an occlusion. It is a matter of a knowledge which does not consider man as already attained, but which aims at the *transformation of his life and history according to the horizon of truth.* For this reason, science and philosophy—the latter understood as the rational sense of the truth of human and historical praxis—are not abstractly separable, and the condemnation of philosophy in the name of the "neutral" sciences is but a symptom of the crisis. This crisis is expressed in an eminent form in the rejection of the dialectic and the reality operating in it, and in the rejection of human subjectivity. This rejection is ultimately none other than the rejection of the meaning of historical truth.

[70] *Ambiguity and the*
      Intersubjective Dialectic

MERLEAU-PONTY WRITES, in *Sense and Non-Sense:*

> If it is neither a "social nature given outside ourselves, nor the
> "World Spirit," nor the movement appropriate to ideas, nor col-
> lective consciousness, *then what is, for Marx, the vehicle of his-*
> *tory and the motivating force of the dialectic?* It is man involved
> in a certain way of appropriating nature in which the mode of his
> relationship with others takes shape; it is concrete human inter-
> subjectivity, the successive and simultaneous community of exist-
> ences in the process of self-realization in a type of ownership
> which they both submit to and transform, each created by and
> creating the other.[1]

Further on he says that "Marxism is not a philosophy of the subject, but it is just as far from a philosophy of the object: it is a
philosophy of history." [2] This must be understood in terms of
what has been said in the preceding pages. Certainly, man is
the moving force of the dialectic. However, we must remember
that man as a disembodied subject is inconceivable. The subject
is always concrete and contains the world. To the extent that he
is concrete and rooted in the precategorial material world, man
lives in a material structure. Materialism is not a metaphysical

1. Maurice Merleau-Ponty, *Sense and Non-Sense,* trans. Hubert
L. Dreyfus and Patricia Allen Dreyfus (Evanston: Northwestern
University Press, 1964), p. 129.
2. *Ibid.,* p. 130.

and naturalistic necessity. It is not the reduction of man to an object-thing; it is the struggle against objectification. In this sense it is true that

> throughout the history of Marxism, in fact, the fetishism of science has always made its appearance where the revolutionary conscience was faltering: the celebrated Bernstein exhorted Marxists to return to scientific objectivity. As Lukács notes, scientism is a particular case of alienation or objectification (*Verdinglichung*) which deprives man of his human reality and makes him confuse himself with things.[3]

This must be clarified. The subject is always in the world, even if, in order to become aware of the way in which he experiences the world, he must first carry out the epochē. Instead of saying "subject," Merleau-Ponty says "existence." Thus, the existence living in its actual presence and in the modalities of the first person is subjectivity which contains reality. This reality includes matter, precategorial causal determinism, and the world of needs and satisfactions. In Merleau-Ponty's usage, "existence" may appear as an indeterminate something which does not become aware of the endured objectification. The subject is converted into an object by another subject. In a given social situation, man is reduced to the level of a thing by another man (i.e., by a part of intersubjectivity or society). In other words, he is exploited. But even when exploited and conditioned by the material and economic situation, the exploited man can attain consciousness of his own situation and will to transform it for himself and for all men.

The proletariat is a part containing a totality, i.e., humanity and its *telos*. In Husserl, the whole-part relationship is basic and is already investigated in the third of the *Logical Investigations*. This relationship lies at the source of all phenomenology and can be grasped only through the subjective and precategorial foundation. The sciences are objectified in a given historical situation. Phenomenology does not fight the sciences; it fights the loss of their *function*. The function is understandable if the subject is also the world of all subjects (their *Umwelt*). The dialectic among subjects is a dialectic among the respective worlds of the subjects. This applies, with good reason, to the dialectic of groups, communities, and classes. Man as the subject and motive force of the dialectic includes his temporality,

3. *Ibid.*, p. 126.

his genesis, his history, his *milieu,* his class, and the way he fully experiences his living environment and his class, i.e., matter, his own body, soul, consciousness, and spirit.

The endured alienation refers to the whole man and all that is human within him. In work man becomes adjusted to nature and obeys it in order to dominate it: he becomes a thing in order to shape things. This process of becoming a thing turns into alienation if the subject, who becomes a thing in order to work and make his tools, is reduced by another subject to the level of a thing or tool. The internality of the subject contains *his own world*. Objectification understood as alienation operates in such a way that this very world of mine becomes *foreign* to me by becoming someone else's property. Interpreted in this fashion, Merleau-Ponty is correct in talking about "submitted to" and "transformed" property, in the sense that, if I become someone else's property, I want to regain my own property, which is the result of my own labor. In order to do so within the historical situation of capitalism, I cannot fight just for my emancipation. Since I am denied my individualized subjectivity which intentionally contains all of humanity—the *species-being*, as Marx put it—I must fight for all the real and concrete humanity which I represent. Therefore, I must fight for the essence of the humanity which is negated in me. In the negation of the negation, this essence becomes consciousness, will, and praxis. It is not essence in the categorial sense but it is real humanity which, as the totality and its intentional meaning, acts in that part of humanity which is negated by another part.

It must be emphasized that the subjects contain their full human reality: they are integral subjects. Every group is composed of real subjects. But while the group which exploits and alienates another group only represents itself, the exploited group represents itself and the totality of humanity as the negation of a humanity free from alienation. If I consider my body and my precategorial material reality, with my labor and needs, as external objects, I consider my world as external to me. But I live my world in the first person. It is I-myself in flesh and blood, my soul and my very own material body, who endures the alienation imposed by someone else. Can I call my world, which is no longer my own and which has become foreign to me, the objective world? In that case I would have to distinguish a subject containing all of its objectivity, because he contains his entire world, from this subject deprived both of his liberty and of his world. From this viewpoint, the master-slave relationship, or the exploiter-exploited relationship, obtains between two subject-objects, one of whom appropriates the subjectivity or the world of the other.

My full and concrete ego, with its own world, i.e., the subject-object of our example, is objectified to the utmost. He becomes a man rendered non-man by the other man who exploits him. What is negated is precisely the subjectivity with its entire world and the operations that it performs.

When the sciences occlude their human and precategorial foundation and transform man into an object of study, we do not criticize them for studying man. In fact, all of the sciences are branches of a first total science which studies man. What is objectionable is that, in given situations, even if they are progressing as sciences or technologies, they can lose their intentionality, i.e., their function of constituting the human rationality demanded by every scientific operation. The rationality of the sciences and technology becomes alienated. This generates a contradiction within the rationality of the man who undertakes the scientific and technological operations.

When capitalism uses scientific and rational techniques for a nonrational society, it enters into a contradiction with itself. By doing so, as Marx put it, it will never reach its complete self-realization: like Goethe's sorcerer's apprentice, mentioned in the *Manifesto*, it neglected to learn the magic words able to halt the forces it has unchained. The logical consequence is the total reduction of human subjectivity to a dead reality: something which could happen in an atomic war. The situation imposes its own modalities. But if communism is the movement of emancipation for all of humanity, its first duty is precisely to avoid at all costs an atomic war and what could cause one. The development of the problem of the dialectic leads inexorably to concrete individuation and to the actual situation. This is because in reality we cannot avoid departing from ourselves and our concrete subjectivity which contains the world. If the dialectic obtains between subject and object, we must not confuse the object that we contain, our world, and the endured objectification.

Merleau-Ponty knows that the subject always contains his material reality. However, he stresses that the subject cannot be the prisoner of causal determinations.[4] This is true: but if the

4. Maurice Merleau-Ponty, *Phenomenology of Perception*, trans. Colin Smith (New York: Humanities Press, 1962), p. 171 n.

totality of the world is in us (Husserl's *Weltall*), we are also rooted in the precategorial structure of needs and in precategorial causal nature. If it is not naturalized, this nature can be recognized in its reality, which precedes man's presence on earth. As material beings, we are in a reciprocal and circumstantiated complexity. We are in a causal relationship, even if this causality is not that of physics (which, today, would have to be considered a form of probability). We could say that the precategorial economic structure is concrete insofar as it is existential. However, we must remember that the existential here cannot be contraposed to the *subjective*, since the phenomenological subject is always concrete and rooted in the world and matter. The danger lies in using the term "subjectivity" as it is used in idealism, and the term "existence" as it is used in realism. This would lead to Merleau-Ponty's somewhat unclear claim concerning the impossibility of separating idealism from realism (or, *ambiguity*). Idealism and realism are categorial constructions which are derived from a precategorial reality from which we must always depart, i.e., from a subject which contains the world, or from an internal which contains its external or, better yet, Husserl's *Umschlagspunkt* of the internal and the external. Insofar as I contain the world, the matter I experience or work with is the same matter of which I am made and which conditions me even if my consciousness does not realize it. Science may study the material or organic body, or the psyche. But since the subject is the whole man, the intentional totality of the sciences or of the ontologies corresponds to this totality of man. We know that the teleological idea of history is the idea of the agreement of all ontologies and well-founded sciences. Ultimately, it is this very idea which returns their function to the sciences, and in studying man (e.g., in anthropology) I can very well make use of mathematics, physics, biology, and the other sciences, never forgetting, however, that it is men who found the sciences and give them their meaning of truth.

Merleau-Ponty writes: "Because economics is not a closed world, and because all motivations intermingle at the core of history, the external becomes internal and the internal external." [5] More precisely: "History by its nature never transcends . . . economics." [6] As we have already seen in Labriola, what is involved here is the precategorial structure of economics, and

5. *Ibid.*, p. 172 n.
6. *Ibid.*, p. 173 n.

not of political economy as a science which claims to be independent of the temporal, historical, and precategorial situation. Because of the precategorial nature of economics, Marx criticizes bourgeois political economy. Evidently, even when dealing with economics, we must return to the root and see how, from this root which is the full man, diverse economic relationships arise in different situations. Economics is a science which, like all others, cannot carry on without history, but within which the problem of the function of the sciences is particularly important. This is why we have called it the *science of decisions*.

In connection with the dialectic of the internal and the external—which will be further developed by Sartre—we must keep in mind that there is no "internal" subject which does not contain its world. This dialectic is resolved in the intersubjective temporal dialectic in which each subject, with his world and his praxis, is "conditioned" by other subjects, their world, and their praxis. This is valid in two senses: in point of fact I am always in a genetic line; I am "made" by my parents in the same way that I am constituted by their environment and by their education. The historical milieu will even decide whether I will be born or not, since my parents can have various reasons for wanting or not wanting children, according to economic and other conditions. This is a theme which Sartre will clarify in the *Critique,* and which he seems to derive, in certain respects, from some of Merleau-Ponty's suggestions.[7] Second: I am conditioned by others, by the environment in which I live, by the modes of struggle imposed upon me, by the way in which others react to me, and by the way in which my actions are interpreted. Given all these modalities, my actions can very well result in something I did not want, or, at any rate, result in something very different from what I intended. Here we rediscover the theme of ambiguity.[8] Anyway, we must remember the principle according to which the totality is present in every part, even when the meaning of the truth of the historical totality in process is denied (i.e., it is present as negation).

Therefore, the true ambiguity is not that of realism and idealism. It is that which in determined historical circumstances characterizes the initiative and its results. The true ambiguity is in the transformation of both intentions and their actual inter-

7. Andrea Bonomi, "Materialismo Storico e Questione Esistenzale," *Aut-Aut,* no. 75 (1963).
8. For the presence of this in Lukács, see Bonomi, "Materialismo."

connected practical results, in the course of their temporal realization and in their reciprocal conditioning.

> It is the essence of liberty to exist only in the practice of liberty, in the inevitably imperfect movement which joins us to others, to the things of the world, to our jobs, mixed with the hazards of our situation.[9]

The meaning of truth must itself move in a dialectic which continually runs the risk of losing it, and which would not be possible if it were ever definitely lost.

[71] *Ambiguity and Reconsideration.*
The Loss of the Function of the Sciences
and the Fetishism of Commodities

WHEN PHILOSOPHIES ARE DOGMATIC AND CATEGORIAL, when they are either idealistic or realistic systems, they stand still. In their actual movement, on the other hand, theoretical constructions are very often transformed and refined. But phenomenology is not a construction insofar as it continually departs and redeparts from actual experience where it reconsiders previous experiences and their results in the present for the future. Idealism and realism become worn out in the temporal course of praxis insofar as they are abstract and constructed philosophies.

Thus, the complex texture of the temporal dialectic, in its continuous rebirth in subjects and groups, is hardly reducible to the dialectic of a categorial philosophy of subject and object. Merleau-Ponty criticizes Weber for failing to "relativize" subject and object.[10] Unlike Lukács, Weber failed to catch the ambiguity, i.e., the interpenetration of idealism and realism in terms of which the dialectic is the tormented dialectical relationship of subject and object. Even though we are concerned with a dialectic of subject and object, and we find it in Marx also, we need not reduce the subject to idealism and the object to realism. In

9. Maurice Merleau-Ponty, *Humanism and Terror*, trans. John O'Neill (Boston: Beacon Press, 1969), p. xxiv.
10. Maurice Merleau-Ponty, *Les Aventures de la dialectique* (Paris: Gallimard, 1955), pp. 42–44. [For an English translation of this, see *Telos*, no. 6 (Fall, 1969), pp. 140 ff.]

fact, we find in the concrete dialectic the progressive decline of idealism and realism as philosophies, rendering impossible a third philosophy which would be the synthesis or the ambiguity of the other two. Therefore, when the two terms are used, "realism" and "idealism" have meanings which depend on the active historical situation. Lenin's defense of realism in *Materialism and Empirio-criticism* is the result of the need to fight idealism in a determinate situation. What Lenin really does is neither idealism nor realism: he continuously reconsiders the meaning of Marxism. At that given moment, Lenin may have had to stress a simple and efficient ideology like realism. As Merleau-Ponty points out, in 1922 Lenin will somehow return to Hegel. When Lenin launched the password "Communism is the Soviets plus electrification," he was thinking of what needed to be done in the actual present in which he was operating. Yet, even at that given moment, the intentional movement of communism was not exhausted in electrification, which is only one operation through which it is necessary to pass in order to undertake others. Lenin needed a kind of technical action, similar to that of an engineer building a bridge: this does not mean that communism is exhausted in building bridges. Technique and that for which it is technique should not be confused. The distinction is important. Without it, every technical operation becomes a communism and the latter loses its direction, thus becoming indistinguishable from capitalism. The same is true of idealism and realism. The fact that, at a certain point, Lenin stresses the importance of realism, and subsequently talks about the necessity of restudying the Hegelian dialectic, implies that he stops neither with the first nor with the second. The valuation of realism is tied to the situation in which Lenin finds himself. Lenin's true philosophy, which is not a construction, is more than realism. It is not a simple polemic against idealism. Departing from the self-revelation of an actual situation, that in which one operates, it is possible to act historically, i.e., to realize in praxis an end which is not exhausted in separate and disconnected operations. Hence, praxis is not pure empiricism, but rather a continuous and renewed process of becoming-conscious. The present is not simply one instant of atomic time, and the sum total of atomic instants can never give a direction to the dialectic. This means that praxis must not be considered in terms of a *historical relativism*. It is not mere pragmatism precisely because it must continually reconsider its own results and its own projects. The *reconsideration* (*Rückfrage*), the beginning anew that maintains, corrects, and criticizes at the same time, does not allow for continuity as if praxis were deduced from an already completely elaborated theory. Rather, it allows for a dialectical continuity. The reconsideration is necessary in order not to lose sight of the goal: relationships with others, among the diverse tendencies of a group, and between groups, operate in terms of subjective reconsiderations. Members of the group can separate themselves from the group for personal, psychological, or other reasons. This is a fact to be taken into consideration. But this does not alter the need for the reconsideration, i.e., for an unbiased analysis of the situation, its conditioning elements, and its possibilities. That the adversary forces me to alter the project does not affect the need for continuity and the necessity that the totality and its meaning remain in a part of that same totality. This is the meaning of the totality that Lukács discusses in *History and Class Consciousness*. In the reconsideration, the actual present can always reveal its rational and historical meaning and its teleological sense. The uncertainties of the future, or accidents, are to be considered for what they are and in terms of their influence on the actual project. The most common error is to consider unavoidable what is expected and to consider anticipation or prefiguration (*Vorerinnerung*) as a mathematical prediction or fatality. This would prevent me from trying to effect what I think should happen. The projecting prefiguration must guide my actions by departing from the reconsideration in the present and controlling my actions according to a style of reciprocal conditioning of individualities and groups. The ideal situation would be one in which a leader is not needed, since the presence of a leader always indicates historical immaturity or the insufficiency of the reconsideration, irrespective of whether the leader becomes the focus of hopes or delusions and errors.

The phenomenological analysis of the temporal structure of praxis engulfs the subjects. Yet it is something more complex than a dialectic of idealism and realism. We have used the terms "protention" and "*Vorerinnerung*": we could also have used "retention," the permanence of the present praxis in its "period," and remembering (*Wiedererinnerung*) the past praxis based on its results and the chain of results extending to the present. The act of becoming-conscious is itself, in the present, a temporalization, and it is never separable from the concrete subjects who become conscious. Thus Lukács is correct in saying that consciousness is not something to be added to the proletariat, but that it is inseparable from it, in the same way that in phenome-

nology the soul (*Seele*) is not separable from the body (*Leib*), or
the subject from his world. Lenin's insistence on consciousness
as the reflection of things is correct if the reflection, or, better
yet, the reconsideration, is understood not as an anticipated system but as what continually unveils and reveals reality by freeing it from biases and occlusions. The correction of a mechanistic theory of reflection must recognize the truth along with the
falsity of such a theory. Because of this, Lukács says that "insofar as the 'false' is an aspect of the 'true,' it is both 'false' and
'non-false.' " [11] This contains recognition of the concreteness of
the individual who, in the acting presence, reconsiders history in
order to act in it. At the same time, it implies the meaning of
truth. The emphasis on consciousness is an indication of the
need to return to the concrete subject and its reconsideration.

We must remember that the need to return to the concrete
subject is a Marxian requirement. As we shall see, in the "Economic and Philosophic Manuscripts of 1844," and elsewhere,
Marx continually stresses the *return to concrete individuality*.
He also stresses that "man's being is not separate from consciousness and thought." Such separation is expressed in fetishism,
i.e., in the objectification in which the worker is reduced to a
commodity, and it occludes man's essence. Man is essentially
characterized by the fact that he is a part which contains the
totality. It is impossible thus to separate the individual from the
social in the real man. This inseparability clarifies what Merleau-
Ponty seeks in ambiguity. The ambiguity must catch the *internal*
immanence of society in individuals. This is an immanence of
monads and individuals in one another (Husserl's *Ineinander*),
given that "society" is as abstract a term as "state." As abstract
terms, "society" and "state" are "occluded" and become objectifications of abstractions which are contraposed to the individual
and his labor, i.e., to concrete operations. In fact, phenomenological analysis reveals "society" and "state" as complexes of
operations which are performed by concrete individuals.

Marx not only tends to destroy objectification but, in so doing, he also clarifies *how* it is produced, i.e., its genesis. The
contraposition of the concrete individual and the abstract society
which is posed as concrete (a society which in turn objectifies
the individual, thus reducing him, in bourgeois society, to a
commodity) arises from the fact that a group of individuals con-

11. Georg Lukács, *History and Class Consciousness*, trans.
Rodney Livingstone (Cambridge, Mass.: M.I.T. Press, 1971), p.
xlvii.

ceives of society as a means to its own domination over others, thus constituting itself as a class. Disoccluded, the contraposition of society and individual turns out to be the *class struggle,* and the state becomes one of its tools. Philosophy becomes occlusive when it posits society as opposed to the individual and abstractly contraposes the two terms. Like objectification understood as alienation, this occlusion also originates in the class struggle.

The human world is constituted by concrete subjects and by the *relationships* among them. These relationships are, in turn, *operations of subjects.* A society which appears as an abstraction before the individual does so not for theoretical or *categorial* reasons, but because of precategorial ones, i.e., because of actual operations of concrete individuals in the *Lebenswelt.* Because these operations are forgotten or occluded, that which is in fact occluded is that one class of individuals operates through the state against another class of individuals. Similarly occluded is the fact that capital is produced by labor, i.e., by the operations of concrete individuals. Thus, capital becomes the tool with which a class of individuals subtracts from another class the product of its labor. Therefore, Marx insists: "To be avoided above all is establishing 'society' as an abstraction over against the individual." [12] Consequently, communism must intentionally strive toward the suppression of the state to the extent that the state stands in the way of the individual and his reintegration. The return to the concrete and individual subject is therefore a necessary moment in the revolutionary movement. It is the moment when the individual becomes conscious. To reiterate, it is not a matter of "constructing" a philosophy or of "theoretically" resolving the relationship between subject and object. By returning to the subject and opposing mundane fetishism, the existing society, and the state, phenomenology returns man to his own operations and permits new ones. The problem of the "constitution of the other" by the subject is the phenomenological history of the individual in relation to other individuals and the inherence of "society" in the individual. In fact, the individual finds others within himself even if he becomes an absolute solipsist. However, because of the method of disocclusion, he must begin from the *solus ipse* of solipsism. That which is social in the individual is not given to him by the state. The state is "bracketed,"

12. Loyd D. Easton and Kurt H. Guddat, trans. and eds., *Writings of the Young Marx on Philosophy and Society* (Garden City, N. Y.: Doubleday, 1967), p. 306.

and the individual then truly finds the others and society within himself. Society is not external to individuals, just as the species is not external to individuals. As Marx writes in the "Manuscripts": individual life and species life (*Gattungsleben*) are not different. The species is not an abstract category; it indicates the operations that can be considered within a "species" of concrete individuals. In this sense it is the essence of individuals, which is not a self-contained reality but a *typical complex* of operations. Marx insists on the return of man to his *essence*.

One need not think that every pairing (*Paarung*) and every group constitute a class. The phenomenology of types and human groups is full of serious difficulties. Groups of various types are possible even in a classless society. The phenomenology of groups is important because it clarifies the relationship between classes and nation, e.g., between the struggle of national liberation and the class struggle, and the relationship among the various types of proletariats in various nations. The missing clarification of these relationships breaks "proletarian unity."

The proletariat is a group, but it is also a class. What characterizes it is the fact that it is a part which contains the whole in such a way as to vindicate for every human group the totality which is immanent in them. In other words, it *is both a real and a typical group*. It is the *norm* of all groups, since by its very existence it affirms that there must not be groups without humanity. This is asserted by the proletariat at the very moment (and precisely because of this) when it is denied the right to be a human group, i.e., at the very moment when another class, in constituting it as the proletariat, constitutes it as a class. Having established this, the proletariat sees that its struggle against the bourgeois class which constitutes it as a class must necessarily have as its aim the suppression of that very same proletariat as a class. It is clear that the proletarian struggle must be a struggle of liberation against what renders the proletariat what it is. Therefore, it must aim at the elimination of the proletariat. The *present proletarian class consciousness* seeks to change the proletariat, and it can do so only by struggling against the bourgeois class and against every class distinction (beginning with the class to which it belongs). Class consciousness, therefore, is consciousness of the negation of this negation, i.e., the class.

The proletariat *is* insofar as it aims at *not being*, and it *is not* to the extent that it realizes its own *telos. It is insofar as it is not; and it is not, insofar as it is*. It is not by accident that this partial definition resembles the definition of time. Hegel, however, lacks the structural sense of time, whereas phenomenology vindicates it and Marxism points out that time is not a category but is the concreteness of the real dialectical process. At any rate, the point of departure is the *actual presence*.

What is called "ideology" in Marxism is seen as part of the process of occlusion in phenomenology. In Husserl, liberation from occlusion is necessary for the constitution of a rational society, while in Marx it is needed for the constitution of a classless society. In this sense, the march of humanity aims for the realization of society (*Vergesellschaftung der Gesellschaft*). The march goes through capitalism which, by means of industrialization, leads to the emergence of the proletariat. In other words, capitalism poses the problem of the relationship of man to man at the same time that it occludes it. In this sense, Merleau-Ponty points out in Lukács the importance of the distinction between capitalist and precapitalist society.

Therefore, the need to industrialize defines communism only if what is obtained by means of industrialization is not forgotten. Capitalism also can defend a neutral and nonoriented industrialization. Here technistic alienation and the loss of the function of the sciences reappear. Marxism must not be reduced to technologism, historicism, or relativism. In fact, in order to fight technistic alienation one must keep in mind that Marxism is not a relativism. Lukács remarks that a "theoretical act" is necessary —we will call it an *immanent reconsideration of praxis*, or the act of becoming-conscious—to make us understand the essential character of the "Marxist method." In this sense, for Lukács, Lenin's thought is "theoretical":

> His effectiveness rests on the fact that he has developed the *practical essence* of Marxism to a pitch of clarity and concreteness never before achieved. He has rescued this aspect of Marxism from an almost total oblivion and by virtue of this *theoretical action* he has once again placed in our hands the key to a right understanding of Marxist method.[13]

There is an uncertainty in Lukács that can lead one to think about a dualism between theory and practice. He observes that the Marxist method is theoretical in the sense that "its principal aim is *knowledge of the present*." The dialectic cannot be abandoned, and to correct Hegel means to bring the Hegelian dialectic back to the actual present; it means to make it function as "*a*

13. Lukács, *History and Class Consciousness*, p. xlii.

vital intellectual force for the present." [14] The present reveals its secret to the proletariat.[15] This is a secret that capitalism wants to keep, since the proletariat is the beginning of the ending of the present world. In order to keep the secret, capitalism is forced to hide the totality in particular problems. The totality is *removed*, and this removal is typical of technistic alienation and of the loss of the function of the sciences. What is lost in the removal is intentionality, or in Lukács' words, the "course of action." [16] Technistic alienation and the fall of intentionality reduce man to an object which cannot become conscious, cannot reflect, and cannot reconsider. Man himself comes to be reduced to the level of an object-commodity, i.e., he is fetishized as a commodity. This reveals the *connection between the loss of intentionality and the function of the sciences in the fetishism of commodities*. In terms of our phenomenological analysis, centered on the concept of presence, becoming-conscious, and *reconsideration*, we can agree that the problem of the commodity, as Lukács argues,

> must not be considered in isolation or even regarded as the central problem in economics, but as the central, structural problem of capitalist society in all its aspects. Only in this case can the structure of commodity-relations be made to yield a model of all the objective forms of bourgeois society together with all the subjective forms corresponding to them.[17]

There is thus a correspondence between objectivity and subjectivity. But this means that the objectification of commodities, and the occlusion, in the exchange, of the fact that commodities are man's labor, is the alienation of man.

The prototype clarifies the nature of alienation (*Verdinglichung*), i.e., the reduction of the subjects to the level of things. Marx says that

> a commodity is . . . a mysterious thing, simply because in it the social character of men's labour appears to them as an objective character stamped upon the product of that labour; because the relation of the producers to the sum total of their own labour is presented to them as a social relation, existing not between themselves, but between the products of their labour.

That is, they exist as objectifications.[18]

14. *Ibid.*, p. xlv.
15. *Ibid.*, pp. 2–3.
16. *Ibid.*, p. 69.
17. *Ibid.*, p. 83.
18. *Ibid.*, p. 86.

In all this, Lukács explains, "what is of central importance here is that because of this situation a man's own activity, his own labour becomes something objective and independent of him, something that controls him by virtue of an autonomy alien to man." [19] Transposed from their legitimate use, exact scientific categories occlude the precategorial. This clearly occurs through the exchange of commodities and the quantitative formalism required by that exchange: "*Objectively,* in so far as the commodity form facilitates the equal exchange of qualitatively different objects, it can only exist if that formal equality is in fact recognized." [20]

Capitalism needs "neutral" exactness, but it forgets that exactness is a human operation. Labor is no longer an operation and exertion of the subject. It is "abstract, equal, comparable labour, measurable with increasing precision according to the time socially necessary for its accomplishment, the labour of the capitalist division of labour." [21] Rationalism here becomes pure "calculation." The principle of rationalization is based upon the possibility of calculation. [22] Rationalization understood in this fashion demands specialization as a *rupture of the totality*. The separate object implies objectification and fetishization of the subject or worker.

> The human qualities and idiosyncrasies of the worker appear increasingly as *mere sources of error*. . . . Neither objectively nor in relation to his work does man appear as the authentic master of the process; on the contrary, he is a mechanical part incorporated into a mechanical system. [23]

As Marx put it, only quantity decides here. Similarly, when it is forgotten that it is a method of a particular field, the method of mathematical physics asserts that only the quantitative is real, and reduces the world and nature to pure quantity. Marx again writes: "Time is everything, man is nothing; he is at the most the incarnation of time. Quality no longer matters." And Lukács reiterates:

> Thus time sheds its qualitative, variable, flowing nature; it freezes into an exactly delimited, quantifiable continuum filled with quantifiable "things." . . . In this environment where time is trans-

19. *Ibid.,* pp. 86–87.
20. *Ibid.,* p. 87.
21. *Ibid.*
22. *Ibid.,* p. 88.
23. *Ibid.,* p. 89.

formed into abstract, exactly measurable, physical space, an environment at once the cause and the effect of the scientifically and mechanically fragmented and specialized production of the object of labour, the subjects of labour must likewise be rationally fragmented.

They become, continues Lukács, "the objectifications of their labour-power into something opposed to their total personality," while mechanical disintegration "destroys those bonds that had bound individuals to a community." [24] The categorial objectification and capitalist rationalization seek to destroy the precategorial, but, if they ever did, they would also destroy themselves. This has the inevitable consequence that the subjects must take over the tools of rationalization and transform them into tools of liberation, even at the cost of submitting to the harshest laws of labor. Typical refutation of dialectic claims that rationalization does not hinge on the subject, on the *elimination of the subject,* on the reduction of rationality and time to pure atomicity, and, in general, on the *elimination of reflection in the name of neutral and formal technology* or the problems separated from the totality. The crisis is the result of the removal of man and the *telos:* it is the result of the purely illusory rationalization of the world. Since it is illusory, it falls back upon *relativism* and skepticism. But precisely through such a falling-back, the crisis reveals the rational meaning of history and its concreteness. *The crisis is the forgetting of the origins, the human roots, the human subject,* and the precategorial genesis. Rationalization itself and its formalism are symptoms of the crisis. Here the importance of the application of Husserl's method becomes clear.

We must remember that the reconsideration maintains the continuity and the "course of action." The meaning of the totality is maintained in the part through the reconsideration of subjects and of the group. It can be said that the revision, in the sense of "revisionism," tends to break the continuity and the unity, while the reconsideration tends to maintain it. Usually, it is precisely the inadequacy of the reconsideration which provokes the rupture of unity and revision. The ambiguity must be resolved in the historical reflection. The reconsideration avoids historicism as relativism and the transformation of the act of becoming-conscious into a preconstituted system from which praxis is "deduced." Similarly, it avoids the transposition of the

24. *Ibid.,* p. 90.

Cartesian dualism of soul and body (*res cogitans* and *res extensa*) into theory and practice.

[72] *Ambiguity, Fallibility, and Truth*

MERLEAU-PONTY'S ALWAYS ACTIVE FREEDOM, the conditioning, the instance, the probability of the future, and the dialectic among groups and subjects of a group, are to be brought back to a temporal science of history, i.e., the temporal becoming-conscious of conditioning and possibility. A science of history makes no sense if we mean by it a science such as classical physics. It does make sense, however, if it is understood as the continual reconsideration of the "course of action" in the actual presence and in temporal modalities. In the present, the past is what has led to the present, and the future is what in the present prepares the future in terms of a precise and possible analysis of historical "maturation," both in relation to precategorial economic structures and in relation to the dialectic among classes and small groups of subjects.

In praxis there is a dialectic of action and reaction. The adversary forces the proletariat to struggle in certain ways, and it is indeed a step forward for the proletariat not to lose the "course of action" in them. Similarly, it is an emancipation to keep the adversary's imposition down to a minimum.

The direction is given by the totalizing intentionality. If, in order to hold power, the adversary class contradicts itself and negates the historical meaning of truth, it can force the proletariat into contradiction if it succeeds in making the proletariat yield its own intentionality and meaning of truth. Thus, the proletariat has the duty to maintain its unity and intentionality. This duty can be threatened by lack of reconsideration and by the failure to pass from A to B, when A was attained only in order to arrive at B. Different modes of reconsideration and different projects arise within the proletariat. As in the relationships among monads, the relationship among groups is also interactive. The science of history is not like astronomy: it cannot make precise predictions, because precategorial causal determinism includes freedom and will. Before the multiplicity of dialectical situations, the analysis of the economic situation is fundamental. Yet it is not decisive, even if one can find a certain analogy in the reappearance of economic cycles. Moreover, historical change takes place in a certain order wherein an operation is conditioned by the preceding one: I cannot do B unless I have already done A. Therefore, in order to attain B, I must first pass through A even if I do not have to remain at A. This type of relation reintroduces the conditioning structure and the relationship between conditions and motivations. The attainment of socialism requires, as a precondition, a certain abundance of products and therefore a certain productive capacity which necessitates planning. The future is open, but the project can result in a future which can be predicted only within certain limits and which can change as a result of its being predicted. Planning is a mode of predicting and conditioning the future. This mode changes in the process of its realization.

The dialectic with the adversary and within the group itself must be continually reconsidered. It can lead therefore into conflicts between feelings and comprehending, between popular spontaneity and management. "The popular element senses, but it does not always know or comprehend; the intellectual element knows, but it does not always comprehend; especially, it does not always sense." [25] Thus economic planning must be preceded by organization. In Gramsci we find the Jacobins as the historical incarnation of Machiavelli's *Prince*. The Party must take the place of the "divinity" and of the "categorical imperative." Luckily, Gramsci stresses that this situation obtains only at the beginning of a movement. The same relative separation between intellectuals and the populace, between knowing and sensing, also occurs in a given historical situation. What counts is that, in principle, such a separation should not remain. In the last analysis, this means that sensing and knowing must coincide in the concrete man who is the unity of sensing and knowing. Management as the categorical imperative—in historical situations where the term "imperative" could have a pejorative meaning—must no longer mean the incarnation of the principle of an imperative, but the reconsideration and the limiting idea of the meaning of truth.

The universal aim must be kept in the situations within which praxis takes place in spite of the many forms of the dialectic. This aim is the emancipation of all humanity. The proletariat has a hegemony because it has a duty and aims toward an end.

25. Antonio Gramsci, *Il Materialismo Storico e la Filosofia di Benedetto Croce* (Turin: G. Einaudi, 1948), p. 114.

Marx emphasizes that, in order to realize its own end, i.e., a classless society, the proletariat must suppress or "remove itself" as a class and "raise itself" to the level of humanity. In fact, the proletariat is the negation of a negation. And the nature of the negation is such that in order to negate it the proletariat must bear the negation of humanity in order to make it positive in the transformation of the totality of humanity. This will allow humanity to realize in time its meaning of truth. This means that proletarian culture is *in principle* human culture. The proletariat is not just the heir of classical German philosophy; it is the heir of all human culture to the extent that such a culture resists criticism.

Cultural works, and especially art works, are socially and historically conditioned. Yet they transcend any given historical and social situation. Marx remarks that it is impossible to imagine Achilles with lead and gunpowder. And yet Achilles means something to us as well as to the Greeks, even if his meaning varies with the varying of history. Greek epic and art are bound to certain forms of social development. "The difficulty," writes Marx, "lies in understanding why they still constitute with us a source of aesthetic enjoyment and in certain respects prevail as the standard and model beyond attainment." Man cannot return to childhood, "but does he not enjoy the artless ways of the child and must he not strive to reproduce its truth on a higher plane?" [26] Thus the sociohistorical conditions which produced Greek art cannot return, although we can reproduce the meaning of Greek art. Similarly, we do not want to return to bourgeois or feudal conditions. Yet we can "reproduce," i.e., render alive and reenact for ourselves, the meaning of truth of the artworks produced during feudal and bourgeois periods. This follows necessarily from the fact that the proletariat is the heir of all humanity: it is a part which acts for the totality. In the ultimate analysis, the proletariat should be able to comprehend the always renewed meaning of artworks for all humanity by discovering the root of a work in the social situation, thus understanding the historicity of an epoch. This will enable the proletariat to judge the universal character of its cultural products much better than otherwise. As such, the proletariat should ultimately come to comprehend bourgeois art better than the bourgeoisie itself has been able to, known how to, or wanted to. It is a matter of dis-

26. Karl Marx, *A Contribution to the Critique of Political Economy*, trans. N. I. Stone (Chicago: Charles H. Kerr, 1904), pp. 311–12.

covering the directly or indirectly expressed intentional direction which is contained in bourgeois art and which, in the case of true art, is the same intentional direction of history toward its horizon of truth.

The true hegemony of the proletariat is broader than the hegemony that can be demanded in specific situations of struggle. Little by little, all humanity should be represented by communism, to the extent that communism is able to maintain its own direction in spite of the conditions of struggle imposed upon it by its adversaries. Art is a particular instance of the dialectic of the reciprocal conditioning and the possible development of a dialectic of groups within the struggling group. In the advanced conditions of assertion, the proletariat can and must defend the freedom of art.

The separation between knowing and feeling, or, as Marx put it, between the *head* and the *heart*, can have two meanings. One can fail to understand an idea or a work of art not because the creator does not *feel* it, but because he feels something unusual and new which needs time to be felt. In principle, art does not exist just for artists. As Husserl put it, art belongs to the whole man and is for all men.[27] It can happen, however, that men recognize themselves in a work of art only after many years and after many changes in their social and psychological conditions. The aim of Marxism is to place man in certain conditions where he can comprehend and relive the meaning of truth of art. Marxism's aim would also include what is or will be produced in a socialist society. The dialectic of the artist and his public is not to be confused with the dialectic of socioeconomic forces or with the necessary overcoming of capitalist society. Capitalism, in fact, seeks to industrialize everything, including art. Communism, on the other hand, should coherently defend the humanity of art.[28] In a socialist society, the abundance of products must not be allowed to reduce man to the level of a pure consumer, since the goal of communism is not only economic well-being, but the harmonious development of individuals, their faculties, and their personalities. Economic well-being allows more free time and aims toward a polytechnical culture where man is not

27. Edmund Husserl, *Die Krisis der europäischen Wissenschaften und die transzendentale Phänomenologie: Eine Einleitung in die phänomenologische Philosophie*, ed. Walter Biemel (1954; 2d printing, The Hague: Nijhoff, 1962), pp. 506–7.

28. See my paper, "Per un Incontro Intenzionale," *Questo e Altro*, no. 2 (1962).

reduced to his profession but remains whole. The man who has to a great extent satisfied his economic needs will increasingly participate in cultural life, in the positive dialectic of cultures, in their renovation and reinterpretation, and, ultimately, in the dialectic of those who have produced culture in the past, produce in the present, and will produce in the future. In Husserl's terminology this is the dialectic of tradition and renovation. It is the dialogue between the living and the dead, and those yet to come.

Today, communism finds itself able to represent all human culture, reinterpret it, and renew it in new creations. It is important for Marxism to vindicate artistic freedom against the alienation of the welfare state. This could be a vindication of all human art and its value. Ultimately, Marxism will have to defend the value and the meaning of the works of art of the past, works which, as such, imply a meaning of truth that bourgeois society could neither realize nor recognize because by doing so it would have had to reject itself or render explicit its own contradiction.

The relationship between Marxism and religion is even more complex. As positive religions, the various human religions are bound to historical situations and to particular psychological needs, sedimented in the tradition, that can express various tendencies. It would be very difficult to say that these are all positive. But the critique and analysis of religion must understand, overcome, and resolve on the level of the horizon of truth of the historical process. Generally speaking—or, better yet, phenomenologically speaking—comprehension itself is a religion. It teaches man that each action and part contains a meaning, or a negation of a meaning, even if no part—and this is essential— can ever exhaust the meaning and present itself as the whole. Here faith means faith in intentional rationality which is also indirectly present when negated and recoils upon him who negates, thus provoking the negation of the negation. Each man contains the principle of truth. Yet no man can ever be the truth; this would be idolatry. Critical Marxism could rediscover its own secret religious tone as the overcoming of every idolatry and as the movement of liberation from every type of alienation. This is parallel to the way that a society must be freed from that basic idolatry represented by the fetishism of commodities, which is ultimately the pretense of possessing man and the meaning of truth.

The meaning of truth is infinite and cannot be exhausted in means and in time, even though it must begin with the struggle against economic alienation, and it is historically individuated according to the modality whereby "in order to do *B* I must first do *A*." We should recall with Gramsci the "cultural unification of mankind," whereby "spirit is not a point of departure but of arrival." The meaning of truth continues to live in each subject because it essentially reveals itself in the experience in the first person of each subject. No dialectic among subjects and groups can eliminate it, as it cannot be eliminated by *the ambiguity* of praxis discussed by Merleau-Ponty. Meaning is not a system or an abstract philosophical construction. Meaning must move in a dialectic where it is continually in danger of being lost, although the possibility of there being meaning at all demands that it never be definitely lost.

In the phenomenological sense, beginning from the subject means beginning from that nucleus of truth which, although minimal, the subject contains precisely because he is a subject who departs from the evidence of what he directly experiences in the first person. Man can lose himself in his path and make errors in what Merleau-Ponty calls the crisscrossing of ambiguities. According to Ricoeur, man is *fallible,* and must realize that he is fallible. Ricoeur recalls Descartes's fourth *Meditation:* "I find myself subject to an infinity of imperfections, so that I should not be surprised if I err." He observes that fallibility designates a characteristic of being human.[29] Yet man has another characteristic: that which allows him *to recognize his own fallibility* by departing from the intentionality which lives in him and which is never the same as attained truth. For phenomenology, man is original self-revelation who knows that, because of his essence, he will never coincide with truth, and who still considers the movement toward the truth as the meaning of his life, the world, and history.

29. Paul Ricoeur, *Fallible Man,* trans. Charles Kelbley (Chicago: Regnery, 1965), pp. 3–4.

[73]   *Irreversibility and Economic Structure.*
        The Duty of the Transformation
        of Irreversibility into Meaning

FOR SARTRE, intentional consciousness is consciousness
that "explodes toward"[1] the object. Consciousness is the self-
negation of being in the presence in order to transcend itself.
This is true to the extent that each subject transcends himself in
meaning. Although the subject explodes toward the object, he
nevertheless remains a subject in the presence from which and
in which he explodes. If we think about being in terms of traditional philosophy—or in terms of any ontological philosophy—
we must say that consciousness is annihilation insofar as it is
the negation of being. But for phenomenology the word "being" is
only a category or a bias. As such, it must be bracketed. If we return to the original subject, i.e., the ego in flesh and blood, rather
than the word "subject" which is but a category, we realize that
"being" refers to the categorial operations of my subject in flesh
and blood and its reflection or consciousness. I am always already in the world and I contain the world; among other operations, I can carry out that abstractive operation which leads me
to speak of being. What is lacking in Sartre is the epochē, i.e.,
the return to the concrete subject and his intentionality.

The subject is negation to the extent that it becomes presence, outdistances the past, and denies it as presence. To the extent that it succeeds in remaining in the epochē and aims at

1. Jean-Paul Sartre, *Situations* (Paris: Gallimard, 1947), I, 33.

transforming the mundane according to the meaning of truth, it is also the negation of the mundane. But truth is a horizon which is never equivalent to being. We understand the meaning of truth, free from the danger of considering "truth" as a category, if we think of the *telos* which operates in each past and the various relations of its parts. ("Truth" can be considered as a category when, in formal logic, we say that truth is tautologous, i.e., that it is based on certain operations which lead to a tautology.) Truth appears as a relation among subjects, or as a society of subjects in which no subject is an object for another subject. For example, in the case of the dialectic that Sartre rediscovers within existential psychoanalysis, truth is the overcoming of both sadism and masochism. However, without having the idea of a sexual relation which goes beyond the sadistic and the masochistic, one cannot even talk about the sadist and the masochist. This means that the meaning of truth lives in the sexual relation even when one pretends to deny it. This is a particular instance of the Husserlian principle whereby it is only by recognizing the normal within me that I can talk about the abnormal. The subject is self-revelation to himself. Departing from the evidence in the first person, he discovers in the universal correlation the possibility of knowing all that his evidence implies. The subject contains the initial truth that he discovers only by negating the mundane and the biases. Yet he discovers it as the original point of departure.

The subject can never be the whole truth. He is a nucleus surrounded by dark zones which must be discovered. Their discovery is infinite and, to the extent that the subject is intentional, he always goes beyond himself. He aims at a meaning which is not yet realized but which can be gradually attained. Here, transcendence is negation, but not a total negation: the subject negates only that part of himself that must be transformed, since he continues to realize himself in transformative operations.

That the subject is never self-sufficient and always depends *on something* precategorially, i.e., in the domain of economic need, is connected to the fact that consciousness is never separable from its own body (*Leib*) and causality. Here, the negative element that constitutes the subject is the economic need which is bound to precategorial causality, the organic body, and the environment. To the extent that the subject has needs, he is *presence* as lack of a satisfaction which is necessary if he is to be maintained alive. By the same token, presence is finite: the precategorial structure of needs is temporal, and organic bodies gradually wear out and die, just as, in order to live, they must rest and sleep. The principle of irreversibility is not the same as the second principle of thermodynamics. Since we cannot go back in time, we experience in the first person the irreversibility of time in fatigue and in the aging of our bodies. This is a principle which is really a factual experience. As we can subsequently discover, ours is ultimately the reality of each temporal entity which wears out, begins, and ends.

The irreversibility of the second principle of thermodynamics derives from a precategorial experience which we live in the first person and which is valid both for us and for things, since, as concrete monads, we are both body and thing. Our reality is structured as a reality which is always *in need of something,* i.e., as precategorial economic reality. This is why economics is a decisive science and we are always conditioned by the economic structure: we experience a world and, if we want to live, the world must satisfy our needs. In this sense, the relationism whereby nothing is isolated and each thing and subject needs other things and other subjects is the opposite of the principle whereby substance needs nothing in order to exist. As in Husserl, relationism also discovers the modalities of time in the basic structures of the life-world. In temporal modalities there is irreversibility and, therefore, economic need.

Pure freedom is thus impossible: freedom must always pass through the economic structure, i.e., necessity. Sartre makes this clear in his *Critique de la raison dialectique*. The fact that in this work he arrives at the principle of irreversibility, by means of a path other than mine, confronts me with the scope of my analyses of 1951–54.

As I said then, the problem of man is that of living according to a value and a meaning, even if he lives in irreversibility. Irreversibility must be transformed into a direction which has a value and a meaning of truth. This is the work of culture and civilization which, given irreversible and basic structures, cannot jump to the "spiritual" level without passing through economic necessity. Thus, culture and civilization can be considered as human answers to becoming and death.

Man is rooted in irreversibility and in the precategorial economic structure. His consciousness is always consciousness-of-something. It is intentional. It always transcends itself by going toward a truth at which it aims: the man-subject is transcendental. But consciousness has a body and a world. Furthermore, it needs an environment in order to live. Its intentional motion toward truth is conditioned by the economic structure, and, therefore, by labor, production, and distribution. It is impossible for man not to have needs which begin and end in time. If the temporal structure is fundamentally the economic structure, and the precategorial base is undeniable, it is impossible to occlude the economic structure.

I breathe in the first person: I can say that the air I breathe is *external* to me, since I lack it and must introduce it into my lungs. Here I experience in the first person the lack of something: Husserl has hinted at this type of experience in connection with hunger and food. Hunger can be indeterminate. It constitutes a special relationship between me and the objects that can satisfy my hunger. This is the subject's original experience of the *external*. Sexual impulse is a particular form of hunger. Husserl writes:

> The drive towards the other sex. The drive in one individual and the reciprocal drive in the other. The drive can be in the stage of the indeterminate hunger that does not yet contain within itself its object as its goal. Hunger in the ordinary sense is more determinate when there is a drive towards the food—determinately directed in the original mode (even before the hunger has been satisfied by such a food and this food already has that certain character which allows its recognition, the typical character, of course, of a "food" of a familiar object which can satisfy a hunger).[2]

What do I experience in hunger? That I lack something and that this something is away from me: I want it close enough to me to make it my own, i.e., "internalize it." I therefore experience the external as that which is lacking in me and as that which I must make my own. When I am hungry, the whole world that I experience is valid for me only as a complex of foods which can satisfy my hunger. I pay attention only to foods—in the same way that the baby pays attention only to the maternal breast that can feed him. Before he is born, he probably does not experience the world. "Within procreation," to use Husserl's terminology, there is no distinction between the internal and external. To the extent that it is external, the world is not constituted. Here, we clearly see how the "world" is bound to genetic concatenation, irreversible temporality, the original economic structure, and, therefore, *historicity*. We rediscover Marxism's *precategorial phe-*

2. See manuscript E III 5, published as "Universal Teleology," in *Telos*, no. 4 (Fall, 1969), pp. 176–77.

nomenological foundations or, in terms of what we said earlier, its transcendental foundations. Economic structure, reality, and historicity are inextricably connected. To the extent that it is temporal, the precategorial structure is *necessary. Possibility depends on this basic necessity.* There cannot be a possibility that is not conditioned by necessity. Temporality as the irreversible and necessary structure is the real and transcendental foundation of possibility. Irreversibility is the very structure of history, where we find an authentic historicism. The economic structure conditions freedom but, at the same time, also makes it possible.

To be in history means to be originally and precategorially mortal and to have to satisfy hunger. Since, as a real economic and precategorial subject, I must nourish myself, I must work. Also, another subject can make me work for him. This is the social origin of alienation. For Marx, alienation is always an intersubjective social relation: this is why he poked so much fun at the example of Robinson Crusoe in political economy. This alienation can be overcome only if the economic problem is resolved. There must be an abundance of economic goods. For Sartre, the *base* of the problem is the *scarcity* of goods. This scarcity entails the work needed to produce them, the importance of the type of environment, and the quantity of the population in relation to it. Here a reevaluation of Malthus is in order.

Marx had good reasons to discard Malthus; he does so for the same reasons that Engels criticizes the theory of the *struggle for existence.* The scarcity of products as such does not cause true and genuine alienation. This is not to deny that man is mortal and that death is the total externalization which makes him a cadaver. Here, it is nature which alienates man. In war, however, it can also be another man. I can say that, if death comes because of hunger, it is due to a natural law, "scientific" in the naturalistic sense of the self-multiplication of population. In this case, history is dominated by an inviolable scientific law and alienation is unavoidable, i.e., there will always be exploitation of man by man. Marx objects by saying that true and genuine alienation is an intersubjective relation. It is possible that a subject exploits another because the latter is hungry. Alienation would be impossible if man were not rooted in the precategorial economic structure. However, it does not follow from this that man cannot act upon nature in such a way as to satisfy his needs and, if necessary, regulate population in terms of a global plan.

In fact, an environment without resources leads to misery. But Marx recognizes man's ability to modify the environment

through labor. Alienation obtains to the extent that the subjects
are in a relationship of labor and production. In labor, my operations are my own: I am in the product of my labor. If someone
else, or another class, expropriates my labor and hides the fact
that the *value* of labor is in the subject's operations by saying
that the belabored object is only a commodity, I, who work, am
reduced from a subject to an object and become estranged from
myself. Alienation is *a reversal of subjectivity*.

The center of the whole problem is, and remains, the return
to subjectivity. We have alienation when social relations do not
allow this return. Now, we know that subjectivity is the point of
departure of truth. The struggle against alienation is a struggle
for emancipation and for the liberation from exploitation. The
latter is a struggle for the meaning of truth, which departs from
the becoming-conscious of the subject. Thus, the meaning of
truth is the very meaning of history.

All this indicates that Sartre's investigations must be phenomenologically founded. In general, Sartre's work comes out
clearer and more valid if reconsidered from within phenomenology, i.e., if based on the precategorial foundation (irreversibility)
and on the discovery of the subject as the original nucleus of
truth, operations, and intersubjective relationships. The subject
is in time, in irreversibility: he is hungry and discovers food. If
we depart from the "internal" subject and analyze his operations,
we find everything—not only our being as material things, but
also our experiencing of the distant and the near, of what is lacking, and of what can allow for its satisfaction. The nothingness
that is rooted in man is actually experienced as economic need.
The "external" which I experience by departing from myself in
the first person is the difference between need and satisfaction.

The relationship between man and food, however, is not the
same as the relationship between man and woman. The woman
is not a substance with which to work. Here we have a matter of
relationships among subjects. Similarly, the relationship between
the exploited worker and he who exploits him is not the same as
that between the worker and the matter with which he works. It
is, rather, a relationship between two subjects where one exploits
the other by taking advantage of economic need. But exploitation
does not necessarily follow from economic need in the same way
that economic need does not necessarily lead to the reduction of
the worker to a thing or a packhorse. Similarly, the sexual relationship does not necessarily entail that I must be the object of
some subject or vice versa (sadomasochism). The same is true of

war. This is what becoming-conscious means: it is the discovery that exploitation, sadomasochism, or war are historical facts which are neither fatalistic nor necessary and insuperable. The precategorial structure of needs and satisfactions remains perpetually valid: it is a permanent structure of the life-world. However, this permanence does not entail the permanence of the ways through which I can satisfy my needs in order to live. Relations of production and social relations are alterable.

The irreversible temporal structure is dialectical and is not a function of temporal changes. In Sartre's terms, in every society the present negates the past and the future negates the present. In every society I will have to compensate for consumption by nourishing myself, by sleeping, or by undertaking similar actions. In every society I must still be born—and I would be born even if artificially—and, although I could prolong my youth and my old age, I will eventually die. In every society I will have to depend on an artificial or natural environment. In fact, in the ultimate analysis, any artificial environment will fall back on the natural. But the fact that I cannot avoid death is different from the fact that I can kill or be killed. The duty of the revolutionary class must be that of abolishing the dialectic of war and exploitation in the new society. This is related to the modalities of the struggle, and to the abolition by the liberating class of the ways through which the bourgeoisie has come into being.

Returning to the subject, I discover in myself and in others the ways in which the external is given to me. Each one of us contains the external. In the intersubjective and social dialectic, this fact is exploited by the exploiter who seeks to make me external to myself. He will impose a way of life in which the environment and my working relationships make me external to myself. When I say that I internalize the environment which is imposed upon me, it is the same as saying that the other prevents me from being a subject. However, my rebellion proves to the other that I am still a subject. Thus, the dialectic of internalization and externalization is a dialectic among concrete subjects in which one class does not allow the other to live in or have an environment of its own.

The problem remains: everything is based on irreversibility and the structure of needs and satisfactions. The man who satisfies one level of needs finds himself confronting new ones. Ultimately, even if he has abolished misery and war, he can become aware of the desire to escape death as well as every type of social exploitation. If I consider my answer to the challenge of death as my assertion of superiority, the solution to this problem can re-introduce war and the negated dialectic on a new level.

At any rate, even within the limitations of my life, if I want to become a subject who is compensated for death by his own imposition upon others, and who asserts himself in proportion to the degree to which he negates others and therefore reduces them to objects, I would be, according to Sartre, on the road of self-deification. Since self-deification is impossible, it becomes a "useless passion." This obtains on the level of the phenomenology of impure consciousness. In order to constitute a society of subjects and, therefore, in order not to absolutize myself, I must develop a relationship, between myself and the other, in which neither of the two negates the other in order to assert himself. The revolutionary group which negates a constituted order where relationships between subjects are reciprocally alienating must not reproduce the same relationship that it negates, or it will repeat the dialectic of alienation.

The problem of the psychological, social, and cultural relationships among men remains even after economic alienation has been overcome. These relationships are expressed in the dialectic of tradition and renewal, the heredity received from those who have preceded us—including negative heredity—and the renewal of the meaning of life. Here, the formation of personality among other personalities becomes as fundamental a task as culture.

The constitution of a human society according to the meaning of truth, and its intentional life in each work and each man, must permit a society of subjects in which no subject can assert himself by negating another as a subject, i.e., a society in which the assertion of a subject requires the assertion of the other as a subject as well.

This goal is a meaning of truth as well as the reengagement, the retotalization, of the tradition and its renewal in daily life activities. It is the problem of irreversibility in an infinite temporal transformation toward the direction of truth.

[74]   *Practico-Inert Praxis*
         and the Sociohistoric Dialectic

THERE IS NO EXPLICIT REFERENCE TO HUSSERL in the *Critique de la raison dialectique*. But, whether or not he knows it, the path that Sartre treads is a phenomenological one, if by phenomenology we understand what has been outlined in Part II of this volume. The recall to subjectivity in the *Critique* is compelling and obtains even where it is not explicitly declared. Naturally, it is a matter of returning to the individual and concrete subject: "The only practical and dialectical reality, the motive force of all, is *individual action*." [3]

The subject is the very possibility of praxis: "Praxis, in fact, insofar as it is the praxis of an organism that reproduces its life by reorganizing the environment, is man." [4] It is man who transcends himself in his own subjectivity while remaining subjectivity and persisting as such. For the subject, "the consciousness of its praxis as free efficacy, remains, throughout all the constraints and all the exigencies, the constant reality of itself insofar as it is the perpetual supersession [*dépassement*] of its ends." [5] It is the supersession of its immediate ends for the meaning of truth and the totalization in progress.

Man as the subject contains inertia. In order to realize himself and his ends, he must pass through material inertia. However, inertia must not "externalize" man and his human relations. Through inert praxis, I must work and dominate matter. This does not necessarily mean that I must be externalized or rendered into an object by another man. Ultimately, my praxis must come to terms with the precategorial economic structure in which I live: with the environment (*Umwelt*) and with the scarcity of products. Man lives with nature in a symbiosis which is constituted by labor. In order to dominate nature, satisfy economic needs, and overcome the scarcity of products, man must use his own body in "practico-inert praxis." From the phenomenological viewpoint, this is possible because man is not just an organic body (*Leib*). He is also the material original thing (*Ursache*) at the very center of the causal series. According to Sartre, social life is dominated by inertia, and human activity goes through inertia in order to dominate it.

Therefore, the constitution of social life is a struggle, using all the technical means, against dominating inertia. Technical means are, in fact, the true and genuine symbiosis with nature. The constitution of a society free from exploitation is impossible if nature dominates man. On the other hand, man's domination

3. Jean-Paul Sartre, *Critique de la raison dialectique* (Paris: Gallimard, 1960), p. 361.
4. *Ibid.*, p. 367.
5. *Ibid.*, p. 366.

of nature, the inert praxis through which one must pass, must not reduce man to nature.

If human organization (which must pass through the practico-inert praxis) does not overcome inertia, society remains dominated by naturalization, which renders men external to one another. A class can take advantage of the fact that man must pass through inertia in order to be rendered external to himself. This is crucial. Social inertia is due to a usage of labor, technology, and science that have lost their intentionality. That man must pass through labor does not necessarily imply that he must live in an alienated society. Alienation is a result of the organization of labor and the relations of production. Thus the social struggle is a struggle against nature. This struggle is possible because man externalizes himself in labor and uses his body as an instrument. The social dialectic, which in order to be understood must return to the man-nature symbiosis, is not a direct struggle against nature. Rather, it is a struggle mediated by man and by the group: it is rendered possible by the fact that one class naturalizes another class, or that one man naturalizes another man.

The scarcity of products is conditioning. However, capitalist exploitation could remain even in a situation of abundance. In the final analysis, what renders man external to himself is the fact that he works and, as such, passes through the inert praxis. But a man is exploited by another man only when the latter forces him to remain inert praxis. The dialectic is, therefore, a struggle among subjects. Only through the relationships among subjects, who are also nature, does it become the struggle against natural inertia. Sartre seems to stress the fact that the dialectic among classes and groups is ultimately due to the *symbiosis* of man and nature. Now, symbiosis is necessary but not sufficient to explain the historical dialectic, which is explained only in terms of the operations whereby one man naturalizes the other. Not all poor societies which are forced to live with scarcity are capitalist. In fact, the contrary is the case. The dialectic is intelligible if we clarify the fact that the inert praxis to which nature forces us does not require that inertia dominate human relationships. Labor overcomes inertia. The relation of exploitation obtains when the victory of a man, a class, a group, or a people is exploited by another class, group, or people, who take advantage of the victory over inertia to appropriate to themselves the results of that victory.

The fact that the subject has needs, and works, does not invariably necessitate exploitation, even if products are scarce. The naturalization of man is not a naturalistic fact. Recognition of the necessary character of inert praxis, i.e., the precategorial economic structure, does not entail that the sociohistorical dialectic is a result of inert praxis. I must pass through necessity in order to reach freedom: labor gives me freedom, which is taken away from me in the social relation of labor. The struggle for emancipation is the struggle for the freedom of the worker to conquer himself through his own labor.

Theoretically, capitalism is in a position to overcome the *scarcity* of products. This is why socialism presupposes capitalism. The contradiction of capitalism lies in the fact that, although it is in a position to overcome scarcity, it holds peoples and classes in inertia as if it were impossible to do so and as if scarcity were the only problem. This also explains Soviet planning, which, although it has goals opposed to capitalist ones, has been forced to reproduce the state of practico-inert praxis in order to reach the abundance of goods already attained by capitalism. This explains the Soviet race with capitalism. But the goal is not the abundance of goods. Rather, it is the reorganization of society on the basis of abundance. Here is where the quantitative must change into the qualitative. If the goal were only the abundance of goods, then the Soviet planning of production would run the risk of being indistinguishable from that of capitalism. However, these two types of planning become distinct in the process of realizing the plan. In becoming realized, Soviet production planning does not lose sight of the *telos*. If this were to happen, it would be the whole man who would be planned, and not just his work. De-Stalinization has a meaning to the extent that it is the regaining of subjectivity on the part of each subject who, in order to become a subject, has had to pass through necessity and alienation in order to avoid being reduced to the mere necessity of economic need.

The struggle against natural necessities demands the *telos: logical* use of labor, technology, and the sciences. Otherwise, nature rebels against us with its counterfinalities. Here, Sartre's viewpoint becomes valid once again. For instance, in their secular march, the Chinese peasants clear the land. But deforestation causes landslides, the obstruction of rivers, and catastrophic floods. The Chinese peasants' praxis must be rationally organized. Unless we become aware of natural and historical necessities, we vainly exalt ourselves in an abstract scientism or in a sterile idealism (Sartre speaks of a "Stalinist idealism"). It is possible to avoid deforestation and landslides even in a capitalist society by retaining the state of exploitation of the peasants. I can avoid counterfinality without removing the exploitation of man, and, having avoided the counterfinality and having attained a state of abundance, I can force man to consume the products that capitalist production deems necessary. As Sartre puts it, capitalism can place me in the situation of desiring and of doing precisely what capitalism wishes me to desire and do. Sartre's critique of the idealistic organization of labor that overlooks the finality remains valid. However, the organization that overcomes the counterfinality is not yet socialism and must not lose its own socialist intentionality. Science and technology must rediscover their function and their meaning while becoming conscious of praxis.

This helps us understand the importance of Sartre's critique of a nonoriented praxis which is not guided by reason. What is criticized is praxis for its own sake. Therefore, praxis must not be separated from theory. "The separation of the theory and practice resulted in transforming the latter into an empiricism without principles; the former into a pure, fixed knowledge." [6] This amounts to the submission of men and things to abstract ideas. This is why one can talk about idealism and the "idealist violation." Such a position is not in accordance with Marxism "as the interpretation of man and history." Thus, it is necessary for the epochē to free us from prejudices and these positions. Praxis must always reconsider itself, its own results, and its own projects.

Realism demands consciousness and reflection: It "necessarily implies a reflective point of departure." As in phenomenological analysis, here reflection is considered as a point of departure in the actual present. Sartre continues: Reflection allows the *"revelation"* of a situation "in and through the practice which changes it." The term "revelation" [*dévoilement*] is crucial: that which is hidden must therefore become disoccluded, i.e., must become a *phenomenon*. Sartre criticizes the dualism of consciousness and practice as if the former were a *res cogitans* separated from *res extensa*.

> We do not hold that the first act of becoming-conscious of the situation is the originating source of an action; we see in it a necessary moment of the action itself—the action, *in the course of its accomplishment*, provides its own clarification. That does

6. Jean-Paul Sartre, *Search for a Method*, trans. Hazel Barnes (New York: Random House, 1968), p. 22.

not prevent this clarification from appearing in and by means of the attainment of awareness on the part of the agents; and this in turn necessarily implies that one must develop a theory of consciousness.

It is, therefore, recognized that the agent, i.e., the subject who is already in the world and in praxis, must depart from the act of becoming-conscious. The theory of consciousness needed here is no different from the continuous retention of intentionality in the praxis, i.e., from the fact that the subjects are the ones who become conscious. Therefore, realism is not the negation of subjectivity. It is not to be understood as an absolute reality which confronts us as if we ourselves, the subjects, were not reality. If knowledge were knowledge of a reality already fully displayed before us, we could not fit in it, know it, or modify it, precisely because of the pretense of catching "a world of objects inhabited by object-men." [7] Here Sartre's discussion of objectification is a Husserlian critique and, as such, it demands a return to subjectivity. Within himself the subject always discovers matter, labor, and what Sartre calls externality. The subject has a body which is a point of transformation and reciprocal encounter of the internal and the external (*Umschlagspunkt*). Alienation begins when the other reduces me, or tries to reduce me, to pure matter by using science and technology devoid of their function and intentionality.

The dialectic is clarified in the ongoing praxis. This means that the subject is always in the already given world and he has become what he is. He finds within himself the world that has preceded him, and before himself the world as a project to be realized. Subjectivity as presence in time has historically become what it is, in intersubjective history, in an irreversible dialectical and temporal process of being fulfilled and totalized. Thus it is not a matter of deducing praxis from a theory or philosophy. It is necessary to begin historically from the presence by continually reconsidering past experiences and projects. Historicism demands the reconsideration, the act of becoming-conscious, and the retotalization of previous consciousnesses and their results. Continuity obtains by always undertaking anew the analysis and the critique. Otherwise, praxis is always right simply because it has been performed. More concretely, it is precisely the lack of consciousness and the loss of the intentional continuity of meaning that lead my praxis into contradictory counterfinalities. True

7. *Ibid.*, p. 32 n.

empiricism is the reconsideration of temporal modalities: it is conscious work in the movement of the precategorial structure, and the retention of the intentionality of the totality in every part, and the retotalization of every group and *whole*.

Relativistic empiricism prevents praxis from examining counterfinalities and continually forces it to change direction, thus annulling the results or resulting in the same situation that has to be transformed. We must remember here that experience and reason are never abstractly separable, and that experience is valid only to the extent to which it retains the meaning of truth. So conceived, experience is bound to the irreversible temporal structure, to the precategorial economic level, to matter, and to necessity, without thereby blocking man in necessity.

For Sartre, in pragmatic and relativistic empiricism, "success is substituted for the notion of truth." A scientific and technological success which is not the realization of humanity in history, or a qualitative transformation of the subject and social relations, is a technological but not a human and social success. It is certainly not technological and scientific success that differentiates socialism from neocapitalism. If the problem is only practical and technological, and praxis itself is reduced to technology in both the socialist and the capitalist camps, it becomes increasingly difficult to distinguish the neocapitalism that claims the abundance of goods as its goal from the empirico-pragmatic Marxism which aims only at the same abundance.

Neocapitalism stresses a neutral and nonoriented science. Sartre correctly claims that dialectical reason is contraposed to dualistic reason: science loses its function and society hides the meaning of praxis through technistic ideology.

> Science is not dialectical. . . . The contradiction is not here: it is between the bourgeois resolution to adhere to scientific positivism, and in the progressive effort of the proletariat . . . to dissolve positivism in the dialectical movement of human praxis. In reality, it is simply a matter of the existence of a self-conscious dialectic in the movement of the working class and of the tactical negation of this very same reason in the movement (in fact, dialectical) of the bourgeois class. It is in fact dehumanization by bourgeois oppression that leads the workers to humanity and to praxis organized as a constituted dialectic (i.e., to a positive supercession [*un dépassement positif*] of abstract and destructive Reason); but, conversely, it is this dialectic itself as praxis-totalization which reinforces analytical Reason in the bourgeoisie.[8]

8. Sartre, *Critique,* p. 742.

Therefore, when the working class accepts analytical reason and bourgeois technism, i.e., when it accepts the bourgeois thesis that everything must be reduced to particular technical problems, the proletariat is already at the mercy of the bourgeoisie and renounces its own totalizing praxis. This is how the problem appears on the level of a concrete self-conscious praxis. Technism, pure pragmatism, and relativistic historicism are ideological masks of a praxis which has renounced its own duty, leading to a situation in which man, consciously or unconsciously, accepts dehumanization and objectification.

The proletariat has a universally human mission: the annihilation of itself as a class through the *return of the sciences to their functions*. Science and technology are no longer neutral, and they become necessary to the totalizing meaning of the subjects' concrete operating. For neocapitalism, science is reconciled with technistic alienation and dehumanization, even in the maximum abundance of products and in a wealthy society. But for Marxism, the original function of science is the elimination of alienation. Technistic alienation tends to atomize and divide. It tends to hinder the attainment of consciousness as the unification of groups. Technistic exploitation seeks to extinguish the subjects' consciousness of their having become objects. As a subject, I understand that I am being exploited and alienated by another subject, *"departing from the object that I am for him."* [9] The rebellion against technistic alienation allows man to rediscover his own subjectivity and to get together with others. "He who says: 'I will not force others to do more than they can do, so that another will not force me to do more than I can do,' he is already a master of dialectical humanism." And Sartre observes that, even if verbally refuted, the dialectic can be actually instrumentalized and used by capitalism in spite of analytical reason and "positivistic mystification."

> The boss departs from the analytic viewpoint of atomization and competition: each is free, if he is able, to work more than his neighbor and gain an advantage over him; and the neighbor is free to enter into competition. But dialectical Reason, insofar as it is a carefully hidden mystery, establishes in fact for management that the raising of a norm of labor for and on the part of some, is the elevation (to a lesser degree) of all. [10]

9. *Ibid.*, p. 746.
10. *Ibid.*, p. 743 n.

[75]   *Individuation and the*
       Intentional Horizon of Truth

SARTRE CHARGES DOGMATIC MARXISM with using a preconstituted a priori method.

> It does not draw its concepts from experience—or at least not
> from the new experiences which it seeks to interpret. It has
> already formed its concepts; it is already certain of their truth; it
> will assign to them the role of constitutive schemata. Its sole
> purpose is to force the events, the persons, or the acts considered
> into prefabricated molds.[11]

This inevitably leads one to ignore the concrete particular by reducing it to an abstract universal. The "different" is suppressed.
"The aim is not to integrate what is different as such, while pre-
serving for it a relative autonomy, but rather to suppress it. Thus
the perpetual movement *toward identification* reflects the bureau-
crat's practice of unifying everything." [12] Marx did precisely the
opposite: in a letter to Lassalle he defines his own method as a
pursuit which "rises from the abstract to the concrete." For Marx,
the concrete was the "hierarchical totalization of determinations
and of hierarchized realities." Ultimately, what is most concrete
are men, human relations, and relations among subjects.[13]

Sartre shows a certain amount of interest in Henri Lefebvre's
method, which departs from an actual situation or from an actual
presence which is indicated as a horizon. Each horizontal presence is also *vertical* or historical. Considered with respect to the
horizontal presence, every actual presence is regressive. From the
present I regress to its genesis, in order to return subsequently to
the present which is now "elucidated and explained." The method
must use the various auxiliary disciplines, i.e., the various sciences and technologies. However, it must use them genetically in
order to subsequently return to the present that it wants to explain. This is acceptable to Sartre, who observes that Lefebvre's
method, "with its phases of phenomenological descriptions and
its double movement of regression followed by progress, is valid
—with the mediations which its object may impose on it—*in all*

11. Sartre, *Search for a Method*, p. 37.
12. *Ibid.*, p. 48.
13. *Ibid.*, p. 50.

the domains of anthropology." [14] If rigorously pursued, such a method demands the foundation of the sciences in man's actual presence, temporally situated among other men and in the world, in the now. This involves the problems of the presence and its modifications, of the reenactment of the past, of the ongoing temporal reflection, of the relationship of temporality and truth, of the relation of subjectivity and intersubjectivity, and of the relation of the categorial and precategorial structures of the various sciences.

An immediate identification of an individual or "collective" fact and the abstract universal is impossible. Some *mediations* are therefore necessary. The mediations must allow for the explanation of "this man," e.g., Flaubert, and his work in his time in relation to us, to our time, and to the *project* of our time. We are dealing with the "subject" Flaubert. Thus, the mediations, and all that they imply, are connected to the problem of subjectivity and its relations, to the problem of the relations between the subject Flaubert and the document he has left us *sedimented* in his writings, and to the problem of the relations between the subject Flaubert and the subject Sartre or *us*. Clearly, in his own examination, Sartre cannot occlude his own subjectivity: the regressive-progressive method obviously also involves its user.

One's subjectivity in the *first person* must always be disoccluded. One must find a principle of scientificity without thereby considering himself as already disoccluded a priori. He must find, in his very being, a "part" or something which can be valid not only *for itself*. This leads to the principle of *universal correlation*, which in turn implies the presence of the totality in the part, and, more precisely, in that part which is *us*. I can investigate it because I have discovered myself as a *practical whole*, i.e., because I know that my investigation is not just *mine*, but that it also belongs to society, the world in which I live, ongoing history, and its meaning of truth. In reality, I know myself in the world and in others. To use Sartrean language, to know myself amounts to knowing the externality that has made me and the internality that I make of it. My history is separable neither from the history which has constituted me nor from its critical investigation. To disocclude myself is to discover myself in the world and to understand the meaning of the truth of my *individuation* in relation to others who have constituted me from infancy in the society that has led to my birth. This is precisely the problem of the *first per-*

14. *Ibid.,* p. 52 n.

son and his experiences in relation to the world and its history. It is the problem of the historico-genetic concatenation. Sartre does not overlook this problem, precisely because of its unavoidable theoretical and practical implications, which are connected with the analysis of the *practical whole*. The dialectical subject-object relation as praxis is valid for me and for my humanity in the first person. Thus it is also valid for all the first persons and their intersubjective relations. Praxis is the point of departure: a passage "from the objective to the objective through internalization." Here, "objective" indicates the situation that changes into another situation. It is the world in which I live and which I want to transform.

> The project as the subjective supersession of objectivity toward objectivity, and stretched between the objective conditions of the environment and the objective structures of the field of possibles, represents *in itself* the moving unity of subjectivity and objectivity, those cardinal determinants of activity. The subjective appears then as a necessary moment in the objective process. If the material conditions which govern human relations are to become real conditions of *praxis,* they must be lived in the particularity of particular situations.[15]

The project is certainly connected to the horizon of truth, to the meaning of the totalization and its *intentionality*. It seems that to understand the other is to go beyond, with, and through him according to a praxis. This praxis is not just common, but is in some sense "cooperative." Thus, intentionality acquires a pregnant sense in actual praxis and in its self-transcendence, and, as such, in the totalizing movement of the dialectic. Sartre elaborates the meaning of intentionality in connection with temporalization. He writes:

> Man defines himself by his project. This material being perpetually goes beyond the condition which is made for him; he reveals and determines his situation by transcending it in order to objectify himself—by work, action, or the gesture. The project must not be confused with the will, which is an abstract entity, although the project can assume a voluntary form under certain circumstances. This immediate relation with the Other, beyond the given and constituted elements, this perpetual production of oneself by work and *praxis*, is our peculiar structure. It is neither a will nor a need nor a passion, but our needs—like our passions or like the

15. *Ibid.,* p. 97.

most abstract of our thoughts—participate in this structure. They are always *outside of themselves toward.*[16]

Here, "to exist" means *to be outside of oneself toward,* i.e., to overcome one's own condition in the intentional negation. On the other hand, this presupposes that existence is in an already given world (*vorgegebene Welt*).

The subject has always been in the genetic intersubjective concatenation. He has already become. Therefore, he has always had a past and has become in it. But he knows this only if, by recognizing this necessity that has conditioned him, he negates it in relation to the liberty of the project, i.e., in relation to the meaning of the truth of the future. Here, dialectical laws appear as temporal laws. Yet they are not laws in which the project has always been preliminarily realized. Rather, they appear as laws which include, in dialectical necessity, i.e., in temporality, temporalization as reflection, and, therefore, the freedom of reflection as temporalization. Subjective reflection is an integral part of the "objective" dialectic which is always negated in the subjectivity included in it. The project (or the future) is not a simple deduction or a simple causal dependence. Similarly, it is not independent of genetic-temporal conditioning. Thus, in the final analysis, it is not independent of causal circumstantiality (precategorial with respect to each category of cause understood in the physicomathematical sense). All of this entails a "circularity" which must be investigated. The implied problems are connected with the problem of the counterfinality and what Sartre indicates as the "antidialectical" dimension in relation to the dialectical one. In other words, the project for the future does not coincide with its meaning of truth, even though I must think about the future as the realization of a horizon of truth. The expectation can remain unfulfilled, and my work can result in a future which is different from that toward which my project aims, depending on my relations with others and on the nature of the situation. Yet it would be erroneous to hold that, in every case, the "failure" of a project is a failure of others or of "things," since I myself do not exist independently of others and things.

This leads to the problem of the reality and intelligibility of the dialectic. Sartre is interested in what he sometimes calls the "formal" conditions of intelligibility of the dialectic. These formal conditions concern the "theme" of intelligibility. Actually, for Sartre, these conditions are never purely formal, but are al-

16. *Ibid.,* pp. 150–51.

ways concrete and individuated. They are always a function of individual situations, and, therefore, of the actual presence, i.e., the actual historical presence. In other words, dialectical reason always starts from a particular historical moment. It becomes "historicized" by continually reenacting, in the historical moment when it arises, a past which under certain conditions becomes "a present that has passed," i.e., the historical past. At the same time, however, it finds in the present the expectation and the project for a future present which may or may not be oriented according to the horizon of truth. This is where the philosophical tradition poses the problem of the negative that will have to be recognized as the *negation of the negation*. Insofar as it is intelligible, dialectical reason *departs* from an individuated historical presence in which totalization is in progress. As Sartre observes:

> We will see later on in the paragraph reserved for "The Critique of Dialectical Experience" how the dialectic can be at the same time historical reason and self-historicization departing from a particular moment of history.[17]

This note refers to the second volume of the *Critique*. However, even in the first volume, the dialectic must depart from its "historicization" of the actual presence.

The critique of reason is thus inextricable from a *critique of experience*. Rather, it is a function of the critique of experience and, therefore, of the actually "lived" temporality or of the temporalizing of reflection. In other words, the "categories" of dialectical reason are a function of "how" these categories operate in experience. Here we find a critique of Kant similar to Husserl's. For us, the critique of experience must be the precategorial foundation. The Kantian analysis offers us the necessary forms of experience, but, in principle, the Kantian dialectic separates the dialectic from experience. The reverse also obtains: the dialectic is immanent in experience. Therefore, a critique of dialectical reason must also be a critique of dialectical experience. Hegel's answer to the problem leads to the identification of dialectical experience with its intentional horizon of truth, of the actual with the rational, or, as Sartre puts it, of being with thought. We hold that the dialectic is obscured if it does not operate in experience. Furthermore, it presupposes the nonidentity of the actual and the

17. Sartre, *Critique*, p. 741 n. [The section on "The Critique of Dialectical Experience" appears in the projected second volume of Sartre's *Critique*, which has not yet been published (1972).]

rational, of being and thought. This nonidentity is the assertion of intentionality. On one hand, it is the inclusion of the totality in the part, of the infinite in the finite, and of truth in individuality; on the other hand, it is the identification of the part and the whole, of actuality and rationality, and of individuality and totality. There are *mediations* between abstract individuals and the abstract totality. Along with all "science and auxiliary technology," both individuals and the totality are grounded in the "historicization" of dialectical reason, "starting from a particular moment of history," i.e., the moment that *we* live and experience.

The *we* and the subjectivity are therefore constituted by the *intentional difference* between the actual presence and its horizon of truth which never coincides with the being-present as such. Contrary to what Heidegger claims, it is not a matter of an *ontological difference* between being and the presumed *being-in-itself*. The latter, along with determinate being (*Dasein*), is an abstraction. If this *being-as-such* [*Sosein*] replaces the intentional horizon of truth, such a horizon is compromised and rendered impossible, and man's concrete subjectivity is denied in the name of an abstract being which is nothing but the product of a particular form of alienation. It is a great achievement of the *Critique* to have dealt with the theme of the horizon of truth and the intentional orientation toward truth. Time, through reflection, and therefore through *subjectivity*, appears in us not only as a project, but also as action for a project directed toward the intentional horizon of truth.

[76]   *Irreversibility and Repetition*

I REDISCOVER THE WORLD and history within myself, but not as pregiven things separated from me: this would presuppose a mythological absolute consciousness in opposition to which these things would be "being." I rediscover them as things among which I am also a thing precisely because I am a subject. I know myself in the praxis of this relation which is ultimately a common project. It is a project which is directed toward the future and the orientation of its truth. I depart from myself as original and incomplete praxis which is, and makes itself to the extent that it aims at realizing the totalization in the historical process, in myself, and in others. In this sense, Sartre's observations seem important:

The critical experience will start out from the immediate, i.e., from the individual attaining himself in his abstract *praxis,* to rediscover, through deeper and deeper conditionings, the totality of his practical links with others, and thereby the structures of the diverse practical multiplicities and, through the contradictions and the struggles among these, the concrete absolute: historical man.

Thus, historical man is not concrete because he declares himself to be concrete. Evidently, I am individuated and historically concrete from the very beginning. Yet, *I must discover myself-as-such,* not as the man who I already am, but as the man who makes himself concrete "through the contradictions and the struggles" of practical multiplicities. Here, concrete praxis is constituted in a project which is oriented toward the horizon of truth. My historical concreteness consists in completing myself by departing from the actual presence which is recognized as negative and incomplete. This completion obtains in a praxis which is oriented toward the meaning of intentional truth. In this context, Sartre notes:

> I understand "abstract" here in the sense of "incomplete." From the point of view of his singular reality, the individual is not abstract (one might say that he is the concrete itself), but *on condition that* more and more profound determinations have been discovered which constitute him in his very existence as an historical agent, and, at the same time, as a product of history.[18]

Here we encounter irreversibility: the real subject is "a structure of irreversibility" [19] who allows the possibility of a future and its determination.[20] The totalization in process of the practical individualities obtains in the concrete temporal dialectic. It is in the reciprocal encounter of subjects: in the constitution of individual subjectivities in *series* and in *groups.* Inert praxis and externality characterize the *series,* while the *group* is constituted as freedom only in opposition to the externalizing coexistence of the series. According to Sartre, the series ultimately appears as repetition and circularity, unlike the progressive meaning which is implicit in the irreversibility which shatters the repeti-

18. *Ibid.,* p. 143 n. This may also be found in *The Philosophy of Jean-Paul Sartre,* ed. Robert D. Cumming (New York: Random House, 1965), p. 427 n. [In this and the passage quoted immediately above, we have used Professor Cumming's translation.]
19. *Ibid.,* p. 472.
20. *Ibid.,* p. 473.

tion. Irreversibility is opposed to repetition, and if the dialectic is progressive temporality, the serial repetition generates the counterdialectic.

Sartre's position must be clarified and corrected. Temporal irreversibility, which for physicists is the increase in entropy, appears to man's precategorial experience as the necessity of satisfying the needs which arise from the consumption of his body (the increase of entropy). This necessity forces him to eat, work, or make others work for him. Precisely because time is irreversible and everything wears out, everyone must repair his own consumption with food and rest—or risk death, which will eventually come anyway. Everyone must sate his own hunger. The need to eat always reappears. If this repetition is a serialization, then the series and the need to eat *always* reappear, precisely because irreversibility cannot be overcome. This is parallel to the impossibility of perpetual motion and circular reversibility (the living being cannot eat itself).[21] It may seem paradoxical, but I have needs because I change in time, and because I always change in time I have needs which must be continually satisfied. From this follows the need for work, and practico-inert praxis. This does not prevent me from making someone else work for me, and thus I become a master, i.e., it does not prevent the exploitation of man by man. Now, the inexorable reappearance of needs because of irreversibility and consumption does not entail the reappearance of exploitation. Thus the group that fights serialization also fights the exploitation of practico-inert praxis. Therefore, one fights a *kind* of intersubjective dialectic and not the fact that needs reappear. Once again, scarcity of food does not entail that I must be exploited. If by working I make myself practico-inert praxis, this is not equivalent to exploitation: the latter is different from the former even if it is a function of the former. More precisely, the fact that needs reappear makes exploitation possible, but it does not make exploitation necessary and insurmountable. The sophism of exploitation is as follows: since needs always reappear, exploitation must always reappear. Or, since this land is inadequate and its goods are scarce, the exploitation of man by man is unavoidable. The revolutionary group must overcome the circle of exploitation, so that a man does not come to be used as an inert means by another man. Ultimately, social inertia can be overcome because it is due to human relations, unlike the serialization of needs which is in-

21. *Ibid.*, p. 155.

evitable. What must be overcome is the externalization of a man rendered into a thing by another man, and not the fact that I am also a natural thing, i.e., that I experience my own inertia and that of things among which I live in a causal precategorial relation. What must be broken is the reduction of man to the level of a thing or commodity (*Verdinglichung*). The externalization which I always contain, whereby I always live and experience nature, is not social alienation, even if it is the origin of this alienation. History is nature, but it is not simply nature or natural history. If social inertia were to reappear in the same way that needs do, and if the externalization of a subject in relation to another were inevitable, exploitation could never be avoided. The laws of political economy that Marx criticized for reducing human relations to "scientific," naturalistic, and insuperable laws would then be eternal. According to economic naturalism, however, men become abstractions. They are degraded to the level of natural things in the same way that the worker is forced to live abstractly and not as a man. Thus serialization is the reduction of man to the level of a natural thing, and the struggle against serialization is the struggle against *Verdinglichung*. The struggle agaist serialization brings us to the discovery that, although man has to pass through necessity and practico-inert praxis, he can still constitute a society of subjects.

[77]   *Marxism and Scientism.*
        The Separation of Abstract Politics
        from Public and Social Life

IN MARX, IS THERE THE PROBLEM of human subjectivity
and of the wholeness of man? Does Marx see man solely as an
object of Marxism—understanding the latter as a science in the
positivistic sense? The truth is that the problem of man is at the
center of Marxist thought. However, this problem is not at all
obvious. Certainly Marx trusts the objectivity of science, but this
trust does not mean that Marxism is a science in the naturalistic
sense. Even Feuerbach's paradigm of mineralogy did not have
this meaning. In January, 1843, Marx writes: "In the investigation of *political* conditions one is too easily tempted to overlook
the objective nature of the relationships and to explain everything from the *will* of the persons acting." Thus not everything
depends on the subject, who is himself conditioned by the con-
textual and historical situations (e.g., by the context of Moselle,
of which Marx is speaking). At any rate, the subject, his will,
and his freedom are not abstractions. The peasants of Moselle
become conscious of their situation, i.e., of the fact that their
rights as men are being abused: it is a matter of a *subjective
becoming-conscious* on the part of the peasants. Through the
peasants, however, it also concerns man himself: it is the first
indication of the universality of the proletariat's task.

      Marx emphasizes that the analysis of the struggling parts
must not be disturbed by prejudices, moral or otherwise. The
analysis must bracket value judgments. However, this does not

[371]

mean that the results will be neutral. Ultimately, the proletariat turns out to be the historical agent, and ethical meaning is rediscovered as *founded* and not as *preconstituted*. If we consider the factual data in the political struggle, "one will not presuppose an exclusively good or bad will on either side. Rather, one will observe relationships in which only persons appear to act at first." This passage seems to deny the person. Actually, in his intellectual development, Marx does not deny the person, but only the person separated from the situation. Marx does not consider persons as situations, or situations as the conditions that in chemistry make a compound possible. In fact, he explicitly criticizes this approach in the Preface of *Capital*. Marxism is not a social physics, as might be supposed from the following passage:

> As soon as it is demonstrated that something was *necessitated* by conditions, it will not be difficult to figure out under which external circumstances this thing *actually* had to come into being, and under which other circumstances it could not have come about although a need for it was present. One can determine this with almost the same certainty as a chemist determines under which *external* circumstances some substances will form a compound.[1]

If we read this passage and all of Marx's work in a scientistic way, then Marxism becomes positivism in the Comtean sense, i.e., a social physics or a naturalism. But Marx's thought aims in precisely the opposite direction, even if the positivistic interpretation is the easiest and most persistent one. In fact, the scientific aspect of Marxism has, above all, a negative sense: it is the opposite of "utopian." What subsequently corrects the scientistic perspective is the "historical" element, i.e., the critique of science that claims to fix eternal laws, and the problem of the historical foundation of science. Marx sees this problem as soon as he comes in contact with political economy. What he says in the "Economic and Philosophic Manuscripts of 1844" is certainly elaborated, but the elaboration does not give us anything qualitatively different. If there is some of Marx's youthful thought which somehow conflicts with *Capital*, it is not in the "Manuscripts." Rather, it is in the passage quoted in conjunction with

1. Karl Marx, "The Defense of the Moselle Correspondent: Economic Distress and Freedom of the Press," in *Writings of the Young Marx on Philosophy and Society*, trans. and ed. Loyd D. Easton and Kurt H. Guddat (Garden City, N. Y.: Doubleday, 1967), p. 145.

chemistry, which is bound up with Feuerbach's criticism of theology. It is a moment of enthusiasm provoked by Feuerbach's "stream of fire" criticism of religion and speculative philosophy: "the stream of fire [*Feuer-bach*] is the *purgatory* of the present times." [2] Speculative philosophy turns out to be ideology. But the criticism of philosophy does not reject reflection on *praxis in praxis*, i.e., true philosophy. It does not reject self-reflecting praxis which continually reconsiders itself by departing from the present situation in relation to the obtained results and the ends that it wants to reach. This last point is essential to Marx's notion of historicism. Scientificity does not conflict with the *reconsideration*. Therefore, it does not deny freedom of analysis and the will, even if they are made possible, within their concrete limits, by the situation. To believe that Marxism is a science like physics amounts to transforming Marxism into an ideology or scientistic *utopianism*. What interested the young Marx from the very beginning was the human subject in his full concrete and universal meaning, which is both real and transcendental. This is the fundamental point for *any* Marx. If this is forgotten, it becomes absurd to claim that the proletariat, as a part, contains the totality of humanity-in-becoming and its meaning of truth. That the human subject is both real and transcendental is the meaning of humanity-in-becoming, i.e., of ongoing human history, allows meaning to be removed from speculative philosophy and given back to real men, their praxis, and its horizon. Thus, universality is no longer an abstract category, and the foundation of meaning is precategorial rather than categorial.

Genuine philosophical thought, then, departs from the actual historical situation and its comprehension. To the extent that it is directed, this comprehension gives a function to all the sciences, which, if truly pure and disinterested, have the duty of constructing a rational society. Hence, whoever uses them irrationally contradicts himself. This is the *authentic* scientific character of Marxism: the historical and the scientific meanings of truth coincide. The positivist interpretation is a bourgeois interpretation. In capitalist society, science unavoidably enters into a crisis, not because of technical results, but because of its function. Similarly, if the economic structure is scientistically interpreted, economic operations lose and the categories of bourgeois political economy become eternal. Political economy becomes a scientistic theology. Generally speaking, every category which is

2. "Luther as Arbiter between Strauss and Feuerbach," in *Writings of the Young Marx*, p. 95.

separated from the human subject is abstract, and every category that returns to its foundation in the man-subject is not only universal but also concrete.

On the 10th of August, 1844, Marx writes in "Vorwärts":

> We have seen that a social revolution involves the standpoint of the *whole* because it is a protest of man against dehumanized life even if it occurs in only *one* factory district, because it proceeds from the *standpoint* of the *single actual individual*, because the *community* against whose separation from himself the individual reacts is the *true* community of man, human existence.[3]

Notice how Marx vindicates concreteness insofar as it is founded upon the *"single actual individual"*: although the universal is embodied in the part ("in only *one* factory district") it is valid for humanity. Man rebels at the fact that the community, camouflaged as the German state, appears as something separated from, extraneous to, man's humanity. Separated from man, "politics" itself is abstract: the German state, something abstract, appears as the concrete reality. *It is a category that operates as a real fact.* Thus it forces man to become an abstract "isolated" worker like the isolated "political community." Here Marx criticizes the "separation": the categories separated from their precategorial human foundation and from man's physical and spiritual humanity. Marx never abandoned this position, and any reading of his works that fails to take it into account, that substitutes separatism for Marx's relationism, makes the very same error that Marx continually criticized.

The "community" is concrete society grounded on concrete individuals. The "political community" is the abstract state which appears as abstract and brings about the isolation.

> Do not all uprisings without exception, however, break out in *disastrous isolation of men from the community*? Doesn't *every* uprising necessarily presuppose this isolation? Would the Revolution of 1789 have occurred without the disastrous isolation of the French citizens from the community? Its aim, after all, was to end this isolation. But the community from which the worker is *isolated* is a community of a very different order and extent than the *political* community. This community, from which *his own labor* separates him, is life itself, physical and spiritual life, human morality, human activity, human enjoyment, *human* existence. *Human existence* is the *real community* of man. As the disastrous

3. Karl Marx, "Critical Notes on 'The King of Prussia and Social Reform,'" in *Writings of the Young Marx*, pp. 356–57.

isolation from this existence is more final, intolerable, terrible, and contradictory than isolation from the political community, so is the ending of this isolation. And even a partial reaction, a *revolt* against it, means all the more, as *man* is more than *citizen* and *human life* more than *political life*. Hence, however *partial* the *industrial* revolt may be, it conceals within itself a universal soul: no matter how universal a *political* revolt may be, it conceals a *narrow-minded* spirit under the *most colossal* form.[4]

This passage should be studied carefully. Marx's man is whole because he is both physical and spiritual: he is the *subject* of human activities. To the extent that he is whole, this subject is the essential foundation of all his operations. Man's essence is precisely this wholeness of his precategorial operating which grounds everything. In functioning as if they were concrete, abstract categories which are separated from this subjective foundation render man abstract. Marx does not criticize simply a formal dialectic of "ideas": he criticizes the fact that the bourgeoisie make ideas function as reality. This is similar to the way economics makes its "scientific" categories function as reality, and finds it scientific to discuss the worker abstractly. Separated from man, the worker's own labor poses itself against the worker, because the owner does not consider the worker as a man but as a "scientific" term of the economic calculus. "His *own labor*" separates man from the community, since it leads the worker into becoming abstract, as Marx will unequivocably clarify in the "Manuscripts of 1844."

[78]   *The Whole Man, Civil Society,*
         and the State

ALL OF THIS is connected to "Toward the Critique of Hegel's *Philosophy of Law*," the Introduction to which has already been mentioned in conjunction with Husserl, since it illustrates that, for Marx, man is the true *original root*. We must emphasize that Marx's program against abstractions is "to return to the things themselves." "To be radical is to grasp things at the root. But for man the root is man himself." [5] The return to man is es-

4. *Ibid.*, p. 356.
5. "Toward the Critique of Hegel's *Philosophy of Law*: Introduction," in *Writings of the Young Marx*, p. 257.

sential if philosophy is to be understood by the masses. To be understood is to be addressed to concrete persons *ad hominem.* It is possible to return to man by criticizing religious alienation in Feuerbach's sense, i.e., in the sense that man, in religion, projects his own essence outside himself. "The criticism of religion ends with the doctrine that man is the highest being for man." [6] This critique does not say that man is God, or that man's meaning of truth projects man outside himself. Rather, it says the contrary: truth cannot be considered as human reality (or turned into idolatry), and the deification of man is idolatry. It may be necessary to recall once again that, when we speak of "being," it is easy for us to fall into abstractions, even if being is not always the supreme being.

Man is the supreme being for man. But the proletariat is forced into the condition of not being able to realize its own human essence (we may speak of essence as not separate from human operations). In fact, the proletariat is treated as if it were a thing, an animal, or a factor of the economic calculus. Therefore, man's essence, which religion posited as beyond man, becomes a task: to realize the *highest human* essence in history, i.e., man's meaning of truth in a society of subjects and man. Reason becomes the movement of realization of the meaning of truth in history.

Man's reality cannot be isolated. However, it is in fact isolated by the bourgeois *state* which, as such, takes man's human reality away from him. The "community" from which the worker is isolated is called by Marx *Gemeinwesen* (from *Gemein,* meaning "common"). In this case it refers to what every man has in common with every other man: that humanity which is taken away from the proletariat [7] and which the proletariat must reestablish for all with its praxis. *Gemeinwesen* therefore also means *common essence.* That which is common does not boil down to politics: the politics of the proletariat is inseparable from the constitution of humanity. With the praxis of the proletariat, politics returns to the subject. It is no longer a separate category or an abstraction. It must return to precategorial *life.* Hence, it is concretely individuated and contains, in its own individuation, the universal *common essence.* Politics is only one kind of human action: human life is *something more* than political life. For Husserl, precategorial life (*Lebenswelt*) has

6. *Ibid.*
7. "Critical Notes on 'The King of Prussia and Social Reform,'" p. 356.

an infinite historical task. To the extent that it is concretely individuated it is finite. It is a part containing an infinite totality
which must gradually be realized in history. For Marx, the goal
of communism is not the abundance of goods but the common
harmony among whole men: "physical and spiritual life, human
morality" (recall Gramsci's "spirit").

> Communism represents the superior form of economy and social
> life, but the classics of Marxism did not at all consider it the
> ultimate goal of humanity. . . . The ultimate goal is the har-
> monious development of all the capacities and attitudes of each
> member of society.[8]

Marx writes that the attempt to negate the inhuman, "even
[if it is] a partial reaction" originating in the proletariat, "means
all the more as *man* is more than *citizen* and *human life* more
than *political life*." The human being is infinite in his essence.
He is embodied in human precategorial life, which is not outside
time, history, and precategorial economic structures. The workers' insurrection has a universal soul which, in its universality,
is not *separate* from the live body of the insurrection (Husserl
would call it *Leib*). This holds even if the insurrection is only
partial. In fact, Marx speaks of a revolution against industry as
necessary because capitalist industry dehumanizes man (technistic alienation), and he emphasizes that the industrial insurrection is total, since industry does not oppress an abstract industrial worker but suppresses, in the worker, the whole man.
Therefore, the revolution is not an abstract political fact separated from the whole man. To the extent that he engages in
politics, the worker fights with his whole self and not as a political "technician." Politicians who claim to be only "political
technicians" lose man's "universal soul." Marx writes: "However
partial the industrial revolt may be, it conceals within itself a
universal soul: no matter how universal a *political* revolt may
be, it conceals a narrow-minded spirit under the *most colossal*
form."

Historically, capitalist industrialization gives rise to the maturation which permits the rise of the proletariat, and therefore of
man, so that he can reconquer himself in the class struggle. Industrialization is unavoidable. However, this does not mean that
communism is just industrialization. Clearly, it is precisely the

8. Stanislav Strumilin, *Il Passaggio dal Socialismo al Commu-
nismo*, trans. L. Foa (Turin: G. Einaudi, 1961), pp. 29–30.

opposite: it places industry, science, and technology in their real historical *functions*.

Man's return to the concrete subject, *individuated and universal*, is the hinge of Marx's critiques of Hegel.

> The separation of civil society and the political state appears necessarily to be a separation of the political citizen, the citizen of the state from the civil society, i.e., from his own actual empirical reality; for as a state-idealist he is a being who is completely other, distinct, different from and opposed to his own actuality.[9]

> Civil society and the state are separated. Consequently, the citizen of the state and member of civil society, are also separated. The individual must thus undertake an essential schism [*wesentliche Diremption*] within himself.[10]

Here, the expression *wesentliche Diremption* refers to the distinction between the concrete man and the political man, i.e., man is split in his *human essence*. The state is an abstract idea which operates as if it were concrete and, as such, divides man from himself and from his own essence. Only the concrete individual contains universality: the state's will is contraposed to the will of man, to the will of the society of men. The will has its own true existence as the general will only in the self-conscious species-will (*Gattungswille*).[11] Here *Gattungswille* refers to the will of the individual as the species-being containing the essence of mankind which, if negated, is the cause of the *essential schism* (*wesentliche Diremption*). By departing from the humanity that is denied to it, from the endured exploitation, and from the being considered as an object or as a thing, the proletariat becomes conscious of containing the will of mankind. The proletarian revolution is the result of the negation of what is human in itself and in all men.

Marx criticizes the legislative power in terms of the "essential schism" which is produced in man by the distinction between real social-individual man and the political state. He observes that if the political state were not separate from man, then the legislative power would fail as the representative power. With the

9. Marx, *Critique of Hegel's "Philosophy of Right,"* trans. Annette Jolin and Joseph O'Malley (Cambridge: At the University Press, 1970), p. 78.
10. *Ibid.*, p. 77.
11. *Ibid.*, p. 58.

disappearance of the separation, representative power would be representative

> in the same sense in which every function is representative. For example, the shoemaker is my representative insofar as he fulfills a social need, just as every definite social activity, because it is a species-activity, represents only the species; that is to say, it represents a determination of my own essence the way every man is the representative of the other. Here, he is representative not by virtue of something other than himself which he represents, but by virtue of what he is and does.[12]

Each man represents other men, i.e., each man as an individual contains mankind in his human essence. In his trade, the shoemaker is a determination of mankind. However, the determination must not deprive the shoemaker of the humanity whereby each man "represents" others. His humanity does not boil down to the shoemaker's trade. The whole man obtains in what he *is* and what he *does:* man is not simply his abstract determination. Strictly speaking, the social man cannot be represented. If he is represented, it is because the social man is not a concrete individual in a concrete society which is not an abstraction opposing the individual and rendering him abstract. From this follows the warning (already mentioned in the "Manuscripts of 1844"): "To be avoided above all is establishing 'society' once again as an abstraction over against the individual." [13]

[79]   *Real Humanism and Ideology*

FOR MARX, the individual is both the starting point and concrete reality. In fact, we always begin with an individual who lives with other individuals. Outside of this factual and actual relation, society is an abstraction and, therefore, a form of alienation in Feuerbach's sense. Moses Hess undoubtedly influenced Marx, since for Hess the critique of religion is connected with the critique of private property. The close relation between Hess and Proudhon is undeniable. But Hess seems to be more "concrete" than Proudhon, since Hess's problem is not to order the categories or the "spirits of real men." It is to bring back the

12. *Ibid.*, pp. 119–20.
13. "Economic and Philosophic Manuscripts of 1844," in *Writings of the Young Marx*, p. 306.

"bodies [*Leiber*] of these spirits into *civil society*." [14] Marx's critique of Proudhon's conception of money seems to echo Hess, and it is reminiscent of other religious suggestions whereby money and circulation imply subtle problems of religious idolatry (Marx will recall this point in conjunction with the "fetishism of commodities").

Marx's critique of Proudhon is the critique of "the metaphysics of political economy" and represents a stable point of arrival in Marxian thought ("The Poverty of Philosophy" was written in 1847–48). We must emphasize what Marx means by the critique of the "metaphysics of political economy." He means the critique of necessarily abstract economic categories which are transformed into a false concreteness. The categories are not pure reason and are not independent of real relationships. Real relationships are, in turn, precategorial and human relationships, or, to use Marx's terminology, they are the very movement of life, since they are "active and busy [*das bewegte und bewegende Leben*]." [15] Categories and human operations originate in this life. Economics must rediscover the foundation of the categories in men. The "subject matter" of economics is not the economists' dogma, but man's operating.

> The economists explain how production takes place in the relations given, but they do not explain how these relations themselves are produced, that is, the historical movement which gave birth to them. Having taken these relations as principles, categories, and abstract thoughts, M. Proudhon has only to put order into thoughts which are already alphabetically arranged at the end of every treatise of political economy. The material of the economists is the active and busy life of men; the materials of M. Proudhon are the dogmas of the economists. [16]

In this sense, the categories are the "expressions of the relations of production." It is important here to avoid considering relations of production as categorial and independent of the men who produce them, just as society must not be considered as categorial and abstractly contraposed to the individuals who form it.

14. Moses Hess, "Die letzten Philosophen," in *Die Hegelsche Linke*, ed. Karl Löwith (Stuttgart: F. Frommann, 1962), p. 50.

15. "The Poverty of Philosophy," in *Writings of the Young Marx*, p. 476; and Karl Marx and Friedrich Engels, *Werke* (Berlin, D.D.R.: Dietz, 1956–69), IV, 126.

16. "Poverty of Philosophy," p. 476; Marx and Engels, *Werke*, IV, 126.

Something similar to this must be said of Marx's ambiguous use of the neuter noun *Wesen*. Originally, *Wesen* meant "condition" or "state." But it also means "being alive" and "essence." Clearly, Marx does not want to construct a theory of *essences in themselves,* considering them as if they were real beings with their particular nature and particular status. More precisely, each man carries the human essence of mankind, but this essence is not an abstract term that becomes concrete. In fact, it ultimately coincides with real human society, i.e., the constitution of human society which realizes the true essence of man, that which is essential in man and his meaning. So understood, this society is not already constituted: it is in the process of being constituted and it is the task of the proletariat to constitute it. Thus, "knowledge" of man's essence coincides with the knowledge of the concrete humanity which is constituted and is in the process of being constituted. But precisely because this constitution is the developing historical realization of the essence of the human species, it is a meaningful praxis, and a reflection on the praxis in the praxis. It is a continual reconsideration. Therefore, Marx can easily use the term "essence" [*Wesen*], except that its use involves the danger of its being always exposed to an abstract and categorial interpretation.

This is what is at issue in the not always clear polemics of *The Holy Family* (written between September, 1844, and February, 1846). The polemic aims at defending a real or radical *humanism* against a humanism that is considered to be concrete simply because it talks about man and is called concrete (this self-declaration is Hess's own). Spiritualism and speculative idealism are dangerous because they are abstractions that seek to pass as concrete. Furthermore, by speaking in the name of concreteness, they occlude the real individual men as subjects in the first person.

Marx's defense of man as an individual does not mean that he contraposes society to the individual. His criticism of the transubstantiation of concrete individuals into self-consciousness or spirit does not mean that he denies that the individual can become conscious or perform the concrete operations which constitute "spiritual" works, art, for example. Marx's emphasizing of real relations of production does not mean that these relations, or the economic structure, are separable from society. Furthermore, their being conditioned by nature does not entail that all human relations are naturalistic. If one reads Marx without keeping the organic development of his thought in mind, one risks falling into the reverse of Bauer's position. The critique of speculative philosophy is the vindication of the operating human subject. As already indicated, this subject is necessarily conditioned, but neither sufficiently nor exhaustively, by nature and the economic structure. Furthermore, the critique of speculative philosophy is not the opposition of praxis to theory. The human essence is unthinkable apart from the historical actualization of the essence of the human species, but this does not mean that it must not be thought. Rather, it means that thinking is possible only in terms of each concrete individual in his historical becoming and self-realization as a man or woman in the horizon of the meaning of mankind. For Marx, this is positive humanism and not idealistic, naturalistic, or, in Feuerbach's sense, anthropological humanism. This is how the Preface to *The Holy Family* is to be understood: *"Real humanism* has no more dangerous enemy in Germany than *spiritualism* or *speculative idealism* which substitutes, *'self-consciousness'* or the *'spirit'* for the real individual man." [17] Thus, self-consciousness or the comprehension of oneself does not replace the real man: self-consciousness as reflection is not denied. What is denied is a consciousness of oneself which is not a consciousness of real and active man and his operations. Man is real and active to the extent that he operates and produces. His dependence on economic operations and nature does not mean that all human operations must be reduced to natural ones, even if those operations cannot be realized other than in and through nature. Active men are in time and are conditioned by a determinate social structure. Yet they can change both the social structure and nature.

Men's being is their live and real process. Consciousness is consciousness of this process departing from the actual present. *The German Ideology* is closely connected with the "Theses on Feuerbach." According to *The German Ideology*, Marxism is the "science of history." [18] History is human history conditioned by natural history. However, human history is not a *naturalistic science* like physics, biology, or the Darwinian law of the "struggle for existence." In fact,

> The history of nature, so-called natural science, does not concern us here; but we will have to examine the history of men, since

17. Marx and Engels, *The Holy Family or Critique of Critical Critique*, trans. R. Dixon (Moscow: Progress Publishers, 1956), p. 15.

18. Marx and Engels, *The German Ideology*, trans. S. Ryazanskaya (Moscow: Progress Publishers, 1968), p. 28.

almost the whole ideology amounts either to a distorted interpretation of this history or to a complete abstraction from it.[19]

In the preceding passage we find the simplest and most original meaning of ideology: *ideology is a distorted interpretation* of the operations that real men actually carry out in time and history. If human operations are reduced to purely spiritual ones, we have an abstract man which is only spirit; if they are reduced to natural operations, we have another abstract man reduced to nature or to an object-thing. After all, this is what capitalism tries to do through *Verdinglichung*. Yet even though it is abstract, ideology affects history: it is a real historical fact that the worker is reduced to the level of a thing, a workhorse, or an "abstract worker." Ideology is not the assertion of naturalism against idealism. There can also be a naturalistic ideology which very often is nothing other than the correlation of idealistic or spiritualistic ideology. Naturalism and realism, and idealism and spiritualism, are philosophical systems. Thus, they are constructed. Marxism, on the other hand, is not a philosophical system. It departs from real men in their actual situation as conscious beings who must always become conscious of what in fact is. Ideology makes things appear different from what they are. Hence, to take things at their roots, and to discover man who is his own root, is to discover what ideology hides. This is a disoccluding analysis which is, *ante litteram*, a phenomenological analysis. Marx will hold this position to the very end: in fact, it is reiterated in a writing dated 1881–82 ("Randglossen zu Adolph Wagners *Lehrbuch der politischen Ökonomie*").

Beyond ideology one discovers real man, i.e., we discover ourselves precisely as we are, in the actual situation and in the actual ongoing historical society. "Ourselves" here refers to the operations of the whole man even if he has been rendered abstract. In fact, capitalism forces the worker to live as if he were abstract. Actually, however, the worker remains a man and, because of this, he is alienated.

History is the history of real individuals, "their activity and the material conditions under which they live." "The first premise of all human history is, of course, the existence of living human individuals." [20] Man lives in nature and modifies it insofar as he produces his own means of existence and, indirectly, his very

19. *Ibid.*
20. *Ibid.*, p. 31.

own "material conditions." When we begin to reflect, material life is already a product of human operations.

What is important is how men produce. The analysis therefore must pay much attention to this "how." Society is the totality of all types of operations. These operations *appear different* from what they are, and so do the subjects operating in the vital process: hence, the need for an analysis which discovers the real life-process and becomes conscious of it: "Consciousness can never be anything else than conscious existence, and the existence of men is their actual life-process." [21] Consciousness is conditioned by life. It is life that becomes conscious of the practical developmental process of men: *"des praktischen Entwicklungsprozess der Menschen."* [22] Marxism is the science of human development under given conditions. It is neither "abstract empiricism" nor "idealism" (understanding idealism to be "the imagined activity of imagined subjects.") [23] It is "practical materialism." However, this does not entail the reduction of man to a naturalistic being who is unable to become conscious of his own operations, conditions, and real possibilities. The science of history is the science of all human operations: man is not a natural fact; he is the subject of sensible, commercial, and industrial operations. However, this—unlike capitalism—does not mean that every human operation is reducible or must be reduced to industrial operations. Against Feuerbach, Marx stresses commerce and industry as operations of human subjects who are not reducible to mere scientific objects of physics or chemistry:

> Feuerbach speaks in particular of the perception of nature; he mentions secrets which are disclosed only to the eye of the physicist and chemist; but where would natural science be without industry and commerce? [24]

The (precategorial) economic structure is a function of the fact that men, in order to affect history, must be alive and able to satisfy their needs. In turn, satisfied needs create new ones: human operations are totally human. Marx does not contrapose separate economic and industrial operations to Feuerbach. In fact, he reproaches Feuerbach for his failure to see the sensible

21. *Ibid.*, p. 37.
22. *Ibid.*, p. 38; and *Werke*, III, 27.
23. *German Ideology*, p. 38.
24. *Ibid.*, p. 58.

world as the totality of human operations, "as the total living sensuous activity of the individuals." [25]

[80] *Crisis of Society and Economics as a Science.* Verdinglichung

THE ANALYSES IN *The German Ideology* presuppose those in the "Economic and Philosophical Manuscripts of 1844." In Marx, the economic factor does not appear as something separate, but as what is essentially inherent in society. The "separation" (between the state and the community) falls back on the worker. The abstract separation among capital, land, and labor renders the worker abstract and no longer a man. To the extent that he is forced to live as if he were abstract, the worker is forced to *live as if he were dead.* This is consistent with the fact that wages are determined through "the hostile struggle between capitalists and workers." "For the worker, therefore, the separation of capital, ground rent, and labor is fatal." [26] The separation of the three categories is the work of economics as a science: in phenomenological terms, it is the work of the "naturalism" of political economy. As a constituted science, political economy forgets to return to the subjective and precategorial foundation of the categories which it employs. In the case of the category "labor," it fails to return to the man who works. Conversely, man is forced to live as a scientific-naturalistic category.

If economics were pushed to its logical consequences, the worker could not live. His existence would be reduced to the most simple humanity, i.e., to an animallike existence. In other words, man becomes just another commodity among many. "According to Smith, the normal wage is the lowest which is compatible with common humanity, that is, with a bestial existence." [27] The reduction to the level of an animal does not exclude the reduction to the level of a machine:

Thus, the existence of the worker is reduced to the same conditions as the existence of any other commodity. The worker has

25. *Ibid.,* p. 59.
26. Marx, "Economic and Philosophic Manuscripts of 1844," in *Early Writings,* trans. and ed. T. B. Bottomore (New York: McGraw-Hill, 1963), p. 69.
27. *Ibid.*

become a commodity and he is fortunate if he can find a buyer. And the demand, upon which the worker's life depends, is determined by the caprice of the wealthy and the capitalists.[28]

To the extent that it is abstract, the worker's activity can be more easily studied by the economist. It is the economist's very object of study and coincides with the "reduction to the level of a machine" which industry needs, and with the "reduction to the level of a commodity" which the market also needs. To reiterate, economists ignore the real subject who works and, through his own labor, produces a product. The working subject interests them only in terms of the result of labor and not as an original subject. The economist "tells us that originally, and in principle, the *whole product* of labor belongs to the worker." [29] But he subsequently forgets the real originality of the worker. "This reduction of the greater part of mankind to abstract labor" occurs because "in political economy *labor* appears only in the form of acquisitive activity." [30] From the industrial viewpoint, the result of labor is scientific: economics studies products and not men, i.e., it studies labor as separate from the worker. What results is capital which "is accumulated labor." [31] Capital renders men into abstractions, and abstract categories become subjects: what happens here is a genuine and true reversal which can be expressed by the term "objectification." The situation is self-contradictory. Therefore, political economy as a science of objectified man is also *in crisis*. We can easily see how the problem can be clarified by dealing with it in terms of a phenomenological analysis. Furthermore, the crisis of economics as a science is actually a symptom of the crisis of the society within which that economics obtains. Thus it indicates the fall of intentionality and the function of science.

According to Adam Smith, the function of economics is to bring happiness to the majority of society. And Marx observes:

Since, however, according to Smith a society is not happy in which the majority suffers, and since the wealthiest state of society leads to suffering for the majority, while the economic system (in general, the society of private interests) leads to this

28. *Ibid.*, pp. 69–70.
29. *Ibid.*, p. 74.
30. *Ibid.*, p. 77.
31. *Ibid.*, p. 72.

wealthiest state, it follows, that social *misery* is the goal of the economy.[32]

Marx's comment is relevant today if it is taken to refer to the entire population of the planet Earth. As a separating science, economics is the science "of nations" [*Nationalökonomie*] and is also "categorial" and "industrial." As a categorial and industrial science, it "knows the worker only as a draught animal, as a beast." [33]

Accumulated labor becomes embodied in commodity capital. In order to accumulate crystallized and objectified labor, and exchange it, capital must reduce both man and labor to the level of a commodity.[34]

It is self-evident that political economy treats the *proletarian*, i.e., one who lives, without capital or rent, simply from labor, and from one-sided, abstract labor, merely as a *worker*. It can, therefore, propound the thesis that he, like a horse, must receive just as much as will enable him to work. Political economy does not deal with him in his free time, as a human being, but leaves this aspect to the criminal law, doctors, religion, statistical tables, politics, and the workhouse beadle.[35]

The reduction to the level of an object brought about by political economy implies still other reductions, i.e., it leads to the objective separation of the various activities and sciences which break man down into as many objects as there are domains: law, medicine, statistics, politics. Naturally, all these are considered separate from civil society. The alternative to the fragmentation of man is the totalizing unity of the sciences as precategorially founded by real and whole men.

The reductions to the level of an animal or a machine are part of the reduction of man to the level of a thing through alienation understood as *Verdinglichung*: "Political economy considers labor abstractly as a thing. Labor is a commodity." [36] Therefore, the reduction to the level of a thing or commodity coincides with the reduction of man to the level of an object of study of political economy, i.e., it coincides with the reduction of the subject to the level of an abstract category of a science that has

32. *Ibid.*, p. 74.
33. *Ibid.*, p. 79.
34. *Ibid.*, p. 83.
35. *Ibid.*, p. 76.
36. *Ibid.*, p. 82.

lost its precategorial foundation and function. For the subject who is reduced to the level of a category, to return to the subject is to become conscious of his own situation and *to attain revolutionary consciousness by departing from the endured objectification*. The attainment of consciousness reveals that man, as a categorial object, is reduced to the zoological level. History follows a similar path. It follows that the abstract worker vindicates his own human essence in his praxis. This essence unveils to humanity its self-contradiction: humanity has lost its own meaning and the historical *telos*. Similarly, the sciences have lost their function in relation to the constitution of a society of men-subjects who are not reduced to the level of things or animals. In all its variations, alienation is to be understood in relation to the situation we have just analyzed.

Materialism should not be interpreted without reference to the analysis of alienation. Otherwise, the "reduction of man to the level of matter" becomes, along with the "reduction to the level of a thing," a form of alienation. The same applies to referring to nature while forgetting the human and historical operations. For example, the fertility of the soil is not a distinctive characteristic of landownership. Rather, landownership is characterized by the way in which the owner of land uses it, especially during the passage from feudal to industrial property.

> Landed property had to develop in both these ways, in order to experience in both of them its inevitable decline. So also industry had to ruin itself both in the form of monopoly and in the form of competition, in order to arrive at faith in man.[37]

Marx began from the factual situation presented by political economy as a science. Precisely because he did so, his demonstration shows that the man-object of political economy is not man. Rather, he is a man only insofar as he rejects his own dehumanization, i.e., his own transformation into a category of political economy understood as the "science of wealth." The man in question here is, obviously, precategorial.

"We have begun from the presuppositions of political economy. We have accepted its terminology and its laws." The analyses in *Capital* follow the same method. If the method of economics is abstraction, one need not confuse the abstraction that does what it is meant to do with the active abstraction imposed by capitalist society—an abstraction that Marx himself must follow

37. *Ibid.*, p. 119.

as a factual datum. The liberation from capitalist abstraction demands the becoming-conscious of the subject who is rendered abstract. Thus this becoming-conscious becomes revolutionary praxis. The abstractions which Marx takes into account in *Capital* aim at the same end, i.e., a radical transformation of man and society. *Capital* is not simply a history of economics; it is the return to the subject as the founder and the economic operator who must negate the negation endured under a capitalist economy.

[81]   *Estrangement and the*
       Return to the Subject

MARX CONTINUES:

We have begun from the presuppositions of political economy. We have accepted its terminology and its laws. We presupposed private property; the separation of labor, capital and land, as also of wages, profit and rent; the division of labor; competition; the concept of exchange value, etc. From political economy itself, in its own words, we have shown that the worker sinks to the level of a commodity, and to a most miserable commodity; that the misery of the worker increases with the power and volume of his production; that the necessary result of competition is the accumulation of capital in a few hands, and thus a restoration of monopoly in a more terrible form; and finally that the distinction between capitalist and landlord, and between agricultural laborer and industrial worker, must disappear, and the whole of society divide into the two classes of property *owners* and *propertyless* workers.[38]

All this is in relation to scientific laws which are not "explained," i.e., not brought back to the subject. As we know, the explanation creates a revolutionary subject. Economics as a science does not understand man and ends by generating in him a need to reconstitute the negated humanity. Economics does not understand the coherence of the historical-economic movement and becomes a decisive factor in the beginning of a new historical period.

These considerations necessarily depart from the actual presence and from the attainment of consciousness in order to arrive at the reshaping of history. Political economy, with its social and

38. *Ibid.*, p. 120.

human crisis, is part of the actual presence. "We shall begin from a *contemporary* economic fact." [39] Subjects become conscious of the presence, and, precisely to the extent that they discover themselves as objects, they recognize themselves as *estranged*. Estrangement follows alienation.

> The worker becomes poorer the more wealth he produces and the more his production increases in power and extent. The worker becomes an ever cheaper commodity the more goods he creates. The *devaluation* of the human world increases in direct relation with the *increase in value* of the world of things.

Therefore, the more commodities are worth as *things*, the less men are worth *as men*. It follows that "labor does not only create goods; it also produces itself and the worker as a *commodity*, and indeed in the same proportion as it produces goods." [40] At this stage of the analysis, alienation is perceived as the *reduction to the level of a thing* (*Verdinglichung*). But let us proceed:

> The object produced by labor, its object, now stands opposed to it [i.e., the worker's labor, and thus the worker] as an *alien being*, as a *power independent* of the producer. The product of labor is labor which has been embodied in an object and turned into a physical thing; this product is an *objectification* of labor.

Therefore, alienation turns out to be *objectification*—the very same *objectification* into which political economy as a science has fallen. Marx says that the labor that has become objective 'is an *objectification* of labor." Here, by "objectification," Marx does not mean that in labor, technology, or science my activity is objectively expressed. *When I work I always work on something:* labor is intentional. But in intentionality there is a continuity between the subjective operation that intends the object and the object itself. Here, however, as in the case of Husserl's scientific objectification, the continuity is broken. The object is no longer *my own:* it is no longer my property. In fact, it is taken away from me to the extent that it becomes a commodity owned by *someone else* who can say that the object of labor that I have produced is *his own*. Thus, my labor becomes owned by someone else: it is now *extraneous* to me. What the other owns, however, is my subjectivity which has worked and has remained crystallized in the worked product. Since *it is* really *I-myself* that comes to be owned by the other, I become extraneous to myself. This is

39. *Ibid.*, p. 121.
40. *Ibid.*

a phenomenological analysis of the situation described by Marx. However, Marx says precisely what results from the phenomenological analysis. "The performance of work appears in the sphere of political economy"—and, therefore, is described by political economy as a science that has lost its own function—"as a *vitiation* of the worker, objectification as a *loss* and as *servitude to the object*." In other words, the worker is vitiated by the produced object and he becomes the slave and serf of the one who takes it away from him by transforming the produced object into a commodity. It is the worker who, together with the object of his work, becomes a slave and a serf, since the vitiation is of his laboring subjectivity and its appropriation by someone else. In the act in which the worker appropriates what is his own, he expropriates himself. Appropriation becomes alienation as *estrangement*.[41]

The worker transforms nature into the worked object, but nature also furnishes foods (recall Husserl's analysis of foods). Estrangement ends up by affecting the worker's very nature (*Umwelt*). It thus changes his way of experiencing and living the world.

Marx has brought to light what political economy as a science has hidden. He began from the "data" and discovered what the data were hiding. His analysis is phenomenological, since it has transformed the data into *phenomena*. The same thing happens when an ideology is examined: the reality hidden beyond the ideological construction is eventually discovered. What is discovered is precategorial. This explains why what has remained hidden was hidden in the first place. Marx himself speaks of the occlusion which was implicit in the very functioning of political economy as a science which does not know that it is founded on the precategorial, and which thus "covers" its own human foundation.

> *Political economy conceals the alienation in the nature of labor in so far as it does not examine the direct relationship between the worker (work) and production. . . . The direct relationship of labor to its products is the relationship of the worker to the objects of his production.*[42]

There is no doubt that by *labor* Marx means the laboring subject, and his analysis is possible only in terms of the return to the subject.

41. *Ibid.*, p. 122.
42. *Ibid.*, p. 124.

[82]   *The Goal of Dialectical Materialism.*
         Man and Mankind. Language.
         Nature as the Inorganic Body of Man
         and Intersubjective Constitution

ALIENATION AFFECTS THE PRODUCING SUBJECT IN THE
"productive activity itself." [43] The product is nothing other than
the result of the subjective producing activity.

> First, that the work is *external* to the worker, that it is not part of
> his nature; and that, consequently, he does not fulfill himself in
> his work but denies himself, has a feeling of misery rather than
> well-being, does not develop freely his mental and physical ener-
> gies but is physically exhausted and mentally debased. The
> worker, therefore, feels himself at home only during his leisure
> time, whereas at work he feels homeless. His work is not voluntary
> but imposed, *forced labor*. It is not the satisfaction of a need, but
> only a *means* for satisfying other needs. Its alien character is
> clearly shown by the fact that as soon as there is no physical or
> other compulsion it is avoided like the plague. External labor,
> labor in which man alienates himself, is a labor of self-sacrifice,
> or mortification. Finally, the external character of work for the
> worker is shown by the fact that it is not his own work but work
> for someone else, that in work he does not belong to himself but
> to another person.
>   Just as in religion the spontaneous activity of human fantasy,
> of the human brain and heart, reacts independently as an alien
> activity of gods or devils upon the individual, so the activity of
> the worker is not his own spontaneous activity. It is another's
> activity and a loss of his own spontaneity.
>   We arrive at the result that man (the worker) feels himself to
> be freely active only in his animal functions—eating, drinking
> and procreating, or at most also in his dwelling and in personal
> adornment—while in his human functions he is reduced to an
> animal. The animal becomes human and the human becomes
> animal.
>   Eating, drinking and procreating, are of course also genuine
> human functions. But abstractly considered, apart from the en-
> vironment of human activities, and turned into final and sole
> ends, they are animal functions. [44]

43. *Ibid.*
44. *Ibid.*, pp. 124–25.

Thus, abstraction and separation, and therefore political economy as a science that objectifies man, reduce him to the level of an animal—as already indicated. However, this reduction is a consequence of "naturalism." In naturalistic objectification, man becomes an animal, and vice versa. Here, his transformation into an animal refers to what is "diabolic" in religions. At any rate, my becoming an animal is due to the fact that I, as a worker, become the property of someone else: I am turned into an object by another subject. On the other hand, the activity of the other subject who appropriates me can be said to be diabolical. The diabolic here appears to be a consequence of capitalism.

Marx refers explicitly to religion: religious fantasy elaborates an object. It is a subjective operation which produces a fantastic object. This object is a product of the heart as well as *of the brain*. Up to this point there is nothing negative. The conceived fantastic object is a *cogitatum:* it can be a fantasy or an idea. But it can also be a meaning of truth, since even what is intended by fantasy has its meaning of truth as fantasy. But the *cogitatum* becomes blocked. It is no longer a *cogitatum:* it becomes a real being. As Hegel would put it, the rational becomes actual. This actual being to which I myself have given the status of reality becomes opposed to me and dominates me from the outside as if it were *divine* or *diabolical*. But what happens if I disocclude this procedure? The *cogitatum* is once again found to be what it is: a fantasy or meaning of truth which is not condensed in a being or in reality. In this case, religion returns to the subject. However, this does not mean that, having avoided transforming the fantasy or truth into a being, religion does not have its function. Marx himself has laid the foundations for a phenomenology of religion beginning with the denunciation of the connection between religion and the diabolical character of capitalism. Thus he returns to religion its own subjective foundation which cannot allow a *cogitatum* to dominate man from the outside, as if it were a real being. Here, however, the meaning of truth is not denied, since it is not a real being and can never be definitively owned. To claim to own it is, again, diabolical.

The disocclusion of the economic structure and religion would transform human society by eliminating *human sacrifice*, i.e., the forced self-sacrifice of the individual to society. This concerns both religion and society. But Marx says more than this. He allows us to understand the *telos* of dialectical materialism, and to picture it (a communist society), even if he always claimed that he was not doing so. In a communist society work must not be external to the worker. It must therefore become internal: it must belong to the very being of the subject. It must become what I experience by working as a subject. In work, man must feel happy in developing a free physical and spiritual energy, and he must feel himself *at home*. Work must not be a means to satisfy other needs: it must be the satisfaction of the need to work. The whole man must feel work as a need. The communist society must be a society in which all subjects feel this. In this idealized work, I would not do *A* in order to obtain *B*, but would do *A* in order to obtain *A*. Work thus becomes the continual presence and continual presentification of man, the world, and human society, to man himself. The estranged man contains this positive sense of himself and of others. In the very nucleus of evidence which cannot be expropriated, he contains the principle of a constitution of human individual and social life according to the meaning of truth. Clearly, Marx offers us a meaning which is the truth of knowledge and praxis. When pushed to the limit, this meaning is an infinite idea which is concretized and individuated in the temporal maturation of the historical dialectic as the totalization in progress within each determinate and partial realization which, at the very moment it is realized, is also transcended. Thus, the negation produces the negation of the negation as the qualitative transformation and the will to qualitatively transform human history.

Marx summarizes the analysis of alienation by observing that it has led to two interconnected results: (1) in alienation, the produced object dominates the subject that has produced it; and (2) subjectively, in this situation, the subject becomes estranged to himself in working.

There is a third point closely connected to the way in which we have interpreted and reconsidered Marx's analysis. Marx says that man is a species-being (*Gattungswesen*). He explains that man "treats himself as the present, living species, as a *universal* and consequently free being." [45] That which is universal in the subject is that which is common to all subjects. Each individual man, and all men, *contain the world*. The "theoretical aspect" [46] of human consciousness contains, as a part, "plants, animals, minerals, air, light, etc." Science can study plants, animals, and

45. *Ibid.*, p. 126.
46. *Ibid.*

light to the extent that man (and mankind) contains the world. In Husserl's language, this is the transcendental consciousness present in every subject. This is true both for the sciences (which are, therefore, founded and foundable by each concrete monad which experiences and contains the world) and for art.[47] Generally speaking, it is true of every spiritual operation. This kind of knowledge is broader than the world which is "present and living" within me with the species-life (in Marx's terminology). This means that I do not have everything present: I do not simultaneously experience the totality of the universe. I see the moon but I cannot touch it. However, even if it is present in me only as a "vision" (Husserl's phantasm), I know that I could touch the moon were I to go there. In the same way, I cannot touch Julius Caesar, but I know that I could have touched him had I lived in his epoch and been a friend of his. This indirect knowledge appears here as *theoretical human consciousness* to the extent that it is consciousness of mankind, and is, in fact, spatiotemporally embodied in concrete individuals. It must be added that theoretical consciousness is also the becoming-conscious of the present living situation and its alienation. In him who bears alienation, it is the becoming-conscious of all humanity. This is the situation that defines the proletariat along with every man and group which, in a present and determinate historical society, discovers itself as alienated. This becoming-conscious is also the discovery that all humanity, mankind, its reality, and its meaning of historical truth are also alienated in the process.

Marx elaborates his analysis in another sense which is also crucial in relation to all the indicated phenomenological analyses. Marx says that the natural world, both as scientific and as aesthetic, is part of my spiritual life: I must feed myself from this natural world. This means that language, art, and science elaborate the natural world and express in it the universality of the human species and its *telos* (recall what was said of von Humboldt and of the relationship between language and economic structure). Therefore, art and science have a *function* with respect to the intentional *telos*. They indicate to man a not yet attained universality. It is an aspect of man's civil and cultural way of living which has a universal character because it is not just peculiar to an epoch, but is valid for the human species (recall the example of Greek art in the 1857 Introduction to *A Contribution to the Critique of Political Economy*). Inorganic

47. *Ibid.*

material nature, the world which is mine and which I contain, here becomes an instrument, a vehicle, a sedimentation, for the purpose of historically uniting mankind (in Husserl's language: in order to unite the living with the dead). Because of this, Marx says that in a determinate epoch, the physical world, studied by the sciences and elaborated by art, constitutes, in the individual, mankind's inorganic spiritual nature.

The essence of mankind lives in the individual as a *telos*. But Marx does not want theoretical consciousness or spiritual life to be separated from the physical body: he rejects the dualism of *res cogitans* and *res extensa*. Consequently, he rejects a separate essence. Phenomenologically, essence is nothing other than the typical character of operations which are precategorially performed by concrete subjects. Marx later sees in Feuerbach, in the "Theses," precisely this separation. In *The German Ideology* he reproaches Feuerbach for confusing being (*Sein*) with essence.[48] The individual is not the essence, but the essence of the human species lives in the individual. Knowledge therefore refers to mankind's natural and human operations. It is never knowledge of a categorial essence which is not brought back to its fundamental operations.

Now, the species present in the individual which becomes conscious of the human essence negated in the individual and in the proletariat is the becoming-conscious of the praxis that must transform the negated humanity. The proletariat must realize for all of mankind the human universality toward which science and art aim. History is not the self-consciousness of a soul, or of a separate spirit, but the *becoming-conscious* of alienation. To the extent that the alienation of the proletariat reflects the alienation of all humanity, the proletariat's becoming-conscious and its praxis move within the totality of history and, therefore, as stated in *The German Ideology*, constitute world history (*Weltgeschichte*).[49]

The fact that consciousness and the soul are not separate, but have a body which needs food, connects the *telos* of world history with the concrete economic structure. The essence is not a known object but mankind's typicality or the universality in the individual who recognizes this universality if it is negated in him, i.e., if the operations and actions in and because of which he is a man are negated in him. Essence which is not brought back to the

48. *German Ideology*, p. 55.
49. *Ibid.*, pp. 49, 60–61.

operations, the structure, and the nature *which is in man* must be recognized as abstract (this also includes artistic and scientific operations, such as painting, writing, experimenting, drawing, writing logical symbols, etc.). What is reasserted is the fact that the species and mankind's *telos* live in the individual. Furthermore, the individual can negate the negation of the life of the species through revolutionary praxis.

All depends on a radical change which, as such, moves history to the extent that the change is a becoming-conscious that contains the structure. It is not a separate soul or a separate consciousness. Language is praxis in which real and physical structure and consciousness become united: "Language is as old as consciousness, language *is* practical consciousness that exists also for other men." [50]

"Language, like consciousness, only arises from the need, the necessity, of intercourse with other men. . . . Where there exists a relationship, it exists for me." [51] Language is already intersubjective and social: it is rooted in body and matter. Language can become fetishized in *exchange* in the same way as commodities. Art and science must defetishize language and its reproduction. However, we must remember that such defetishization is always rooted in the world of corporeal and material structures. Even language is manifested in sounds and physical signs and can express an aspect, a phase, or a way of expressing the world that is valid for all humanity and its *telos*. This is what happens in spiritual operations where man is free to express the universality of the human species which is always present in him, even if it is negated. In this sense, art has a collective value and expresses the "personal freedom" which is not just the freedom of those who depend on the dominating classes.

Spiritual operations can reassert personality against the society which is contraposed to the individual as the state: "The proletarians, if they are to assert themselves as individuals, will have to abolish the very conditions of their existence hitherto (which has, moreover, been that of all society up to the present), namely, labor." [52] This means that the proletarians must fight in order to be able to freely perform the spiritual and human operations which they are unable to perform because they are alienated and do not have any "free time." This presupposes a positive evaluation of spiritual operations and a negation of those social

50. *Ibid.*, p. 42.
51. *Ibid.*
52. *Ibid.*, p. 96.

situations which make them possible for only one class. However, this does not mean that Homer or Dante does not express a universal value for the proletariat. In the Introduction to the *Contribution to the Critique of Political Economy*, one finds: "It is well known that certain periods of highest development of art stand in no direct connection with the general development of society, nor with the material basis and the skeleton structure of its organization." [53]

There is no spirit or consciousness separate from the body, nature, society, and the world that man experiences and contains. Language is evidence of this. The basic material structure is always conditioning. In Husserl too, the precategorial material structure of things is always conditioning, along with the fact that, as a man, I am also an "original thing." I am in the world and I live in it even if I am not conscious of my dependence on, e.g., causality, or chlorophyll and, therefore, sunlight.

In its material reality, the planet Earth is my planet. More specifically, as Husserl put it in the unpublished manuscripts D 17 and D 18, it is my body. My live body (*Leib*) is rooted in inorganic nature. From this follows the admirable phenomenological and Marxian concept of the nature which is *in me* as man's inorganic body. This nature allows the real physical expression of my spiritual activity. This is why Marx speaks of the "spiritual inorganic nature."

Man's human essence (*Gattungswesen*) must have its inorganic body. The scientific study and aesthetic elaboration of such a body is intentional. Its aim is to move history toward the constitution of a free society in the horizon of the meaning of truth. "Spirit" obtains in the operations of the whole man. But the whole man does not have only his own body (*Leib*): he contains nature as his inorganic body. He contains what is external to him because man is the point of insertion and encounter (*Umschlagspunkt*) of the internal and of the external. In the "Manuscripts of 1844," Marx writes:

> The universality of man appears in practice in the universality which makes the whole of nature into its inorganic body: 1) as a direct means of life; and equally, 2) as the material object and instrument of his life activity. Nature is the inorganic body of man; that is to say nature, excluding the human body itself. To say that man *lives* from nature means that nature is his *body*

53. Marx, *A Contribution to the Critique of Political Economy*, trans. N. I. Stone (Chicago: Charles H. Kerr, 1904), pp. 309–10.

with which he must remain in a continuous interchange in order not to die.[54]

To die is to be reduced to a mere inorganic body or to pure externality. Marx's analysis here clarifies the problem of internality and externality as posed by Sartre. For Marx, the continuous interchange with nature is the work which, with its product, repairs the consumption necessary for the irreversibility of the temporal structure. Culture (spiritual operations) and civilization are the continuous progress over death and answer to the human need of not being reduced to the level of a mere inorganic body. In Egypt, social revolutions were fought against the aristocratic class which claimed to be the only one to enjoy immortality: the people were vindicating for all the right to be Osirides. Capitalist inequality obtains both in life and in death. This is why Marx emphasizes that culture, art, and civilization are human needs in which the proletariat must participate. If culture and art are alienated, it is because not everyone can practice them. In order for the proletariat to participate in them, and in order to fight what we have called the spiritual blackmail, the economic organization of humanity must be valid *for the whole of the planet Earth* and for those other planets that man will be able to make his *own*.

Marx writes: "The statement that the physical and mental life of man, and nature, are interdependent means simply that nature is interdependent with itself, for man is a part of nature." Nature must not be only a means for life: true life is always free material and spiritual nature rooted in the inorganic. Work is not work-in-order-to-satisfy-another-need: it is the human need to live in nature and to give a meaning to itself and nature. As such, we have an anticipation of the communist society as the overcoming of the dualism and the separation of man from nature, which is also the overcoming of both abstract spiritualism and abstract materialism.

> Since alienated labor: (1) alienates nature from man; and (2) alienates man from himself, from his own active function, his life activity; so it alienates him from the species. It makes species-life into a means of individual life or to a class reduced to the level of a means by the dominating class which considers itself as the goal. In the first place, it alienates species-life and individual life. Here, estrangement appears as the separation of man from

54. "Economic and Philosophic Manuscripts," *Early Writings,* pp. 126–27.

his human essence and his humanity: from this follows the criticism of Feuerbach's separate essence. . . . Secondly, it turns the latter [i.e., individual life], as an abstraction, into the purpose of the former [i.e., species-life], also in its abstract and alienated form.[55]

This brings us back to nonalienated work, i.e., to work as the satisfaction of a need. "For labor, *life activity, productive life,* now appear to man only as a *means* for the satisfaction of a need, the need to maintain his physical existence. Productive life is, however, species-life. It is life creating life." [56] Man must not fight irreversibility only with his own conservation. Mankind and the genetic concatenation live in him. Death itself is a function of life (recall Husserl's dictum: without life there is not death). It is a function of a living society free from exploitation and from the mere task of conserving physical existence, i.e., free to live according to the meaning of truth of humanity.

Marx fights the appropriation of human life by human life. This is why he fights private property, which is the appropriation of human life, since my own labor becomes someone else's. As such, Marx anticipates the phenomenological problem of the constitution of the other as a subject and gives the problem its most real and profound meaning. In the constitution of a *society of subjects* (the communist society), each man constitutes the other. According to Marx, he "makes" the other man, but he must not reduce the other to the level of a mere means or instrument. The object produced by my labor contains me and my subjectivity. If my own object becomes someone else's, I myself become someone else's property. My individual subjectivity is immediately realized in the produced object. In a society of individual subjects, a society which is concrete precisely because it is a society of individual subjects and not of abstract men or objectified workers, the object is mine in the same way that the object of the other subject is his own. At the same time the object, although everyone's object is one's own, is also *our object.* The other recognizes my subjectivity in my labor. He recognizes, for himself as existence in the first person, my existence in the first person similar to his own, while I do the same for him. Marx anticipated Husserl and, moreover, unveiled the foundation of intersubjective alienation (Sartre's existential psychoanalysis) in the subject's claim to possess the other, through irreversibility and need,

55. *Ibid.,* p. 127.
56. *Ibid.*

in order to objectify him. The foundation of morality and the meaning of truth are implicit in Marx's account.

We have seen how, on the assumption that private property has been positively superseded, man produces man, himself and then other men; how the object which is the direct activity of his personality is at the same time his existence for other men and their existence for him.[57]

57. *Ibid.*

21 / The Reversal of the Subject into the Object

[83] *The Definitive Clarification
of the Return to the Subject*

IN 1867, MARX PRESENTS *Capital* as the continuation of
the *Contribution to the Critique of Political Economy* (1859).
This work is preceded by an Introduction written in September,
1857. The wealth of material found in *Capital* can be traced
back, not only to the *Contribution*, but also to the manuscripts of
1857–58 [*Grundrisse der Kritik der politischen Ökonomie*] and
the manuscripts of 1863–65 [*Resultate des unmittelbaren Produktionsprozesses*]. The continuity with the "Manuscripts of 1844"
becomes evident when one considers the problems of alienation
and objectification. As already indicated, alienation here refers
to the reduction of one man to an object by another man. More
specifically, it is the reduction of man to a commodity (fetishization) through the relations of production. This is what gives rise
to the accumulation of capital and surplus-value. In the manuscripts of 1857–58, the relationship between alienation and commodity fetishism is clearly defined in such a way as to explain the
accumulation of capital.

From the "Manuscripts of 1844" to *Capital*, all the problems
on which Marx elaborated are part of the theme of alienation.
The accumulation of capital is possible as a result of the "estrangement of the working conditions of labor" (*Entfremdung
der Arbeitsbedingungen der Arbeit*).[1] The fundamental distinc-

---

1. Karl Marx, *Grundrisse der Kritik der politischen Ökonomie*
(*Rohentwurf*), *1857–1858* (Berlin, D.D.R.: Dietz, 1953), p. 715.

tion is found to be between the subjective living labor which produces its objects and the transformation of produced objects into alienated ones. Man produces objects and lives in them with his living labor. Thus, in this sense, the produced objects are subjective labor. The presence of the workers' labor in the object yields the living labor of the worker and his product as two correlated and inseparable moments. However, under capitalist working conditions, the objective product becomes autonomous in relation to subjective operations: it is no longer the workers' living body. Yet the objective product is social wealth. In a noncapitalist society this labor would remain part of all the workers: it would become the increasingly stronger body (*Leib*) of all the working subjects. The objective moment would be the embodiment of the subjective moment. Such a development is impossible under capitalist working conditions. The wealth produced by the subject becomes fetishized, autonomous, and contraposed to the subjects as extraneous. "The moment of societal activity—objective labor—does not become the increasingly stronger body of the other moment, of the subjective, living labor." [2] Working conditions always broaden objectivity: the *object* containing living labor, yet separated from it, becomes alienated along with the subject. Social wealth is contraposed to labor as an extraneous and domineering force. As long as the subject has his own objective product there is no alienation. Alienation as estrangement results when the object becomes separated from the subject. What is alienated is the object which no longer belongs to the worker and which now alienates him.

Attention must be paid to the working conditions within which living labor produces its own object. Separated from the subjects, these objective conditions become autonomous and acquire a kind of subjectivity. They become personified: "The objective working conditions assume an increasingly more colossal autonomy [*Selbständigkeit*]." [3] From the viewpoint of capital, the "colossal" product is no longer recognized as the product of working subjects. The capitalist no longer views it as commensurate with the immediate working capacity of the subjects: he cares only about the appropriated products, while the worker finds himself in estrangement. For the workers—subjects turned into objects—working conditions become personified as if they were subjects themselves. Things such as matter, the means of production, and exchange really become persons, while workers

2. *Ibid.*
3. *Ibid.*

become things. The working subject produces his own object: he objectivizes himself in his own object while remaining a subject. When the object becomes autonomous and develops into a subject, however, the working subject becomes an object. Therefore, he is estranged. Objective labor is necessary but not sufficient for estrangement. In order for estrangement to occur, the objective working conditions must become subjective or personified. As is said in *Capital:* the subjects become things and things become subjects.

By becoming estranged and separated through the objective working conditions (e.g., with the passage from manufacture to industry), objective labor transforms the factory into a colossal monster for which the workers become objects.

> Here we have, in the place of the isolated machine, a mechanical monster whose body fills whole factories, and whose demon power, at first veiled under the slow and measured motions of his giant limbs, at length breaks out into the fast and furious whirl of his countless working organs.[4]

This monster is a subject who embodies personified working conditions. Initially, this monster's development as a subject-person has been limited, since "its characteristic instrument of production, the machine, owed its existence to personal strength and personal skill, and depended on the muscular development, the keenness of sight, and the cunning of hand." [5] Its original function was to extend the organic body of persons, i.e., to strengthen the workers' *Leib* and, therefore, to increase individual and social wealth. But the function becomes reversed: in capitalist society it becomes a subject that makes the real subjects into objects. Therefore, we have a reversal (*Verkehrung*) of the subject into the object. Simultaneously, this is also the reversal of the function of science and technology: the last phase of this reversal is the atomic bomb, which becomes the subject and threatens to reduce all living subjects into objects, i.e., into dead inorganic nature. Alienation leads to the disappearance of subjects. It is the reduction of what is living to the level of a thing (*Verdinglichung*).

Therefore, what is crucial is not that subjective labor becomes objective but that the object becomes the subject, i.e., capital becomes personified (this point is not too clear in the

4. Karl Marx, *Capital*, trans. Samuel Moore and Edward Aveling (Moscow: Progress Publishers, n.d.), I, 381–82.
5. *Ibid.*, p. 382.

"Manuscripts of 1844"). This is why Marx says that we must emphasize not objective being (in the sense of labor becoming objective) but estranged being which subsequently becomes personified in capital. This is how capital comes into being as the subject:

> The emphasis is placed not on objectified being [*Vergegenständlichtsein*], but upon estranged, alienated, externalized being, on the nothing of the worker [*das Entfremdet-, Entäussert-, Veräussertsein, das Nicht-der-Arbeiter*], but the personified working conditions of capital are emphasized: the monstrous objectified power that social labor has contraposed to itself as one of its moments.[6]

The objective moment has become contraposed to the subjective moment or the worker. Here, society enters into a contradiction with itself because of the contraposition, and, therefore, because of capital. The logic of capital renders conditions and products increasingly more objective: left to itself and forced to expand (imperialism), capital leads to war. The economic contradiction is already war: it is production which annihilates the subject. Capitalists themselves are prisoners of capital and its logic. The atomic bomb is not an accidental development: it is the logical consequence of the reversal of the subject into the object.

Labor becomes objectified, and even if labor becomes the satisfaction of his need to work, man must live in nature and realize himself in it. However, he can live in nature as if it were not his organic body, and on the planet Earth as if it were not the organ of human society. Today he is in a situation of producing sufficient objective labor. Yet the planet Earth is divided because of the personification of capital and its inevitable and contradictory expansion. Consequently, the answer to this situation, i.e., mere peace, is already nascent socialism. Conversely, socialism must lead to the economic organization of the planet Earth. Communism is essentially universal. It is the movement of totalization of all the parts containing the totality, humanity, and its meanings. The reversal of the subject into the object can be answered only with the return to the subject who uses objective products and the real function of labor, and who supervises the function of science and technology so that humanity can truly transform the planet into its own body, and labor into the satisfaction of the need to work. However, this *is* the passage from socialism to communism. The return to the subject is, therefore, the beginning of the negation of the reversal into the object. This

6. *Grundrisse*, p. 716.

reversal is the negation of capital and its inherent contradictions. To return to man the atomic energy which is contraposed to him as an extraneous power is to organize a society in which production is not contraposed to it as an extraneous power. Obviously, peace, as the first step, is valid for all. However, the first step contains its own consequences: the radical change of working conditions, the social structure, and all human relationships.

[84] *The Crisis of the Sciences*
and the Enslavement to Capital

IN THE 1859 PREFACE TO THE *Contribution to the Critique of Political Economy*, Marx attempts to outline the road that he has traveled—the same road which we have briefly attempted to reconstruct. It is a road which shows the relevance of the Marxian analysis to the atomic age. Marx writes: "The entire material lies before me in the form of monographs, written at long intervals not for publication but for the purpose of clearing up those questions to myself." [7] It might have been better if he had published them, even though only today is it possible to fully understand them. In the Preface, Marx explains matters much more simply than he did in the manuscripts, which, however, he always keeps in mind. For example, even in the manuscripts of 1863–65 he contraposes "the life-process" to estrangement specifically defined as "the reversal of the subject into the object [*die Verkehrung des Subjekts, in das Objekt*]." [8]

In the Preface, Marx writes:

It is not the consciousness of men that determines their existence, but, on the contrary, their social existence determines their consciousness. At a certain stage of their development, the material forces of production in society come in conflict with the existing relations of production, or—what is but a legal expression for the same thing—with the property relations within which they had been at work before. From forms of development of the forces of production these relations turn into their fetters. Then comes the period of social revolution. With the change of the economic foundation the entire immense superstructure is more or less rapidly

7. Karl Marx, *A Contribution to the Critique of Political Economy*, trans. N. I. Stone (Chicago: Charles H. Kerr, 1904), p. 9.
8. Marx, *Resultate des unmittelbaren Produktionsprozesses* (Frankfurt: Verlag Neue Kritik, 1969), p. 18.

transformed. In considering such transformations the distinction should always be made between the material transformation of the economic conditions of production which can be determined with the precision of natural science, and the legal, political, religious, aesthetic or philosophic—in short ideological forms in which men become conscious of this conflict and fight it out. Just as our opinion of an individual is not based on what he thinks of himself, so can we not judge of such a period of transformation by its own consciousness; on the contrary, this consciousness must rather be explained from the contradictions of material life, from the existing conflict between the social forces of production and the relations of production. No social order ever disappears before all the productive forces, for which there is room in it, have developed; and new higher relations of productions never appear before the material conditions of their existence have matured in the womb of the old society. Therefore, mankind always takes up only such problems as it can solve; since, looking at the matter more closely, we will always find that the problem itself arises only when the material conditions necessary for its solution already exist or are at least in the process of formation. In broad outlines, we can designate the Asiatic, the ancient, the feudal, and the modern bourgeois methods of production as so many epochs in the progress of the economic formation of society. The bourgeois relations of production are the last antagonistic form of the social process of production—antagonistic not in the sense of individual antagonism, but of one arising from conditions surrounding the life of the individuals in society; at the same time the productive forces developing in the womb of bourgeois society create the material conditions for the solution of that antagonism. This social foundation constitutes, therefore, the closing chapter of the prehistoric stage of human society.[9]

All this must be interpreted in terms of the indicated reconstruction and reconsideration. Marx means that it is not consciousness which determines social being, but, on the contrary, that consciousness is not separate from the historical process within which it occurs. It does not exist independently of man's live and inorganic body, nature, or society. If the process of becoming-conscious is determined, it can modify the situation by departing from the endured alienation and in relation to the dialectic of what is one's "own" and what is "extraneous," which is in contradiction because of the accumulation of capital. The revolutionary situation presupposes capitalist maturation and must go through capitalism. At the base of all this we find the

9. *Contribution,* pp. 11–13.

structure of needs and the relations of production that can be studied with the precision of the "natural sciences." Now, there is no doubt that science can and must be applied to the study of the structure and its genesis. However, science must not lose its function and reduce man to an objective and inorganic body. Otherwise, what Marx generally calls "ideological forms" "would not allow men to perceive the conflict and fight it." Therefore, there is a process of becoming-conscious of the crisis, and there is an intentional praxis which is oriented toward the overcoming of such a crisis.[10] The real point of departure, the actual present or the living presence (*lebendige Gegenwart*), is not a consciousness separate from the material and historical situation. It is the becoming-conscious of a part of the totality which contains the totalization in process. Because of this, it makes possible the proletarian praxis in the dialectic of the parts. We must necessarily depart from the presence and from the social and material world which constitutes it. This presence is discovered to be alienated through the becoming-conscious of a part, i.e., the exploited class. The praxis directed toward the overcoming of alienation converts science and neutral or enslaved technology, and transforms them in relation to the constitution of a nonalienated social world. Thus, the actual present contains "tendential laws": capitalism itself offers the means for the transformation of the relations of production and their noncapitalist use. The recall to the presence is the recall to historicity. This historicity is in crisis and forces those who endure it to plan its transformation within the existing historical conditions. Therefore, historicism must indicate "the historical propensities of a certain epoch," i.e., "the presence of a historical direction." This allows the recognition of the possibility of overcoming capitalism and of the peculiar character of a situation, and, finally, the discovery of the means necessary for such an overcoming. The latter can be the very means of capitalism (industry and technology), if they are taken over by those who endure the alienation and the negation in order to negate both. Historicism itself is not necessarily Marxist; [11] it becomes Marxist if it appropriates the means whereby capital has asserted itself and uses these means in order to abolish capital, and if it does not lose the totalizing intentionality.

10. Some recent Italian studies of Marxism, particularly those connected with Gramsci's thought, have dealt with "the process of becoming-conscious of historical intentionality." See N. Badaloni, *Marxismo come Storicismo* (Milan: Feltrinelli, 1962), p. 239.

11. *Ibid.*, p. 206.

All this is connected to the problem of the "return of the product to the subject" [12] and to the discovery "of the tendency of a consciously directed historical becoming." [13] Consciousness is not ideological if it does not become a system from which the actual presence is deduced, but remains reflection on the actual presence in order to reshape the world according to its immanent tendency. Ideologies are in crisis to the extent that they hide the situation of crisis or transform it into something perennial and insuperable, thus hiding the very possibility of acting to overcome it. Ideology appears here in its original negative meaning which, however, unveils the positive meaning of the act of becoming-conscious. Gramsci claimed that the subordinate classes have an interest in knowing all the truth, i.e., the meaning of truth. Ideology covers reality and truths. According to Marx, "one cannot judge a man by the concept which he has of himself," or an epoch "by the consciousness that it has of itself." That is, it is possible that superstructures do not present the real situation. In phenomenological terms, this possibility entails the epochē and the return to the concrete presence, and things-themselves and their contradictions, i.e., the endured alienation and the realization that the sciences have lost their function.

The act of becoming-conscious leads us back to the situation in which we actually live, and to the possibility of actually overcoming the real endured contradictions. In order to do so, it is necessary to return to the precategorial operations of the foundation of the sciences and the economy. In a capitalist situation, the sciences appear fetishized by the theory of the impossibility of overcoming capitalist contradictions. This is a theory which has already lost its own scientific function.

If man is conditioned by the structures, then, as Gramsci argued, the economic factor must not be isolated. Scientificity must not become "the abstract scheme of a given economic society." [14]

When Marx says that "the material development of the economic conditions of production can be determined with the precision of the natural sciences," he puts forth more than one claim. The study of the development can require all of the sciences, from geography to mathematics. However, this develop-

12. *Ibid.*, p. 183.
13. *Ibid.*, p. 179.
14. Antonio Gramsci, *Il Materialismo Storico e la Filosofia di Benedetto Croce* (Turin: G. Einaudi, 1948), p. 99. Also see Badaloni, *Marxismo*, p. 176.

ment is not the objective domain of any isolated science—not even of economics, which is not a natural science although it can and must use mathematics. In other words, in reading the quoted passage, one must be on guard for naturalism and the objectification of the sciences. Since this objectification is a fact of bourgeois society, it must be examined, along with its genesis, the possibilities of changing it, and its meaning.

Marx was very well aware that basic economic structures cannot be studied with the methods of any given natural science. In the Preface to *Capital* he writes: "In the analysis of economic forms, moreover, neither microscopes nor chemical reagents are of use. The force of abstraction must replace both." [15] The force of abstraction starts from the way things actually appear from the capitalistic viewpoint, which yields the reality of capitalist society and the endured alienation. Marx begins his analyses with actual society and with the recognition that exchange relations are given as the fetishism of commodities. This means that the relations of production and exchange, in their "classical setting," England, appear *typically* as the reversal of the subject into the object, i.e., in capitalist operations which must be studied not according to what they claim to be, but according to what they are behind the ideologies and the appearances, behind their "phenomenal forms" (as Marx says in the commentary on Wagner). This study leads us back to the real operations and contradictions which are hidden by the capitalist abstractions which have become reality. We can analyze these abstractions by grasping their temporal, structural, and operative genesis, i.e., their historical genesis, and by reconstructing the process of capitalist abstraction. Marx's analysis presupposes and reconstructs the process of capitalist abstraction in order to unveil its foundation and discover how to transform the whole process. Thus, Marx can say that "the march of our analysis compels this splitting-up of the subject-matter, a splitting-up which is quite in keeping with the spirit of capitalist production." [16] This allows a scientific analysis on the industrial level, while, for manufacturing, it excludes a really scientific analysis of the process of production, given the restricted technological base. Here manufacture is the mechanism of production and the organism of men: the *concours de forces* [Destutt de Tracy]. Although industry can be scientifically analyzed, at this stage science enters into a crisis and loses its function. The accumulation of capital becomes contraposed to

15. *Capital,* I, 8.
16. *Ibid.,* p. 325.

the producing subjects. The consciousness of the meaning of science is lost. Science itself becomes a capitalist means. It thus falls into objectification and creates the dualism between consciousness and reality or the alienation of both what is one's "own" and the "other."

> It is a result of the division of labor in manufactures, that the laborer is brought face to face with the intellectual potencies of the material process of production, as the property of another, and as a ruling power. This separation begins in simple cooperation, where the capitalist represents to the single workman, the oneness and the will of the associated labor. It is developed in manufacture which cuts down the laborer into a detail laborer. It is completed in modern industry, which makes science a productive force distinct from labor and presses it into the service of capital.[17]

Husserl's sciences in crisis are the objectified sciences, at the service of capital, that have lost both their foundation and their function. The proletarian movement must lead the sciences back to their function and overthrow their capitalist use. Yet the proletariat is produced by large industry and its abstractions, which function as if they were concrete. Marx's analysis reconstructs the genesis of the abstraction. This is why Labriola claimed that *Capital* was "not the first book of critical communism, but the last great book of bourgeois economics." [18] Since it takes place within bourgeois society, the becoming-conscious of the realities of bourgeois economics is from the beginning the discovery of the possibility of their being overcome, precisely because "a social formation does not perish until all the productive forces to which it gives rise have been fully developed."

The Preface of the *Contribution to the Critique of Political Economy* is filled with problems, and it is certainly not to be considered as a total and definitive synthesis of dialectical materialism. If we study it, we arrive at *Capital:* we move with Marx, who had already traveled the path of the manuscripts. With *Capital*, "prehistory is completed and history begins." The work is a junction which analyzes the old and prepares the new. The passage from prehistory to history implies the crisis of the sciences, i.e., the reduction of the sciences to technistic alienation and to the

17. *Ibid.*, p. 361.
18. Antonio Labriola, *Essays on the Materialist Conception of History*, trans. Charles H. Kerr (1903; 2d printing, New York: Monthly Review Press, 1966), p. 86.

level of an ideology whose function is to hide the fact that science is at the service of industrial capitalism. The beginning of history coincides with the return of science to its precategorial and human foundation, i.e., to the conquest of the function of all the sciences and their intentionality. Technism is the ideology of industrial capitalism. To the extent that, even as politics, praxis becomes a pure technique, it loses the intentional historical meaning, and, because it is impossible to avoid passing through industrial technism, one infers that it is not possible to escape technistic alienation. Actually, technistic alienation is capitalist alienation in its most perfect and mature stage. Thus Marx's abstraction is qualitatively different from capitalist abstraction, even though his analysis necessarily follows the spirit of capitalism in order to overcome it, i.e., it passes through the negation in order to negate it. If we try to go behind the word "abstraction" and attempt to follow the Marxian method, we discover much more than what might appear at first sight, along with the most profound and most authentic aspects of Marx's work.

[85]   *The Point of Departure*
       of the Investigation

IN THE INTRODUCTION TO THE *Contribution to the Critique of Political Economy,* Marx tries to clarify for both the reader and himself the kind of analysis that leads to *Capital:*

> When we consider a given country from a political-economic standpoint, we begin with its population, then analyze the latter according to its subdivision into classes, location in city, country, or by the sea, occupation in different branches of production; then we study its exports and imports, annual production and consumption, prices of commodities, etc. It seems to be the correct procedure to commence with the real and concrete aspect of conditions as they are; in the case of political economy, to commence with population which is the basis of the entire productive activity of society. Yet, on closer consideration it proves to be wrong. Population is an abstraction, if we leave out, e.g., the classes of which it consists. These classes, again, are but an empty word, unless we know what are the elements on which they are based, such as wage-labor, capital, etc. These imply, in their turn, exchange, division of labor, prices, etc. Capital, e.g., does not mean anything without wage-labor, value, money, price, etc.

If we start out, therefore, with population, we do so with a chaotic conception of the whole, and by closer analysis we will gradually arrive at simpler ideas; thus we shall proceed from the imaginary concrete to less and less complex abstractions, until we get at the simplest conception.[19]

Initially, Marx considers population to be concrete and to refer to all the subjects who contain nature and to all of the subjective operations performed in a given historical situation, which is subsequently the actual presence in which I find myself. We say all of them: in fact, at the base we find the operations meant to satisfy needs and labor with all that follows. But men in a specific historical society perform many other operations along with the economic ones. The economic operations are taken separately so that they can be studied without being dualistically contraposed to the others. They are the *theme* of my study. In their reality, however, they are not separable from all other operations. The population and the subjects refer to all the subjects. Taken as such, the concrete population is not actually the true concrete but is a very general abstraction. It is a presupposition which is similar to the one concerning the already given world (*vorgegebene Welt*). But population implies an already historically formed whole *when* I begin the analysis. For example, it is organized in the forms of production and exchange of a capitalist society, and I live in this society as a capitalist, a worker, or in a "mixed" situation which is unclear. I can be a scientist at the service of capital. However, at least in certain respects, I can work against the crisis of the sciences: I can once again bring their function to light and, with this, I can perform the first anti-capitalist act. Beliefs, world-views, and capitalist ideologies can condition me and prevent me from judging things as they are, after having made me absorb their prejudices. Therefore, my first act as a scientist is to reject prejudices, i.e., perform the epochē. This is an act of scientific autonomy: it is a rejection of the world as it is, the *mundane*. Marx does not talk about the epochē, but he performs it, as the Preface to the *Contribution to the Critique of Political Economy* testifies:

This account of the course of my studies in political economy is simply to prove that my views, whatever one may think of them, and no matter how little they agree with the interested prejudices of the ruling class, are the results of many years of conscientious

19. *Contribution*, p. 292.

research. At the entrance of science, however, the same requirement must be put as at the entrance to hell:

Qui si convien lasciare ogni sospetto
Ogni viltà convien che qui sia morta.[20]

Marx defends the autonomy and disinterestedness of scientific research which, freed from prejudices and dominant interests, becomes independent of the servility of society in order to
subsequently give a meaning of truth to praxis.

Considering the preceding, it is not surprising to discover that
"population" is not really a concrete concept: it is a false concreteness. Population is only abstractly "the subject of the entire
social act of production." Therefore, population is an abstract
category. We must go back to something more simple and less
indistinct and chaotic. "Population is an abstraction if I forget
classes." However, in order not to remain in that false concreteness that has been revealed to be abstract, from the analysis of
classes we must go to wage-labor, to capital, and to even more
simple concepts: "to always more subtle abstractions, until I arrive at the simplest determinations." The "more subtle" abstractions should be less abstract than the generic abstraction of "population." But what are these simple abstractions? If the more
subtle abstractions are always less abstract, the original determinations will be concrete precisely because they are simple.
Now, the simplest concepts are those of real subjects and men,
without whom there would be no social operations and no consequent abstractions. The "subject of the whole social act" is, in
fact, the dialectical product of subjective labor. Under capitalism, this objective product becomes contraposed to the subjects
who have produced it, and renders them objects. By returning to
the subject and his operations, I can discover that appearances
are abstractions that have become real and have transformed
workers into abstractions, while actually the worker is the concrete man. This is precisely what Marx clarifies in *Capital* by
rediscovering men behind the phenomenal forms that have been
turned into a false reality by exchange, wage-labor, and capital.

Therefore, the original concreteness, from which Marx in
fact departs, is the subjects. Among these subjects, the starting
point is Marx himself, who lives among others in the English society of his epoch, and who studies its *typical character*, genesis,
alienation, and possibility of transformation. English society is in
a real contradiction and Marx unveils it as typical of the capitalist

20. *Ibid.*, p. 15.

epoch. This typical character is the basis of the return to the whole subject and the process of the constitution of other subjects, for the dialectic of what is one's "own" and the "other," alienation, and all kinds of factual contradictions, is always reducible to "the reversal of the subject into the object." It is I-myself who am reversed, and the analysis is the first reconstitutive praxis. It is the first historical act which must begin from the actual presence, which includes the subjects doing the analysis.

Marx begins with subjects, and, by studying what happens behind the phenomenal forms that have falsely become concrete, e.g., the fetishism of commodities, he discovers commodities as crystallizations of subjective human labor. Having reached the simplest determinations of "population," he must now deal with society and the population as it is. In addition, he must explain how it came to be in the state of alienation and contradiction. We must "start on our journey" from the subjects, i.e., what Marx calls the simplest determinations, "until we would finally come back to population, but this time not as a chaotic notion of an integral whole, but as a rich aggregate of many conceptions and relations." [21] This totality is so rich that it includes all that we have attempted to analyze in the whole of this work, by beginning from the relation between nature and history. The nonchaotic kind of "population" is actually composed of men engaged in struggles and in their complex determined dialectic. They are individuated in every part of the ongoing totalization in process, yet always in relation to the meaning of truth. This is so whether we recognize it or not: either indirectly and contradictorily, or directly and positively, in the movement of the emancipation of the proletariat.

Marx observes that the seventeenth-century economists attempted to begin with society but ended by beginning with the simple. And he says that this is correct, if the simple is a man who lives in time and in a given society. It is incorrect if economics substitutes the category man and other abstract categories for man, thus forcing the worker to live abstractly. This is why Marx criticizes political economy, by denouncing its situation, i.e., the claim of scientifically justifying exploitation. By rediscovering man, Marx returns to the precategorial foundation of political economy and to the temporal structure of the need-satisfaction relationship. He shows that the allegedly eternal scientific laws of political economy must constantly be reconsidered

21. *Ibid.*, p. 293.

in terms of the concrete historical operations of the precategorial economic life which gives rise to the categories and the various economic systems. The fundamental point is that, since economics is a science that can even be mathematized, while the foundation of economics is temporal, human, social, and historical, the alleged laws by which a system becomes fixed in a categorial construction are scientific *sui generis,* yet can be overcome. By using them, praxis can transform them into other laws and thus transform society. A new kind of economics cannot be abstractly deduced from the old kind, because a new social formation would then exist which would be different from the old social formation. If economics is not kept separate from men and society but is brought back to man, i.e., is unveiled and founded, it provokes the transformation on the part of that class of the society that is dehumanized and that fights this negation by negating it both for itself and for humanity.

Therefore, precategorial economic life is the projection of scientific abstractions onto men *only* in a capitalist society. Precategorial economic life did not have to wait for economics as a science in order to exist, just as the terrain does not exist solely because there are geographical maps. Furthermore, if the maps change, it is not because the new is deduced from the old, but because either the terrain comes to be better known or it changes altogether through men's efforts: rivers can take different courses, forests can be cleared, and islands, let us say, can disappear while others may emerge. Similarly, "scientific" economic systems change because society changes. Bourgeois political economy has forced the real worker to live as a sign on the map. The worker, however, does not want to change the maps but the real social situation: "The origin of [political economy] *as a science* does not by any means date from the time to which it is referred *as such.*" [22] A historically changeable economic and social life exists prior to the economics which is founded on it, and scientific economics, understood as an attempt to analyze the becoming of society and its economic relations, has always existed, even when it was not recognized as a science.

For us, the concrete is we-ourselves engaged in the economic relations of our society. The concrete of the feudal world was the feudal "we." There is no history of economics that is devoid of solutions to the problem of continuity, i.e., as a history of a pure science, without bringing science back to the concrete society

22. *Ibid.,* p. 302.

from which it has arisen and to which it always returns in order to be reconstituted in a broken continuity conditioned by social changes. (Here, recall what Husserl says about the discontinuity of the history of philosophy.) Marx poses this problem when he asks whether simple categories have a historical existence where the temporal coincides with the logical. Such a coincidence of the temporal and the logical would be Hegel's categorial dialectic. The temporal unfolding cannot coincide with the categories. On the other hand, if I begin from the actual presence of the society in which I live, and the determined or the simple is not a category but social and individual reality, then the actual society is both the result of the performed concrete sociohistorical operations and the (negative and positive) function exercised by the various categorial economic systems—even though they must always be brought back to the society from which they arose. When I reflect upon the actual presence and how we arrive at it, I reconstruct its genesis. In my reflection, I re-present the social structure and the categories that I meet and, eventually, discover and rediscover. This process is parallel to Husserl's notion of the modification of the presence. I re-present both the original social situations and the economic systems that have arisen from them. This is why Marx can say that "the abstract definitions lead to the reproduction of the concrete subject." [23] This path reconstructs the history that has led to the present, that "rises from the simple to the complex," i.e., that rediscovers the structural and precategorial human foundation of the categories of past as well as present society. But if I claim that the movement of the categories removed from their foundation (as in Hegel) coincides with the real historical movement, then I falsify history by imposing upon it an abstract categorial scheme. This is what bourgeois society wants me to do, since this society understands the past only by departing from its own categorial and "scientific" construction which is presented as eternally valid.

This explains why Marx writes as follows:

The concrete is concrete, because it is a combination of many objects with different destinations, i.e., a unity of diverse elements. In our thought, it therefore appears as a process of synthesis, as the result, and not as a starting point, although it is the real starting point and, therefore, also the starting point of observation and conception. [24]

23. *Ibid.*, p. 293.
24. *Ibid.*

In other words, I depart from the concrete which is myself and others in the actual historical society. I reflect upon this society and seek its genesis. In fact, I must begin from the society in which I live and from reconsidering it. I discover the genesis by departing from a given beginning in the past that can very well not have been considered as a beginning by those who lived at that time. This is the problem of historical periods, which are founded on the birth of certain social relationships, their end, and their transformation. This problem is also connected to the elementary problems of birth and death, fatigue, sleep, and what Husserl calls "the impoverishing of the ego" which is due to temporal rhythms and irreversible precategorial structures of consumption, needs, and satisfactions. Therefore, by reconstructing past history and interpreting documents, I depart in reflection from the point of arrival which is the actual present. In other words, in reflection I travel the same path in thought. The actual present appears to me as a result: the synthesis of the process that I reconstruct, the end point of a process of synthesis, the unity of a multiplicity of dialectical situations and their results. The real *concrete* which I can experience only in the first person appears as a unity or as the totalization of a multiplicity of processes. This is how it appears in reflection and in recollection which constitutes the present that has passed, i.e., the historical past, and which can, with new reconsiderations, reconstitute it anew. Yet the concrete, which appears to reflection as the result, is the true point of departure, the true origin. It is prior to the recalling reflection insofar as it is given to me as it is, in flesh and blood, *in intuition and in representation,* precisely as the present that has passed was given to those who lived then. Insofar as the actually concrete reflects upon itself and upon its own genesis, its genesis can be said to be reconstructed. With Marx, we can say that the concrete "is reproduced in our mind as a concrete." [25] The movement of the categories of reflection appears as the "real act of production." But the concrete is prior to categories in the same way that the "need-satisfaction" relationship is prior to political economy and its categories. In fact, the concrete is given by intuition (Husserl's *evidence*) and representation. Moreover, it is given to me by the evidence of the needs that I live in the first person and by the produced work which is taken away from me, thus estranging me in the endured negation. Therefore, the real subject is

25. *Ibid.*, p. 294.

the present concreteness that rediscovers its own genesis, endures the negation, becomes aware of what it endures, and plans the negation of the negation. The project is realized by being reformulated in the praxis that must bring about a new society in terms of the analysis of the present and its genesis. The starting point is the "abstraction" which is endured through political economy, which posits its categorial laws as insurmountable in order to prevent the process of the negation of the negation based on the factual situations that condition political economy and make it possible.

Therefore, it is necessary to keep in mind that in the concrete presence in which I live, I find myself as an abstract worker and as an abstract man. This is due to alienation and the categorial pretenses of political economy, which present the phenomenal forms of reality, and which force me to live as a phenomenal form in the fantastic and enigmatic relations of fetishization. The abstract appears as the concrete. Commodity relations (that *appear* as subjects) make me into a commodity without, however, my ceasing to be a man. Commodity relations appear as personal relations, and personal relations appear as relations among things. What is important for Marx *is to unveil what is hidden behind this false appearance,* which is presented in society as a factual and insuperable reality. We must analyze this reality, since it is where, paradoxically and contradictorily, capitalist society can exist only by making the producing workers live in contradictions, which are not revealed as such. The contradictions are hidden, along with the fact that the value of commodities is the product of labor which is contraposed as an extraneous subject to the worker, according to the reversal of the subject into the object. The abstractions and the enigmatic paradoxes of capitalist society are abstractions that function and live as if they were reality. Although they are abstractions brought about because of certain relations of labor and production, if I want to begin from things as they are, I must assume them to be real, since they actually appear as insurmountable laws. However, I must show that actually they are only apparent forms and abstractions that can be overcome. Thus I discover the true concrete from which I can depart in order to transform capitalist society on the basis of the class which endures dehumanization, and which is forced by capitalist society to live as if it were abstract. The abstraction is the reality of the proletariat in the contradiction. In order to remove it, the proletariat must become conscious of it so that the proletariat can realize its own human concreteness and intentional truth. As already indicated, this is the concreteness and the meaning of truth of all humanity.

Marx accepts the passage through the capitalist abstraction, which is presented as a fact, so that he can disocclude and overcome it. Thus, in his analysis, and in our continuation of it, the concrete as a point of departure is men struggling for their true concreteness and the overcoming of the purely apparent concreteness of capitalist society. The dialectic of the abstract and the concrete is also the dialectic of appearance and reality. Already, in Kant, the dialectic was one of appearances. Hegel has investigated it, no longer in the antinomies, the paralogisms, and the ideal of pure reason, but in the process of the genesis of spirit: the phenomenology of spirit. But, by means of absolute spirit, Hegel covered *us as concrete men* [26] living in a real society and rendered abstract, phenomenal, and alienated. This "phenomenal" existence must be investigated and rediscovered by departing from the actual abstraction that appears as reality. What is needed is a phenomenological analysis: this is what Marx performs in *Capital.*

26. See my paper on "Anthropology, Dialectics, and Phenomenology in Hegel," *Radical America,* IV, no. 6 (September–October, 1971), 33–53.

22 / The Dialectic of the Concrete and the Abstract

[86]   *Fetishism and the*
        Dialectic of Appearance

THE READER OF *Capital* who follows the dynamics of the analysis cannot fail to be struck by the continuous metamorphosis of appearance and reality. It may seem strange that dialectics is seldom mentioned in *Capital*. In fact, in his analysis, Marx does not talk about dialectics: *he is in the dialectic.* Overlooking this unprecedented situation, whereby the analysis is itself praxis, can give rise to serious misunderstandings. This is what happens in all the analyses of *Capital,* beginning with exchange-value and extending to the tendency of the falling rate of profit and the transformation of values into prices. Capital becomes a "personalized" historical agent. *It appears so,* and this appearing becomes a reality. Ultimately, however, there are always authentic agents, hidden by the continually changing play of the transformation of that which appears and that which is. In the struggle with the omnipotent abusive agent, i.e., capital, the true agents are always men. But we do not have only one appearance and one reality: that would be too simple. We have appearance functioning as if it were not appearance, functioning as an appearance which has become real and which, therefore, is *real.* The tension guiding the entire analysis is the search for what is hidden beyond the appearances, the ideologies, and the constructions whose real nature as arbitrary constructions has been forgotten. These constructions are ghosts of a very special nature that act as if they were real. Although real men know that they are subjects, they feel themselves transformed into ghosts: this is the sort of thing that happens in Kafka's *Metamorphosis*. The possibility of losing oneself is continually present: the labyrinth changes the moment one enters it. It becomes a world of magic, enchantment, and masks. "Value . . . does not stalk about with a label describing *what it is*. It is value, rather, that converts every product into a social hieroglyphic."[1] Marx wants to decipher the hieroglyphic, beginning with the "mystery" of the fetishism of commodities.

The critique of economics aims at discovering *what is hidden behind* the enigmatic character of the fetishism of commodities. Bourgeois economics is not a neutral science: it forces society into fetishization. Hence, Marx begins his analysis with a study of the two factors that characterize commodities: use-value and exchange-value. He says that exchange-value is the "phenomenal form of value." In general, use-value is what it is only because "human labor in the abstract has been embodied or materialized in it."[2] The values of commodities are "crystals of this social substance,"[3] i.e. "human labor." This crystallization ignores the concrete individuals and therefore makes concrete society impossible. The *abstract categories* of economics as a science and their improper use hide the value of labor behind the commodity. Because of this, it is very difficult to analyze commodities. "A commodity appears, at first sight, a very trivial thing, and easily understood. Its analysis shows that it is, in reality, a very queer thing."[4]

In order to explain this complexity, Marx points out that the relation among commodities *qua* values must not be understood as a relation between two physical things. He writes:

> In the same way, the light from an object is perceived by us not as the subjective excitation of our optic nerve, but as the objective form of something outside the eye itself. But, in the act of seeing, there is at all events, an actual passage of light from one thing to another, from the external object to the eye. There is a physical relation between physical things. But it is different with commodities. There, the existence of the things *qua* commodities, and the value-relation between the products of labor which stamps them as commodities, have absolutely no connection with their

1. Karl Marx, *Capital*, trans. Samuel Moore and Edward Aveling (Moscow: Progress Publishers, n.d.), I, 74.
2. *Ibid.*, p. 38.
3. *Ibid.*
4. *Ibid.*, p. 71.

physical properties and with the material relations arising there-from. There it is a definite social relation between men, that assumes, in their eyes, the fantastic form of a relation between things.[5]

Therefore, in a determinate social relation (capitalism), fetish-ism transforms social relations into physical relations between physical things, and social relations cease to be relations between workers who create value. Marx calls these relations "fantastic," since "they have absolutely nothing to do with their physical nature." Naturally, this does not mean that the real and concrete man does not labor upon material and natural objects, or that he does not live nature as his inorganic body. It means that social relations must not be reduced to naturalistic relations. In this sense, Marx is against the *naturalization* of social rela-tions and the labor produced by the concrete, social, and living worker. Naturalization is the transformation of living into dead labor. This transformation is typical of capitalism. Capital is dead, and only the labor which produces value is alive. Thus capitalism forces the producer of value, the worker, to live as if he were dead. For instance, colonialism forces colonialized people to live only so much as to allow their exploitation, with colonialism's having the recurring temptation to destroy them.

Marx further clarifies his analysis when he explains that the crystallization of labor into commodities is abstract natural-ism insofar as it ignores history and fails to realize that social relations are historical. Thus the naturalized relations of the bad use of economics are also historical. The categories of economics are founded on real history, and this is what capitalism does not want to recognize. Conceived outside their foundation in con-crete men living in the world and nature—even if only as concrete men who are forced to live as if they were abstract—the categories became intellectual abstractions. However, these abstract categories reflect an objective society, because in bour-geois society *abstract categories function as if they were con-crete,* i.e., because in bourgeois society the worker really lives as if he were an abstraction, and the relations among workers are conceived as if they were physical relations.

The categories of bourgeois economy consist of suchlike forms. They are forms of thought expressing with social validity the

5. *Ibid.,* p. 72.

conditions and relations of a definite, historically determined mode of production, viz., the production of commodities,[6]

which is characterized by fetishism.

It is thus typical of the capitalist mode of production that abstract categories become concrete. A capitalist society is organized according to abstract categories which have become *objective* and, at the same time, according to social relations conceived as if they were physical. Here we have an abstraction and a fetishization, or naturalization. Capitalist society does not want to recognize that abstractions and fetishizations are historically founded and must be transformed.

Marxism is a critique of badly used science. The bad use of economic categories is abstract insofar as it is contrary to real development and its meaning of truth. Therefore, even capitalist society, which is reflected in the false use of economics, is the opposite of real society. It is an overturned society in which the abstract is concrete and the concrete is abstract: physical nature turns into social relations, and social relations become physical nature.

> Man's reflection on the forms of social life, and consequently, also, his scientific analysis of those forms take a course directly opposite to that of their actual historical development. He begins, *post festum*, with the results of the process of development ready to hand before him. The characters that stamp products as commodities, and whose establishment is a necessary preliminary to the circulation of commodities, have already acquired the stability of natural, self-understood forms of social life, before man seeks to decipher, not their historical character, for in his eyes they are immutable, but their meaning.[7]

The analysis must study capitalist society and must begin with its data. Since capitalist society is inverted, the analysis is forced to follow a movement opposite to the real one. But the analysis is *correct if it is aware of this abstraction into which it is forced*. It traces the data and the commodities already fixed in circulation back to their *origins*. It discovers the contradictions of capitalist society, because it discovers that the capitalist use of science, unaware that it reflects an inverted movement, is a mistaken one. It is very important to understand this point, which is connected to the way Marx uses "abstraction" in *Capital*. He moves from the abstract to the concrete. He begins with the analysis of the abstract which functions as if it were

6. *Ibid.*, p. 76.
7. *Ibid.*, p. 75.

concrete, and he discovers that this contradiction is transformed into a praxis which is aimed at the constitution of a society free from fetishized abstractions.

Real things appear *as what they are not* in capitalist society. However, real things appear as *what they are* to the extent that the worker is always a concrete man, even if he is forced to live abstractly because of the abstraction that functions as if it were concrete. In other words, according to Marx, capitalist relations are *natural relations among persons and social relations among things.* Consequently, in so appearing,[8] they hide the *partial man* by presenting him as total. Here the real is the untrue. Capitalist reality is contradictory because it is not the true reality. The becoming-conscious of this situation guides the praxis which has as its task the constitution of a reality according to the meaning of truth.

To the extent that it wants to bring about a concrete, harmoniously developing human society, Marxism is the true defense of the human person, his reality, and his truth. The society that Marxism aims at bringing about is the society of living and true men, i.e., the society of living labor.

Capital opposes reality and truth. The same must be said of land, as Marx demonstrates in his analysis of rent. In the inversion of the relation, products dominate the living producers who now become dead. This is why Marx says that, for capitalism, individual subjects are always implicit but never recognized. He writes: "Labor-power exists only as a capacity, or power of the living individual. Its production consequently presupposes his existence." [9] Capitalism denies the existence of concrete individuals and ends by denying the existence of the world. In capitalism's attempt to hide man's concrete life and meaning, it ends by losing and destroying reality. For Marx, the analysis must lead appearance back to reality and reveal the real situation.[10] The analysis must lead to the awareness that the capitalist situation is distorted and that it opposes the true direction and end of the historical process and its meaning of truth. It is important that things themselves appear and become *phenomena.* It is even more important that men develop themselves by becoming true men. This is why the task of phenomenology is to return to the things-themselves by allowing them to be *revealed* so that man can move toward his own *telos.*

8. *Ibid.*, p. 72.
9. *Ibid.*, p. 171.
10. *Capital* (Moscow: Progress Publishers, 1962), III, 806.

Social relations are not what they appear to be even if, in a given historical situation, they must appear precisely as they do:

It is clear that capital presupposes labor as wage-labor. But it is just as clear that if labor as wage-labor is taken as the point of departure, so that the identity of labor in general with wage-labor appears to be self-evident, then capital and monopolized land must also appear as the natural form of the conditions of labor in relation to labor in general.[11]

The key point here is that something is covered and hidden. We must discover and reveal that which is *implicit* and how it has been hidden through the identification of labor in general with wage-labor. Capital and monopolized land appear as "natural forms" because of the factual conditions of capitalist society. This "given" society has constituted a *model* according to which capital appears as the natural, perennial, and scientific form of the conditions of labor. This model is a "construction," but it is not merely another epistemological construction, since society acts according to it. Even though it is constructed with abstract categories, the "trinity formula" (capital-profit, land-ground rent, and labor-wages) functions as if it were real. This is "the trinity formula which comprises all the secrets of the social production process." [12]

Capital, land, labor! However, capital is not a thing, but rather a definite social production relation, belonging to a definite historical formation of society, which is manifested in a thing and lends this thing a specific social character. Capital is not the sum of the material and produced means of production. Capital is rather the means of production transformed into capital, which in themselves are no more capital than gold or silver in itself is money. It is the means of production monopolized by a certain section of society, confronting living labor-power as products and working conditions rendered independent of this very labor-power, which are personified through this antithesis in capital. It is not merely the products of laborers turned into independent powers, products as rulers and buyers of their producers.[13]

The "trinity formula" is a mystery that Marx wants to bring to light and phenomenologically transform into a *phenomenon*.

In capitalist society, the abstract *functions as if it were*

11. *Ibid.*, p. 804.
12. *Ibid.*, p. 194.
13. *Ibid.*, pp. 794–95.

concrete, and, in spite of its being abstract, it leads to serious consequences: *social relations* appear and function as if they were things, while they are not things. Capital appears and functions as if it were a sum, while it is not a sum. The products of labor appear and function as if they were autonomous, while they are not separable from living labor-power. In capital, they are personified as separate entities, while they are not persons. Marx says elsewhere that the capitalist is not a man: he is personified capital.

Marx reveals the basic meaning of living and non-fetishized labor-power. *For him, this living force belongs to the subject understood as a concrete individual.* "Labor-power exists only as a capacity, or power of the living individual. Its production consequently presupposes its existence." [14]

The individual is always presupposed: the subject or the human person is always *implicit* as living labor. To the extent that it is implicit, subjectivity is stolen from man and becomes embodied in the labor process. Yet the trinity formula is an abstraction, and it must be considered as such. It is useful to employ the trinity formula if we remember that it is an abstraction which, however, functions as if it were reality.

Thus, although we must use abstractions and models, it is important that we know their genesis. The employment of abstractions does not imply that we must keep them. Furthermore, we should not forget that, ultimately, the basis of all this is always man as concrete subjectivity with his living labor.

It is, however, just this ultimate money-form of the world of commodities that actually conceals, instead of disclosing, the social character of private labor, and the social relations between the individual producers. When I state that coats or boots stand in a relation to linen, because it is the universal incarnation of abstract human labor, the absurdity of the statement is self-evident. Nevertheless, when the producers of coats and boots compare those articles with linen, or, what is the same thing, with gold or silver, as the universal equivalent, they express the relation between their own private labor and the collective labor of society in the same absurd form. The categories of bourgeois economy consist of suchlike forms. [15]

Although they are constructions, categories and abstractions function as if they were reality. Thought-forms hide man and

14. *Capital,* I, 171.
15. *Ibid.,* p. 76.

human labor. Marx's approach can be best characterized as a
search for the precategorial. Categories do not remain in books
and in thought: they act in society.

> They are forms of thought expressing with social validity the
> conditions and relations of a definite, *historically determined* mode
> of production, viz., the production of commodities. The whole
> mystery of commodities, all the magic and necromancy that sur-
> rounds the products of labor as long as they take the forms of
> commodities, vanishes therefore, so soon as we come to other
> forms of production.[16]

They vanish because of the analysis. But in the meantime we
actually live in witchcraft. In feudal society,

> for the very reason that personal dependence forms the ground-
> work of society, there is no necessity for labor and its products to
> assume a fantastic form different from their reality. They take the
> shape, in the transactions of society, of services in kind and pay-
> ments in kind. Here the particular and natural form of labor, and
> not, as in a society based on production of commodities, its general
> abstract form, is the immediate social form of labor. Compulsory
> labor is just as properly measured by time, as commodity-pro-
> ducing labor; but every serf knows that what he expends in the
> service of his lord, is a definite quantity of his own personal labor-
> power. The tithe to be rendered to the priest is more a matter of
> fact than his blessing. No matter, then, what we may think of the
> parts played by the different classes of people themselves in this
> society, the social relations between individuals in the performance
> of their labor, appear at all events as their own mutual personal
> relations, and are not disguised under the shape of social relations
> between the products of labor.[17]

What we have here are masks, camouflage, and theater. Perhaps
Marx was thinking of Hamlet, who does not appear accidentally
when there is something rotten in the state of Denmark.
Pirandello, Brecht, and Sartre also treat the problem of masks
and camouflages.

"In the course of our investigation we shall find, in general,
that the characters who appear on the economic stage are but
the personifications of the economic relations that exist between
them."[18] Ideology is not based on masks: the personae move,
descend from the stage, live, and act in the theater of the world,

16. *Ibid.*
17. *Ibid.*, p. 77.
18. *Ibid.*, p. 85.

and they are not recognized as personae or *apparent forms*. They become operative laws which are expressible in precise formulae.

The circulation of commodities is capital's point of departure. Commerce is its historical presupposition. If we examine the process we find that its final product is money. Hence: money-commodity-money. This last product of the circulation of commodities is the *first phenomenal form of capital*.[19] However, money is also capital's first form of appearance. "We can see it daily under our very eyes. All new capital, to commence with, comes on the stage, that is, on the market . . . in the shape of money that by a definite process has to be transformed into capital." Thus, we have money as money and money as capital. They initially differ only in their form of circulation.

> The simplest form of the circulation of commodities is *C-M-C*, the transformation of commodities into money, and change of money back into commodities; or selling in order to buy. But alongside of this form we find another specifically different form: *M-C-M*, the transformation of money into commodities, and the change of commodities back again into money; or buying in order to sell. Money that circulates in the latter manner is thereby transformed into, becomes capital, and is already potentially capital.[20]

Subjective labor, turned into a separate object crystallized in the commodity, has had its play: a construction without life, capital has become a living and *unique* person who knows and plays all the parts in the comedy. "Both circuits are resolvable into the same two antithetical phases, *C-M*, a sale, and *M-C*, a purchase. In each of these phases the same material elements —a commodity and money, and the same economic *dramatis personae*, a buyer and a seller—confront one another." [21]

What moves the whole process which begins and ends with *M*? Is it simply a matter of an initial, identical equality (money with itself)? Does anything change along the route? Money constitutes the beginning and the end. With the poet, it can claim that "in my beginning is my end" and "in my end is my beginning." [22] However, something happens in this circle. The capitalist does not want equality, but *something more*. Value must beget value by itself. This is the goal of capitalist produc-

19. *Ibid.*, p. 146.
20. *Ibid.*, pp. 146–47.
21. *Ibid.*, pp. 147–48.
22. T. S. Eliot, *Four Quartets* (London: Faber and Faber, 1958), pp. 15, 23.

tion which requires the objectification of human labor in commodities: the reversal of the subject in the object can be found in all of Marx. The reversal makes possible *something more* than equality: *surplus-value.* As Engels says in the Preface to the second volume of *Capital,* the theory of surplus-value (*Mehrwert*) is the crux of political economy.[23] It is also the crux of the history of political economy, as is demonstrated in the fourth, fifth, and sixth volumes of *Capital* (*Theories of Surplus Value*). In order to break the identity of the formula, surplus-value requires the living labor performed by the living subject.

> The capitalist anticipates . . . not only in order to reproduce the capital invested but also to reproduce an excess of value over it. He can convert into a higher value the value of the anticipated variable capital only through the exchange of the latter with living labor, through the exploitation of living labor. Furthermore, he can exploit labor only to the extent that he simultaneously anticipates the presuppositions for the execution of that labor—tools and objects of labor, machinery and raw material—i.e., only to the extent that he changes a sum of value that he owns into the form of the conditions of production: as in general he is a capitalist and can undertake the process of the exploitation of labor only to the extent that, as the owner of the combinations of labor, he contraposes himself to the worker as the simple owner of labor-power.[24]

Here, the emphasis is on the temporal modality of *anticipation,* i.e., exploitation connected with the modality of *working* and *circulation time.* In other words: the capitalist transforms time, as the worker's needs and consumption (irreversibility), into the exploitation of time and the production of surplus-value.

The tautological formula $M = M$ corresponds to the formal principle of identity. This is a logical formal principle which is valid independently of the meaning of M. It can indicate sensible, determinate, and material finitude which, precisely because it is determinate and tautological, subsequently makes the dialectic possible. However, if it is a formal principle, it cannot be valid as a factual principle. In fact, we never have $M = M$, but we have the exploitation of the worker which permits the capitalist to obtain more than the original M: something, i.e., surplus-value. For the capitalist, this happens as a result of the properties

23. *Capital* (Moscow: Progress Publishers, 1961), II, 2.
24. G. Della Volpe, *Logica come Scienze Positiva* (Florence: G. d'Anna, 1956), p. 159.

of capital. In fact, it happens because of the exploitation of the worker through the conversion of subjective labor into commodities.

The capitalist considers surplus-value to be independent of the exploitation of labor. He sees surplus-value as an abstract product of capital and of the circulation of commodities. In fact, surplus-value originates in the worker's own labor which is taken away from him in the detached results which are transformed into objects and commodities. Profit cannot be explained by claiming that the capitalist exchanges a present good (wage) for a future good (the product of labor). The present good (wage) must be lower than the future return: the future M must be $M+$ something. This "something," of course, is surplus-value. This means that the working time actually expended by the worker is not fully repaid, for, if it were, M would be equal to M. If, at the end of M, we have $M+$ something, it is precisely because something has entered into the equation between M and M. This something is not a result of M but of real labor and its temporality. More precisely, it is a result of the labor which the worker originally expended in order to repair consumption and to satisfy needs, but which was subsequently transformed into the accumulated capital which is contraposed to labor as an alien power. Thus, time as need and as the reparation of need is contraposed to the pure abstract form. These times are transformed not into the concrete satisfaction of needs but into surplus-value. The contradiction pertains first of all to the worker who endures it. The capitalist *anticipates* capital but he does not want to end up with only the recovery of what he has anticipated. Instead, he wants surplus-value, which he considers a result of the virtue of anticipation, while in fact it results from exploitation. All is consumed except capital, which increases instead. What remains hidden is that capital increases as a function of consumption and the deferred satisfaction of needs.

For Marx, the circle can ultimately be broken only if work itself becomes the satisfaction of a need, in addition to producing goods that satisfy needs in proportion to the expended labor. Today this requires the precondition that the workers own the means of production and use them, along with their labor, and eventual surplus-labor, not for capital, but for society. They must bring about working conditions that allow them to work and realize their own humanity in labor, without having labor turn against them. The isolated worker can never succeed in this task, which is connected to the relations of workers, to the con-

trol of means of production, and to the collective project of production based on the anticipation of the results of labor and their
circulation. In the ultimate analysis, the workers have to anticipate and regulate the whole process, thus preventing the possibility that an anticipation external to them could be contraposed
to labor as an alien power: the production of surplus-value derived from surplus-value.

Surplus-value is bound to labor-time and must maximize
production in the minimum amount of time. Here, technology
intervenes as a "relationship with nature" and as the transformation of nature into the inorganic body of man. Therefore, the
emancipation of the worker is connected to the use of a science
and a technology which are not enslaved by capital. The worker
must prevent science and technology from being used solely to
produce surplus-value. The struggle is directed against technistic
and scientistic alienation so that the sciences can be led back to
their function. They cannot be if capital remains personified and
a separate nature comes to dominate man, even though nature
is man's inorganic body. The passage from necessity—which in
capitalism becomes surplus-value in order to end in the decline
of profit—must lead to freedom. "In fact, the realm of freedom
actually begins only where labor which is determined by necessity and mundane considerations ceases; thus in the very nature
of things it lies beyond the sphere of actual material production."
Had Marx not written this, who could have saved the author of
the passage from the charge of "spiritualism"?

> Just as the savage must wrestle with Nature to satisfy his wants,
> to maintain and reproduce life, so must civilized man, and he must
> do so in all social formations and under all possible modes of
> production. With his development this realm of physical necessity
> expands as a result of his wants; but, at the same time, the forces
> of production which satisfy these wants also increase. Freedom in
> this field can only consist in socialized man, the associated pro-
> ducers, rationally regulating their interchange with nature, bring-
> ing it under their common control, instead of being ruled by it as
> by the blind forces of Nature; and achieving this with the least
> expenditure of energy and under conditions most favorable to, and
> worthy of, their human nature.[25]

For Marx, the goal of communism is man's dignity, which capital
prevents. Because of its internal contradictions, however, capitalism ends by making the realization of dignity impossible, because

25. *Capital,* III, 799–800.

capitalism rules need in such a way that man cannot find himself but can only lose himself.

[87] *The Return to the Concrete*

THE DISTINGUISHING FEATURE of capitalism is its tendency to make abstract categories live as if they were concrete. The categories become subjects or persons (in the Latin sense of "masks"). Capital is the abstract first person who acts as if he were concrete against man's authentic and unmasked experience of himself, others, and the world in the first person (in Husserl's sense). The capitalist himself is personified capital: in him, capital as the subject has replaced the human subject. The capitalist is a man who has become a mask of capital. He produces for the love of production and not for the consumption of what is produced. Production for the sake of production is surplus-value for the sake of surplus-value. Capitalism does two things: it produces commodities and their consequent fetishism; and it results in the "production of surplus-value as the direct aim and the determining motive of production. Capital produces essentially capital, and does so only to the extent that it produces surplus-value." [26] It is important to note that the "direct aim" is surplus-value and, consequently, profit. That is, the aim is not to satisfy real human needs: surplus-value goes its own way. Real human needs are *essentially* interested in *use-value*, which is precisely what interests the concrete man who thinks about consuming commodities, and is only indirectly interested in the money needed to buy these commodities.

From the very beginning, Marx *abstracts from use-value*, not because it is inessential, but because this is the only way that we can analyze capitalism and its foundations in commodities, exchange, and capitalist circulation: *M-C-M'*. In circulation, money becomes surplus-value and surplus-value becomes profit. What is hidden is the concrete worker who becomes abstract, and the surplus-value which creates surplus-value. The process is complex and implies the separation of constant capital (e.g., the machines) from variable capital (the labor-power of the workers). It is thus possible to talk about the "organic composition of capital" which consists in the relation between the mass of labor employed and the means of production used. Obviously, this re-

26. *Ibid.,* p. 858.

lation is connected with the transformation of the value of commodities in costs of production. In all of these metamorphoses, however, value originally derives from labor, and, in commodities, labor becomes an object. The determination of prices is a function of the analysis of the market and wages and of the market and competition. For Marx, profits tend to decline (the law of the falling rate of profit in Part III of the third volume of *Capital*). No matter how one interprets Marx's "law" and criticizes the way in which it is introduced, it is difficult to deny that capitalism as a closed system leads to the falling rate of profits. The tendency for profit to fall is countered by various antagonistic forces, e.g., technological inventions and scientific discoveries, as well as imperialist expansion which removes the law from the closed system for which it was formulated. The contradiction inherent in capitalism is not a function of the law of the falling rate of profits. The contradiction develops in two immediately obvious complementary directions: (1) the fall of the intentionality of the function of the sciences, i.e., the crisis of the sciences and technistic alienation (science at the service of capital); and (2) war, and science at the service of war. The result is the alienated use of atomic energy and the possible total alienation of all humanity. The atomic bomb is the last metamorphosis of capital: its extreme *persona* and subjective incarnation vis-à-vis the men-objects. It is the final consequence of the reversal of the subject into the object, and, if humanity does not want to be alienated and degraded to the level of inorganic nature, it must bring about the reversal of the reversal, i.e., the *return to the subject*.

This historical development is connected with the process of the personification of capital. Therefore, it is also connected with the concrete functioning of abstractions, the *metamorphosis of the abstract into the concrete*, and the correlative *metamorphosis of the concrete into the abstract* on the part of man who becomes an abstract worker, a category or a number, a "draught animal," or, as in Kafka's *Metamorphosis*, a cockroach, or the tupaia which builds its shelter but *does not live in it*. In the logic of capitalism, what counts is exchange-value and not use-value. The goal of production is not human consumption and, therefore, real human needs. Capitalist wealth does not exclude hunger for large sectors of the population. The needs of this population remain outside the exchange of commodities in the cycle *M-C-M'*. For the same reason, in an affluent society, what consumers desire as real and concrete men does not matter. The important thing is that men become consuming animals or a *commodity which consumes* those commodities that abstract capitalism needs to have consumed. From the very beginning, capitalism has put aside use-value in order to produce commodities needed not by consumers but by exchange-value. Therefore, it is once again a function of the reversal of the subject. Even real use has become *abstract*.

Capital does not produce for man or society, but for itself. This is its limit and its basic contradiction. To the extent that this contradiction has become concretized from an abstraction, it does not mechanically produce its contrary. Better yet: the force contraposed to and generated by the contradiction is the concrete reality *against* which the contradiction operates. This concrete reality contains the revolt of the negated humanity and its principle of emancipation of all humanity, even if it is expressed only in one of its parts. What is concrete is the proletariat and its historical forms.

The proletariat grows in proportion to alienation. This happens for everyone: from the peasant to the assembly-line worker, from the immigrant to the consumer of the affluent society. The last is forced to become a machine for preestablished consumption. Eventually, he spontaneously desires what capital wants him to desire, even alienation, on every level of life, psychological as well as sexual. This situation generates the opposite process. The act of becoming-conscious begins from the increasingly greater endured alienation that capital produces, both quantitatively and qualitatively. As *capital-in-itself* is revealed as the sole aim of production, it forces man to return to himself. In fact, the moment of the contradiction of that abstract which has become concrete becomes connected with that moment in which the concrete (man) becomes abstract. To the extent that it realizes itself, capital provokes its own negation. Thus, the negation of the negation becomes a reality. Capitalist production must expand and improve, but in doing so it produces its own negation and *prepares* the means for such a negation. The goal is no longer capital, but man. Capitalism develops all these for its own eventual destruction: technology, goods, invention, the expansion of markets, colonialism, technistic alienation, and even war. It provides those whom it has used in becoming capital with the means to negate capital and lays the groundwork for a socialist society. And these means are the very same ones developed by capitalism. How this inversion is going to take place cannot be defined a priori, nor can it be left to an abstract revolutionary will or to a revolution for the revolution. Furthermore, the model of one inversion cannot be applied to another situation, except for the gravest situations which are common to all men (e.g., the atomic bomb).

What ultimately provokes the negation of capitalist production is capitalist production itself.

> The *real barrier* of capitalist production is *capital itself*. It is that capital and its self-expansion appear as the starting and the closing point, the motive and the purpose of production; that production is only production for *capital* and not vice versa, the means of production are not mere means for a constant expansion of the living process of the *society of* producers.[27]

Capital appears as it is to the producers, who consequently must appropriate the means of production. Here, "the means of production" must be understood in a very broad sense.

The capitalist contradiction obtains between use-value and exchange-value, and between the authentic means of production and technology and the expansion of capital as the principle and the goal (capital for capital's sake). Marx emphasizes that capitalist production does not aim at use-value, but at exchange-value. Thus science and technology must be contraposed to the authentic goal of production, which is not the accumulation of money for its own sake, but the production of means to satisfy human needs, and the transformation of labor itself into the satisfaction of a need.

The analysis thus reveals to us the situation as it is. It leads us back to things and to their reality which is hidden behind the appearances that have become objective reality. Reality is no longer presented in disguises and *apparent forms*. Instead, it is presented along with the function of production and the historical function of capital and its contradictions. In fact, the dialectic of the abstract and the concrete, of appearance and reality, also holds for the dialectic as the discussion and struggle among and within groups. As such, it is sometimes transformed into sophistry, the "theatrical" play of sudden reversals, and the reciprocal self-projection of motivations and accusations. This also shows the inevitable acceptance of the adversary's means of struggle and the necessity of never losing the meaning of truth in every concrete situation and determined praxis.

27. *Ibid.*, p. 245.

[88]   *The Typicity of Economics*
        as the Science of Decisions

THE RETURN TO CONCRETENESS is the negation of capital's function as an abstract category. Therefore, it is the return to the precategorial and to man. To the extent that it is a "critique of political economy," Marx's *Capital* is a critique of an unfounded and nonoriented science. With Smith, economics had a direction, since its aim was "the happiness of the greatest number." However, it led to the opposite. The intentionality of science does not exclude its "scientificity"; rather, the intentionality guarantees it through the regaining of the meaning of truth. Economics encompasses all the problems that deal with the crisis of the sciences and the return of their function. As a science, it needs mathematics, but it is also historical. In its domain, economics is the analysis of economic phenomena. These economic phenomena, however, must not be separated from sociohistorical phenomena. Economics needs models, but they must always be reconstructed and are not abstractly derivable from one another. The model itself can function as a concrete and empirical datum. However, economics can lose its foundation insofar as it is categorial, and can, therefore, affect precategorial experience. More than any other science, economics must continually be reconsidered by our rediscovering the historical, social, and human roots of theories and economic analyses. The reconsideration begins from the actual present which contains both economic studies and the sociohistorical situation.

Economics as a science must be continually redeemed from *objectification* so that its sociohistorical function can be discovered, i.e., the continuity of the intentional effort for the constitution of a human society of subjects free from exploitation. Joseph Schumpeter says:

> By history of economic analysis, I mean the history of the intellectual efforts that men have made in order to *understand* economic phenomena or, what comes to the same thing, the history of the analytic or scientific aspects of economic thought.[28]

28. Joseph A. Schumpeter, *History of Economic Analysis*, ed. Elizabeth Boody Schumpeter (New York: Oxford University Press, 1954), p. 3.

However, the analytic aspects and categorial constructions are not analytically deducible and must always be brought back to the history of human society and the precategorial foundation of sciences. In fact,

> The significance and validity of both problems and methods cannot be fully grasped without a knowledge of the previous problems and methods to which they are the (tentative) response. Scientific analysis is not simply a logically consistent process that starts with some primitive notions and then adds to the stock in a straight-line fashion. It is not simply progressive discovery of an objective reality—as is, for example, discovery in the basin of the Congo. Rather, it is an incessant struggle with creations of our own and our predecessors' minds and it "progresses," if at all, in a criss-cross fashion, not as logic, but as the impact of new ideas or observations or needs, and also as the bents and temperaments of new men dictate.[29]

Phenomenological themes spontaneously arise here. One does not pass from logical construction to logical construction, i.e., it is not a matter of an analytical categorial passage. Needs are temporal, social, and precategorial, and there is an interplay between categories and models, categories and reality, and categories that become concrete, and man's precategorial operations, according to the complex dialectic of the concrete and the abstract.

For Schumpeter, logic becomes both praxis and teleological orientation. The history of economics reveals "logic in the concrete, logic in action, logic wedded to vision and to purpose."[30] Schumpeter's rhapsodic and unordered observations can be understood only if one poses the phenomenological problem of the foundation of economics and sees its solution in terms of the return of economics to its precategorial structure, beginning with a critique of objectification. Economics can and must use mathematics. However, it is not mathematical physics and, unlike psychology, it must not fall into "naturalism." In fact, to the extent that it falls into naturalism, it ceases to be a science. Schumpeter writes:

> Thus, in everyday parlance as well as in the lingo of academic life . . . the term [science] is often used to denote mathematical physics. Evidently, this excludes all social sciences and also economics. Nor is economics as a whole a science if we make the use

29. *Ibid.*, p. 4.
30. *Ibid.*, p. 5.

of methods similar to those of mathematical physics the defining characteristic (*definiens*) of science. In this case only a small part of economics is "scientific." Again, if we define science according to the slogan "Science is Measurement," then economics is scientific in some of its parts and not in others.[31]

This statement clearly indicates the need for a precategorial foundation in the *Lebenswelt*. This foundation is man in his environment, in nature considered as his inorganic body, and in the inevitability of consumption, needs, and satisfaction, required by temporal irreversibility. Furthermore, the precategorial structure poses the problem of labor, its value, alienation, the dialectic, and the return to the concrete.

Economics has its own domain, but it must continually return to that which grounds and constitutes this domain. It must emerge from its own categorial abstraction and stop functioning as if it were concrete in the abstraction. In fact, economics often functions categorially, even if it does not know precisely what it is doing. The precategorial must be sought in a dimension prior to political economy that ultimately gives rise to economic categories. For example, Keynes talks about a *psychological law* as the *key to his whole system*. To the extent that it "depends on the psychological characteristic of the community," this law exists in the categorial picture of economics, as we can see by analyzing the principle of the "propensity to consume." [32] Naturally, a psychological factor is not abstract, and the reference to psychology is a reference to man's fullness and concreteness, even though Keynes does not say so. The other constitutive factor of Keynes's *General Theory* is the *temporal* dimension, which was already decisive for Marshall. Time, however, is the very foundation of historicity.

When Keynes asserts that "all production is for the purpose of ultimately satisfying a consumer," [33] he returns to use-value, and the *General Theory* needs to be reframed with regard to the problem of the relation of use-value and exchange-value. The true problem does not concern circulation-time. Ultimately, it is the problem of working-time and value. Even if one criticizes Marx's theory of value within the closed system of categorial economics, the fact remains that, in Marx, value is the foundation of economics. Thus, it grounds the *function* of economics as

31. *Ibid.*, p. 6.
32. John Maynard Keynes, *General Theory of Employment, Interest and Money* (New York: Harcourt, Brace, 1936), p. 28.
33. *Ibid.*, p. 46.

a science in human history. For example, Keynes's analysis, in
the second paragraph of the fifth chapter of the *General Theory*,
is based on the temporal modalities of expectation and actual
presence. Thus it refers to an analysis of precategorial time, not
at the level of capitalist circulation, but at the level of the precategorial temporal experience which gives rise to every abstract
categorial structure that functions as if it were concrete. In other
words, the theory of full employment and the reevaluation of the
function of money must return to *concreteness*, in the sense
indicated, with respect to the dialectic of the abstract and the
concrete. This is a return to the foundation of economics as a
science in the horizon of historical truth.

Economics is a decisive science to the extent that it encompasses and highlights all the problems analyzed with respect to
the crisis of the sciences and the return to their function. Now
we can understand one of the most important aspects of *Capital*,
which is not just a treatise of political economy. It is first and
foremost a "critique of political economy." Here, the term "critique" must be understood in a Kantian sense. *Capital* is the
answer to the question: How is political economy as a science
possible? The answer is the following: Political economy is truly
scientific to the extent that its scientificity coincides with the
critique of the categorial abstraction that functions as if it were
real, and with the return to concreteness. On the other hand, the
return to concreteness is not possible without the constitution of
a new society and a new humanity. All that has been said can be
called "transcendental" in Husserl's terminology, and it reveals
the essence of the expression "transcendental foundation." Political economy rediscovers its intentional function precisely
when it reveals its scientific foundation. Thus it becomes constituted as praxis according to the meaning of truth. The case of
political economy is paradigmatic. Ultimately, the root of *objectification* and of the crisis of the sciences can be revealed through
the analysis of political economy, its historical foundation, and
its goal. Here we rediscover the need to return the sciences to
their function, and the full meaning of the return to the concreteness of the subject. The concreteness of the subject is the
meaning of man and the meaning of truth of the historical constitution of a society of subjects free from objectification. Therefore, in analyzing the problem of the sciences in Husserl, we have
called political economy the *science of decisions*. The paradigmatic character of the problem of the foundation of political
economy as a science is its typicity. What are typical are the

problems of analysis and disocclusion to which we are forced by political economy as the founded and intentional science [34] of economic operations. The problems of typicity and disocclusion also involve the typicity of the dialectic of objectification, and of the reconquering, on the part of the sciences, of their function. The reconquering of this function is the self-revelation of the meaning of man.

[89]   Philosophia Perennis

POLITICAL ECONOMY MUST TAKE INTO ACCOUNT the capitalist categorial system which functions as concrete reality. The struggle against capitalism is the return to man and, therefore, to the proletariat in all its levels of alienation.

The categorial contradiction is not a naturalistic law and is not deterministically repeated, unlike Darwin's "struggle for existence" mentioned by Engels. It requires a human foundation and the movement of the negation of that which is abstract and categorial. Therefore, it demands the critique of what is only illusory and apparent. In a rigorous sense, it demands the critique of ideology. Once again, the meaning of the term "ideology" reappears.

Since phenomenal forms function as if they were real, the analysis that transforms the apparent forms which hide the things-themselves into phenomena of things (into a *Schein of Sein*) is not a speculative analysis but is *essentially a praxis.*[35]

34. See my essay, "Nuove ricerche fenomenologiche," *Aut-Aut*, no. 68 (1962).
35. See Marx, "Randglossen zu Adolph Wagners *Lehrbuch der politischen Ökonomie*," in Marx and Engels, *Werke* (Berlin, D.D.R.: Dietz, 1956–69), XIX, 369: "What I begin with is the simplest social form in which the product of labor presents itself in present society, and this is as a *commodity*. I analyze this, and indeed first of all in the *form in which it appears*. Here I now find that, on the one hand, it is in its natural form a *useful thing*, alias *use-value*, while on the other hand it is the *carrier* of *exchange-value*, and from this point of view is itself 'exchange-value.' A further analysis of this shows that exchange-value is only an appearance form [*Erscheinungs*form], a mode of self-presentation independent of the *value* contained in the commodity, and I can then pass to the analysis of the latter . . . a commodity is use-value or object of use, a 'value.' It presents itself as a double of what it is, as if it possesses a *value* of its own in its *appearance form,* exchange-value, which is different from its nat-

This transformation is exactly what *phenomenological* analysis accomplishes, because phenomenal forms function as if they were real, and praxis is a real negation of that which is apparent and illusory. To the extent that the movement of real negation is the return to the subject's concreteness and operations, it is a return to a subject who becomes aware of the specific situation and precise character of alienation in which he lives and operates. The subject is in the negation of the negation, with specific historical modes of praxis, and always departs from the present, according to the movement of reflection which always moves from the origin and presence (*lebendige Gegenwart*). This movement is the exercise of the phenomenological doing and reflecting. It is the movement of reconsideration that must return to all that has been said of phenomenology. Here we must stress what we have clarified. The analysis is already a praxis as reflection. For phenomenology, reflection is temporalization and necessarily develops into a concrete negation, since the categorial abstraction functions as if it were concrete. It is a *human operation of negating* that negation which is appearance. Appearance operates by negating and alienating man. Therefore, it operates in different forms which change according to time and place. Reconsideration and the epochē must prevent these forms from once again becoming prejudicial. The analysis forces man to *reshape* and *transform* the world. Praxis, consequently, obtains in the reconsideration which is reflection in praxis to the extent to which praxis is negative and reconstitutive action according to the meaning of truth and the uncovering of the things-themselves.

To the extent that the critique of ideology is a critique of phenomenal appearances which function as if they were reality, it requires—already in reflection—the return to the subject. It is an exercise, an *ascesis* in the Greek sense of the term. It is a return to the subject's responsibility. An ethical direction can easily be discerned in this movement.

The return to the subject is a return to the precategorial and to the foundation of the sciences and, therefore, to the discovery of their functions. Hence, the critique is not itself an ideology,

---

ural form. I therefore do not divide use-value and exchange-value as opposites, splitting abstract and 'value,' but consider the *concrete social form* as the product of labor; the '*commodity*' is on the one hand use-value, and on the other hand, value, not exchange-value, since this is the simple appearance form and not its own content."

nor is ideology the responsibility that requires avoiding repetition of the negativity that must be negated.

To the extent that the critique is not and must not be ideology, it is not speculative philosophy. The meaning of truth is revealed by uncovering that which the phenomenal forms hide through the dialectic of appearance and reality, and of the abstract and the concrete. But what lies behind the phenomenal forms is not a thing-in-itself. Things-themselves appear as real in the light of a teleological movement. They appear as a reality that must be transformed and constituted in concrete relations in a real society which can be constituted in a given historical stage according to the horizon of truth. The infinite limiting idea of this is not separated from the actual presence as a being-in-itself or a noumenal reality, but lives and acts in every finite historical situation and in its praxis. The reconsideration in the present situation is also a corrective and repairing praxis. Therefore, it is an implicit recognition of man's fallibility and his practical self-correction. In this, the meaning of truth, which requires the non-identification of the subject with the horizon of truth and the noncrystallization of truth in being (and, therefore, non-fetishization), here acquires its ethical meaning.

When the abstract categories operating in their phenomenal forms are disoccluded, the *phenomenal* is transformed into the *phenomenological*. The sciences regain their function. Philosophy as ideology is negated as an occluding system. But the negation of speculative philosophy is not the negation of authentic philosophy, which rises again precisely from the negation of ideology and is constituted to the extent to which it disoccludes the phenomenally apparent forms and transforms them into phenomenological forms. Authentic philosophy does so by departing from the return to the subject who overcomes every prejudice with the epochē and discovers in himself, as an individual who endures alienation, part of a totality in the process of becoming. He discovers the negated humanity, the *universality of the meaning of man,* and, therefore, the inherence of the universal in the particular in his own experience in the first person. The disoccluding analysis, or the return to the human operations and to the subject, coincides with the discovery of what in the subject is not "subjective" (in the sense of "relative"). It therefore coincides with the discovery of the *typical* and *intentional* character of reality to the extent that it is transformed by the subject's praxis. This is the reality which is constituted according to truth. Because the occluded operates concretely, its critique becomes concrete praxis which is aimed at the transformation of the real. The contradiction of the category that functions as if it were concrete is negated as a negation by the real praxis that continually implies reflection and reconsideration.

Here theory and praxis are no longer dogmatically separated: we no longer have a blind praxis, just as, in principle, all reconsideration is already praxis. The whole mystery of the dualism between theory and praxis is dissolved, along with the fetishism of commodities, when it is discovered why the latter appear in the way that they do in exchange. Abstract capital acts as if it were concrete and forces the worker to act as an abstraction. Subsequently, however, it allows him to become conscious of the endured abstraction. This is the beginning of the return to concreteness and of the revolutionary class movement by alienated humanity. The goal is to constitute, through the negation of the negation, a society so concrete that it disoccludes appearances and discovers what lies behind the forms, and, therefore, discovers the intentionality of the things-themselves.

"Speculative" philosophy and ideology as occlusion give way to authentic philosophy. Philosophy also moves from prehistory to history and realizes the intentionality of all the philosophies that have preceded it. It thus becomes a philosophy which is not a system or a construction. By means of the epochē, it preliminarily negates every prejudice and, therefore, every ideology. The original praxis of debunking what is not founded on evidence, on experience in the first person, and on man as he is today in his society and in his world, reshapes and transforms the world by departing from the living presence and its reconsideration. This philosophy is phenomenology as we have reconstructed it, corrected it, and transformed it. Thus, phenomenology is the transforming and constitutive praxis of a new human society.

Paradoxically, the self-correcting philosophy that departs from the present and transforms itself and the world is the only philosophy, or *philosophia perennis*, that is antinomical to any speculative philosophy constructed by systems which seek to deduce man and the world. This is the philosophy which gives the sciences back their function and gives man back his meaning of truth. The negation of speculative philosophy, as the negation for praxis, is not sufficient for the oriented praxis, while the negation of praxis by speculative philosophy (and the fetishized sciences) is already a praxis and a political act. Correlatively, the negation of reconsideration is a negation of the meaning of truth of praxis, and the praxis that does not reconsider itself ends by provoking a series of counterfinalities that annul what praxis wants to attain, or repeat what it wants to negate. The discovery of philosophy is the discovery of the phenomenological analysis necessary for praxis to achieve its desired successes. It is the critique of the past departing from the present. It is rehabilitation and reparation. It is the continual analysis of the situation and the negation of already rendered judgments. It is the inherence in determined and localized presence of the unitary efforts to maintain, in the many parts, the unitary movement and its teleological horizon of truth in the precise evaluation of the various types of alienation and in the recognition of the unitary function of science and culture. It is the discovery of phenomenology within Marxism. The discovery that the sciences are at the service of capital is the discovery of Marxism within phenomenology. The struggle against the categorial, and the return to the subject for the foundation of science and philosophy, is the struggle against capitalism. Similarly, the disoccluding analysis is a return to the things-themselves and to a praxis which, departing from the endured alienation, operates in the maturity of the actual historical situation in order to construct a free socialist society. We have seen that phenomenology is closely connected to the foundation and meaning of political economy, which essentially encompasses the problem of the function of the sciences and of the meaning of man in an intentional horizon which gives him back his integrity, his inorganic body, the planet Earth, and the authentic function of philosophy.

In the positive yet dangerous path that he is treading, man's success in the struggle for his own material and moral emancipation does not depend on ideologies, but on the energy with which he will maintain the meaning of truth in his praxis, by always departing anew from reflection and reconsideration.

Appendix

Short Phenomenological Dictionary

THE TERMS IN THIS DICTIONARY are not definitions, much less axioms; rather, they suggest the kinds of operations that the phenomenologist must carry out in order to understand and transform himself, others, and the world. Words cannot be substituted for operations. As the reader proceeds with the text, he will be able to seek help in the dictionary, where he can find the exercise he needs in order to learn how to perform active phenomenological analysis.

Background (Hintergrund)
The background is that which I do not clearly perceive in the actual evidence. Nonetheless, it is given to me, even if in a confused way, as a totality from which actual perception comes to the fore as a first level. The actual limited perception always inheres in a broader horizon that must be investigated.

Beginning and Ending
That which I experience in the first person, every experience (*Erlebnis*) that I live directly, has a beginning and ending. "All the life-processes [*Erlebnisse*] belonging to the ego that can ever be found reflectively must present themselves as temporally ordered, temporally beginning and ending" [Husserl, *Cartesian Meditations: An Introduction to Phenomenology*, trans. Dorion Cairns (The Hague: Nijhoff, 1960), p. 43]. This does not prevent their being connected, even in their relativity, according to essential modalities and structures.

Being
For Husserl, being never has a finished meaning and, therefore, we must always constitute it. The loss of meaning and inten-

tionality is due to the attempt to identify truth with being. Therefore, truth is always intentional and never real. It is a direction, a rational representation (*eidos*), a limiting concept, and a task. Intentional, true life is never its own being; it always goes beyond itself and, paradoxically, constitutes itself for and in the "end" toward which it aims. It makes and experiences itself in the aiming, in the movement where it is and where it goes beyond itself. It is in this being-already-beyond-itself that intentional life appears as intentionality. Intentional life is not in the springboard, but in the jump itself and in the direction toward which it jumps. In the Husserlian sense, truth is the goal. While Heidegger wants to "go back" to being, Husserl wants to transform the world according to the meaning of truth.

Being-at-hand
This is the mode of immediate utility (*Vorhandenheit*), which, however, is never connected in its parts and ordered according to a meaning, although it appears obvious and finished. The epochē brackets the *Vorhandenheit* and things become useful *for something* and, according to a rational project, for a unitary end.

Cause
Cause is a lived experience before it is a category. The category of "cause" is constituted and founded scientifically and categorially by means of determinate operations through which the subject experiences a whole series of causal dependencies. For Husserl, therefore, there is a precategorial causality that connects things in determinate ways. These connections give rise to circumstantiality. Insofar as it is surrounded by other things, the thing is said to be original (*Ursache*). The real living body (*Leib*) of the subject or man is localized as a thing in its field of localization (*Lokalisationsfeld*) and is, therefore, subject to precategorial causality.

Cogito
We must not confuse Husserl's *cogito* with the Cartesian axiomatic *ego cogito,* and even less with the *res cogitans.* It is in the world of the *cogito* (or transcendental domain)

> that the complex forms of my manifold and shifting spontaneities of consciousness stand related: observing in the interests of research the bringing of meaning into conceptual form through description; comparing and distinguishing, collecting and count-

ing, presupposing and inferring, the theorizing activity of consciousness, in short, in its different forms and stages. Related to it likewise are the diverse acts and states of sentiment and will: approval and disapproval, joy and sorrow, desire and aversion, hope and fear, decision and action. All these, together with the sheer acts of the Ego, in which I become acquainted with the world as *immediately* given me, through spontaneous tendencies to turn toward it and grasp it, are included under the one Cartesian expression: *Cogito* [Husserl, *Ideas: General Introduction to Pure Phenomenology*, trans. W. R. Boyce Gibson (New York: Humanities Press, 1931), pp. 103–4].

The *cogito* is the living presence which operates and experiences things which are lived (*Erlebnisse*) in their original givenness, in their typicality and essentiality, and in their intentional meaning.

Concrete Monad
The ego is always a concrete monad to the extent that it is always already in the world and is constituted by the psyche and the real body (*Leib*). The concrete monad, even remaining as such, discovers itself as transcendental subjectivity and can investigate itself and other monads in all constitutive and founding operations. The concrete monad always experiences the world and, therefore, always lives in an environment and in a "surrounding world" (*Umwelt*). Reciprocal constitution gives rise to an intermonadic surrounding environment in the intersubjective relation. Intersubjective constitution makes the world of society and culture possible to the extent that it is experience of what is "thereness-for-everyone" [*Für-jedermann-da*] (Husserl, *Cartesian Meditations*, p. 92).

Consciousness
Consciousness as such is intentional and relational. It always goes beyond itself toward what it intends, and, in so doing, as the reflection of the presence it gives a meaning of truth to the presence of which it is a consciousness. As a relation of the ego with itself, consciousness grasps the past again in order to intend, in the present, the future as the meaning that renews the past, lives it, and transforms it according to an end (*telos*). Consciousness is an "absolute" only to the extent that it discovers meaning after the epochē, i.e., only to the extent that it is the "field from which the meaning is derived" (*Feld der Sinngebung*). (See Husserl, *Ideas*, p. 165.)

Constitution

To constitute does not mean to create. Constitution presupposes the epochē as a suspension of judgment. After the suspension, I must discover how things, the world, and others are presented and constituted for me. "The constitution of the object is a title [*Titel*] which indicates the system of the experiences [*Erlebnisse*] lived by knowing subjectivity" (manuscript B I 33, p. 7). To constitute is to see how things are formed around me. An experience is constituted if I discover its *genesis* by departing from the actual presence and its operations. If a category or habit has been constituted in the past, the genesis departs from the recollection of a past presence which I render present in remembrance, thus reliving it as it was in the present which is now past.

Constitution of Things

The thing is not a finished datum; it is formed in all my sensory experiences, the perceptive relation, and the dialectic of the hypothetical and the verified. Thus, the thing turns out to be a theme, a horizon in the movement of the progressive self-implication of the horizon of things in the horizon of the world. The dynamic self-constituting of things (forms, colors, and sounds) makes possible the *transformation of things into meanings*.

Empathy (Einfühlung)

When, after performing the epochē, we have returned to the ego and its transcendental field, we must see how the ego constitutes another ego. In order to constitute the other, I must begin by recognizing what is *my own* (the reduction to *property*). [The etymological source of *proprio* is important here. "Property" and what is "appropriate" are herein intimately connected.] For example, I must begin with my own body, from which I distinguish the body that belongs to another subject in the same way that my body belongs to me. Therefore, in order to constitute the other subject, I must pass from my own body and *feel* the body of the other. This "feeling the other," this affective penetration which is a kind of "inner identification," is called *Einfühlung* (a term derived from Theodor Lipps). Since I perceive the body of the other and see it as animated, just as mine is animated in my perception of it, what is revealed to me is that the other finds the world by departing from a subjectivity which is analogous to mine (analogous apperception).

Thus, the other is present to me as other. "My appresentation of the other is an original self-offering of the other men" (manuscript A V 10/2, p. 155).

Epochē

Literally, the epochē signifies "suspension of judgment." All that is not given to me in my original experience must be "bracketed." All is "obvious" prior to the epochē. After the epochē, everything that was obvious becomes a problem and all my acts must be genetically clarified, by departing from the operations which I perform directly and by departing from the evidence. Genetic clarification transforms what is obvious and obscured by biases into *phenomena*, and constitutes the world by departing from the concrete operations of the subject.

Erlebnis

The *Erlebnis* is every experience which is "lived," which is present and directed into the various modalities of feeling, perceiving, and intending.

Evidence

Evidence is that which is experienced in a direct and apodictic way, i.e., in such a way that it cannot be different from how it is. As such, evidence is the "original phenomenon of intentional life." It can be adequate or inadequate, hypothetical or verified. In a negative sense, it is the contrary of what is symbolic, deduced, predicted, or unwitnessed. It is the original meaning-structure to which every discourse refers. Evidence can be considered as presence that discovers itself. As the primary phenomenon, it is limited and finite in its center, but in its nucleus it also implies what has not yet been but can be revealed. As "meaning-structure" (*Sinngebung*), the evidence is the self-testimony of the meaning of truth and, therefore, the intentional horizon which is implicit in the presence.

Factuality

What is factual appears as it is without being capable of further modification or reduction. The things-themselves are factual. "Being-as-such" (*Sosein*) is also factual, e.g., being red, resistant, caused, or unreal. To the extent that he is experienced in the first person, the subject himself is a fact (see Husserl, *Ideas*, pp. 52, 64). However, we must not forget that, for Husserl, every fact is *typical*, i.e., it is the index of all the facts of its type. Therefore, its typicality is the essence of a fact that can appear in time either as irreducible or as the result of operations which are themselves reducible to the original and founding operation.

Functioning Life
The "sourceful functioning" originality is the functioning and operating of my ego, understood not as a category, word, or theory of the ego (even if in an active sense), but as factual concreteness in my situation that may still be unanalyzed and not fully understood. I live physiologically and psychically, even if I do not know it and am ignorant of physiology and psychology. In my functioning life, as a part I am connected to the whole, and in self-reflection the functioning life always reproposes itself to me as the clarification and the demand to discover and reveal, i.e., to render phenomenal and analyze phenomenologically that which remains unconscious and hidden. By analyzing my functioning life and its modalities, I analyze the world, its silent and hidden functioning, its causal conditioning and motivated concatenations, its passivity, and its freedom. Life functions in time and reflects upon itself in time. We must keep in mind that reflection is a temporalization, a continuous discovery, and a continuous recognition of meaning.

Horseman of Dürer (from the etching of 1513)
For Husserl, this is the symbol of the struggle for the meaning of truth, and, therefore, of the struggle for the transformation of time and history according to the teleological and totalizing idea of the dialectic. He must proceed without ever letting himself be tempted by death and the devil (i.e., by fetishism and idolatry); otherwise truth will come to be considered as attained and coinciding with reality. Truth, on the contrary, is the meaning of reality. (See Husserl, *Ideas*, p. 311.)

I-Can
The ego is not only reflection, or separate consciousness (*res cogitans*); it is also the I that can, do, and make. It is never pure possibility, but always caused possibility. It is conditioned and motivated, which is tantamount to saying that it is the temporal present that can act and defeat passivity by using that very same passivity. The I-can is the "I can always again" (*Ich kann immer wieder*). (See Husserl, *Cartesian Meditations*, p. 60.)

Inorganic Body (Körper)
This is the inert and exterior body which presents itself to the subject as resistance and obstacle: I live myself as myself, not only as a *Leib* but also as an inert body. On the one hand, the inorganic body permits the inert praxis of labor (Sartre). On the other hand, both nature and the planet Earth can present themselves to me as *my* inorganic *body* (Marx). The inorganic body

must be intimately bound with the extraneous body (of a subject for the other subject). The dialectic of one's own body and the extraneous body renders possible not only the encounter of the *Einfühlung* but also estrangement.

Intentionality

Intentionality is everything toward which the subject directs himself as consciousness, perception, and experience of *something*. If the subject is designated as *cogito,* the *cogitata* are the themes intended by the subject. According to the way the intentional operation is performed, that which is intended can be real, possible, fantastic, ideal, etc. To the extent that the subject intends another subject as a subject, the intentional operation constitutes intersubjectivity which is concrete, since it is formed by concrete monads. But it is also teleological to the extent that it aims at the constitution of a *society of subjects.* Departing from the presence, intentionality aims beyond the presence, thus recapturing the past and moving toward the future. It is consciousness, in time, of the flux of temporal experiences (*Erlebnisstrom*). To the extent that, in the flux, typical operations (and, therefore, typical essences) present themselves anew, intentionality aims toward the teleological meaning and the intentional task of the temporal and historical realization of the meaning of truth, while it constitutes what is permanent.

Intersubjectivity

In terms of the *Einfühlung* and the encounter with the other (*Paarung*), intersubjective life is constituted in temporal contemporaneity and, ultimately, in the relation between the present and the past, in the generative concatenation. Each subject implies the existence of the other and constitutes the communion or coexistence of subjects. Since this coexistence is temporally formed, it has an essentially historical character. History is constituted in each subject and in the encountering and clashing of subjects. Everyone has his experiences, but each lives according to those common experiences which he calls "ours." The result of the encounters and the clashes depends on the will and direction of the praxis.

We are a multiplicity of sensible subjects but, to the extent that we communicate, the meaning of all serves each and every subject, and in such a way that each finds himself in front of a world that has been constituted with all those meanings, and knows that, in this respect, he experiences the same world as everyone else. It is as if there were a collective world correlative to a unique subject [manuscript F I 33, p. 126].

We must never forget that Husserl's subject is "unique" in the already indicated sense.

Irreversibility

According to the second law of thermodynamics (Carnot's principle), the productive capacity of a machine depends on the difference in temperatures of the source and the refrigerator. In terms of Clausius' postulate, the principle affirms that heat cannot pass from a colder to a warmer body *without work* and the adequate phenomenon of compensation.

Therefore, what results in an isolated system is an irreversible thermodynamic transformation. In other words, energy is consumed, and the compensation of energy is represented by *entropy*. Irreversibility dominates the whole universe and *in fact* renders repetition impossible. The second principle of thermodynamics gives us an intersubjective and measurable demonstration of temporal irreversibility. All this is valid on the categorial level, where it is admissible, by means of mathematical idealization, to present the second principle of thermodynamics in such a way that repetition becomes formally possible. Phenomenologically, however, irreversibility is a fact: it is the impossibility of *really* turning back in time, of denying need and consumption. On the precategorial level, consumption is something "lived," a necessity, just as I can never again live exactly what I have already lived.

Kinesthesis

There is always an evolution and a mutation of the perception of the way in which things appear to our concrete and corporeal ego and its movements. The ways in which the world appears to the subject (and subjects) is the domain of the phenomenological analysis of kinestheses. In these kinetheses, the monad reveals itself in its dynamism and its praxis, and in the meaning of its praxis in relation to the praxis of other monads which move and act in the surrounding nature and, in general, in the world. The phenomenology of kinetheses is the study of sensibility in its actual functioning character of both the body and its organs. Real corporeality in the first person of the *Leib* is functioning corporeality.

Life-world (Lebenswelt)

The life-world is the original experience that precedes every scientific and philosophic category. Although it is relative, it has its fundamental structures. This makes a science of the life-world possible, reducible to the perceptions and the operations of the subjects in their spatiotemporal and causal environment. By space, time, and causality, we must understand spatial experience with its modalities, the temporal experiencing with the modifications of the presence, and the precategorial causal experiencing upon which every causal scientific category is founded. Husserl also refers to the *Lebenswelt* as the world of experience (*Erfahrungswelt*).

Loss of the World (Weltverlorenheit)
Man is lost in the world to the extent that he remains a prisoner of prejudices or uninvestigated obviousness. Liberation from the mundane is possible through the epochē and becoming-conscious. When Husserl speaks of negating the world (*Weltvernichtung*) in order to lead us to the return to the subject, by "world" he means the mundane and those prejudices and obviousnesses which must not be taken into account.

Materialism
The problem of materialism is connected with the problem of unconscious and external experience. The *internal* is not to be confused with the *interior*. The *external* appears as a direct mode of experiencing that which makes the subject passive, conditions him, and binds him to causality and need. The experience of need and the relation of need and satisfaction can be considered as the precategorial structure of political economy, i.e., as constitutive of the regional ontology of political economy as a science.

Matter or Hyle
The subject lives in matter, and the experience of matter is his basic experience. The animal and spiritual worlds are constituted on this basis. The three regions—material, animal, and spiritual —are encapsulated one in the other: the third is not possible without the second, and the second is not possible without the first. The regions are united in original and precategorial experience understood as the *Lebenswelt*. The sciences of this "primary" experience study some typical and specific aspects (the worlds of mathematics, physics, biology, etc.). These aspects, founded in their categories with operations derived from the *Lebenswelt*, give rise to regions or *regional ontologies*. The *Lebenswelt*, with its material and original experience, is the point of origin of the regions and regional ontologies (*Quellpunkt der Ontologien*). As the original material thing (*Ursache*) and real body (*Leib*) in its function as the organ of the organs of sense, the subject is the

center of constitutive operations. The origin of both *material* ontologies (e.g., the bodies studied by physics) and *formal* ontologies (e.g., formal logic) is based on logical judgments.

Meaning

Meaning is that which, divested of false appearances and prejudices, I rediscover as mine, as having an origin in me, in others, and in humanity. Meaning is that which is unveiled. It is that which becomes clear from what was hidden, that which has a significant direction which was not imposed but is lived by myself as autonomous. The loss of meaning is the loss of intentionality, and in its loss everything becomes equivalent (truth is equal to falsehood, good to bad, real to fantastic, etc.). Things acquire meaning only if I remove them from mundane skepticism and, by bracketing what they pretend to be by means of the epochē, transform them into phenomena (phenomenological reduction). The thing that is revealed, or the phenomenon, offers itself in its intrinsic form (*Gehalt*), its content (*Inhalt*), and its origin (*Ursprung*), which in turn illuminates the end (*telos*).

Meaning-Structure (Sinngebung)

Every category, technique, and abstraction has a meaning insofar as it originates from the prescientific concrete operations by means of which the categories, abstractions, and techniques are constructed and founded. If the foundation is forgotten, abstraction which is valid as such is substituted for concreteness and loses the meaning-structure. If we return from the isolated abstraction to the origin of the operations which are based on original experience, we find that this appears as the *meaning-structure*.

Memorative Anticipation (Vorerinnerung)

This is a modification of the presence that is turned toward the future and is parallel to memory, which is turned toward the past. The anticipation of the future is not a projection toward it. Rather, it is the imagining or the thinking of the future as real, as if it had already happened, in relation to the project and the praxis. The ego makes itself future to the extent that, both from and in the present, it already *has a future*. Memorative anticipation is always a hypothesis, but we do not know whether or not it will obtain. Fundamentally, it is a "prefiguration which delineates an image of what may happen, of what we may expect" (see manuscript C 4, p. 5). The prefiguration of the future is bound to the present and the past, and it is intimately connected not only to causality and conditioning but also to the relationship between means and ends.

Ontogenesis, Phylogenesis
According to a hypothesis suggested by Meckel and elaborated by Haeckel, the individual recapitulates in his genetic development (*ontogenesis*) the stages of development of the species (*phylogenesis*). Husserl knew this hypothesis and did not consider it a genuine and true law. However, he used the two terms ("ontogenesis" and "phylogenesis") to indicate that, in the genetic chain, every individual starts from the beginning with respect to his parents.

Origin, Original
That which is original, for Husserl, is all that stems from the experience of the subject in the first person, considered not only as a consciousness but also as a concrete monad. Therefore, we can speak of original sensations, original perceptions, etc. In his own presence, the subject discovers the modifications of the presence, and, therefore, he discovers matters such as his own origin in the past. In the latter case, the original term acquires a genetic, temporal, and historical significance.

Passive Constitution
The monad is not absolutely free. It has been formed and caused by historical time and is conditioned by the precategorial causal structure of the pregiven world. Causality and conditioning allow for the concrete freedom which is never a theory or a category; rather, to be free is to operate in the actual situation according to a rational direction, i.e., according to a meaning of truth. From the very beginning it is bound to genetic concatenation in the same way that it is bound to need, to the experiences of the resistance and exteriority of matter, and to the effort that matter requires in order to be worked. The corporeal spatiality and aesthetic experiences conjoin me to the others by means of the *Einfühlung*, yet they do not allow me an absolute comprehension or identification which would annul concrete individuations. The fundamental witness of passive genesis is the fact that every living presence as life in the first person is always *inherited*. Also, the content of a perception is passive to the extent that I do not create it, but rather receive it as it is given to me.

Pause
Pause is the loss of perception and presence in sleep, fainting, and, in the extreme case, death. From the actual presence to its

modifications, there is no uninterrupted linearity, but rather a discontinuity connected to an individuation that has a beginning and an ending.

Praxis

Action is first and foremost the functioning of every bodily perception. To act means to place or detach oneself in space and time. Praxis always occurs in the present, in relation to past and future, and is in a means-end *relation*. Since it encounters material resistance and depends on causality, acting is passively conditioned in the same way that it is conditioned by need. Inert praxis is a passive bodily way to act. To the extent that it is rooted in the temporal and historical situation, praxis is a *faculty* of the subject and appears not only in the need-satisfaction and means-end relationship, but also in the dialectic of interest and disinterest (and, therefore, in relation to the subject who is awake or asleep in relation to continuity, discontinuity, and individuation). Praxis presupposes the passive genesis which, from "the passive having of the world," becomes transformed into a presence that acts according to a *telos*. For Husserl, the *field of praxis* is the world in its historical becoming. Praxis loses its meaning if it is not guided by the meaning of truth, even in dialectical contrasts.

Presence

What is present is what is directly experienced in the actual now. What I feel, think, perceive, or dream, as I feel it, perceive it, think it, and dream it, is present to me in the first person. Above all, presence is the evidence that, being apodictic, cannot be different from what it is, independent of any philosophic or scientific theory. In order to catch the presence as it is, we must free ourselves from every prejudice so that we can describe the thing-itself as it is given in flesh and blood (*Leibhaft*). The central experience of every subject is a nucleus (*Kern*) surrounded by penumbrae (*Abschattungen*). It is a part which implies the whole and the horizon of the whole, but which appears only as a part. The presence is original, and every genesis starts from it by undertaking the genesis both as subjectivity and as the beginning in the present that has passed. To the extent that it is original and founding (and everything is founded by the original experience), the presence is said to be *living presence* (*lebendige Gegenwart*). The original presence (*Urpräsenz*) can make present—or presentify—the past within itself, and attend to and anticipate the future in the same way that it can make present the other (*Appräsenz*) and constitute a common presence with the other (*Kompräsenz*). The latter depends on *Einfühlung*.

Presentification (Vergegenwärtigung)

Presentification is the operation whereby I render present what has been forgotten. I can, for instance, presentify a past span of my life, or, with respect to others, an indirect knowledge that I transform in direct original knowledge, in actual presentification (*Gegenwärtigung*). Presentification occurs every time that I have the experience of another presence in my presence. To the extent that I remove myself from my presence in order to come near to the presence of others, I perform a de-presentification (*Ent-gegenwärtigung*) within myself.

With the de-presentification, I tend toward the other, I couple myself with the other (*Paarung*), and I begin the constitution of intersubjectivity and sociality. Just as, by detaching myself from the present, I remember how I have been before in my life, and then, from the detachment, I return to the synthesis (the present), so, by departing and becoming detached from myself until I go out of myself, I find others. When I return to the synthesis (the present), I rediscover myself in intersubjectivity.

Protention

Protention is one of the modalities of the presence. In relation to the future, it is parallel to *retention*, which, on the contrary, regards the past. The protention is to protend oneself forward, to expect, to hypothesize. In hearing a sound, I expect that it will be followed by another one, or be resolved in a certain accord. To protend oneself means *to be disposed* toward what is about to happen. In the modality of protention, that which is about to happen, and which I experience as such, is continually transformed into what happens, just as, in retention, what happens is continually transformed into what has just happened.

Protention and retention are connected. What is now present is the realization of what a little while ago was future, which, in being realized, will become something just passed.

Real or Live Body [Corpo proprio] (Leib)

The real body is the organic living body insofar as it is lived by me as mine (while the body of the other is not mine). The real body is the point of reference of spatial experiences: it is the zero-point (*Nullpunkt*) of the lived space (i.e., directly perceived space). It is also the point of insertion into the environment (*Umwelt*) and into the causal precategorial world. This insertion gives rise to psychophysical causality in the same way that it is the meeting point of reciprocal insertion of the internal and the external (*Umschlagspunkt*).

Reconsideration (Rückfrage)

Reconsideration is the operation whereby, in the actual historical present, I continually reflect anew upon the past for a praxis oriented toward a future guided by the meaning of truth. Reconsideration is also a continual correction and renewal. It is not a "turning-back" to original being, meaning by "being" something metaphysically original with respect to the present and the subject. The Husserlian reconsideration is continually founded anew by the presence in the historical process. The interpretation of *Rückfrage* as a "return to being" is due to that "genial lack of scientificity" which Husserl attributed to Heidegger.

Reduction

Generally speaking, the reduction is the transformation of that which is obscure into that which is clear, of that which is hidden by prejudices into that which is given and revealed as it is by becoming a *phenomenon*. The *phenomenological reduction* presupposes the epochē or suspension of judgment. To the extent that it is a phenomenon, that which is revealed is essential and eidetic. The intuition of the essence is the intuition of the typical form of every phenomenon (*eidetic reduction*). The *eidos* of a phenomenon is constituted by the operations that ground it, and these are operations of the subject in the first person, of the concrete individual ego and *every ego* that experiences in the first person. In this sense, this is the reduction to the transcendental ego, and it is called the *transcendental reduction*, which subsequently becomes the reduction to the *Lebenswelt*. The reduction to that which is *properly* of the ego allows the recognition of the *other* subject and, therefore, the foundation of intersubjectivity.

Reflection

Reflection is the becoming-conscious in the actual present, which also attributes the antecedent world to reflection. If we live in the world reflectively, our interests change, and we aim at a meaning in the sense that we decide to transform the world according to a rational *telos*. Phenomenology is the self-development of the given world through reflection, the study of *how* the world is valid and can be valid for us. Then, phenomenology appears in reflection as a science of how the world is given to us and can be given to us in a new way. The self-development of the naïvely accepted world (the *ontic*), in the reflection that leads it to be transformed into a *phenomenon* according to various levels and regions, transforms the *ontic* into the *ontological*. For Husserl, the ontological is not a theory or metaphysics of being; it is the self-revelation of the meaning of experience and, therefore, is resolved into a phenomenological analysis.

Rememorization (Wiedererinnerung)
What happens in the present detaches itself from the present even if it is retained. Ultimately, it is submerged and forgotten. It is, therefore, increasingly more detached, thus allowing the ego to have a certain freedom and power. The past that moves away from the present is constituted as "what has become" (*Gewordenheit*). The action passes, even if that which it has accomplished remains and constitutes us and becomes incorporated into our history. It is in us even if it is forgotten. The forgotten past gives rise to the awakening (*Weckung*), the discovering (*Aufdekkung*), and reproduction (*Wiederholung*). Rememorization, with all of its operations, allows for the reconstruction of the succession (*Nacheinander*) and stabilization of the historical past.

Retention or Primary Recall
Retention is a modality of the presence. The presence becomes modified by itself. It is not closed but "broadened" and constituted by its own continuous self-modification. That which is now present, the musical note that I hear, passes, but yet remains in the present, even if a new note is being heard at the same time. Retention is something which begins to detach itself from the immediate nucleus of presentation and which, although detached, is retained. It is the temporal modification closest to evidence and immediate perception [see Husserl, *The Phenomenology of Internal Time-Consciousness*, ed. Martin Heidegger, trans. James C. Churchill (Bloomington: Indiana University Press, 1964), pp. 57, 75]. The present passes in retention, but we can always hold (*noch-im-Griff-behalten*) what is passing. The beginning of perception in the present *is* passive (we are not the ones who create the note that we hear), while the passing of the original perception already allows a detachment from passivity. When what is past is forgotten and then recalled, we can re-present and reconstruct it according to our interests, our projects, and our praxis, which must, however, establish the present which has passed (the historical past). The temporal dialectic is thus connected to the dialectic of history.

Reversal of the Past into the Future
This is the fundamental operation in which the present transforms the past and its comprehension into a task and a goal (*telos*) for the future; the unattainable past origin, and the impossibility of going back to it, becomes a praxis, a project, and a task.

Telos
The *telos* is the goal. Phenomenology is a teleology. But this teleology is not the substitution of finalistic explanations for "causal" ones. Rather, it is the analysis of the meaning-structure and meaning of causality itself. The *telos* is not the substitution of finalism for "scientific" laws, but is the meaning of the operative foundation of all the sciences—we do not distinguish between the natural and social sciences. The *telos* does not leave the choice within the domain of the irrational. Rather, it grounds the choice in the precategorial and investigates its causality, its conditioning, and the motivation which inheres in the life which experiences the world, along with the praxis that transforms the world according to a direction and meaning. The *telos* is realized in the intersubjective relation, where it appears as the constitution of a society and culture according to the meaning of truth.

Temporality of the Ego
The ego is temporal to the extent that it is present to itself. It remains identical to itself even though it extends itself in its own past and in its own future. By reflecting upon itself, the present ego removes itself, as an object of reflection, but the two moments are always reunited in the actual experiencing of the ego, and the two moments realize a difference and a unity. The ego upon which I reflect is the ego which I was "a little while ago" and which I retain in my actual reflection. The ego that performs the reflection becomes the ego that I was "a little while ago" and toward which I have moved. Reflection is thus constituted in permanency, while permanence itself is the self-temporalization of the presence and the temporal reflection of the ego upon itself.

Theme
The theme is that which is the object of my actual analysis, actual interest, and praxis. To thematize means to examine what in the passive background appears as clarifiable and transposable into significant phenomena. Thematization gives rise to the dialectic of the center and the periphery, the nucleus (*Kern*) and the penumbrae (*Abschattungen*). Thematization is perceptive

and analytic awareness: it allows praxis to mediate means and end, organization and project. Phenomenological experience is the continuous changing and connecting of the themes, their instantaneous silence, their return, their coming to the foreground, and their self-submersion. The orchestration of themes is possible in the self-constitution of an intentional texture where the origin never falls into oblivion, and where praxis always moves toward the horizon of the truth of the world.

Transcendental Aesthetic

This is the analysis of the various modes through which we perceive with the senses (sight, touch, etc.), and, in general, the analysis of the modes through which we bodily live in the world. Here, the body is meant as the *organ of the organs of sense.* Aesthetic experience is intersubjective to the extent that, in it, the monads are constituted in one another. *Einfühlung* is basically one of the fundamental modalities of aesthetic experience. The transcendental aesthetic is connected to the study of the dynamics of the body. While in Kant it is only the elaboration of the a priori forms of intuition, in Husserl the transcendental aesthetic appears as the *critique of corporeal experience.*

Transcendental Phenomenology

In Kant, that which is transcendental is the knowledge which, although a priori with respect to experience, can be applied only within the limits of experience itself. Husserl is more radical because of the necessity, essential to phenomenology, of always beginning from the root. He analyzes Descartes's *ego cogito* and Kant's *I think,* but since, for man, the root is man himself, he never separates the Cartesian *ego* and the Kantian *I* from the concrete man ("Can the ego which posits itself, of which Fichte speaks, be anything other than Fichte's own?" [p. 202]). All the analyses of the *Logical Investigations* must be connected to the transcendental ego so conceived (see manuscript B II 1, September, 1907). Consequently, all knowledge and all human operations are founded on experience (*Erlebnis*), on the passage of temporal perception (this is clear as early as 1904). The typical or eidetic character of every *Erlebnis,* and the fact that every experience is connected to all others, allow the radical and original ego to discover a priori knowledge in the *transcendental field* lived as direct experience. Thus, Husserl speaks of an empirical a priori, an a priori of the life-world, and an a priori of history. If man—not the concept and the category "man," but each one of us in flesh and blood (*Leibhaft*)—has suspended every judgment and has reduced himself to himself, it is precisely this "commitment to poverty" that gives him the maximum wealth, since the reduction allows him to catch the self-constitution of the world and its meaning of truth.

Rooted in experience, immanence, and intentionality, the truth I discover is not a reality possessed and reduced to idolatry, or a separate reality (e.g., as the *res cogitans* is separated from the *res extensa*), but is the meaning of my operations in the intersubjective relation. My acts, and those of every ego which is an ego in the same way as *I am*, i.e., the acts of the original ego, are transcendental, not because they are syntheses of an immanence and a transcendence which, in reality, once separated can no longer be reunited, but because they have in my ego a meaning valid for all humanity.

Thus transcendental phenomenology reveals the *radical responsibility* of every living man to constitute society and history (p. 271). We say "reveal" because to reveal is to render phenomenal, since "phenomenon" literally means "what has come to the light of day," and "φάοςβλέπειν" means "to live."

Universal Correlation

For Husserl, universal correlation is the fundamental principle of phenomenology. Every "lived thing" is connected to others according to typical relations. All that I experience is correlated and can be assumed as a model. Every individual implies the others and, although unique, is connected to all real and possible relations. The analysis of the relations starts from an individual presence which, as such, is non-repeatable, but which, as an index, is typical and essential. Every moment, although temporally distinct from others, is constituted according to relations which also constitute the other moments. It is fundamental to comprehend that *essence* is not a reality and, therefore, that essence can characterize a concrete individual.

Veil of Ideas (Ideenkleid)

This is the set of prejudices and categorial constructions that have been removed from their origin and, therefore, from their meaning-structure. Phenomenology is never a construction of ideas, and it must, therefore, always begin anew from what is original. Broadly speaking, the *Ideenkleid* is every ideology. Phenomenology is the critique of all ideologies to the extent that it aims at *revealing*, i.e., turning what is hidden into a *phenomenon*.

Index